SIX MONTHS IN THE
SANDWICH ISLANDS

A NIGHT SCENE IN THE CRATER OF THE VOLCANO OF KILAUEA, HAWAII. [*Frontispiece.*]

THE HAWAIIAN ARCHIPELAGO

SIX MONTHS

AMONG THE

PALM GROVES, CORAL REEFS AND VOLCANOES

OF THE

SANDWICH ISLANDS

by ISABELLA L. BIRD

author of *Unbeaten Tracks in Japan*

with an introduction to the new edition by
TERENCE BARROW Ph.D.

"Summer isles of Eden lying
In dark purple spheres of sea."

SEVENTH EDITION

CHARLES E. TUTTLE COMPANY
Rutland, Vermont & Tokyo, Japan

Representatives

British Isles & Continental Europe:
SIMON & SCHUSTER INTERNATIONAL GROUP, *London*
Australasia: BOOKWISE INTERNATIONAL
1 Jeanes Street, Beverley, 5009, South Australia

Published by the Charles E. Tuttle Co., Inc.
of Rutland, Vermont & Tokyo, Japan
with editorial offices at
Suido 1-chome, 2-6, Bunkyo-ku, Tokyo, Japan

Library of Congress Catalog Card No. 73-77575

International Standard Book No. 0-8048-1112-1

First edition, 1890 by John Murray, London
First Tuttle edition, 1974
Ninth printing, 1990

Printed in Japan

TO

MY SISTER,

TO WHOM THESE LETTERS WERE ORIGINALLY WRITTEN
THEY ARE NOW AFFECTIONATELY

Dedicated.

TABLE OF CONTENTS

LETTER I.

LETTER II.

LETTER III.

LETTER IV.

LETTER V.

LETTER VI.

LETTER XXIX.—*continued.*

LETTER XXX.

LETTER XXXI.

LIST OF ILLUSTRATIONS

INTRODUCTION TO THE
NEW EDITION

ISABELLA LUCY BIRD won fame in her own lifetime as the most remarkable woman traveler of the nineteenth century. *Six Months in the Sandwich Islands*, which describes her visit to the Hawaiian Islands in 1873, is one of the gems of Pacific literature. Much of the charm of Isabella Bird's writing is due to her use of personal letters for conveying her experiences and reflections. The thirty-one letters that make up the body of the book were written to her beloved sister Henrietta, who dutifully stayed at home in Edinburgh to take care of the household.

Six Months in the Sandwich Islands is an authentic record of daily life in Hawaii in the late nineteenth century. It describes a life style during the brief reign (1873–74) of King Lunalilo, before the grand flamboyance of King David Kalakaua's court and the sad reign of Queen Liliuokalani ended in the queen's dethronement by revolution. Some of the places Isabella Bird visited are virtually unchanged today, and much of the charm remains throughout Hawaii. However, as the Hawaiian scene has changed, the old-time Hawaiians and the colorful characters she met along the way have disappeared. We should note here that though *The Hawaiian Guide Book for Travelers* (published in Honolulu in 1875 and reissued in 1970) was two years too late to be of help to Miss Bird, it remains an interesting companion to *Six Months in the Sandwich Islands* because of its description of Hawaii in the mid-1870's.

Honolulu's facilities for tourists had a grand start in the opening of Hawaii's first public house, the Hawaiian Hotel, just before Isabella's visit, and there she stayed while in Honolulu. *The Hawaiian Guide Book for Travelers* assured the traveler that the Hawaiian Hotel was "elegant" and "first class in every particular," with livery stable and "single or double carriages, and four-in-hand, with polite and trusty drivers." Honolulu would have been immobilized without horses. Miss Bird had the impression that there were more horses than people in Hawaii. The Hawaiians themselves were passionately fond of horses, a new feature to their culture introduced by Europeans. Miss Bird was to see Hawaii from the back of a horse.

What made Isabella Bird such an unusual traveler? The most evident facts are that she used her eyes, she shunned well-beaten tracks, and she was fearless. Also, she was British, a nationality of great significance in her time. The British of the nineteenth century were the greatest travelers the world had ever seen, and Isabella Lucy Bird was typically British and at heart an adventurer. She had the bearing of her beloved Queen Victoria and was proud to be a member of an empire on which the sun never set. Unlike the wives of colonial administrators and missionaries whom she met in distant places and who regarded themselves as exiles, Isabella traveled to out-of-the-way places with zest and enthusiasm. Hardship meant nothing to her. The tourist meccas through which she had to pass she disliked, and she was never happier then when on yak, horse, donkey, camel, or elephant, heading for the hinterland.

There are surprising facts about Isabella Bird that readers of her books should know. She was about forty years of age when she set off on her travels. In Victorian terms she was therefore an "old" woman. Also, she had suffered since childhood from a spinal disease that sometimes required her to wear a steel support and often to write her letters lying on her back. Headaches, backaches, and mental depressions were her companions at home.

It was only when she escaped the "constant murk of Scottish skies" that she really came alive. Her voyage to the Pacific was in search of health—a standard cure for chronic invalids who could afford the passage money. It was Dr. Bishop, the medical adviser to her sister Henrietta, the man whom Isabella later married, who suggested that she take a long sea trip, little knowing that it would launch her on a career of adventure.

Miss Bird did not plan an extended stay in Hawaii. She was on another voyage when the unexpected visit occurred. Traveling through Melbourne and Auckland, she was disappointed. She found the heat and dust of a hot southern summer too much to endure. Also, the provincialism of the colonial inhabitants wilted her spirits. She left Auckland to cross the Pacific in search of the cool mountain air of California. By fate she boarded a leaky old paddle steamer named the *Nevada*, en route to San Francisco via Honolulu.

It was on the journey to Honolulu that Miss Bird found her soul, for this old tub of a vessel, which should never have put to open sea, ran into a tropical storm and barely survived high seas. The nearness of disaster and a watery grave, and the companionship of others in danger, gave Isabella a new sense of life. Her zestful spirit of youth returned to her, and old complaints seemed to disappear. (It is interesting to note that, however much she disdained danger on land or sea thereafter, Miss Bird never conquered her fear of cockroaches or other insects. The giant cockroaches of the *Nevada* kept her from sleeping in her berth.)

By miracle or luck the ancient *Nevada* sailed into Honolulu harbor, listing and with bilge pumps working overtime, but still afloat. Isabella Bird disembarked in Honolulu, not out of fear of continuing the voyage to California but in response to the pleas of a fellow passenger named Mrs. Dexter. Miss Bird agreed to be her companion in the strange town and to help with Mrs. Dexter's son, who had become dangerously ill on the voyage from Auckland.

Isabella's decision to stay in Hawaii was a happy one for both herself and Hawaiian letters. The charm of Hawaii and its people captured the imagination of this unusual British lady. She reached out with gusto, trying to see and do everything, then industriously writing letters about her experiences to her sister at home. The visit was from January to August, covering the cooler winter months when vigorous travel is most endurable. However, what is called winter in Hawaii is smiling summer to anyone from Scotland, and so it seemed to Miss Bird.

Honolulu was a lively Pacific port town in 1873, and capital of the Hawaiian kingdom. It was gay with bright, happy people, rich in their aloha spirit. Hospitality went out immediately to Miss Bird, especially from the elite missionary families, with whom she had much in common. Regardless of this friendship, she found the social life so intense and the chitchat so continuous that she took leave of Honolulu happily and headed for the more out-of-the-way parts of the Hawaiian Islands. She had fascinating adventures, as this book relates, on Hawaii, Maui, Kauai, and Lanai.

At the time of Miss Bird's visit, horses were as vital to daily life as the automobile is to Hawaiian life today. The old foot trails could not take a carriage, but a good horse could go almost anywhere, even along the cliffside trails that led in and out of valleys, the only other means of access to these being sea landings in hazardous Pacific surf. Isabella Bird was an able horsewoman who adapted herself to the massive cowpuncher's saddle of Hawaii and to the astride stance forbidden to polite European ladies of her time because of its supposed indecency. With an innovative bloomer suit, New Zealand boots, and Mexican spurs, she galloped along at a pace that endeared her to local Hawaiians, who were themselves expert horsefolk. They did not expect to see a pale-faced stranger riding, as they said, like a paniola. (Hawaiians had coined the word "paniola" from the Spanish word *español* meaning "Spanish." King Kamehameha III had brought from Mexico some Spanish vaqueros to teach his people how to ride down and to lasso the wild cattle of the mountains. Dashing Hawaiian cowhands are still called paniola and may be seen in all their glory in public parades.)

On the matter of horses and horsemanship there was complete understanding between Isabella and the Hawaiians; however, quite naturally she did not fully understand their attitudes in other areas. She found Hawaiians "peculiar." She was a strange mixture of liberal thinking and severity. We must remember that she had a severe moral upbringing that colored her view of others. She was a Victorian lady, born in Yorkshire, England, in 1831, of an Anglican clergyman father. Her strict home culture classified mankind as heathen or non-heathen, and she shared her father's belief in the need for Christian foreign missions.

Isabella Lucy Bird's character is well expressed in her letters. As she was a strict Christian, we need not be surprised at the sermon style of writing which she often adopts, nor at some of her judgments that are obviously invalid today. We must not condemn her for being a child of her time. In fact, she was in many respects extremely liberal by the standards of her day. Her personality was that of a demure lady of the upper middle class of Victorian society, conforming to social standards when at home but, once abroad, becoming a zestful, eccentric individual. People generally tired her if she had any prolonged contact. Rather than being with people, she sought wild places where danger and the hardships of travel were abundant.

Hawaii was the first of Isabella's great adventures, and she calls it her "bright tropic dream." She came to love Hawaii just as much as did Mark Twain, who also expressed his views on this subject through letters. Reluctantly after her brief six months' sojourn, she left Hawaii for California, never to return.

In California she wrote *A Lady's Life in the Rocky Mountains*, and thereafter for almost half a century she traveled and wrote in remote foreign lands, including Korea, China, Kashmir, Tibet, the Malay Peninsula, and Japan.

Isabella Lucy Bird died in 1904, long after those whom she loved with such devotion had gone to death. Her husband, Dr. Bishop, whom she had married in 1881, died just five years after their marriage. Her last years were sad indeed, yet she labored on in humanitarian causes. Even at home she followed the ideal of practical aid, working with missionary fervor in the slums of Edinburgh. She was no mere Sunday Christian and disapproved of the ladies of her class who did nothing other than needlework, music, and approved reading. She was always a woman of action, never quite happy at home, although her physical limitations seemed great indeed. There is little doubt that during the last lonely years of her life her thoughts filled often with the memories of Hawaii and its happy people, scented days, rich landscapes, indigo sea and pure sky, and the valleys of flowering plants she had visited.

Six Months in the Sandwich Islands is a book to be read and read again. This reprint is from the edition published in London in 1890, which has the advantage of revisions made by Miss Bird. The book moves from mystical responses to nature to the mass of facts that every Victorian expected in a travel book. Today, a century after Isabella Bird wandered over Hawaii, her book is as fresh as the day it was written. Her observations help us to a better understanding of modern Hawaii and deepen our appreciation of the natural beauty of the Sandwich Islands.

TERENCE BARROW, Ph.D.

PREFATORY NOTE TO THE
SECOND EDITION

THE kindness with which this volume has been received by the press and public, both in this country and on the Hawaiian Islands, renders the preparation of another edition a pleasant task. When the book was published last year I was under some apprehension that several errors, arising from hasty observation, had been made, and it is a source of much gratification to me, that the verdict of the Hawaiian press and people is unanimous both as to the accuracy of the facts stated, and the conclusions which have been drawn from them.

Under these circumstances few alterations are necessary. The concluding chapters have been revised, and the statistical information brought down to the latest date, a few repetitions have been omitted, and I have withdrawn a passage regarding the prospects of the " Honolulu Mission," which, in the opinion of those interested in its success, was calculated to cause discouragement.

I. L. B.

EDINBURGH,
June, 1876.

PREFACE

WITHIN the last century the Hawaiian islands have been the topic of various works of merit, and some explanation of the reasons which have led me to enter upon the same subject is necessary.

I was travelling for health, when circumstances induced me to land on the group, and the benefit which I derived from the climate tempted me to remain for nearly seven months. During that time the necessity of leading a life of open air and exercise as a means of recovery, led me to travel on horseback to and fro through the islands, exploring the interior, ascending the highest mountains, visiting the active volcanoes and remote regions which are known to few even of the residents, living among the natives, and otherwise seeing Hawaiian life in all its phases.

At the close of my visit, my Hawaiian friends urged me strongly to publish my impressions and experiences, on the ground that the best books already existing, besides being old, treat chiefly of aboriginal customs and habits now extinct, and of the introduction of Christianity, and subsequent historical events. They also represented that I had seen the islands more thoroughly than any foreign visitor, and the volcano of Mauna Loa under specially favourable circumstances, and that I had so completely lived the island life, and acquainted myself with the existing state of the country, as to be rather a *kamaina** than a stranger, and that consequently I should be able to write on Hawaii with a degree of intimacy as well as freshness. My friends at home, who were interested in my narratives, urged me to give them to a wider circle, and my inclinations led me in the same direction, with a longing to make others share something of my own interest and enjoyment.

The letters which follow were written to a near relation, and often hastily and under great difficulties of circumstance, but even with these and other disadvantages, they appear to me the best form of conveying my impressions in their original vividness. With the exception of certain omissions and abridgments, they are printed as they were written, and for such demerits as arise from this mode of publication, I ask the kind indulgence of my readers.

ISABELLA L. BIRD.

January, 1875.

* A native word used to signify an old resident.

THE
HAWAIIAN
ARCHIPELAGO

MAP
Shewing the Position
of the
SANDWICH ISLES
OR
HAWAIIAN ARCHIPELAGO

KAUAI

OAHU

MOLOKAI

MAUI

LANAI

KAHOOLAUI

HAWAII

KONA

KAU

PUNA

HILO

HAMAKUA

KOHALA

J.D.Cooper Sc.

To face page 1 of Narrative.

TRAVELS

IN THE

SANDWICH ISLANDS.

INTRODUCTORY CHAPTER.

CANON KINGSLEY, in his charming book on the West Indies, says, "The undoubted fact is known I find to few educated English people, that the Coco palm, which produces coir rope, cocoanuts, and a hundred other useful things, is not the same plant as the cacao bush which produces chocolate, or anything like it. I am sorry to have to insist upon this fact, but till Professor Huxley's dream and mine is fulfilled, and our schools deign to teach, in the intervals of Greek and Latin, some slight knowledge of this planet, and of those of its productions which are most commonly in use, even this fact may need to be re-stated more than once."

There is no room for the supposition that the intelligence of Mr. Kingsley's "educated English" acquaintance is below the average, and I should be sorry to form an unworthy estimate of that of my own circle, though I have several times met with the foregoing confusion, as well as the following and other equally ill-informed questions, one or two of which I reluctantly admit that I might have been guilty of myself before I visited the Pacific: "Whereabouts are the Sandwich Islands? They are not the same as the Fijis, are they? Are they the same as Otaheite? Are the natives all cannibals? What sort of idols

do they worship? Are they as pretty as the *other South Sea*
Islands? Does the king wear clothes? Who do they belong
to? Does any one live on them but the savages? Will anything grow on them? Are the people very savage?" etc.
Their geographical position is a great difficulty. I saw a gentleman of very extensive information looking for them on the
map in the neighbourhood of Tristan d'Acunha ; and the pub-
lishers of a high-class periodical lately advertised "Letters
from the Sandwich Islands" as "Letters from the South Sea
Islands." In consequence of these and similar interrogatories,
which are not altogether unreasonable, considering the imperfect teaching of physical geography, the extent of this planet,
the multitude of its productions, and the enormous number of
islands composing Polynesia, Micronesia, and Melanesia, it is
necessary to preface the following letters with as many preliminary statements as shall serve to make them intelligible.

The Sandwich Islands do not form one of the South Sea
groups, and have no other connexion with them than certain
affinities of race and language. They constitute the only important group in the vast North Pacific Ocean, in which they
are so advantageously placed as to be pretty nearly equidistant
from California, Mexico, China, and Japan. They are in the
torrid zone, and extend from 18° 50' to 22° 20' north latitude,
and their longitude is from 154° 53' to 160° 15' west from
Greenwich. They were discovered by Captain Cook in
1778.

They are twelve in number, but only eight are inhabited, and
these vary in size from Hawaii, which is 4000 square miles in
extent, and 88 miles long by 73 broad, to Kahoolawe, which
is only 11 miles long and 8 broad. Their entire superficial
area is about 6,100 miles. They are to some extent bounded
by barrier reefs of coral, and have few safe harbours. Their
formation is altogether volcanic, and they possess the largest
perpetually active volcano and the largest extinct crater in the
world. They are very mountainous, and two mountain summits
on Hawaii are nearly 14,000 feet in height. Their climate for
salubrity and general equability is reputed the finest on earth.
It is almost absolutely equable, and a man may take his choice
between broiling all the year round on the sea level on the
leeward side of the islands at a temperature of 80°, and enjoying
the charms of a fireside at an altitude where there is frost
every night of the year. There is no sickly season, and there
are no diseases of locality. The trade winds blow for nine

months of the year, and on the windward coasts there is an abundance of rain, and a perennial luxuriance of vegetation.

The Sandwich Islands are not the same as Otaheite nor as the Fijis, from which they are distant about 4000 miles, nor are their people of the same race. The natives are not cannibals, and it is doubtful if they ever were so. Their idols only exist in missionary museums. They cast them away voluntarily in 1819, at the very time when missionaries from America sent out to Christianise the group were on their way round Cape Horn. The people are all clothed, and the king, who is an educated gentleman, wears the European dress. The official designation of the group is " Hawaiian Islands," and they form an independent kingdom.

The natives are not savages, most decidedly not. They are on the whole a quiet, courteous, orderly, harmless, Christian community. The native population has declined from 400,000 as estimated by Captain Cook in 1778 to 49,000, according to the census of 1872. There are about 5000 foreign residents, who live on very friendly terms with the natives, and are mostly subjects of Kalakaua, the king of the group.

The Hawaiians show a great aptitude for political organization, and the islands have a thoroughly civilized polity. They constitute a limited monarchy, and have a constitutional and hereditary king, a parliament with an upper and lower house, a cabinet, a standing army, a police force, a Supreme Court of Judicature, a most efficient postal system, a Governor and Sheriff on each of the larger islands, court officials, and court etiquette, a common school system, custom houses, a civil list, taxes, a national debt, and most of the other amenities and appliances of civilization.

There is no State Church. The majority of the foreigners, as well as of the natives, are Congregationalists. The missionaries translated the Bible and other books into Hawaiian, taught the natives to read and write, gave the princes and nobles a high class education, induced the king and chiefs to renounce their oppressive feudal rights, with legal advice framed a constitution which became the law of the land, and obtained the recognition of the little Polynesian kingdom as a member of the brotherhood of civilized nations.

With these few remarks I leave the subject of the volume to develop itself in my letters. In correcting them I have availed myself of the very valuable " History of the Hawaiian Islands," by Mr. Jackson Jarves, Ellis' " Tour Round Hawaii," Mr.

Brigham's valuable monograph on " The Hawaiian Volcanoes,"
and sundry reports presented to the legislature during its
present session. I have also to express my obligations to the
Hon. E. Allen, Chief Justice and Chancellor of the Hawaiian
kingdom, Mr. Manley Hopkins, author of " Hawaii," Dr. T.
M. Coan, of New York, Professor W. Alexander, Daniel Smith,
Esq., and other friends at Honolulu, for assistance most kindly
rendered.

ISABELLA L. BIRD.

LETTER I.

STEAMER NEVADA, NORTH PACIFIC, *Jan. 19th.*

A WHITE, unwinking, scintillating sun blazed down upon Auckland, New Zealand. Along the white glaring road from Onehunga, dusty trees and calla lilies drooped with the heat. Dusty thickets sheltered the cicada, whose triumphant din grated and rasped through the palpitating atmosphere. In dusty enclosures, supposed to be gardens, shrivelled geraniums, scattered sparsely, alone defied the heat. Flags drooped in the stifling air. Men on the verge of sunstroke plied their tasks mechanically. Dogs, with flabby and protruding tongues, hid themselves away under archway shadows. The stones of the sidewalks and the bricks of the houses radiated a furnace heat. All nature was limp, dusty, groaning, gasping. The day was the climax of a burning fortnight of heat, drought, and dust, of baked, cracked, dewless land, and oily, breezeless seas, of glaring days, passing through fiery sunsets into stifling nights.

I only remained long enough in the capital to observe that it had a look of having seen better days, and that its business streets had an American impress, and, taking a boat at a wharf, in whose seams the pitch was melting, I went off to the steamer *Nevada*, which was anchored out in the bay, preferring to spend the night in her than in the unbearable heat on shore. She belongs to the Webb line, an independent mail adventure, now dying a natural death, undertaken by the New Zealand Government, as much probably out of jealousy of Victoria as anything else. She nearly foundered on her last voyage, and her passengers unanimously signed a protest against her unseaworthy condition. She was condemned by the Government surveyor, and her mails were sent to Melbourne. She has, however, been patched up for this trip, and eight passengers, including myself, have trusted ourselves to her. She is a huge paddle-steamer, of the old-fashioned American type, deck above deck, balconies, a pilot-house abaft the foremast, two monstrous walking beams, and two masts which, possibly in case of need, might serve as jury masts.

Huge, airy, perfectly comfortable as she is, not a passenger stepped on board without breathing a more earnest prayer than usual that the voyage might end propitiously. The very first evening statements were whispered about to the effect that her state of disrepair is such that she has not been to her own port for nine months, and has been sailing for that time without a certificate ; that her starboard shaft is partially fractured, and that to reduce the strain upon it the floats of her starboard wheel have been shortened five inches, the strain being further reduced by giving her a decided list to port ; that her crank is "bandaged," that she is leaky, that her mainmast is sprung, and that with only four hours' steaming many of her boiler tubes, even some of those put in at Auckland, had already given way. I cannot testify concerning the mainmast, though it certainly does comport itself like no other mainmast I ever saw ; but the other statements, and many more which might be added, are, I believe, substantially correct. That the caulking of the deck was in evil case we very soon had proof, for heavy rain on deck was a smart shower in the saloon and state rooms, keeping four stewards employed with buckets and swabs, and compelling us to dine in waterproofs and rubber shoes.

In this dilapidated condition, when two days out from Auckland, we encountered a revolving South Sea hurricane, succinctly entered in the log of the day as " Encountered a very severe hurricane with a very heavy sea." It began at eight in the morning, and never spent its fury till nine at night, and the wind changed its direction eleven times. The *Nevada* left Auckland two feet deeper in the water than she ought to have been, and laboured heavily. Seas struck her under the guards with a heavy, explosive *thud*, and she groaned and strained as if she would part asunder. We held no communication with each other, or with those who could form any rational estimate of the probabilities of our destiny ; no officials appeared ; the ordinary invariable routine of the steward department was suspended without notice ; the sounds were tremendous, and a hot, lurid obscurity filled the atmosphere. Soon after four the clamour increased, and the shock of a sea blowing up a part of the fore-guards made the groaning fabric reel and shiver throughout her whole bulk. At that time, by common consent, we assembled in the deck-house, which had windows looking in all directions, and sat there for five hours. Very few words were spoken, and very little fear was felt. We understood by intuition that if our crazy engines failed at any moment to keep the ship's head to the sea, her destruction would not occupy half an hour. It was all palpable. There was nothing which the most experienced seaman could explain to the merest novice. We hoped for the best, and there was no use in speaking about the worst. Nor, indeed, was speech possible, unless a human voice could have outshrieked the hurricane.

In this deck-house the strainings, sunderings, and groanings were hardly audible, or rather were overpowered by a sound which, in thirteen months' experience of the sea in all weathers, I have never heard, and hope never to hear again, unless in a staunch ship, one loud, awful, undying shriek, mingled with a prolonged, relentless hiss. No gathering strength, no languid fainting into momentary lulls, but one protracted, gigantic scream. And this was not the whistle of wind through cordage, but the actual sound of air travelling with tremendous velocity, carrying with it minute particles of water. Nor was the sea running mountains high, for the hurricane kept it down. Indeed during those fierce hours no sea was visible, for the whole surface was caught up and carried furiously into the air, like snow-drift on the prairies, sibilant, relentless. There was profound quiet on deck, the little life which existed being concentrated near the bow, where the captain was either lashed to the foremast, or in shelter in the pilot-house. Never a soul appeared on deck, the force of the hurricane being such that for four hours any man would have been carried off his feet. Through the swift strange evening our hopes rested on the engine, and amidst the uproar and din, and drifting spray, and shocks of pitiless seas, there was a sublime repose in the spectacle of the huge walking beams, alternately rising and falling, slowly, calmly, regularly, as if the *Nevada* were on a holiday trip within the Golden Gate. At eight in the evening we could hear each other speak, and a little later, through the great masses of hissing drift we discerned black water. At nine Captain Blethen appeared, smoking a cigar with nonchalance, and told us that the hurricane had nearly boxed the compass, and had been the most severe he had known for

seventeen years. This grand old man, nearly the oldest captain
in the Pacific, won our respect and confidence from the first,
and his quiet and masterly handling of this dilapidated old ship
is beyond all praise.

When the strain of apprehension was mitigated, we became
aware that we had not had anything to eat since breakfast, a
clean sweep having been made, not only of the lunch, but of
all the glass in the racks above it; but all requests to the
stewards were insufficient to procure even biscuits, and at
eleven we retired supperless to bed, amidst a confusion of
awful sounds, and were deprived of lights as well as food.
When we asked for food or light, and made weak appeals on
the ground of faintness, the one steward who seemed to dawdle
about for the sole purpose of making himself disagreeable,
always replied, "You can't get anything, the stewards are on
duty."   We were not accustomed to recognize that stewards
had any other duty than that of feeding the passengers, but
under the circumstances we meekly acquiesced.   We were
allowed to know that a part of the foreguards had been carried
away, and that iron stanchions four inches thick had been
gnarled and twisted like candy sticks, and the constant falling
of the saloon casing of the mainmast, showed something wrong
there.   A heavy clang, heard at intervals by day and night,
aroused some suspicions as to more serious damage, and these
were afterwards confirmed.   As the wind fell the sea rose, and
for some hours realized every description I have read of the
majesty and magnitude of the rollers of the South Pacific.

The day after the hurricane something went wrong with the
engines, and we were stationary for an hour.   We all felt
thankful that this derangement, which would have jeopardised
or sacrificed sixty lives, was then only a slight detention on a
summer sea.

Five days out from Auckland we entered the tropics with a
temperature of 80° in the water, and 85° in the air, but as the
light head airs blew the intense heat of our two smoke stacks
aft, we often endured a temperature of 110°.   There were
quiet heavy tropical showers, and a general misty dampness,
and the Navigator Islands, with their rainbow-tinted coral
forests, their fringe of coco palms, and groves of banyan and
breadfruit trees, those sunniest isles of the bright South Seas,
resolved themselves into dark lumps looming through a drizzling
mist.   But the showers and the dampness were confined to that
region, and for the last fortnight an unclouded tropical sun has

blazed upon our crawling ship. The boiler tubes are giving
way at the rate of from ten to twenty daily, the fracture in the
shaft is extending, and so, partially maimed, the old ship drags
her 320 feet of length slowly along. The captain is continually
in the engine-room, and we know when things are looking
more unpropitious than usual by his coming up puffing his
cigar with unusual strength of determination. It has been so
far a very pleasant voyage. The moral, mental, and social
qualities of my fellow-passengers are of a high order, and since
the hurricane we have been rather like a family circle than a
miscellaneous, accidental group. For some time our days went
by in reading aloud, working, chess, draughts, and conversation,
with two hours at quoits in the afternoon for exercise ; but four
days ago the only son of Mrs. Dexter, who is the only lady on
board besides myself, ruptured a blood vessel on the lungs, and
lies in a most critical state in the deck-house from which he has
not been moved, requiring most careful nursing, incessant
fanning, and the attention of two persons by day and night.
Mrs. D. had previously won the regard of every one, and I had
learned to look on her as a friend from whom I should be
grieved to part. The only hope for the young man's life is
that he should be landed at Honolulu, and she has urged me
so strongly to land with her there, where she will be a complete
stranger, that I have consented to do so, and consequently
shall see the Sandwich Islands. This severe illness has cast a
great gloom over our circle of six, and Mr. D. continues in a
state of so much exhaustion and peril that all our arrangements
as to occupation, recreation, and sleep, are made with reference
to a sick, and as we sometimes fear, a dying man, whose state is
much aggravated by the maltreatment and stupidity of a dilapidated Scotch doctor, who must be at least eighty, and whose
intellects are obfuscated by years of whisky drinking. Two of
the gentlemen not only show the utmost tenderness as nurses,
but possess a skill and experience which are invaluable. They
never leave him by night, and scarcely take needed rest even
in the day, one or other of them being always at hand to
support him when faint, or raise him on his pillows.

It is not only that the *Nevada* is barely seaworthy, and has
kept us broiling in the tropics when we ought to have been at
San Francisco, but her fittings are so old. The mattresses
bulge and burst, and cockroaches creep in and out, the deck is
so leaky that the water squishes up under the saloon matting
as we walk over it, the bread swarms with minute ants, and we

have to pick every piece over because of weevils. Existence at night is an unequal fight with rats and cockroaches, and at meals with the stewards for time to eat. The stewards out-number the passengers, and are the veriest riff-raff I have seen on board ship. At meals, when the captain is not below, their sole object is to hurry us from the table in order that they may sit down to a protracted meal; they are insulting and dis-obliging, and since illness has been on board, have shown a want of common humanity which places them below the rest of their species. The unconcealed hostility with which they regard us is a marvellous contrast to the natural or purchasable civility or servility which prevails on British steamers. It has its comic side too, and we are content to laugh at it, and at all the other oddities of this vaunted " Mail Line."

Our most serious grievance was the length of time that we were kept in the damp inter-island region of the Tropic of Capricorn. Early breakfasts, cold plunge baths, and the perfect ventilation of our cabins, only just kept us alive. We read, wrote, and talked like automatons, and our voices sounded thin and far away. We decided that heat was less felt in exercise, made up an afternoon quoit party, and played, un-sheltered from the nearly vertical sun on decks so hot that we required thick boots for the protection of our feet, but for three days were limp and faint, and hardly able to crawl about or eat. The nights were insupportable. We used to lounge on the bow, and retire late at night to our cabins, to fight the heat, and scare rats and kill cockroaches with slippers, until driven by the solar heat to rise again unrefreshed to *warstle* through another relentless day. We read the " Idylls of the King," and talked of misty meres and reedy fens, of the cool north, with its purple hills, leaping streams, and life-giving breezes, of long northern winters, and ice and snow, but the realities of sultriness and damp scared away our coolest imagi-nations.

In this dismal region, when about forty miles east of Tutuila, a beast popularly known as the "Flying fox"* alighted on our rigging, and was eventually captured as a prize for the zoological collection at San Francisco. He is a most interest-ing animal, something like an exaggerated bat. His wings are formed of a jet black membrane, and have a highly polished claw at the extremity of each, and his feet consist of five

---

* A Frugiferous bat.

beautifully polished long black claws, with which he hangs on
ʰead downwards. His body is about twice the size of that of
a very large rat, black and furry underneath, and with red, foxy
fur on the head and back. His face is pointed, with a very
black nose and prominent black eyes with a savage, remorse-
less expression. His wings, when extended, measure forty-
eight inches across, and his flying powers are prodigious. He
snapped like a dog at first, but is now quite tame, and devours
quantities of dried figs, the only diet he will eat.

We crossed the Equator in Long. 159° 44′ W., but in consequence of the misty weather it was not till we reached
Lat. 10° 6′ N. that the Pole star, cold and pure, glistened far
above the horizon, and two hours later we saw the coruscating
Pleiades, and the starry belt of Orion, the blessed familiar
constellations of " auld lang syne," and a " breath of the cool
north," the first I have felt for five months, fanned the tropic
night and the calm, silvery Pacific. From that time we have
been indifferent to our crawling pace, except for the sick man's
sake. The days dawn in rose colour and die in gold, and
through their long hours a sea of delicious blue shimmers
beneath the sun, so soft, so blue, so dreamlike, an ocean
worthy of its name, the enchanted region of perpetual calm,
and an endless summer. Far off, for many an azure league,
rims of rock, fringed with the graceful coco palm, girdle still
lagoons, and are themselves encircled by coral reefs on which
the ocean breaks all the year in broad drifts of foam. Myriads
of flying fish, and a few dolphins and Portuguese men-of-war
flash or float through the scarcely undulating water. But we
look in vain for the " sails of silk and ropes of sendal" which
are alone appropriate to this dream-world. The Pacific in this
region is an indolent, blue expanse, pure and lonely, an almost
untraversed sea. We revel in these tropic days of transcendent
glory, in the balmy breath which just stirs the dreamy blue, in
the brief, fierce crimson sunsets, in the soft splendour of the
nights, when the moon and stars hang like lamps out of a lofty
and distant vault, and in the pearly crystalline dawns, when the
sun rising through a veil of rose and gold " rejoices as a giant
to run his course," and brightens by no " pale gradations " into
the " perfect day."

P.S.—To-morrow morning we expect to sight land. In spite
of minor evils, our voyage has been a singularly pleasant one.
The condition of the ship and her machinery warrants the

strongest condemnation, but her discipline is admirable, and so are many of her regulations, and we might have had a much more disagreeable voyage in a better ship. Captain Blethen is beyond all praise, and so is the chief engineer, whose duties are incessant and most harassing, owing to the critical state of the engines. The *Nevada* now presents a grotesque appearance, for within the last few hours she has received such an added list to port that her starboard wheel looks nearly out of the water.

I. L. B.

LETTER II.

HAWAIIAN HOTEL, HONOLULU, *Jan. 26th.*

YESTERDAY morning at 6.30 I was aroused by the news
that "The Islands" were in sight. Oahu in the distance, a
group of grey, barren peaks rising verdureless out of the lonely
sea, was not an exception to the rule that the first sight of land
is a disappointment. Owing to the clear atmosphere, we
seemed only five miles off, but in reality we were twenty, and
the land improved as we neared it. It was the fiercest day we
had had, the deck was almost too hot to stand upon, the sea
and sky were both magnificently blue, and the unveiled sun
turned every minute ripple into a diamond flash. As we approached, the island changed its character. There were lofty
peaks, truly—grey and red, sun-scorched, and wind-bleached,
glowing here and there with traces of their fiery origin; but
they were cleft by deep chasms and ravines of cool shade and
entrancing greenness, and falling water streaked their sides—
a most welcome vision after eleven months of the desert sea,
and the dusty browns of Australia and New Zealand. Nearer
yet, and the coast line came into sight, fringed by the feathery
cocoanut tree of the tropics, and marked by a long line of surf.
The grand promontory of Diamond Head, its fiery sides now
softened by a haze of green, terminated the wavy line of palms;
then the Punchbowl, a perfect, extinct crater, brilliant with
every shade of red volcanic ash, blazed against the green skirts
of the mountains. We were close to the coral reef before the
cry, "There's Honolulu!" made us aware of the proximity of
the capital of the island kingdom, and then, indeed, its existence had almost to be taken upon trust, for besides the lovely
wooden and grass huts, with deep verandahs, which nestled
under palms and bananas on soft green sward, margined by
the bright sea sand, only two church spires and a few grey
roofs appeared above the trees.

We were just outside the reef, and near enough to hear that
deep sound of the surf which, through the ever serene summer
years girdles the Hawaiian Islands with perpetual thunder,
before the pilot glided alongside, bringing the news which
Mark Twain had prepared us to receive with interest, that
" Prince Bill " had been unanimously elected to the throne.
The surf ran white and pure over the environing coral reef, and
as we passed through the narrow channel, we almost saw the
coral forests deep down under the *Nevada's* keel ; the coral
fishers plied their graceful trade ; canoes with outriggers rode
the combers, and glided with inconceivable rapidity round our
ship; amphibious brown beings sported in the transparent
waves ; and within the reef lay a calm surface of water of a
wonderful blue, entered by a narrow, intricate passage of the
deepest indigo.   And beyond the reef and beyond the blue,
nestling among cocoanut trees and bananas, umbrella trees
and breadfruits, oranges, mangoes, hibiscus, algaroba, and
passion-flowers, almost hidden in the deep, dense greenery,
was Honolulu.   Bright blossom of a summer sea !   Fair Paradise of the Pacific !

Inside the reef the magnificent iron-clad *California* and
another large American war vessel, the *Benicia,* are moored in
line with the British corvette *Scout,* within 200 yards of the
shore ; and their boats were constantly passing and re-passing,
among countless canoes filled with natives.   Two coasting
schooners were just leaving the harbour, and the inter-island
steamer *Kilauea,* with her deck crowded with natives, was just
coming in.   By noon the great decrepit *Nevada,* which has no
wharf at which she can lie in New Zealand, was moored alongside a very respectable one in this enterprising little Hawaiian
capital.

We looked down from the towering deck on a crowd of two
or three thousand people—whites, Kanakas, Chinamen—and
hundreds of them at once made their way on board, and
streamed over the ship, talking, laughing, and remarking upon
us in a language which seemed without backbone.   Such rich
brown men and women they were, with wavy, shining black
hair, large, brown, lustrous eyes, and rows of perfect teeth like
ivory.   Everyone was smiling.   The forms of the women seemed
to be inclined towards obesity, but their drapery, which consists of a sleeved garment which falls in ample and unconfined
folds from their shoulders to their feet, partly conceals this
defect, which is here regarded as a beauty.   Some of these

dresses were black, but many of those worn by the younger
women were of pure white, crimson, yellow, scarlet, blue, or
light green. The men displayed their lithe, graceful figures to
the best advantage in white trousers and gay Garibaldi shirts.
A few of the women wore coloured handkerchiefs twined round
their hair, but generally both men and women wore straw hats,
which the men set jauntily on one side of their heads, and
heightened their picturesqueness yet more by bandana handkerchiefs of rich, bright colours round their necks, knotted
loosely on the left side, with a grace to which, I think, no
Anglo-Saxon dandy could attain. Without an exception the
men and women wore wreaths and garlands of flowers, carmine,
orange, or pure white, twined round their hats, and thrown
carelessly round their throats, flowers unknown to me, but
redolent of the tropics in fragrance and colour. Many of the
young beauties wore the gorgeous blossom of the red hibiscus
among their abundant, unconfined, black hair, and many, besides the garlands, wore festoons of a sweet-scented vine, or of
an exquisitely beautiful fern, knotted behind, and hanging half-
way down their dresses. These adornments of natural flowers
are most attractive. Chinamen, all alike, very yellow, with
almond-shaped eyes, youthful, hairless faces, long pigtails, spot-
lessly clean clothes, and an expression of mingled cunning and
simplicity, "foreigners," half-whites, a few negroes, and a very
few dark-skinned Polynesians from the far-off South Seas, made
up the rest of the rainbow-tinted crowd.

The "foreign" ladies, who were there in great numbers,
generally wore simple, light prints or muslins, and white straw
hats, and many of them so far conformed to native custom as
to wear natural flowers round their hats and throats. But
where were the hard, angular, careworn, sallow, passionate
faces of men and women, such as form the majority of every
crowd at home, as well as in America and Australia? The
conditions of life must surely be easier here, and people must
have found rest from some of its burdensome conventionalities.
The foreign ladies, in their simple, tasteful, fresh attire, innocent of the humpings and bunchings, the monstrosities and
deformities of ultra-fashionable bad taste, beamed with cheerfulness, friendliness, and kindliness. Men and women looked
as easy, contented, and happy as if care never came near them.
I never saw such healthy, bright complexions as among the
women, or such "sparkling smiles," or such a diffusion of
feminine grace and graciousness anywhere.

Outside this motley, genial, picturesque crowd about 200 saddled horses were standing, each with the Mexican saddle, with its lassoing horn in front, high peak behind, immense wooden stirrups, with great leathern guards, silver or brass bosses, and coloured saddle-cloths. The saddles were the only element of the picturesque that these Hawaiian steeds possessed. They were sorry, lean, undersized beasts, looking in general as if the emergencies of life left them little time for eating or sleeping. They stood calmly in the broiling sun, heavy-headed and heavy-hearted, with flabby ears and pendulous lower lips, limp and rawboned, a doleful type of the "creation which groaneth and travaileth in misery." All these belonged to the natives, who are passionately fond of riding. Every now and then a flower-wreathed Hawaiian woman, in her full, radiant garment, sprang on one of these animals astride, and dashed along the road at full gallop, sitting on her horse as square and easy as a hussar. In the crowd and outside of it, and everywhere, there were piles of fruit for sale — oranges and guavas, strawberries, papayas, bananas (green and golden), cocoanuts, and other rich, fantastic productions of a prolific climate, where nature gives of her wealth the whole year round. Fishes, strange in shape and colour, crimson, blue, orange, rose, gold, such fishes as flash like living light through the coral groves of these enchanted seas, were there for sale, and coral divers were there with their treasures—branch coral, as white as snow, each perfect specimen weighing from eight to twenty pounds. But no one pushed his wares for sale—we were at liberty to look and admire, and pass on unmolested. No vexatious restrictions obstructed our landing. A sum of two dollars for the support of the Queen's Hospital is levied on each passenger, and the examination of ordinary luggage, if it exists, is a mere form. From the demeanour of the crowd it was at once apparent that the conditions of conquerors and conquered do not exist. On the contrary, many of the foreigners there were subjects of a Hawaiian king, a reversal of the ordinary relations between a white and a coloured race which it is not easy yet to appreciate.

Two of my fellow-passengers, who were going on to San Francisco, were anxious that I should accompany them to the *Pali*, the great excursion from Honolulu; and leaving Mr. M—— to make all arrangements for the Dexters and myself, we hired a buggy, destitute of any peculiarity but a native driver, who spoke nothing but Hawaiian, and left the ship.

This place is quite unique. It is said that 15,000 people are
buried away in these low-browed, shadowy houses, under the
glossy, dark-leaved trees, but except in one or two streets of
miscellaneous, old-fashioned-looking stores, arranged with a
distinct leaning towards native tastes, it looks like a large
village, or rather like an aggregate of villages. As we drove
through the town we could only see our immediate surroundings, but each had a new fascination. We drove along roads
with over-arching trees, through whose dense leafage the noon
sunshine only trickled in dancing, broken lights ; umbrella
trees, caoutchouc, bamboo, mango, orange, breadfruit, candle-
nut, monkey pod, date and coco palms, alligator pears, " prides "
of Barbary, India, and Peru, and huge-leaved, wide-spreading
trees, exotics from the South Seas, many of them rich in parasitic ferns, and others blazing with bright, fantastic blossoms.
The air was heavy with odours of gardenia, tuberose, oleanders,
roses, lilies, and the great white trumpet-flower, and myriads
of others whose names I do not know, and verandahs were
festooned with a gorgeous trailer with magenta blossoms,
passion-flowers, and a vine with masses of trumpet-shaped,
yellow, waxy flowers. The delicate tamarind and the feathery
algaroba intermingled their fragile grace with the dark, shiny
foliage of the South Sea exotics, and the deep red, solitary
flowers of the hibiscus rioted among familiar fuchsias and
geraniums, which here attain the height and size of large rhodo-
dendrons.

Few of the new trees surprised me more than the papaya.
It is a perfect gem of tropical vegetation. It has a soft, indented stem, which runs up quite straight to a height of from
15 to 30 feet, and is crowned by a profusion of large, deeply
indented leaves, with long foot-stalks, and among, as well as
considerably below these, are the flowers or the fruit, in all
stages of development. This, when ripe, is bright yellow, and
the size of a musk melon. Clumps of bananas, the first sight
of which, like that of the palm, constitutes a new experience,
shaded the native houses with their wonderful leaves, broad and
deep green, from five to ten feet long. The breadfruit is a superb
tree, about 60 feet high, with deep green, shining leaves, a foot
broad, sharply and symmetrically cut, worthy, from their exceeding beauty of form, to take the place of the acanthus in
architectural ornament, and throwing their pale green fruit into
delicate contrast. All these, with the exquisite rose apple,
with a deep red tinge in its young leaves, the fan palm, the

chirimoya, and numberless others, and the slender shafts of the
coco palms rising high above them, with their waving plumes
and perpetual fruitage, were a perfect festival of beauty.

In the deep shade of this perennial greenery the people
dwell. The foreign houses show a very various individuality.
The peculiarity in which all seem to share is, that everything
is decorated and festooned with flowering trailers. It is often
difficult to tell what the architecture is, or what is house and
what is vegetation; for all angles, lattices, balustrades, and
verandahs are hidden by jessamine or passion-flowers, or
the gorgeous, flame-like Bougainvillea. Many of the dwellings
straggle over the ground without an upper story, and have very
deep verandahs, through which I caught glimpses of cool, shady
rooms, with matted floors. Some look as if they had been
transported from the old-fashioned villages of the Connecticut
Valley, with their clap-board fronts painted white, and jalousies
painted green; but then the deep verandah in which families
lead an open-air life has been added, and the chimneys have
been omitted, and the New England severity and angularity
are toned down and draped out of sight by these festoons of
large-leaved, bright-blossomed, tropical climbing plants. Besides the frame houses there are houses built of blocks of a
cream-coloured coral conglomerate laid in cement, of *adobe,* or
large sun-baked bricks, plastered; houses of grass and bamboo;
houses on the ground and houses raised on posts; but nothing
looks prosaic, commonplace, or mean, for the glow and
luxuriance of the tropics rest on all. Each house has a large
garden or "yard," with lawns of bright perennial green, and
banks of blazing, many-tinted flowers, and lines of Dracæna,
and other foliage plants, with their great purple or crimson
leaves, and clumps of marvellous lilies, gladiolas, ginger, and
many plants unknown to me. Fences and walls are altogether
buried by passion-flowers, the night-blowing Cereus, and the
tropæolum, mixed with geraniums, fuchsia, and jessamine,
which cluster and entangle over them in indescribable profusion. A soft air moves through the upper branches, and the
drip of water from miniature fountains falls musically on the
perfumed air. This is mid-winter! The summer, they say,
is thermometrically hotter, but practically cooler, because of
the regular trades which set in in April, but now, with the
shaded thermometer at 80° and the sky without clouds, the
heat is not oppressive.

The mixture of the neat grass houses of the natives with the more elaborate homes of the foreign residents has a very pleasant look. The "aborigines" have not been crowded out of sight, or into a special "quarter." We saw many groups of them sitting under the trees outside their houses, each group with a mat in the centre, with calabashes upon it containing *poi*, the national Hawaiian dish, a fermented paste made from the root of the *kalo*, or *arum esculentum*. As we emerged on the broad road which leads up the Nuuanu Valley to the mountains, we saw many patches of this *kalo*, a very handsome tropical plant, with large leaves of a bright tender green. Each plant was growing on a small hillock, with water round it. There were beautiful vegetable gardens also, in which Chinamen raise for sale not only melons, pineapples, sweet potatoes, and other edibles of hot climates, but the familiar fruits and vegetables of the temperate zones. In patches of surpassing neatness, there were strawberries, which are ripe here all the year, peas, carrots, turnips, asparagus, lettuce, and celery. I saw no other plants or trees which grow at home, but recognized as hardly less familiar growths the Victorian Eucalyptus, which has not had time to become gaunt and straggling, the Norfolk Island pine, which grows superbly here, and the handsome Moreton Bay fig. But the chief feature of this road is the number of residences ; I had almost written of pretentious residences, but the term would be a base slander, as I have jumped to the conclusion that the twin vulgarities of ostentation and pretence have no place here. But certainly for a mile and a half or more there are many very comfortable-looking dwellings, very attractive to the eye, with an ease and imperturbable serenity of demeanour as if they had nothing to fear from heat, cold, wind, or criticism. Their architecture is absolutely unostentatious, and their one beauty is that they are embowered among trailers, shadowed by superb exotics, and surrounded by banks of flowers, while the stately cocoanut, the banana, and the candlenut, the aborigines of Oahu, are nowhere displaced. One house with extensive grounds, a perfect wilderness of vegetation, was pointed out as the summer palace of Queen Emma, or Kaleeonalani, widow of Kamehameha IV., who visited England a few years ago, and the finest garden of all as that of a much respected Chinese merchant, named Afong. Oahu, at least on this leeward side, is not tropical looking, and all this tropical variety and luxuriance which delight the eye result from foreign enthusiasm and love of beauty and shade.

When we ascended above the scattered dwellings and had passed the tasteful mausoleum, with two tall Kahilis,* or feather plumes, at the door of the tomb in which the last of the Kamehamehas received Christian burial, the glossy, re-dundant, arborescent vegetation ceased.   At that height a shower of rain falls on nearly every day in the year, and the

The Nuuanu Pali, or Precipice, near Honolulu.

result is a green sward which England can hardly rival, a perfect sea of verdure, darkened in the valley and more than half way up the hill sides by the foliage of the yellow-blossomed and almost impenetrable hibiscus, brightened here and there by the pea-green candlenut.   Streamlets leap from crags and ripple along the roadside, every rock and stone is hidden by

---

* The kahili is shaped like an enormous bottle brush.   The finest are sometimes twenty feet high, with handles twelve or fifteen feet long, covered with tortoiseshell and whale tooth ivory.   The upper part is formed of a cylinder of wicker work about a foot in diameter, on which red, black, and yellow feathers are fastened.   These insignia are carried in procession instead of banners, and used to be fixed in the ground near the temporary residence of the king or chiefs.   At the funeral of the late king seventy-six large and small kahilis were carried by the retainers of chief families.

moist-looking ferns, as aerial and delicate as marabout feathers, and when the windings of the valley and the projecting spurs of mountains shut out all indications of Honolulu, in the cool, green loneliness one could imagine oneself in the temperate zones. The peculiarity of the scenery is, that the hills, which rise to a height of about 4,000 feet, are wall-like ridges of grey or coloured rock, rising precipitously out of the trees and grass, and that these walls are broken up into pinnacles and needles. At the *Pali* (wall-like precipice), the summit of the ascent of 1,000 feet, we left our buggy, and passing through a gash in the rock the celebrated view burst on us with over-whelming effect. Immense masses of black and ferruginous volcanic rock, hundreds of feet in nearly perpendicular height, formed the *pali* on either side, and the ridge extended north-wards for many miles, presenting a lofty, abrupt mass of grey rock broken into fantastic pinnacles, which seemed to pierce the sky. A broad, umbrageous mass of green clothed the lower buttresses, and fringed itself away in clusters of coco palms on a garden-like stretch below, green with grass and sugar-cane, and dotted with white houses, each with its palm and banana grove, and varied by eminences which looked like long extinct tufa cones. Beyond this enchanted region stretched the coral reef, with its white, wavy line of endless surf, and the broad blue Pacific, ruffled by a breeze whose icy freshness chilled us where we stood. Narrow streaks on the landscape, every now and then disappearing behind inter-vening hills, indicated bridle tracks connected with a frightfully steep and rough zig-zag path cut out of the face of the cliff on our right. I could not go down this on foot without a sense of insecurity, but mounted natives driving loaded horses de-scended with perfect impunity into the dreamland below.

This *pali* is the scene of one of the historic tragedies of this island. Kamehameha the Conqueror, who after fierce fighting and much ruthless destruction of human life united the island sovereignties in his own person, routed the forces of the King of Oahu in the Nuuanu Valley, and drove them in hundreds up the precipice, from which they leaped in despair and mad-ness, and their bones lie bleaching 800 feet below.

The drive back here was delightful, from the wintry height, where I must confess that we shivered, to the slumbrous calm of an endless summer, the glorious tropical trees, the distant view of cool chasm-like valleys, with Honolulu sleeping in perpetual shade, and the still, blue ocean, without a single sail to disturb its profound solitude. Saturday afternoon is a gala-day here, and the broad road was so thronged with brilliant equestrians, that I thought we should be ridden over by the reckless rout. There were hundreds of native horsemen and horsewomen, many of them doubtless on the dejected quadrupeds I saw at the wharf, but a judicious application of long rowelled Mexican spurs, and a degree of emulation, caused these animals to tear along at full gallop. The women seemed perfectly at home in their gay, brass-bossed, high peaked saddles, flying along

The Pau or Hawaiian Ladies' Holiday Riding Dress.

astride, bare-footed, with their orange and scarlet riding dresses streaming on each side beyond their horses' tails, a bright kaleidoscopic flash of bright eyes, white teeth, shining hair, garlands of flowers and many coloured dresses ; while the men were hardly less gay, with fresh flowers round their jaunty hats, and the vermilion-coloured blossoms of the *Ohia* round their brown throats. Sometimes a troop of twenty of these free-and-easy female riders went by at a time, a graceful and exciting spectacle, with a running accompaniment of vociferation and laughter. Among these we met several of the

Nevada's officers, riding in the stiff, wooden style which Anglo-Saxons love, and a horde of jolly British sailors from H.M.S. *Scout,* rushing helter skelter, colliding with everybody, bestriding their horses as they would a topsailyard, hanging on to manes and lassoing horns, and enjoying themselves thoroughly. In the shady, tortuous streets we met hundreds more of native riders, dashing at full gallop without fear of the police. Many of the women were in flowing riding dresses of pure white, over which their unbound hair, and wreaths of carmine-tinted flowers fell most picturesquely.

All this time I had not seen our domicile, and when our drive ended under the quivering shadow of large tamarind and algaroba trees, in front of a long, stone, two-storied house with two deep verandahs festooned with clematis and passion flowers, and a shady lawn in front, I felt as if in this fairy land anything might be expected.

This is the perfection of an hotel. Hospitality seems to take possession of and appropriate one as soon as one enters its never-closed door, which is on the lower verandah. Everywhere, only pleasant objects meet the eye. One can sit all day on the back verandah, watching the play of light and colour on the mountains and the deep blue green of the Nuuanu Valley, where showers, sunshine, and rainbows make perpetual variety. The great dining-room is delicious. It has no curtains, and its decorations are cool and pale. Its windows look upon tropical trees in one direction, and up to the cool mountains in the other. Piles of bananas, guavas, limes, and oranges, decorate the tables at each meal, and strange vegetables, fish, and fruits vary the otherwise stereotyped American hotel fare. There are no female domestics The host is a German, the manager an American, the steward a Hawaiian, and the servants are all Chinamen in spotless white linen, with pigtails coiled round their heads, and an air of superabundant good-nature. They know very little English, and make most absurd mistakes, but they are cordial, smiling, and obliging, and look cool and clean. The hotel seems the great public resort of Honolulu, the centre of stir—club-house, exchange, and drawing-room in one. Its wide corridors and verandahs are lively with English and American naval uniforms, several planters' families are here for the season ; and with health-seekers from California, resident boarders, whaling captains, tourists from the British Pacific Colonies, and a stream of townspeople always percolating through the corridors

and verandahs, it seems as lively and free-and-easy as a place
can be, pervaded by the kindliness and bonhomie which
form important items in my first impressions of the islands.
The hotel was lately built by government at a cost of $120,000,
a sum which forms a considerable part of that token of an
advanced civilization, a National Debt. The minister whose
scheme it was seems to be severely censured on account of it,
but undoubtedly it brings strangers and their money into the
kingdom, who would have avoided it had they been obliged as
formerly to cast themselves on the hospitality of the residents.
The present proprietor has it rent-free for a term of years, but
I fear that it is not likely to prove a successful speculation
either for him or the government. I dislike health resorts, and
abhor this kind of life, but for those who like both, I cannot
imagine a more fascinating residence. The charges are $15 a
week, or $3 a day, but such a kindly, open-handed system
prevails, that I am not conscious that I am paying anything !
This sum includes hot and cold plunge baths *ad libitum*, justly
regarded as a necessity in this climate.

Dr. McGrew has hope that our invalid will rally in this
healing, equable atmosphere. Our kind fellow-passengers are
here, and take turns in watching and fanning him. Through
the half-closed jalousies we see breadfruit trees, delicate tamarinds and algarobas, fan-palms, date-palms, and bananas, and
the deep blue Pacific gleams here and there through the
plumage of the cocoanut trees. A soft breeze, scented with a
slight aromatic odour, wanders in at every opening, bringing
with it, mellowed by distance, the hum and clatter of the busy
cicada. The nights are glorious, and so absolutely still, that
even the feathery foliage of the algaroba is at rest. The stars
seem to hang among the trees like lamps, and the crescent
moon gives more light than the full moon at home. The
evening of the day we landed, parties of officers and ladies
mounted at the door, and with much mirth disappeared on
moonlight rides, and the white robes of flower-crowned girls
gleamed among the trees, as groups of natives went by speaking
a language which sounded more like the rippling of water than
human speech. Soft music came from the ironclads in the
harbour, and from the royal band at the king's palace, and a
rich scent of dewy blossoms filled the delicious air. These
are indeed the "isles of Eden," "the sun lands," musical with
beauty. They seem to welcome us to their enchanted shores.
Everything is new but nothing strange ; for as I enjoyed the

purple night, I remembered that I had seen such islands in dreams in the cold, gray North. " How sweet," I thought it would be, thus to hear far off, the low, sweet murmur of the " sparkling brine," to rest, and

> "Ever to seem
> **Falling asleep in a half-dream.**"

A half-dream only, for one would not wish to be quite asleep, and lose the consciousness of this delicious outer world. So I thought one moment. The next I heard a droning, humming sound, which certainly was not the surf upon the reef. It came nearer—there could be no mistake. I felt a stab, and found myself the centre of a swarm of droning, stabbing, malignant mosquitos. No, even this is not paradise ! I am ashamed to say that on my first night in Honolulu I sought an early refuge from this intolerable infliction, in profound and prosaic sleep behind mosquito curtains.

I. L. B.

LETTER III.

An Oahu Sabbath—A State Pageant—An Abrupt Departure—Inter-Island Travelling—Maui—Contradictory Statements—Windward Hawaii— A Polynesian Paradise—Hilo Fascinations.

HAWAIIAN HOTEL, *Jan. 28th.*

SUNDAY was a very pleasant day here. Church bells rang, and the shady streets were filled with people in holiday dress. There are two large native churches, the Kaumakapili, and the Kaiwaiaho, usually called the stone church. The latter is an immense, substantial building, for the erection of which each Christian native brought a block of rock-coral. There is a large Roman Catholic church, the priests of which are said to have been somewhat successful in proselytizing operations. The Reformed Catholic, or English temporary cathedral, is a tasteful but very simple wooden building, standing in pretty grounds, on which a useful institution for boarding and training native and half-white girls, and the reception of white girls as day scholars, also stands. This is in connection with Miss Sellon's Sisterhood at Devonport. Another building, alongside the cathedral, is used for English service in Hawaiian. There are two Congregational churches : the old "Bethel," of which the Rev. S. C. Damon, known to all strangers, and one of the oldest and most respected Honolulu residents, is the minister ; and the "Fort St. Church," which has a large and influential congregation, and has been said to " run the government," because its members compose the majority of the Cabinet. Lunalilo, the present king, has cast in his lot with the Congregationalists, but queen Emma is an earnest member of the Anglican Church, and attends the Liturgical Hawaiian Service in order to throw the weight of her influence with the natives into the scale of that communion. Her husband spent many of his later days in translating the Prayer-Book. As is natural, most of the natives belong to the denomination from which they or their fathers received the Christian faith, and the majority of the foreigners are of the same persuasion. The New England Puritan influence, with its rigid Sabbatarianism, though considerably worn away, is still influential enough to produce a general appearance of Sabbath observance. The stores are closed, the church-going is very demonstrative, and the pleasure-seeking is very unobtrusive. The wharves are profoundly quiet.

I went twice to the English Cathedral, and was interested to see there a lady in a nun's habit, with a number of brown girls, who was pointed out to me as Sister Bertha, who has been working here usefully for many years. The ritual is high. I am told that it is above the desires of most of the island Episcopalians, but the zeal and disinterestedness of Bishop Willis will, in time, I doubt not, win upon those who prize such qualities. He called in the afternoon, and took me to his pretty, unpretending residence up the Nuuanu Valley. He has a training and boarding school there for native boys, some of whom were at church in the morning as a surpliced choir. The bishop, his sister, the schoolmaster, and fourteen boys take their meals together in a refectory, the boys acting as servitors by turns. There is a service every morning at 6.30 in the private chapel attached to the house, and also in the cathedral a little later. Early risers, so near the equator, must get up by candlelight all the year round.

This morning we joined our kind friends from the *Nevada* for the last time at breakfast. I have noticed that there is often a centrifugal force which acts upon passengers who have been long at sea together, dispersing them on reaching port. Indeed, the temporary, enforced cohesion is often succeeded by violent repulsion. But in this instance we deeply regret the dissolution of our pleasant fraternity ; the less so, however, that this wonderful climate has produced a favourable change in Mr. D., who no longer requires the hourly attention hitherto necessary. The mornings here, dew-bathed and rose-flushed, are, if possible, more lovely than the nights, and people are astir early to enjoy them. The American consul and Mr. Damon called while we were sitting at our eight-o'clock breakfast, from which I gather that formalities are dispensed with. After spending the morning in hunting among the stores for things which were essential for the invalid, I lunched in the *Nevada* with Captain Blethen and our friends.

Next to the advent of "national ships" (a euphemism for men-of-war), the arrivals and departures of the New Zealand mail-steamers constitute the great excitement of Honolulu, and the failures, mishaps, and wonderful unpunctuality of this Webb line are highly stimulating in a region where "nothing happens." The loungers were saying that the *Nevada's* pumps were going for five days before we arrived, and pointed out the clearness of the water which was running from them at the wharf as an evidence that she was leaking badly.* The crowd of natives was enormous, and the foreigners were there in hundreds. She was loading with oranges and green bananas up to the last moment,—those tasteless bananas which, out of the tropics, misrepresent this most delicious and ambrosial fruit.

There was a far greater excitement for the natives, for King Lunalilo was about to pay a state visit to the American flag-ship *California*, and every available place along the wharves and roads was crowded with kanakas anxious to see him. I should tell you that the late king, being without heirs, ought to have nominated his successor; but it is said that a sorceress, under whose influence he was, persuaded him that his death would follow upon this act. When he died, two months ago, leaving the succession unprovided for, the duty of electing a sovereign, according to the constitution, devolved upon the people through their representatives, and they exercised it with a combination of order and enthusiasm which reflects great credit on their civilization. They chose the highest chief on the islands, Lunalilo (Above All), known among foreigners as "Prince Bill," and at this time letters of congratulation are pouring in upon him from his brethren, the sovereigns of Europe.

The spectacular effect of a pageant here is greatly heightened by the cloudless blue sky, and the wealth of light and colour. It was very hot, almost too hot for sight-seeing, on the *Nevada's* bow. Expectation among the lieges became tremendous and vociferous when Admiral Pennock's sixteen-oared barge, with a handsome awning, followed by two well-manned boats, swept across the strip of water which lies between the ships and the shore. Outrigger canoes, with garlanded men and women, were poised upon the motionless water, or darted gracefully round the ironclads, as gracefully to come to rest. Then a stir and sway-

---

* A week after her sailing, this unlucky ship put back with some mysterious ailment, and on her final arrival at San Francisco, her condition was found to be such that it was a marvel that she had made the passage at all.

ing of the crowd, and the American Admiral was seen standing
at the steps of an English barouche and four, and an Hawaiian
imitation of an English cheer rang out upon the air.   More
cheering, more excitement, and I saw nothing else till the
Admiral's barge, containing the Admiral, and the King dressed
in a plain morning suit with a single decoration, swept past
the *Nevada.*   The suite followed in the other boats,—brown
men and white, governors, ministers, and court dignitaries, in
Windsor uniforms, but with an added resplendency of plumes,
epaulettes, and gold lace.   As soon as Lunalilo reached the
California, the yards of the three ships were manned, and
amidst cheering which rent the air, and the deafening thunder
of a royal salute from sixty-three guns of heavy calibre, the
popular descendant of seventy generations of sceptred savages
stepped on board the flag-ship's deck.   No higher honours
could have been paid to the Emperor " of all the Russias."   I
have seen few sights more curious than that of the representa
tive of the American Republic standing bare-headed before a
coloured man, and the two mightiest empires on earth paying
royal honours to a Polynesian sovereign, whose little kingdom
in the North Pacific is known to many of us at home only as
" the group of islands where Captain Cook was killed."   Ah !
how lovely this Queen of Oceans is !   Blue, bright, balm-
breathing, gentle in its strength, different both in motion and
colour from the coarse " vexed Atlantic ! "

STEAMER KILAUEA, *January 29th.*

I was turning homewards, enjoying the prospect of a quiet
week in Honolulu, when Mr. and Mrs. Damon seized upon me,
and told me that a lady friend of theirs, anxious for a companion, was going to the volcano on Hawaii, that she was a
most expert and intelligent traveller, that the *Kilauea* would
sail in two hours, that unless I went now I should have no
future opportunity during my limited stay on the islands, that
Mrs. Dexter was anxious for me to go, that they would more
than fill my place in my absence, that this was a golden opportunity, that in short I *must* go, and they would drive me back
to the hotel to pack !   The volcano is still a myth to me, and I
wanted to " read up " before going, and above all was grieved
to leave my friend, but she had already made some needful
preparations, her son with his feeble voice urged my going, the
doctor said that there was now no danger to be apprehended,

and the Damons' kind urgency left me so little choice, that by five I was with them on the wharf, being introduced to my travelling companion, and to many of my fellow-passengers. Such an unexpected move is very bewildering, and it is too experimental, and too much of a leap in the dark to be enjoyable at present.

The wharf was one dense, well-compacted mass of natives taking leave of their friends with much effusiveness, and the steamer's deck was crowded with them, till there was hardly room to move; men, women, children, dogs, cats, mats, calabashes of *poi*, cocoanuts, bananas, dried fish, and every dusky individual of the throng was wreathed and garlanded with odorous and brilliant flowers. All were talking and laughing, and an immense amount of gesticulation seems to emphasise and supplement speech. We steamed through the reef in the brief, red twilight, over the golden tropic sea, keeping on the leeward side of the islands. Before it was quite dark the sleeping arrangements were made, and the deck and skylights were covered with mats and mattresses on which 170 natives sat, slept, or smoked,—a motley, parti-coloured mass of humanity, in the midst of which I recognized Bishop Willis in the usual episcopal dress, lying on a mattress among the others, a prey to discomfort and weariness! What would his episcopal brethren at home think of such a hardship?

There is a yellow-skinned, soft-voiced, fascinating Goa or Malay steward on board, who with infinite goodwill attends to the comfort of everybody. I was surprised when he asked me if I would like a mattress on the skylight, or a berth below, and in unhesitating ignorance replied severely, "Oh, below, of course, please," thinking of a ladies' cabin, but when I went down to supper my eyes were enlightened.

The *Kilauea* is a propeller of 400 tons, most unprepossessing in appearance, slow, but sure, and capable of bearing an infinite amount of battering. It is jokingly said that her keel has rasped off the branch coral round all the islands. Though there are many inter-island schooners, she is the only sure mode of reaching the windward islands in less than a week; and though at present I am disposed to think rather slightingly of her, and to class her with the New Zealand coasting craft, yet the residents are very proud of her, and speak lovingly of her, and regard her as a blessed deliverance from the horrors of beating to windward. She has a shabby, obsolete look about her, like a second-rate coasting collier, or an old American

tow-boat.   She looks ill-found, too ; I saw two essential pieces
of tackle give way as they were hoisting the main sail.   She has
a small saloon with a double tier of berths, besides transoms,
which give accommodation on the level of the lower berth.
There is a stern cabin, which is a prolongation of the saloon,
and not in any way separated from it.   There is no ladies'
cabin ; but sex, race, and colour are included in a promiscuous
arrangement.

Miss Karpe, my travelling companion, and two agreeable
ladies, were already in their berths very sick, but I did not get
into mine because a cockroach, looking as large as a mouse,
occupied the pillow, and a companion not much smaller was
roaming over the quilt without any definite purpose.   I can't
vouch for the accuracy of my observation, but it seemed to me
that these tremendous creatures were dark red, with eyes like
lobsters', and antennæ two inches long.   They looked capable
of carrying out the most dangerous and inscrutable designs.
I called the Malay steward; he smiled mournfully, but spoke
reassuringly, and pledged his word for their innocuousness, but
I never can believe that they are not the enemies of man ; and
I lay down on the transom, not to sleep, however, for it seemed
essential to keep watch on the proceedings of these formidable
vermin.

The grotesqueness of the arrangements of the berths and
their occupants grew on me during the night, and the climax
was put upon it when a gentleman coming down in the early
morning asked me if I knew that I was using the Governor of
Maui's head for a footstool, this portly native "Excellency"
being in profound slumber on the forward part of the transom.
This diagram represents one side of the saloon and the
"happy family" of English, Chinamen, Hawaiians, and
Americans :—

Governor Lyman.	Miss Karpe.	Miss ——.
Afong.	Vacant.	Miss ——.
Governor Nahaolelua	Myself.	An Hawaiian.

I noticed, too, that there were very few trunks and portman-
teaus, but that the after end of the saloon was heaped with
Mexican saddles and saddlebags, which I learned too late were
the essential gear of every traveller on Hawaii.

At five this morning we were at anchor in the roads of
Lahaina, the chief village on the mountainous island of Maui.

This place is very beautiful from the sea, for beyond the blue
water and the foamy reef the eye rests gratefully on a picturesque
collection of low, one-storied, thatched houses, many of frame,
painted white; others of grass, but all with deep, cool verandahs, half hidden among palms, bananas, *kukuis*, breadfruit,
and mangoes, dark groves against gentle slopes behind,
covered with sugar-cane of a bright pea-green. It is but a
narrow strip of land between the ocean and the red, flaring,
almost inaccessible, Maui hills, which here rise abruptly to a
height of 6,000 feet, pinnacled, chasmed, buttressed, and
almost verdureless, except in a few deep clefts, green and cool
with ferns and candlenut trees, and moist with falling water.
Lahaina looked intensely tropical in the roseflush of the early
morning, a dream of some bright southern isle, too surely to
pass away. The sun blazed down on shore, ship, and sea,
glorifying all things through the winter day. It was again
ecstasy "to dream and dream" under the awning, fanned by
the light sea-breeze, with the murmur of an unknown musical
tongue in one's ears, and the rich colouring and graceful group-
ing of a tropical race around one. We called at Maaleia, a
neck of sandy, scorched, verdureless soil, and at Ulupalakua,
or rather at the furnace seven times heated, which is the landing of the plantation of that name, on whose breezy slopes
cane refreshes the eye at a height of 2,000 feet above the sea.
We anchored at both places, and with what seemed to me a
needless amount of delay, discharged goods and natives, and
natives, mats, and calabashes were embarked. In addition to
the essential mat and calabash of *poi*, every native carried some
pet, either dog or cat, which was caressed, sung to, and talked
to with extreme tenderness; but there were hardly any children,
and I noticed that where there were any, the men took charge
of them. There were very few fine, manly dogs; the pets in
greatest favour are obviously odious, weak-eyed, pink-nosed
Maltese terriers.

The aspect of the sea was so completely lazy, that it was a
fresh surprise as each indolent undulation touched the shore
that it had latent vigour left to throw itself upwards into clouds
of spray. We looked through limpid water into cool depths
where strange bright fish darted through the submarine *chap-
paral*, but the coolness was imaginary, for the water was at 80°.
The air above the great black lava flood, which in pre-
historic times had flowed into the sea, and had ever since
declined the kindly, draping offices of nature, vibrated in waves

of heat. Even the imperishable cocoanut trees, whose tall, bare, curved trunks rose from the lava or the burnt red earth, were gaunt, tattered, and thirsty-looking, weary of crying for moisture to the pitiless skies. At last the ceaseless ripple of talk ceased, crew and passengers slept on the hot deck, and no sounds were heard but the drowsy flap of the awning, and the drowsier creak of the rudder, as the *Kilauea* swayed sleepily on the lazy undulations. The flag drooped and fainted with heat. The white sun blazed like a magnesium light on blue water, black lava, and fiery soil, roasting, blinding, scintillating, and flushed the red rocks of Maui into glory. It is all glorious, this fierce bright glow of the Tropic of Cancer, yet it was a relief to look up the great rolling, featureless slopes above Ulupalakua to a forest belt of perennial green, watered, they say, by perpetual showers, and a little later to see a mountain summit uplifted into a region of endless winter, above a steady cloud-bank as white as snow. This mountain, Haleakala, the House of the Sun, is the largest extinct volcano in the world, its terminal crater being nineteen miles in circumference at a height of more than 10,000 feet. It, and its spurs, slopes, and clusters of small craters form East Maui. West Maui is composed mainly of the picturesque group of the Eeka mountains. A desert strip of land, not much above high water mark, unites the twain, which form an island forty-eight miles long and thirty broad, with an area of 620 square miles.

We left Maui in the afternoon, and spent the next six hours in crossing the channel between it and Hawaii, but the short, tropic day did not allow us to see anything of the latter island but two snow-capped domes uplifted above the clouds. I have been reading Jarves' excellent book on the islands as industriously as possible, as well as trying to get information from my fellow-passengers regarding the region into which I have been so suddenly and unintentionally projected. I really know nothing about Hawaii, or the size and phenomena of the volcano to which we are bound, or the state of society or of the native race, or of the relations existing between it and the foreign population, or of the details of the constitution. This ignorance is most oppressive, and I see that it will not be easily enlightened, for among several intelligent gentlemen who have been conversing with me, no two seem agreed on any matter of fact.

From the hour of my landing I have observed the existence of two parties of *pro* and *anti* missionary leanings, with views on all island subjects in grotesque antagonism. So far, the former have left the undoubted results of missionary effort here to speak for themselves ; and I am almost disposed, from the pertinacious aggressiveness of the latter party, to think that it must be weak. I have already been seized upon (a gentleman would write " button-holed ") by several persons, who, in their anxiety to be first in imprinting their own views on the *tabula rasa* of a stranger's mind, have exercised an unseemly over-haste in giving the conversation an anti-missionary twist. They apparently desire to convey the impression that the New England teachers, finding a people rejoicing in the innocence and simplicity of Eden, taught them the knowledge of evil, turned them into a nation of hypocrites, and with a mingling of fanaticism and selfishness, afflicted them with many woes calculated to accelerate their extinction, *clothing* among others. The animus appears strong and bitter. There are two intelligent and highly educated ladies on board, daughters of missionaries, and the candid and cautious tone in which they speak on the same subject impresses me favourably. Mr. Damon introduced me to a very handsome half white gentleman, a lawyer of ability, and lately interpreter to the Legislature, Mr. Ragsdale, or, as he is usually called, " Bill Ragsdale," a leading spirit among the natives. His conversation was eloquent and poetic, though rather stilted, and he has a good deal of French mannerism ; but if he is a specimen of native patriotic feeling, I think that the extinction of Hawaiian nationality must be far off. I was amused with the attention that he paid to his dress under very adverse circumstances. He has appeared in three different suits, with light kid gloves to match, all equally elegant, in two days. A Chinese gentleman, who is at the same time a wealthy merchant at Honolulu, and a successful planter on Hawaii, interests me, from the keen intelligence of his face, and the courtesy and dignity of his manner. I hear that he possesses the respect of the whole community for his honour and integrity. It is quite unlike an ordinary miscellaneous herd of passengers. The tone is cheerful, courteous, and friendly, and people speak without introductions, and help to make the time pass pleasantly to each other.

HILO, HAWAII.

The *Kilauea* is not a fast propeller, and as she lurched very much in crossing the channel most of the passengers were seasick, a casualty which did not impair their cheerfulness and

good humour. After dark we called at Kawaihae (pronounced
To-wee-hye), on the north-west of Hawaii, and then steamed
through the channel to the east or windward side. I was only
too glad on the second night to accept the offer of " a mattrass
on the skylight," but between the heavy rolling caused by the
windward swell, and the natural excitement on nearing the
land of volcanoes and earthquakes, I could not sleep, and no
other person slept, for it was considered " a very rough passage,"
though there was hardly a yachtman's breeze. It would do
these Sybarites good to give them a short spell of the howling
horrors of the North or South Atlantic, an easterly snowstorm
off Sable Island, or a winter gale in the latitude of Inaccessible
Island ! The night was cloudy, and so the glare from Kilauea
which is often seen far out at sea was not visible.

When the sun rose amidst showers and rainbows (for this is
the showery season), I could hardly believe my eyes. Scenery,
vegetation, colour were all changed. The glowing red, the
fiery glare, the obtrusive lack of vegetation were all gone.
There was a magnificent coast-line of grey cliffs many hundred
feet in height, usually draped with green, but often black
and caverned at their bases. Into cracks and caverns the
heavy waves surged with a sound like artillery, sending broad
sheets of foam high up among the ferns and trailers, and
drowning for a time the endless baritone of the surf, which is
never silent through the summer years. Cascades in numbers
took impulsive leaps from the cliffs into the sea, or came
thundering down clefts or "gulches," which, widening at their
extremities, opened on smooth, green lawns, each one of
which has its grass house or houses, *kalo* patch, bananas,
and coco-palms, so close to the Pacific that its spray often
frittered itself away over their fan-like leaves. Above the cliffs
there were grassy uplands with park-like clumps of the screw-
pine, and candle-nut, and glades and dells of dazzling green,
bright with cataracts, opened up among the dense forests which
for some thousands of feet girdle Mauna Kea and Mauna Loa,
two vast volcanic mountains, whose snow-capped summits
gleamed here and there above the clouds, at an altitude of
nearly 14,000 feet. Creation surely cannot exhibit a more
brilliant green than that which clothes windward Hawaii with
perpetual spring. I have never seen such verdure. In the
final twenty-nine miles there are more than sixty gulches, from
100 to 700 feet in depth, each with its cataracts, and wild
vagaries of tropical luxuriance. Native churches, frame-built

and painted white, are almost like mile-stones along the coast, far too large and too many for the notoriously dwindling population. Ten miles from Hilo we came in sight of the first sugar plantation, with its patches of yet brighter green, its white boiling house and tall chimney stack; then more churches, more plantations, more gulches, more houses, and before ten we steamed into Byron's, or as it is now called Hilo Bay.

This is the paradise of Hawaii. What Honolulu attempts to be, Hilo is without effort. Its crescent-shaped bay, said to be the most beautiful in the Pacific, is a semi-circle of about two miles, with its farther extremity formed by Cocoanut Island, a black lava islet on which this palm attains great perfection, and beyond it again a fringe of cocoanuts marks the deep indentations of the shore. From this island to the north point of the bay, there is a band of golden sand on which the roar of the surf sounded thunderous and drowsy as it mingled with the music of the living waters of the Waiakea and the Wailuku, which after lashing the sides of the mountains which give them birth, glide deep and fern-fringed into the ocean. Native houses, half hidden by greenery, line the bay, and stud the heights above the Wailuku, and near the landing some white frame houses and three church spires above the wood denote the foreign element. Hilo is unique. Its climate is humid, and the long repose which it has enjoyed from rude volcanic upheavals has mingled a great depth of vegetable mould with the decomposed lava. Rich soil, rain, heat, sunshine, stimulate nature to vigorous efforts, and there is a luxuriant prodigality of vegetation which leaves nothing uncovered but the golden margin of the sea, and even that above high-water-mark is green with the Convolvulus maritimus. So dense is the wood that Hilo is rather suggested than seen. It is only on shore that one becomes aware of its bewildering variety of native and exotic trees and shrubs. From the sea it looks one dense mass of greenery, in which the bright foliage of the candle-nut relieves the glossy dark green of the bread-fruit—a maze of preposterous bananas, out of which rise slender, annulated trunks of palms giving their infinite grace to the grove. And palms along the bay, almost among the surf, toss their waving plumes in the sweet, soft breeze, not "palms in exile," but children of a blessed isle where "never wind blows loudly." Above Hilo, broad lands sweeping up cloudwards, with their sugar cane, *kalo*, melons, pine-apples, and banana groves suggest the boundless liberality of Nature. Woods and waters, hill and valley are all there, and from the region of an endless summer the eye takes in the domain of an endless winter, where almost perpetual snow crowns the summits of Mauna Kea and Mauna Loa. Mauna Kea from Hilo has a shapely aspect, for its top is broken into peaks, said to be the craters of extinct volcanoes, but my eyes seek the dome-like curve of Mauna Loa with far deeper interest, for it is as yet an unfinished mountain. It has a huge crater on its summit 800 feet in depth, and a pit of unresting fire on its side; it throbs, rumbles, and palpitates; it has sent forth floods of fire over all this part of Hawaii, and at any moment it may be crowned with a lonely light, showing that its tremendous forces are again in activity.

Canoes came off from the shore, dusky swimmers glided through the waters, youths, athletes, like the bronzes of the Naples Museum, rode the waves on their surf-boards, brilliantly dressed riders galloped along the sands, and came trooping down the bridle-paths from all the vicinity till a many-coloured, tropical crowd had assembled at the landing. Then a whale-boat came off, rowed by eight young men in white linen suits and white straw hats, with wreaths of carmine-coloured flowers round both hats and throats. They were singing a glee in honour of Mr. Ragsdale, whom they sprang on deck to welcome. Our crowd of native fellow-passengers, by some inscrutable process, had re-arrayed themselves and blossomed into brilliancy. Hordes of Hilo natives swarmed on deck, and it became a Babel of *alohas*, kisses, hand-shakings, and reiterated welcomes. The glee singers threw their beautiful garlands of roses and *ohias* over the foreign passengers, and music, flowers, good-will and kindliness made us welcome to these enchanted shores. We landed in a whaleboat, and were hoisted up a rude pier which was crowded, for what the arrival of the Australian mail-steamer is to Honolulu, the coming of the *Kilauea* is to Hilo. I had not time to feel myself a stranger, there were so many introductions, and so much friendliness. Mr. Coan and Mr. Lyman, two of the most venerable of the two surviving missionaries, were on the landing, and I was introduced to them and many others. There is no hotel in Hilo. The residents receive strangers, and Miss Karpe and I were soon installed in a large, buff frame-house, with two deep verandahs, the residence of Mr. Severance, Sheriff of Hawaii.

Unlike many other places, Hilo is more fascinating on closer acquaintance, so fascinating that it is hard to write about it in plain prose. Two narrow roads lead up from the sea to one as narrow, running parallel with it. Further up the hill another runs in the same direction. There are no conveyances, and outside the village these lanes dwindle into bridle-paths, with just room for one horse to pass another. The houses in which Mr. Coan, Mr. Lyman, Dr. Wetmore (formerly of the Mission), and one or two others live, have just enough suggestion of New England about them to remind one of the dominant influence on these islands, but the climate has idealized them, and clothed them with poetry and antiquity.

Of the three churches, the most prominent is the Roman Catholic Church, a white frame building with two great towers; Mr. Coan's native church with a spire comes next; and then the neat little foreign church, also with a spire. The Romish Church is a rather noisy neighbour, for its bells ring at unnatural hours, and doleful strains of a band which cannot play either in time or tune proceed from it. The court-house, a large, buff, painted frame-building with two deep verandahs, standing on a well-kept lawn planted with exotic trees, is the most imposing building in Hilo. All the foreigners have carried out their individual tastes in their dwellings, and the result is very agreeable, though in picturesqueness they must yield the palm to the native houses, which, whether of frame, or grass plain or plaited, whether one or two storeyed, all have the deep thatched roofs and verandahs plain or fantastically latticed, which are in harmony with the surroundings. These lattices and single and double verandahs are gorgeous with trailers, and the general warm brown tint of the houses contrasts artistically with the deep green of the bananas which overshadow them. There are living waters everywhere. Each house seems to possess a pure bright stream, which is arrested in bathing houses to be liberated among *kalo* patches of the brightest green. Every verandah appears a gathering place, and the bright *holokus* of the women, the gay shirts and bandanas of the men, the brilliant wreaths of natural flowers which adorn both, the hot-house temperature, the new trees and plants which demand attention, the rich odours, and the low monotonous recitative which mourns through the groves make me feel that I am in a new world. Ah, this is all Polynesian! This must be the land to which the "timid-eyed" lotos-eaters came. There is a strange fascination in the languid air, and it is strangely sweet "to dream of fatherland" . . .

I. L. B.

LETTER IV.

Beauties of Hilo—Palms and Bananas—My First Hawaiian Ride—Hilo Visiting—The Rev. Titus Coan.

I FIND that I can send another short letter before leaving for the volcano. I cannot convey to you any idea of the greenness and lavish luxuriance of this place, where everything flourishes, and glorious trailers and parasitic ferns hide all unsightly objects out of sight. It presents a bewildering maze of lilies, roses, fuchsias, clematis, begonias, convolvuli, the huge grana-dilla, the purple and yellow water lemons, also varieties of passiflora, both with delicious edible fruit, custard apples, rose apples, mangoes, mangostein guavas, bamboos, alligator pears, oranges, tamarinds, papayas, bananas, breadfruit, magnolias, geraniums, candle-nut, gardenias, dracænas, eucalyptus, panda-nus, *ohias*,* *kamani* trees, *kalo*,† *noni*,‡ and quantities of other trees and flowers, of which I shall eventually learn the names, patches of pine-apple, melons, and sugar-cane for children to suck, *kalo* and sweet potatoes.

In the vicinity of this and all other houses, Chili pepper, and a ginger-plant with a drooping flower-stalk with a great number of blossoms, which when not fully developed have a singular resemblance to very pure porcelain tinted with pink at the extremities of the buds, are to be seen growing in "yards," to use a most unfitting Americanism. I don't know how to introduce you to some of the things which delight my eyes here; but you must try to believe that the specimens of tropical growths which we see in conservatories at home are in general either misrepresentations, or very feeble representations of these growths in their natural homes. I don't allude to flowers, and especially not to orchids, but in this instance very specially to bananas, coco-palms, and the pandanus. For example, there is a specimen of the Pandanus odoratissimus in the palm-house in the Edinburgh Botanic Gardens, which is cer-

---

* Metrosideros Polymorpha.
† Colocasia antiquorum (arum esculentum). ‡ Morinda Citrifolia.

tainly a malignant caricature, with its long straggling branches, and widely-scattered tufts of poverty-stricken foliage. The bananas and plantains in the same palm-house represent only the feeblest and poorest of their tribe. They require not only warmth and moisture, but the generous sunshine of the tropics for their development. In the same house the date and sugar-palms are tolerable specimens, but the cocoa-nut trees are most truly "palms in exile."

I suppose that few people ever forget the first sight of a palm-tree of any species. I vividly remember seeing one for the first time at Malaga, but the coco-palm groves of the Pacific have a witchery of their own. As I write now I hear the moaning rustle of the wind through their plume-like tops ; and their long, slender stems and crisp crown of leaves rising above the trees with shining leafage which revel in damp, have a sug-gestion of Orientalism about them. How do they come too, on every atoll or rock that raises its head throughout this lonely ocean ? They fringe the shores of these islands. Wherever it is dry and fiercely hot, and the lava is black and hard, and nothing else grows, or can grow, there they are, close to the sea, sending their root-fibres seawards in search of salt water. Their long, curved, wrinkled, perfectly cylindrical stems, bulging near the ground like an apothecary's pestle, rise to a height of from sixty to one hundred feet. These stems are never straight, and in a grove lean and curve every way, and are apparently capable of enduring any force of wind or earthquake. They look as if they had never been young, and they show no signs of growth, rearing their plumy tufts so far aloft, and casting their shadows so far away, always lonely, as though they belonged to the heavens rather than the earth. Then, while all else that grows is green they are yellowish. Their clusters of nuts in all stages of growth are yellow, their fan-like leaves, which are from twelve to twenty feet long, are yellow, and an amber light pervades and surrounds them. They provide milk, oil, food, rope, and matting, and each tree produces about one hundred nuts annually.

The pandanus, or *lauhala*, is one of the most striking features of the islands. Its funereal foliage droops in Hilo, and it was it that I noticed all along the windward coast as having a most striking peculiarity of aërial roots which the branches send down to the ground, and which I now see have large cup-shaped spongioles. These air-roots are props, and appear to vary in length from three to twelve feet, according to

the situation of the tree.   There is one variety I saw to-day,
the "screw pine," which is really dangerous if one approaches
it unguardedly.   It is a whorled pandanus, with long, sword-
shaped leaves, spirally arranged in three rows, and hard, saw-
toothed edges, very sharp.   When unbranched as I saw them,
they resemble at a distance pine-apple plants thirty times
magnified.   But the mournful looking trees along the coast
and all about Hilo are mostly the Pandanus odoratissimus, a
spreading and branching tree which grows fully twenty-five feet
high, supports itself among inaccessible rocks by its prop-like
roots, and is one of the first plants to appear on the newly-
formed Pacific islands.*   Its foliage is singularly dense,
although it is borne in tufts of a quantity of long yucca-like
leaves on the branches.   The shape of the tree is usually
circular.   The mournful look is caused by the leaves taking a
downward and very decided droop in the middle.   At present
each tuft of leaves has in its centre an object like a green
pine-apple.   This contains the seeds which are eatable, as is
also the fleshy part of the drupes.   It is from the seeds of this
tree and their coverings that the brillant orange *leis*, or garlands of the natives, are made.   The soft white case of the
leaves and the terminal buds can also be eaten.   The leaves
are used for thatching, and their tough longitudinal fibres for
mats and robes.   There is another kind, the Pandanus vacoa,
the same as is used for making sugar bags in Mauritius, but I
have not seen it.

I think the banana comes next in beauty, and I see it in
perfection here for the first time, as those in Honolulu grow in
"yards," and are tattered by the winds.   It transports me intc
the tropics in feeling, as I am already in them in fact, and
satisfies all my cravings for something which shall represent and
epitomize their luxuriance, as well as for simplicity and grace
in vegetable form.   And here it is everywhere with its shining
shade, its smooth, fat, green stem, its crown of great curling
leaves from four to ten feet long, and its heavy cluster of a
whorl of green or golden fruit, with a pendant, purple cone of
undeveloped blossom below.   It is of the tropics, tropical ; a

* I have since learned that it is the same as the Kaldera bush of
Southern India, and that the powerful fragrance of its flowers is the subject
of continual allusions in Sanskrit poetry under the name of Ketaka, and that
oil impregnated with its odour is highly prized as a perfume in India.   The
Hawaiians also used it to give a delicious scent to the *Tapa* made for their
chiefs from the inner bark of the paper mulberry.

thing of beauty, gladness, and sunshine. It is indigenous here, and wild, but never bears seeds, and is propagated solely by suckers, which spring up when the parent plant has fruited, or by cuttings. It bears seed, strange to say, only (so far as is known) in the Andaman Islands, where, stranger still, it springs up as a second growth wherever the forests are cleared. Go to the palm-house, find the Musa sapientum, magnify it ten times, glorify it immeasurably, and you will have a laggard idea of the banana groves of Hilo.

The ground is carpeted with a grass of preternaturally vivid green and rankness of growth, mixed with a handsome fern, with a caudex a foot high, the Sadleria cyathoides, and another of exquisite beauty, the Microlepia tenuifolia, which are said to be the commonest ferns on Hawaii.

Hilo is a lively place for such a mere village; so many natives are stirring about, and dashing along the narrow roads on horseback. This is a large airy house, simple and tasteful, with pretty engravings and water-colour drawings on the walls. There is a large bath-house in the garden, into which a pure, cool stream has been led, and the gurgle and music of many such streams fill the sweet, soft air. There is a saying among sailors, " Follow a Pacific shower, and it leads you to Hilo." Indeed there is a rainfall of from thirteen to sixteen feet annually. These deep verandahs are very pleasant, for they render window-blinds unnecessary; so there is nothing of that dark stuffiness which makes indoor life a trial in the closed, shadeless Australian houses.

Miss Karpe, my travelling companion, is a lady of great energy, and an adept in the art of travelling. Undismayed by three days of sea-sickness, and the prospect of the tremendous journey to the volcano to-morrow, she extemporised a ride to the Anuenue Falls on the Wailuku this afternoon, and I weakly accompanied her, a burly policeman being our guide. The track is only a scramble among rocks and holes, concealed by grass and ferns, and we had to cross a stream, full of great holes, several times. The Fall itself is very pretty, 110 feet in one descent, with a cavernous shrine behind the water, filled with ferns. There were large ferns all round the Fall, and a jungle of luxuriant tropical shrubs of many kinds.

Three miles above this Fall there are the Pei-pei Falls, very interesting geologically. The Wailuku River is the boundary between the two great volcanoes, and its waters, it is supposed by learned men, have often flowed over heated beds of basalt,

with the result of columnar formation radiating from the bottom
of the stream. This structure is sometimes beautifully exhibited
in the form of Gothic archways, through which the torrent
pours into a basin, surrounded by curved, broken, and half-sunk
prisms, black and prominent amidst the white foam of the
Falls. In several places the river has just pierced the beds of
lava, and in one passes under a thick rock bridge, several
hundred feet wide.

Near the Anuenue Fall we stopped at a native house, outside
which a woman, in a rose-coloured chemise, was stringing roses
for a necklace, while her husband pounded the *kalo* root on a
board. His only clothing was the *malo,* a narrow strip of cloth
wound round the loins, and passed between the legs. This was
the only covering worn by men before the introduction of
Christianity. Females wore the *pau,* a short petticoat made of
tapa, which reached from the waist to the knees. To our eyes,
the brown skin produces nearly the effect of clothing.

Everything was new and interesting, but the ride was spoiled
by my insecure seat in my saddle, and the increased pain in my
spine which riding produced. In crossing one stream the horses
have to make a downward jump from a rock, and I slipped
round my horse's neck. Indeed on the way back I felt that on
the ground of health I must give up the volcano, as I would
never consent to be carried to it, like Lady Franklin, in a litter.
When we returned, Mr. Severance suggested that it would be
much better for me to follow the Hawaiian fashion, and ride
astride, and put his saddle on the horse. It was only my strong
desire to see the volcano which made me consent to a mode of
riding against which I have so strong a prejudice, but the result
of the experiment is that I shall visit Kilauea thus or not at all.
The native women all ride astride, on ordinary occasions in full
sacks, or *holokus,* and on gala days in the *pau,* the gay, winged
dress which I described in writing from Honolulu. A great
many of the foreign ladies on Hawaii have adopted the
Mexican saddle also, for greater security to themselves and
ease to their horses, on the steep and perilous bridle-tracks, but
they wear full Turkish trousers and jauntily-made dresses
reaching to the ankles.

It appears that Hilo is free from the universally admitted
nuisance of morning calls. The hours are simple—eight o'clock
breakfasts, one o'clock dinners, six o'clock suppers. If people
want anything with you, they come at any hour of the day, but
if they only wish to be sociable, the early evening is the recog-

nized time for "calling." After supper, when the day's work is
done, people take their lanterns and visit each other, either in
the verandahs or in the cheerful parlours which open upon them.
There are no door-bells, or solemn announcements by servants
of visitors' names, or "not-at-homes." If people are in their
parlours, it is presumed that they receive their friends. Several
pleasant people came in this evening. They seem to take
great interest in two ladies going to the volcano without an
escort, but no news has been received from it lately, and I fear
that it is not very active, as no glare is visible to-night. Mr.
Thompson, the pastor of the small foreign congregation here,
called on me. He is a very agreeable, accomplished man, and
is acquainted with Dr. Holland and several of my New England
friends. He kindly brought his wife's riding-costume for my
trip to Kilauea. The Rev. Titus Coan, one of the earliest and
most successful missionaries to Hawaii, also called. He is a
tall, majestic-looking man, physically well fitted for the extraordinary exertions he has undergone in mission work, and
intellectually also, I should think, for his face expresses great
mental strength, and nothing of the weakness of an enthusiast.
He has admitted about 12,000 persons into the Christian
Church. He is the greatest authority on volcanoes on the
islands, and his enthusiastic manner and illuminated countenance as he spoke of Kilauea, have raised my expectations to
the highest pitch. We are prepared for to-morrow, having
engaged a native named *Upa*, who boasts a little English, as
our guide. He provides three horses and himself for three days
for the sum of thirty dollars.

                                                    I. L. B.

LETTER V.

VOLCANO OF KILAUEA, *Jan.* 31*st.*

BRUISED aching bones, strained muscles, and overwhelming fatigue, render it hardly possible for me to undergo the physical labour of writing, but in spirit I am so elated with success, and so thrilled by new sensations, that though I cannot communicate the incommunicable, I want to write to you while the impression of Kilauea is fresh, and by "the light that never was on sea or shore."

By eight yesterday morning our preparations were finished, and Miss Karpe, whose conversance with the details of travelling I envy, mounted her horse on her own side-saddle, dressed in a short grey waterproof, and a broad-brimmed Leghorn hat tied so tightly over her ears with a green veil as to give it the look of a double spout. The only pack her horse carried was a bundle of cloaks and shawls, slung together with an umbrella on the horn of her saddle. Upa, who was most picturesquely got up in the native style with garlands of flowers round his hat and throat, carried our saddle-bags on the peak of his saddle, a bag with bananas, bread, and a bottle of tea on the horn, and a canteen of water round his waist. I had on my coarse Australian hat which serves the double purpose of sunshade and umbrella, Mrs. Thompson's riding costume, my great rusty New Zealand boots, and my blanket strapped behind a very gaily ornamented, brass-bossed, *demi-pique* Mexican saddle, which one of the missionary's daughters has lent me. It has a horn in front, a low peak behind, large wooden stirrups with leathern flaps the length of the stirrup-leathers, to prevent the dress from coming in contact with the horse, and strong guards of hide which hang over and below the stirrup, and cover it and the foot up to the ankles, to prevent the feet or boots from being torn in riding through the bush. Each horse had four fathoms of tethering rope wound several times round his neck. In such fashion must all travelling be done on Hawaii, whether by ladies or gentlemen.

Upa supplied the picturesque element, we the grotesque.
The morning was moist and unpropitious looking. As the
greater part of the thirty miles has to be travelled at a foot's-
pace, the guide took advantage of the soft grassy track which
leads out of Hilo, to go off at full gallop, a proceeding which
made me at once conscious of the demerits of my novel way of
riding. To guide the horse and to clutch the horn of the
saddle with both hands were clearly incompatible, so I abandoned the first as being the least important. Then my feet
either slipped too far into the stirrups and were cut, or they
were jerked out ; every corner was a new terror, for at each I
was nearly pitched off on one side, and when at last Upa
stopped, and my beast stopped without consulting my wishes,
only a desperate grasp of mane and tethering rope saved me
from going over his head. At this ridiculous moment we came
upon a bevy of brown maidens swimming in a lakelet by the
roadside, who increased my confusion by a chorus of laughter.
How fervently I hoped that the track would never admit of
galloping again !

Hilo fringes off with pretty native houses, *kalo* patches and
mullet ponds, and in about four miles the track, then formed of
rough, hard lava, and not more than 24 inches wide, enters a
forest of the densest description, a burst of true tropical jungle.
I could not have imagined anything so perfectly beautiful,
nature seemed to riot in the production of wonderful forms, as
if the moist, hot-house air encouraged her in lavish excesses.
Such endless variety, such depths of green, such an impassable
and altogether inextricable maze of forest trees, ferns, and lianas !
There were palms, breadfruit trees, *ohias*, eugenias, candle-nuts
of immense size, *Koa* (acacia) bananas, *noni*, bamboos, papayas,
(Carica papaya) guavas, *ti* trees (Cordyline terminalis), tree-
ferns, climbing ferns, parasitic ferns, and ferns themselves the
prey of parasites of their own species. The lianas were there
in profusion climbing over the highest trees, and entangling
them, with stems varying in size from those as thick as a man's
arm to those as slender as whipcord, binding all in an impassable network, and hanging over our heads in rich festoons or
tendrils swaying in the breeze. There were trailers, *i.e.*, (Frey-
cinetia scandens) with heavy knotted stems, as thick as a
frigate's stoutest hawser, coiling up to the tops of tall *ohias* with
tufted leaves like yuccas, and crimson spikes of gaudy blossom.
The shining festoons of the yam and the graceful trailers of the
mailê (Alyxia Olivaeformis), a sweet-scented vine, from which

the natives make garlands, and glossy leaved climbers hung
from tree to tree, and to brighten all, great morning glories of
a heavenly blue opened a thousand blossoms to the sun, and
gave a tenderer loveliness to the forest. Here trees grow and
fall, and nature covers them where they lie with a new vegetation which altogether obliterates their hasty decay. It is four
miles of beautiful and inextricable confusion, untrodden by
human feet except on the narrow track. " Of every tree in this
garden thou mayest freely eat," and no serpent or noxious thing
trails its hideous form through this Eden.

It was quite intoxicating, so new, wonderful, and solemn
withal, that I was sorry when we emerged from its shady depths
upon a grove of cocoanut trees and the glare of day. Two very
poor-looking grass huts, with a ragged patch of sugar-cane beside
them, gave us an excuse for half an hour's rest. An old woman
in a red sack, much tattooed, with thick, short, grey hair bristling on her head, sat on a palm root, holding a nude brown
child ; a lean, hideous old man, dressed only in a *malo*, leaned
against its stem, our horses with their highly miscellaneous gear
were tethered to a fern stump, and Upa, the most picturesque
of the party, served out tea. He and the natives talked incessantly, and from the frequency with which the words " *wahine
haole*" (foreign woman) occurred, the subject of their conversation was obvious. Upa has taken up the notion from something
Mr. S—— said, that I am a "high chief," and related to
Queen Victoria, and he was doubtlessly imposing this fable on
the people. In spite of their poverty and squalor, if squalor
be a term which can be applied to aught beneath these
sunny skies, there was a kindliness about them which they
made us feel, and the *aloha* with which they parted from us
had a sweet, friendly sound.

From this grove we travelled as before in single file over an
immense expanse of lava of the kind called *pahoehoe*, or satin
rock, to distinguish it from the *a-a*, or jagged, rugged, impassable rock. *Savans* all use these terms in the absence of any
equally expressive in English. The *pahoehoe* extends in the
Hilo direction from hence about twenty-three miles. It is the
cooled and arrested torrent of lava which in past ages has
flowed towards Hilo from Kilauea. It lies in hummocks, in
coils, in rippled waves, in rivers, in huge convolutions, in pools
smooth and still, and in caverns which are really bubbles.
Hundreds of square miles of the island are made up of this
and nothing more. A very frequent aspect of *pahoehoe* is the

likeness on a magnificent scale of a thick coat of cream drawn in wrinkling folds to the side of a milk-pan. This lava is all grey, and the greater part of its surface is slightly roughened. Wherever this is not the case the horses slip upon it as upon ice.

Here I began to realize the universally igneous origin of Hawaii, as I had not done among the finely disintegrated lava of Hilo. From the hard black rocks which border the sea, to the loftiest mountain dome or peak, every stone, atom of dust, and foot of fruitful or barren soil bears the Plutonic mark. In fact, the island has been raised heap on heap, ridge on ridge, mountain on mountain, to nearly the height of Mont Blanc, by the same volcanic forces which are still in operation here, and may still add at intervals to the height of the blue dome of Mauna Loa, of which we caught occasional glimpses above the clouds. Hawaii is actually at the present time being built up from the ocean, and this great sea of *pahoehoe* is not to be regarded as a vindictive eruption, bringing desolation on a fertile region, but as an architectural and formative process.

There is no water, except a few deposits of rain-water in holes, but the moist air and incessant showers have aided nature to mantle this frightful expanse with an abundant vegetation, principally ferns of an exquisite green, the most conspicuous being the Sadleria, the Gleichenia Hawaiiensis, a running wire-like fern, and the exquisite Microlepia tenuifolia, dwarf guava, with its white flowers resembling orange flowers in odour, and *ohelos* (Vaccinium reticulatum), with their red and white berries, and a profusion of small-leaved *ohias* (Metrosideros polymorpha), with their deep crimson, tasselled flowers, and their young shoots of bright crimson, relieved the monotony of green. These crimson tassels deftly strung on thread or fibres, are much used by the natives for their *leis*, or garlands. The *ti* tree (Cordyline terminalis) which abounds also on the lava, is most valuable. They cook their food wrapped up in its leaves, the porous root when baked, has the taste and texture of molasses candy, and when distilled yields a spirit, and the leaves form wrappings for fish, hard *poi*, and other edibles. Occasionally a clump of tufted coco-palms, or of the beautiful candle-nut rose among the smaller growths. To our left a fringe of palms marked the place where the lava and the ocean met, while, on our right, we were seldom out of sight of the dense timber belt, with its fringe of tree-ferns and bananas, which girdles Mauna Loa.

The track, on the whole, is a perpetual upward scramble; for, though the ascent is so gradual, that it is only by the increasing coolness of the atmosphere that the increasing elevation is denoted, it is really nearly 4000 feet in thirty miles. Only strong, sure-footed, well-shod horses can undertake this journey, for it is a constant scramble over rocks, going up or down natural steps, or cautiously treading along ledges. Most of the track is quite legible owing to the vegetation having been worn off the lava, but the rock itself hardly shows the slightest abrasion.

Upa had indicated that we were to stop for rest at the "Half Way House;" and, as I was hardly able to sit on my horse owing to fatigue, I consoled myself by visions of a comfortable sofa and a cup of tea. It was with real dismay that I found the reality to consist of a grass hut, much out of repair, and which, bad as it was, was locked. Upa said we had ridden so slowly that it would be dark before we reached the volcano, and only allowed us to rest on the grass for half-an-hour. He had frequently reiterated " Half Way house, you wear spur ;" and, on our remounting, he buckled on my foot a heavy, rusty Mexican spur, with jingling ornaments, and rowels an inch and a half long. These horses are so accustomed to be jogged with these instruments that they won't move without them. The prospect of five hours' more riding looked rather black, for I was much exhausted, and my shoulders and knee-joints were in severe pain. Miss K.'s horse showed no other appreciation of a stick with which she belaboured him than flourishes of his tail, so, for a time, he was put in the middle, that Upa might add his more forcible persuasions, and I rode first, and succeeded in getting my lazy animal into the priestly amble known at home as "a butter and eggs trot," the favourite travelling pace, but this not suiting the guide's notion of progress, he frequently rushed up behind with a torrent of Hawaiian, emphasized by heavy thumps on my horse's back, which so sorely jeopardised my seat on the animal, owing to his resenting the interference by kicking, that I "dropped astern" for the rest of the way, leaving Upa to belabour Miss K.'s steed for his diversion.

The country altered but little, only the variety of trees gave place to the *ohia* alone, with its sombre foliage. There were neither birds nor insects, and the only travellers we encountered in the solitude compelled us to give them a wide berth, for they were a drove of half wild, random cattle, led by a lean bull of hideous aspect, with crumpled horns. Two picturesque native *vaccheros* on mules accompanied them, and my flagging spirits were raised by their news that the volcano was quite active. The owner of these cattle knows that he has 10,000 head, and may have a great many more. They are shot for their hides by men who make shooting and skinning them a profession, and, near settlements, the owners are thankful to get two cents a pound for sirloin and rump-steaks. These, and great herds which are actually wild and ownerless upon the mountains, are a degenerate breed, with some of the worst peculiarities of the Texas cattle, and are the descendants of those which Vancouver placed on the islands and which were under *Tabu* for ten years. They destroy the old trees by gnawing the bark, and render the growth of young ones impossible.

As it was getting dark we passed through a forest strip, where tree-ferns from twelve to eighteen feet in height, and with fronds from five to seven feet long, were the most attractive novelties. As we emerged, "with one stride came the dark," a great darkness, a cloudy night, with neither moon nor stars, and the track was further obscured by a belt of *ohias*. There were five miles of this, and I was so dead from fatigue and want of food, that I would willingly have lain down in the bush in the rain. I most heartlessly wished that Miss K. were tired too, for her voice, which seemed tireless as she rode ahead in the dark, rasped upon my ears. I could only keep on my saddle by leaning on the horn, and my clothes were soaked with the heavy rain. "A dreadful ride," one and another had said, and I then believed them. It seemed an awful solitude full of mystery. Often, I only knew that my companions were ahead by the sparks struck from their horse's shoes.

It became a darkness which could be felt.

"Is that possibly a pool of blood?" I thought in horror, as a rain puddle glowed crimson on the track. Not that indeed! A glare brighter and redder than that from any furnace suddenly lightened the whole sky, and from that moment brightened our path. There sat Miss K. under her dripping umbrella, as provokingly erect as when she left Hilo. There Upa jogged along, huddled up in his poncho, and his canteen shone red. There the *ohia* trees were relieved blackly against the sky. The scene started out from the darkness with the suddenness of a revelation. We felt the pungency of sulphurous fumes in the still night air. A sound as of the sea broke on

our ears, rising and falling as if breaking on the shore, but the
ocean was thirty miles away. The heavens became redder and
brighter, and when we reached the crater-house at eight, clouds
of red vapour mixed with flame were curling ceaselessly out of
a vast, invisible pit of blackness, and Kilauea was in all its
fiery glory. We had reached the largest active volcano in the
world, the " place of everlasting burnings."

Rarely was light more welcome than that which twinkled
from under the verandah of the lonely crater-house into the
rainy night. The hospitable landlord of this unique dwelling
lifted me from my horse, and carried me into a pleasant room
thoroughly warmed by a large wood fire, and I hastily retired
to bed to spend much of the bitterly cold night in watching
the fiery vapours rolling up out of the infinite darkness, and in
dreading the descent into the crater. The heavy clouds were
crimson with the reflection, and soon after midnight jets of
flame of a most peculiar colour leapt fitfully into the air, accompanied by a dull, throbbing sound.

This morning was wet and murky as many mornings are
here, and the view from the door was a blank up to ten o'clock,
when the mist rolled away and revealed the mystery of last
night, the mighty crater whose vast terminal wall is only a few
yards from this house. We think of a volcano as a cone.
This is a different thing. The abyss, which really is at a height of
nearly 4000 feet on the flank of Mauna Loa, has the appearance
of a great pit on a rolling plain. But such a pit ! It is nine miles
in circumference, and its lowest area, which not long ago fell
about 300 feet, just as ice on a pond falls when the water below
it is withdrawn, covers six square miles. The depth of the crater
varies from 800 to 1100 feet in different years, according as
the molten sea below is at flood or ebb. Signs of volcanic
activity are present more or less throughout its whole depth,
and for some distance round its margin, in the form of steam
cracks, jets of sulphurous vapour, blowing cones, accumulating
deposits of acicular crystals of sulphur, &c., and the pit itself
is constantly rent and shaken by earthquakes. Grand eruptions occur at intervals with circumstances of indescribable
terror and dignity, but has Kilauea does not limit its activity to
these outbursts, but has exhibited its marvellous phenomena
through all known time in a lake or lakes in the southern part
of the crater, three miles from this side.

This lake, the Hale-mau-mau, or House of Everlasting Fire
of the Hawaiian mythology, the abode of the dreaded goddess

Pélé, is approachable with safety except during an eruption.
The spectacle, however, varies almost daily, and at times the
level of the lava in the pit within a pit is so low, and the suffocating gases are evolved in such enormous quantities, that
travellers are unable to see anything.   There had been no
news from it for a week, and as nothing was to be seen but a
very faint bluish vapour hanging round its margin, the prospect
was not encouraging.

When I have learned more about the Hawaiian volcanoes, I
shall tell you more of their phenomena, but to-night I shall
only write to you my first impressions of what we actually saw
on this January 31st.   My highest expectations have been in-
finitely exceeded, and I can hardly write soberly after such a
spectacle, especially while through the open door I see the
fiery clouds of vapour from the pit rolling up into a sky, glowing as if itself on fire.

We were accompanied into the crater by a comical native
guide, who mimicked us constantly, our Hilo guide, who
" makes up " a little English, a native woman from Kona, who
speaks imperfect English poetically, and her brother who
speaks none.   I was conscious that we foreign women with our
stout staffs and grotesque dress looked like caricatures, and the
natives, who have a keen sense of the ludicrous, did not conceal that they thought us so.

The first descent down the terminal wall of the crater is very
precipitous, but it and the slope which extends to the second
descent are thickly covered with *ohias*, *ohelos* (a species of
whortleberry), sadlerias, polypodiums, silver grass, and a great
variety of bulbous plants, many of which bore clusters of
berries of a brilliant turquoise blue.   The " beyond " looked
terrible.   I could not help clinging to these vestiges of the
kindlier mood of nature in which she sought to cover the
horrors she had wrought.   The next descent is over rough
blocks and ridges of broken lava, and appears to form part of
a break which extends irregularly round the whole crater, and
which probably marks a tremendous subsidence of its floor.
Here the last apparent vegetation was left behind, and the
familiar earth.   We were in a new region of blackness and awful
desolation, the accustomed sights and sounds of nature all
gone.   Terraces, cliffs, lakes, ridges, rivers, mountain sides,
whirlpools, chasms of lava surrounded us, solid, black, and
shining, as if vitrified, or an ashen grey, stained yellow with
sulphur here and there, or white with alum.   The lava was

fissured and upheaved everywhere by earthquakes, hot underneath, and emitting a hot breath.

After more than an hour of very difficult climbing we reached
the lowest level of the crater, pretty nearly a mile across, presenting from above the appearance of a sea at rest, but on
crossing it we found it to be an expanse of waves and convolutions of ashy-coloured lava, with great cracks filled up with
black, iridescent rolls of lava, only a few weeks old. Parts of
it are very rough and ridgy, jammed together like field ice, or
compacted by rolls of lava which may have swelled up from
beneath, but the largest part of the area presents the appearance of huge coiled hawsers, the ropy formation of the lava
rendering the illusion almost perfect. These are riven by deep
cracks which emit hot, sulphurous vapours. Strange to say, in
one of these, deep down in that black and awful region,
three slender metamorphosed ferns were growing, exquisite
forms, the fragile heralds of the great forest of vegetation,
which probably in coming years will clothe this pit with beauty.
On our right there was a precipitous ledge, and a recent flow
of lava had poured over it, cooling as it fell into columnar
shapes as symmetrical as those of Staffa. It took us a full
hour to cross this deep depression, and as long to master a
steep, hot ascent of about 400 feet, formed by a recent lava-
flow from Hale-mau-mau into the basin. This lava hill is an
extraordinary sight—a flood of molten stone, solidifying as it
ran down the declivity, forming arrested waves, streams, eddies,
gigantic convolutions, forms of snakes, stems of trees, gnarled
roots, crooked water-pipes, all involved and contorted on a
gigantic scale, a wilderness of force and dread. Over one
steeper place the lava had run in a fiery cascade about 100 feet
wide. Some had reached the ground, some had been arrested
midway, but all had taken the aspect of stems of trees. In
some of the crevices I picked up a quantity of very curious
filamentose lava, known as " Péle's hair." It resembles coarse
spun glass, and is of a greenish or yellowish-brown colour. In
many places the whole surface of the lava is covered with this
substance seen through a glazed medium. During eruptions,
when fire-fountains play to a great height, and drops of lava
are thrown in all directions, the wind spins them out in clear
green or yellow threads two or three feet long, which catch
and adhere to projecting points.

As we ascended, the flow became hotter under our feet, as
well as more porous and glistening. It was so hot that a shower

of rain hissed as it fell upon it. The crust became increasingly insecure, and necessitated our walking in single file
with the guide in front, to test the security of the footing. I
fell through several times, and always into holes full of
sulphurous steam, so malignantly acid that my strong, dog-skin
gloves were burned through as I raised myself on my hands.

We had followed a lava-flow for thirty miles up to the crater's
brink, and now we had toiled over recent lava for three hours,
and by all calculation were close to the pit, yet there was no
smoke or sign of fire, and I felt sure that the volcano had died
out for once for our especial disappointment. Indeed, I had
been making up my mind for disappointment since we left the
crater-house, in consequence of reading seven different accounts, in which language was exhausted in describing
Kilauea.

Suddenly, just above, and in front of us, gory drops were
tossed in air, and springing forwards we stood on the brink of
Hale-mau-mau, which was about 35 feet below us. I think we
all screamed, I know we all wept, but we were speechless, for
a new glory and terror had been added to the earth. It is the
most unutterable of wonderful things. The words of common
speech are quite useless. It is unimaginable, indescribable, a
sight to remember for ever, a sight which at once took possession of every faculty of sense and soul, removing one altogether
out of the range of ordinary life. Here was the real " bottomless pit "—the " fire which is not quenched "—" the place of
hell "—" the lake which burneth with fire and brimstone "—the
" everlasting burnings "—the fiery sea whose waves are never
weary. There were groanings, rumblings, and detonations,
rushings, hissings, and splashings, and the crashing sound of
breakers on the coast, but it was the surging of fiery waves
upon a fiery shore. But what can I write ! Such words as
jets, fountains, waves, spray, convey some idea of order and
regularity, but here there was none. The inner lake, while we
stood there, formed a sort of crater within itself, the whole lava
sea rose about three feet, a blowing cone about eight feet high
was formed, it was never the same two minutes together. And
what we saw had no existence a month ago, and probably
will be changed in every essential feature a month hence.

What we did see was one irregularly-shaped lake, possibly
500 feet wide at its narrowest part, and nearly half a mile at
its broadest, almost divided into two by a low bank of lava,
which extended nearly across it where it was narrowest, and

which was raised visibly before our eyes. The sides of the
nearest part of the lake were absolutely perpendicular, but
nowhere more than 40 feet high; though on the far side of
the larger lake they were bold and craggy, and probably not
less than 150 feet high. On one side there was an expanse
entirely occupied with blowing cones, and jets of steam or
vapour. The lake has been known to sink 400 feet, and a
month ago it overflowed its banks. The prominent object
was fire in motion, but the surface of the double lake was continually skinning over for a second or two with a cooled crust
of a lustrous grey-white, like frosted silver, broken by jagged
cracks of a bright rose-colour. The movement was nearly
always from the sides to the centre, but the movement of the
centre itself appeared independent and always took a southerly
direction. Before each outburst of agitation there was much
hissing, and a throbbing, internal roaring, as of imprisoned
gases. Now it seemed furious, demoniacal, as if no power on
earth could bind it, then playful and sportive, then for a second
languid, but only because it was accumulating fresh force. On
our arrival eleven fire fountains were playing joyously round
the lakes, and sometimes the six of the nearer lake ran together
in the centre to go wallowing down in one vortex, from which
they reappeared bulging upwards, till they formed a huge cone
30 feet high, which plunged downwards in a whirlpool only to
reappear in exactly the previous number of fountains in different
parts of the lake, high leaping, raging, flinging themselves upwards. Sometimes the whole lake, abandoning its usual centripetal motion, as if impelled southwards, took the form of
mighty waves, and surging heavily against the partial barrier,
with a sound like the Pacific surf, lashed, tore, covered it, and
threw itself over it in clots of living fire. It was all confusion,
commotion, force, terror, glory, majesty, mystery, and even
beauty. And the colour! Molten metal has not that crimson
gleam, nor blood that living light! Had I not seen this I
should never have known that such a colour was possible.

The crust perpetually wrinkled, folded over, and cracked,
and great pieces were drawn downwards to be again thrown
up on the crests of waves. The eleven fountains of gory fire
played the greater part of the time, dancing round the lake
with a strength of joyousness which was absolute beauty.
Indeed after the first half hour of terror had gone by, the beauty
of these jets made a profound impression upon me, and the
sight of them must always remain one of the most fascinating

recollections of my life. During three hours, the bank of lava which almost divided the lakes rose considerably, owing to the cooling of the spray as it dashed over it, and a cavern of considerable size was formed within it, the roof of which was hung with fiery stalactites, more than a foot long. Nearly the whole time the surges of the farther lake taking a southerly direction broke with a tremendous noise on the bold, craggy cliffs which are its southern boundary, throwing their gory spray to a height of fully forty feet. At times an overhanging crag fell in, creating a vast splash of fire and increased commotion.

Almost close below us there was an intermittent jet of lava, which kept cooling round what was possibly a blowhole, forming a cone with an open top, which when we first saw it was about six feet high on its highest side, and about as many in diameter. Up this cone or chimney heavy jets of lava were thrown every second or two, and cooling as they fell over its edge, raised it rapidly before our eyes. Its fiery interior, and the singular sound with which the lava was vomited up, were very awful. There was no smoke rising from the lake, only a faint blue vapour which the wind carried in the opposite direction. The heat was excessive. We were obliged to stand the whole time, and the soles of our boots were burned, and my ear and one side of my face were blistered. Although there was no smoke from the lake itself, there was an awful region to the westward, of smoke, sound, and rolling clouds of steam and vapour whose phenomena it was not safe to investigate, where the blowing cones are, whose fires last night appeared stationary. We were able to stand quite near the margin, and look down into the lake, as you look into the sea from the deck of a ship, the only risk being that the fractured ledge might give way.

Before we came away, a new impulse seized the lava. The fire was thrown to a great height; the fountains and jets all wallowed together; new ones appeared, and danced joyously round the margin, then converging towards the centre they merged into one glowing mass, which upheaved itself pyramidally and disappeared with a mighty plunge. Then innumerable billows of fire dashed themselves into the air, crashing and lashing, and the lake dividing itself recoiled on either side, then hurling its fires together and rising as if by upheaval from below, it surged over the temporary rim which it had formed, passing downwards in a slow majestic flow, leaving the central surface swaying and dashing in fruitless agony as if sent on some errand it failed to accomplish.

Farewell, I fear for ever, to the glorious Hale-mau-mau, the grandest type of force that the earth holds ! " Break, break, break," on through the coming years,

> " No more by thee my steps shall be,
> No more again for ever ! "

It seemed a dull trudge over the black and awful crater, and strange, like half-forgotten sights of a world with which I had ceased to have aught to do, were the dwarf tree-ferns, the lilies with their turquoise clusters, the crimson myrtle blossoms, and all the fair things which decked the precipice up which we slowly dragged our stiff and painful limbs. Yet it was but the exchange of a world of sublimity for a world of beauty, the "place of hell," for the bright upper earth, with its endless summer, and its perennial foliage, blossom, and fruitage.

Since writing the above I have been looking over the "Volcano Book," which contains the observations and impressions of people from all parts of the world. Some of these are painstaking and valuable as showing the extent and rapidity of the changes which take place in the crater, but there is an immense quantity of flippant rubbish, and would-be wit, in which "Madam Pélé," invariably occurs, this goddess, who was undoubtedly one of the grandest of heathen mythical creations, being caricatured in pencil and pen and ink, under every ludicrous aspect that can be conceived. Some of the entries are brief and absurd, " Not much of a fizz," " a grand splutter," " Madam Pélé in the dumps," and so forth. These generally have English signatures. The American wit is far racier, but depends mainly on the profane use of certain passages of scripture, a species of wit which is at once easy and disgusting. People are all particular in giving the precise time of the departure from Hilo and arrival here, " making good time " being a thing much admired on Hawaii, but few can boast of more than three miles an hour. It is wonderful that people can parade their snobbishness within sight of Hale-mau-mau.

This inn is a unique and interesting place. Its existence is strikingly precarious, for the whole region is in a state of perpetual throb from earthquakes, and the sights and sounds are gruesome and awful both by day and night. The surrounding country steams and smokes from cracks and pits, and a smell of sulphur fills the air. They cook their *kalo* in a steam appa-

ratus of nature's own work just behind the house, and every
drop of water is from a distillery similarly provided. The inn
is a grass and bamboo house, very beautifully constructed
without nails. It is a longish building with a steep roof,
divided inside by partitions which run up to the height of the
walls. There is no ceiling. The joists which run across are
concealed by wreaths of evergreens, from among which peep
out here and there stars on a blue ground. The door opens
from the verandah into a centre room with a large, open, brick
fire place, in which a wood fire is constantly burning, for at
this altitude the temperature is cool. Some chairs, two
lounges, small tables, and some books and pictures on the
walls give a look of comfort, and there is the reality of comfort
in perfection. Our sleeping-place, a neat room with a matted
floor opens from this, and on the other side there is a similar
room, and a small eating-room with a grass cookhouse beyond,
from which an obliging old Chinaman who persistently calls us
"sir," brings our food. We have had for each meal, tea, preserved milk, coffee, *kalo*, biscuits, butter, potatoes, goats' flesh,
and *ohelos*. The charge is five dollars a day, but everything
except the potatoes and *ohelos* has to be brought twenty or
thirty miles on mules' backs. It is a very pretty, picturesque
house both within and without, and stands on a natural lawn
of brilliant but unpalatable grass surrounded by a light fence
covered with a small, trailing, double rose. It is altogether a
most magical building in the heart of a formidable volcanic
wilderness. Mr. Gilman, our host, is a fine picturesque-looking
man, half-Indian, and speaks remarkably good English, but his
wife, a very pretty native woman, speaks none, and he attends
to us entirely himself.

A party of native travellers rainbound are here, and the
native women are sitting on the floor stringing flowers and
berries for *leis*. One very attractive-looking young woman,
refined by consumption, is lying on some blankets, and three
native men are smoking by the fire. Upa attempts conversation with us in broken English, and the others laugh and talk
incessantly. My inkstand, pen, and small handwriting amuse
them very much. Miss K., the typical American travelling lady,
who is encountered everywhere from the Andes to the Pyramids,
tireless, with indomitable energy, Spartan endurance, and a
genius for attaining everything, and myself, a limp, ragged,
shoeless wretch, complete the group, and our heaps of saddles,
blankets, spurs, and gear tell of real travelling, past and future.

It is a most picturesque sight by the light of the flickering fire, and the fire which is unquenchable burns without.

About 300 yards off there is a sulphur steam vapour-bath, highly recommended by the host as a panacea for the woeful aches, pains, and stiffness produced by the six mile scramble through the crater, and I groaned and limped down to it : but it is a most spasmodic arrangement, singularly independent of human control, and I have not the slightest doubt that the reason why Mr. Gilman obligingly remained in the vicinity was, lest I should be scalded or blown to atoms by a sudden freak of Kilauea, though I don't see that he was capable of preventing either catastrophe ! A slight grass shed has been built over a sulphur steam crack, and within this there is a deep box with a sliding lid and a hole for the throat, and the victim is supposed to sit in this and be steamed. But on this occasion the temperature was so high, that my hand, which I unwisely experimented upon, was immediately scalded. In order not to wound Mr. Gilman's feelings, which are evidently sensitive on the subject of this irresponsible contrivance, I remained the prescribed time within the shed, and then managed to limp a little less, and go with him to what are called the Sulphur Banks, on which sulphurous vapour is perpetually depositing the most exquisite acicular sulphur crystals ; these, as they aggregate, take entrancing forms, like the featherwork produced by the " frost-fall " in Colorado, but, like it, they perish with a touch, and can only be seen in the wonderful laboratory where they are formed.

In addition to the natives before mentioned, there is an old man here who has been a bullock-hunter on Hawaii for forty years, and knows the island thoroughly. In common with all the residents I have seen, he takes an intense interest in volcanic phenomena, and has just been giving us a thrilling account of the great eruption in 1868, when beautiful Hilo was threatened with destruction. Three weeks ago, he says, a profound hush fell on Kilauea, and the summit crater of Mauna Loa became active, and amidst throbbings, rumblings, and earthquakes, broke into such magnificence that the light was visible 100 miles at sea, a burning mountain 13,750 feet high ! The fires after two days died out as suddenly, and from here we can see the great dome-like top, snow-capped under the stars, serene in an eternal winter.

I. L. B.

LETTER VI.

HILO, HAWAII, *Feb.* 3.

MY plans are quite overturned. I was to have ridden with the native mail-carrier to the north of the island to take the steamer for Honolulu, but there are freshets in the gulches on the road, making the ride unsafe. There is no steamer from Hilo for three weeks, and in the meantime Mr. and Mrs. S. have kindly consented to receive me as a boarder; and I find the people, scenery, and life so charming, that I only regret my detention on Mrs. Dexter's account. I am already rested from the great volcano trip.

We left Kilauea at seven in the morning of the 1st Feb. in a pouring rain. The natives decorated us with *leis* of turquoise and coral berries, and of crimson and yellow *ohia* blossoms. The saddles were wet, the crater was blotted out by mist, water dripped from the trees, we splashed through pools in the rocks, the horses plunged into mud up to their knees, and the drip, drip, of vertical, earnest, tepid, tropical rain accompanied us nearly to Hilo. Upa and Miss K. held umbrellas the whole way, but I required both hands for holding on to the horse whenever he chose to gallop. As soon as we left the crater-house Upa started over the grass at full speed, my horse of course followed, and my feet being jerked out of the stirrups, I found myself ignominiously sitting on the animal's back behind the saddle, and nearly slid over his tail, before, by skilful efforts, I managed to scramble over the peak back again, when I held on by horn and mane until the others stopped! Happily I was last, and I don't think they saw me. Upa amused me very much on the way; he insists that I am "a high chief." He said a good deal about Queen Victoria, whose virtues seem well known here : " Good Queen make good people," he said, " English very good ! " He asked me how many chiefs we had, and supposing him to mean hereditary peers, I replied, over 500. " Too many, too many ! " he

answered emphatically—"too much chief eat up people!" He
asked me if all people were good in England, and I was sorry
to tell him that this was very far from being the case.   He was
incredulous, or seemed so out of flattery, and said, "You good
Queen, you Bible long time, you good!"   I was surprised to
find how much he knew of European politics, of the liberation
of Italy, and the Franco-German war.   He expressed a most
orthodox horror of the Pope, who, he said, he knew from his
Bible was the "Beast!" He said, "I bring band and serenade
for good Queen sake," but this has not come off yet.

We straggled into Hilo just at dusk, thoroughly wet, jaded,
and satisfied, but half-starved, for the rain had converted that
which should have been our lunch into a brownish pulp of
bread and newspaper, and we had subsisted only on some half-
ripe guavas.   After the black desolation of Kilauea, I realized
more fully the beauty of Hilo, as it appeared in the gloaming.
The rain had ceased, cool breezes rustled through the palm-
groves and sighed through the funereal foliage of the pandanus.
Under thick canopies of the glossy breadfruit and banana,
groups of natives were twining garlands of roses and ohia
blossoms.   The lights of happy foreign homes flashed from
under verandahs festooned with passion-flowers, and the low
chant, to me nearly intolerable, but which the natives love,
mingled with the ceaseless moaning of the surf and the sighing
of the breeze through the trees, and a heavy fragrance, unlike
the faint, sweet odours of the north, filled the evening air.   It
was delicious.

I suffered intensely from pain and stiffness, and was induced
to try a true Hawaiian remedy, which is not only regarded as
a cure for all physical ills, but as the greatest of physical
luxuries; *i.e. lomi-lomi.*   This is a compound of pinching,
pounding, and squeezing, and Moi Moi, the fine old Hawaiian
nurse in this family, is an adept in the art.   She found out by
instinct which were the most painful muscles, and subjected
them to a doubly severe pounding, laughing heartily at my
groans.   However, I must admit that my arms and shoulders
were almost altogether relieved before the *lomi-lomi* was finished.
The first act of courtesy to a stranger in a native house is this,
and it is varied in many ways.   Now and then the patient
lies face downwards, and children execute a sort of dance
upon his spine.*   Formerly, the chiefs, when not engaged in

* "Reef Rovings."

active pursuits, exacted *lomi-lomi* as a constant service from their followers.

A number of Hilo folk came in during the evening to inquire how we had sped, and for news of the volcano. I think the proximity of Kilauea gives sublimity to Hilo, and helps to lift conversation out of common-place ruts. It is no far-off spectacle, but an immediate source of wonder and apprehension, for it rocks the village with earthquakes, and renders the construction of stone houses and plastered ceilings impossible. It rolls vast tidal waves with infinite destruction on the coast, and of late years its fiery overflowings have twice threatened this paradise with annihilation. Then there is the dead volcano of Mauna Loa, from whose resurrection anything may be feared. Even last night a false rumour that a light was to be seen on its summit brought everyone out, but it was only an increased glare from the pit of Hale-mau-mau. It is most interesting to be in a region of such splendid possibilities.

I. L. B.

LETTER VII.

Hilo Homes—Hilo Gossip—Foreign Life—The National Dish—*Pelikia Aloha*—Surf-board Riding.

HILO, HAWAII.

THE white population here, which constitutes "society," is very small. There are two venerable missionaries, "Father Coan" and "Father Lyman," the former pastor of a large native congregation, which, though much shrunk, is not only self-sustaining, but contributes $1200 a year to foreign missions, and the latter, though very old and frail, the indefatigable head of an industrial school for native young men. Their houses combine the trimness of New England, with the luxuriance of the tropics; they are cool retreats, embowered among bread-fruit, tamarind, and bamboo, through whose graceful leafage the blue waters of the bay are visible. Innumerable exotics are domesticated round these fair homesteads. Two of "Father Lyman's" sons are influential residents, one being the Lieutenant-Governor of the island. Other sons of former missionaries are settled here in business, and there are a few strangers who have been attracted hither. Dr. Wetmore, formerly of the mission, is a typical New Englander of the old orthodox school. It is pleasant to see him brighten into almost youthful enthusiasm on the subject of Hawaiian ferns. My host, a genial, social, intelligent American, is sheriff of Hawaii, post-master, &c., and with his charming wife (a missionary's daughter), and some friends who live with them, make their large house a centre of kindliness, friendliness, and hospitality.

There are hardly any young ladies, and very few young men, but plenty of rosy, blooming children, who run about barefoot all the year. Besides the Hilo residents, there are some planters' families within seven miles, who come in to sewing circles, church, &c. There is a small class of reprobate white men who have ostracised themselves by means of drink and bad morals, and are a curse to the natives. The half whites, among whom "Bill Ragsdale" is the leading spirit, are not numerous. Hilo has no carriage roads and no carriages: every one must ride, or travel in a litter. People are very kind to each other. Horses, dresses, patterns, books, and articles of domestic use, are lent and borrowed continually. The small-ness of the society and the close proximity are too much like a ship. People know everything about the details of each other's daily life, income, and expenditure, and the day's doings of each member of the little circle are matters for conversation. Indeed, were it not for the volcano and its doings, conversation might degenerate into mere gossip. There is an immense deal of personal talk; the wonder is that there is not more ill-nature. Not only is what everybody does in Hilo common property, but the sayings, doings, goings, comings, and purchases of every one in all the other islands are common property also, made so by letters and oral communication. It is all very amusing, but not always kindly, and human interests are always interesting; but it has its perilous side. The foreigners are very kind to each other. There is no distress which is not alleviated. There is no nurse, and in cases of sickness the ladies take it by turns to wait on the sufferer by day and night for weeks, and even months. Such inevitable mutual depend-ence of course promotes friendliness.

The foreigners live very simply. The eating-rooms are used solely for eating, the "parlours" are always cheerful and tasteful, and the bedrooms very pretty, adorned with all manner of knick-knacks made by the ladies, who are indescribably deft with their fingers. Light Manilla matting is used instead of carpets. A Chinese man-cook, who leaves at seven in the evening, is the only servant, except in one or two cases, where, as here, a native woman condescends to come in during the day as a nurse. In the morning, the ladies in their fresh pretty wrappers and ruffled white aprons, sweep and dust the rooms, and I never saw women look more truly graceful and refined than they do, when engaged in the plain prose of these domestic duties. They make all their own dresses, and when any lady is busy and wants a dress in a hurry, two or three of them meet and make it for her. I never saw people live such easy, pleasant lives. They have such good health, for one thing, partly no doubt because their domestic duties give them whole-some exercise without pressing upon them. They have abound-ing leisure for reading, music, choir practising, drawing, fern-printing, fancy work, picnics, riding parties, and enjoy sociability thoroughly. They usually ride in dainty bloomer costumes even when they don't ride astride. All the houses are pretty,

and it takes little to make them so in this climate. One novel
fashion is to decorate the walls with festoons of the beautiful
Microlepia tenuifolia, which are renewed as soon as they fade,
and every room is adorned with a profusion of bouquets, which
are easily obtained where flowers bloom all the year. Many
of the residents possess valuable libraries, and these, with
cabinets of minerals, volcanic specimens, shells, and coral, with
weapons, calabashes, ornaments, and cloth of native manufacture, almost furnish a room in themselves. Some of the
volcanic specimens and the coral are of almost inestimable
value, as well as of exquisite beauty.

The gentlemen don't seem to have near so much occupation
as the ladies. There are two stores on the beach, and at these
and at the Court-house they congregate, for lack of club-house
and exchange. Business is not here a synonym for hurry, and
official duties are light; so light, that in these morning hours
I see the governor, sheriff, and judge, with three other gentlemen, playing an interminable croquet game on the Court-
house lawn. They purvey gossip for the ladies, and how
much they invent, and how much they only circulate, can never
be known !

There is a large native population in the village, along the
beach, and on the heights above the Wailuku River. Frame
houses with lattices, and grass houses with deep verandahs,
peep out everywhere from among the mangoes and bananas.
The governess of Hawaii, the Princess Keelikolani, has a house
on the beach shaded by a large umbrella-tree and a magnificent
clump of bamboos, 70 feet in height. The native life with
which one comes constantly in contact, is very interesting.

The men do whatever hard work is done in cultivating the
kalo patches and pounding the *kalo*. This *kalo*, the Arum
esculentum, forms the national diet. A Hawaiian could not
exist without his calabash of *poi*. The root is an object of the
tenderest solicitude, from the day it is planted until the hour
when it is lovingly eaten. The eating of *poi* seems a ceremony
of profound meaning; it is like the eating salt with an Arab,
or a Masonic sign. The *kalo* root is an ovate oblong, as bulky
as a Californian beet, and it has large leaves, shaped like a
broad arrow, of a singularly bright green. The best kinds
grow entirely in water. The patch is embanked and frequently
inundated, and each plant grows on a small hillock of puddled
earth. The cutting from which it grows is simply the top of
the plant, with a little of the tuber. The men stand up to

their knees in water while cultivating the root. It is excellent
when boiled and sliced; but the preparation of *poi* is an elaborate process. The roots are baked in an underground oven,
and are then laid on a slightly hollowed board, and beaten with
a stone pestle. It is hard work, and the men don't wear any
clothes while engaged in it. It is not a pleasant-looking
operation. They often dip their hands in a calabash of water
to aid them in removing the sticky mass, and they always look
hot and tired. When it is removed from the board into large
calabashes, it is reduced to paste by the addition of water, and
set aside for two or three days to ferment. When ready for
use it is either lilac or pink, and tastes like sour bookbinders'
paste. Before water is added, when it is in its dry state, it is
called *paiai*, or hard food, and is then packed in *ti* leaves in
20 lb. bundles for inland carriage, and is exported to the
Guano Islands. It is a prolific and nutritious plant. It is
estimated that forty square feet will support a Hawaiian for
a year.

The melon and *kalo* patches represent a certain amount of
spasmodic industry, but in most other things the natives take
no thought for the morrow. Why should they indeed? For
while they lie basking in the sun, without care of theirs, the
cocoanut, the breadfruit, the yam, the guava, the banana, and
the delicious *papaya*, which is a compound of a ripe apricot
with a Cantaloupe melon, grow and ripen perpetually. Men
and women are always amusing themselves, the men with surf-
bathing, the women with making *leis*—both sexes with riding,
gossiping, and singing. Every man and woman, almost every
child, has a horse. There is a perfect plague of badly bred,
badly developed, weedy looking animals. The beach and the
pleasant lawn above it are always covered with men and women
riding at a gallop, with bare feet, and stirrups tucked between
the toes. To walk even 200 yards seems considered a degradation. The people meet outside each others' houses all day
long, and sit in picturesque groups on their mats, singing,
laughing, talking, and quizzing the *haoles*, as if the primal curse
had never fallen. Pleasant sights of out-door cooking gregari-
ously carried on greet one everywhere. This style of cooking
prevails all over Polynesia. A hole in the ground is lined with
stones, wood is burned within it, and when the rude oven has
been sufficiently heated, the pig, chicken, breadfruit, or *kalo*,
wrapped in *ti* leaves, is put in, a little water is thrown on, and
the whole is covered up. It is a slow but sure process.

Bright dresses, bright eyes, bright sunshine, music, dancing, a life without care, and a climate without asperities, make up the sunny side of native life as pictured at Hilo. But there are dark moral shadows; the population is shrinking away, and rumours of leprosy are afloat, so that some of these fair homes may be desolate ere long. However many causes for regret exist; one must not forget that only forty years ago the people inhabiting this strip of land between the volcanic wilderness and the sea were a vicious, sensual, shameless herd, that no man among them, except their chiefs, had any rights, that they were harried and oppressed almost to death, and had no consciousness of any moral obligations. Now, order and external decorum at least prevail. There is not a locked door in Hilo, and nobody makes anybody else afraid.

The people of Hawaii-nei are clothed and civilized in their habits; they have equal rights; 6,500 of them have *kuleanas* or freeholds, equable and enlightened laws are impartially administered; wrong and oppression are unknown; they enjoy one of the best administered governments in the world; education is universal, and the throne is occupied by a liberal sovereign of their own race and election.

Few of them speak English. Their language is so easy that most of the foreigners acquire it readily. You know how stupid I am about languages, yet I have already picked up the names of most common things. There are only twelve letters, but some of these are made to do double duty, as K is also T, and L is also R. The most northern island of the group, Kauai, is as often pronounced as if it began with a T, and *Kalo* is usually Taro. It is a very musical language. Each syllable and word ends with a vowel, and there are none of our rasping and sibillant consonants. In their soft phraseology our rough surnames undergo a metamorphosis, as Fisk into Filikina, Wilson into Wilikina. Each vowel is distinctly pronounced, and usually with the Italian sound. The volcano is pronounced as if spelt Keel-ah-wee-ah, and Kauai as if Kah-wye-ee. The name Owhyhee for Hawaii had its origin in a mistake, for the island was never anything but Hawaii, pronounced Hah-wye-ee, but Captain Cook mistook the prefix O, which is the sign of the nominative case, for a part of the word. Many of the names of places, especially of those compounded with *wai*, water, are very musical; Wailuku, "water of destruction:" Waialeale, "rippling water;" *Waioli*, "singing water;" Waipio, "vanquished water;" Kaiwaihae, "torn water." Mauna, "mountain," is a mere prefix, and though always used in naming the two giants of the Pacific, Mauna Kea, and Mauna Loa, is hardly ever applied to Hualalai, "the offspring of the shining sun;" or to Haleakala on Maui, "the house of the sun."

I notice that the foreigners never use the English or botanical names of trees or plants, but speak of *ohias*, *ohelos*, *kukui* (candle-nut), *lauhala* (pandanus), *pulu* (tree fern), *mamané*, *koa*, &c. There is one native word in such universal use that I already find I cannot get on without it, *pilikia*. It means anything, from a downright trouble to a slight difficulty or entanglement. "I'm in a *pilikia*," or "very *pilikia*," or "*pilikia!*" A revolution would be "a *pilikia*." The fact of the late king dying without naming a successor was pre-eminently a *pilikia*, and it would be a serious *pilikia* if a horse were to lose a shoe on the way to Kilauea. *Hou-hou*, meaning "in a huff," I hear on all sides; and two words, *makai*, signifying "on the sea-side," and *mauka*, "on the mountain side." These terms are perfectly intelligible out of doors, but it is puzzling when one is asked to sit on "the *mauka* side of the table." The word *aloha*, in foreign use, has taken the place of every English equivalent. It is a greeting, a farewell, thanks, love, goodwill. *Aloha* looks at you from tidies and illuminations, it meets you on the roads and at house-doors, it is conveyed to you in letters, the air is full of it. "My *aloha* to you," "he sends you his *aloha*," "they desire their *aloha*." It already represents to me all of kindness and goodwill that language can express, and the convenience of it as compared with other phrases is, that it means exactly what the receiver understands it to mean, and consequently, in all cases can be conveyed by a third person. There is no word for "thank you." *Maikai*, "good," is often useful in its place, and smiles supply the rest. There are no words which express "gratitude" or "chastity," or some others of the virtues; and they have no word for "weather," that which we understand by "weather" being absolutely unknown.

Natives have no surnames. Our volcano guide is Upa, or Scissors, but his wife and children are anything else. The late king was Kamehameha, or the "lonely one." The father of the present king is called Kanaina, but the king's name is Lunalilo, or "above all." Nor does it appear that a man is always known by the same name, nor that a name necessarily indicates the sex of its possessor. Thus, in signing a paper the signature would be Hoapili *kanaka*, or Hoapili *wahine*, according as the signer was man or woman. I remember that in my first letter I fell into the vulgarism, initiated by the whaling crews, of calling the natives *Kanakas.* This is universally but very absurdly done, as *Kanaka* simply means man. If a Hawaiian word is absolutely necessary, we might translate native and have *maole,* pronounced *maori,* like that of the New Zealand aborigines. *Kanaka* is to me decidedly objectionable, as conveying the idea of *canaille.*

I had written thus far when Mr. Severance came in to say that a grand display of the national sport of surf-bathing was going on, and a large party of us went down to the beach for two hours to enjoy it. It is really a most exciting pastime, and in a rough sea requires immense nerve. The surf-board is a tough plank shaped like a coffin lid, about two feet broad, and from six to nine feet long, well oiled and cared for. It is usually made of the erythrina, or the breadfruit tree. The surf was very heavy and favourable, and legions of natives were swimming and splashing in the sea, though not more than forty had their *Papa-he-nalu,* or "wave sliding boards," with them. The men, dressed only in *malos,* carrying their boards under their arms, waded out from some rocks on which the sea was breaking, and, pushing their boards before them, swam out to the first line of breakers, and then diving down were seen no more till they re-appeared as a number of black heads bobbing about like corks in smooth water half a mile from shore.

What they seek is a very high roller, on the top of which they leap from behind, lying face downwards on their boards. As the wave speeds on, and the bottom strikes the ground, the top breaks into a huge comber. The swimmers appeared posing themselves on its highest edge by dexterous movements of their hands and feet, keeping just at the top of the curl, but always apparently coming down hill with a slanting motion. So they rode in majestically, always just ahead of the breaker, carried shorewards by its mighty impulse at the rate of forty miles an hour, yet seeming to have a volition of their own, as the more daring riders knelt and even stood on their surf-boards, waving their arms and uttering exultant cries. They were always apparently on the verge of engulfment by the fierce breaker whose towering white crest was ever above and just behind them, but when one expected to see them dashed to pieces, they either waded quietly ashore, or sliding off their boards, dived under the surf, taking advantage of the undertow, and were next seen far out at sea preparing for fresh exploits.

The great art seems to be to mount the roller precisely at the right time, and to keep exactly on its curl just before it breaks. Two or three athletes, who stood erect on their boards as they swept exultingly shorewards, were received with ringing cheers by the crowd. Many of the less expert failed to throw themselves on the crest, and slid back into smooth water, or were caught in the combers, which were fully ten feet high, and after being rolled over and over, ignominiously disappeared amidst roars of laughter, and shouts from the shore. At first I held my breath in terror, thinking the creatures were smothered or dashed to pieces, and then in a few seconds I saw the dark heads of the objects of my anxiety bobbing about behind the rollers waiting for another chance. The shore was thronged with spectators, and the presence of the *élite* of Hilo stimulated the swimmers to wonderful exploits.

These people are truly amphibious. Both sexes seem to swim by nature, and the children riot in the waves from their infancy. They dive apparently by a mere effort of the will. In the deep basin of the Wailuku River, a little below the Falls, the maidens swim, float, and dive with garlands of flowers round their heads and throats. The more furious and agitated the water is, the greater the excitement, and the love of these watery exploits is not confined to the young. I saw great fat men with their hair streaked with grey, balancing themselves on their narrow surf-boards, and riding the surges shorewards with as much enjoyment as if they were in their first youth. I enjoyed the afternoon thoroughly.

Is it "always afternoon" here, I wonder? The sea was so blue, the sunlight so soft, the air so sweet. There was no toil, clang, or hurry. People were all holiday-making (if that can be where there is no work), and enjoying themselves, the surf-bathers in the sea, and hundreds of gaily-dressed men and women galloping on the beach. It was serene and tropical. I sympathize with those who eat the lotus, and remain for ever on such enchanted shores.

I am gaining health daily, and almost live in the open air. I have hired the native policeman's horse and saddle, and with a Macgregor flannel riding costume, which my kind friends have made for me, and a pair of jingling Mexican spurs, am quite Hawaiianised. I ride alone once or twice a day exploring the neighbourhood, finding some new fern or flower daily, and abandon myself wholly to the fascination of this new existence.

                                                        I. L. B.

LETTER VIII.

Windward Hawaii—"Gulches"—The Mexican Saddle—Onomea—A Sugar Plantation—Sugar making—The ruling interest.

ONOMEA, HAWAII.
JUDGE AUSTIN'S.

MRS. A. has been ill for some time, and Mrs. S. her sister, and another friend "plotted" in a very "clandestine" manner that I should come here for a few days in order to give her "a little change of society," but I am quite sure that under this they only veil a kind wish that I should see something of plantation life. There is a plan, too, that I should take a five days' trip to a remarkable valley called Waipio, but this is only a "castle in the air."

Mr. A. sent in for me a capital little lean rat of a horse which by dint of spirit and activity managed to keep within sight of two large horses, ridden by Mr. Thompson, and a very handsome young lady riding "cavalier fashion," who convoyed me out. Borrowed saddle-bags, and a couple of shingles for carrying ferns formed my outfit, and were carried behind my saddle. It is a magnificent ride here. The track crosses the deep, still, Wailuku River on a wooden bridge, and then, after winding up a steep hill, among native houses fantastically situated, hangs on the verge of the lofty precipices which descend perpendicularly to the sea, dips into tremendous gulches, loses itself in the bright fern-fringed torrents which have cleft their way down from the mountains, and at last emerges on the delicious height on which this house is built.

This coast looked beautiful from the deck of the *Kilauea*, but I am now convinced that I have never seen anything so perfectly lovely as it is when one is actually among its details. Onomea is 600 feet high, and every yard of the ascent from Hilo brings one into a fresher and purer air. One looks up the wooded, broken slopes to a wild volcanic wilderness and the snowy peaks of Mauna Kea on one side, and on the other down upon the calm, blue Pacific, wrinkled by the sweet trade-wind, till it blends in far-off loveliness with the still, blue sky ; and heavy surges break on the reefs, and fritter themselves away on the rocks, tossing their pure foam over *ti* and *lauhala* trees, and exquisite ferns and trailers mantle the cliffs down to the water's edge. Here a native house stands, with passion-flowers clustering round its verandah, and the great, solitary, red blossoms of the hibiscus flame out from dark surrounding leafage, and women in rose and green *holokus*, weaving garlands, greet us with "*Aloha*" as we pass. Then we come upon a whole cluster of grass houses under *lauhalas* and bananas. Then there is the sugar-plantation of Kaiwiki, with its patches of bright green cane, its flumes crossing the track above our heads, bringing the cane down from the upland cane-fields to the crushing-mill, and the shifting, busy scenes of the sugar-boiling season.

Then the track goes down with a great dip, along which we slip and slide in the mud to a deep broad stream. This is a most picturesque spot, the junction of two bright rivers, and a few native houses and a Chinaman's store are grouped close by under some palms, with the customary loungers on horseback, asking and receiving *nuhou*, or news, at the doors. Our accustomed horses leaped into a ferry-scow provided by Government, worked by a bearded female of hideous aspect, and leaped out on the other side to climb a track cut on the side of a precipice, which would be steep to mount on one's own feet. There we met parties of natives, all flower-wreathed, talking and singing, coming gaily down on their sure-footed horses, saluting us with the invariable "*Aloha*." Every now and then we passed native churches, with spires painted white, or a native school-house, or a group of scholars all ferns and flowers. The greenness of the vegetation merits the term "dazzling." We think England green, but its colour is poor and pale as compared with that of tropical Hawaii. Palms, candlenuts, *ohias*, hibiscus, were it not for their exceeding beauty, would almost pall upon one from their abundance, and each gulch has its glorious entanglement of breadfruit, the large-leaved *ohia* or native apple, a species of Eugenia (*Eugenia Malaccensis*), and the pandanus, with its aerial roots, all looped together by large sky-blue convolvuli and the running fern, and is marvellous with parasitic growths.

The unique beauty of this coast is what is called gulches—

narrow, deep ravines or gorges, from 100 to 2000 feet in depth,
each with a series of cascades from 10 to 1800 feet in height.
I dislike reducing their glories to the baldness of figures, but
the depth of these clefts (originally, probably, the seams caused
by fire torrents), cut and worn by the fierce streams fed by the
snows of Mauna Kea, and the rains of the forest belt, cannot
otherwise be expressed.   The cascades are most truly beautiful,
gleaming white among the dark depths of foliage far away, and
falling into deep limpid basins, festooned and overhung with
the richest and greenest vegetation of this prolific climate,
from the huge-leaved banana and shining breadfruit to the
most feathery of ferns and lycopodiums.   Each gulch opens
on a velvet lawn close to the sea, and most of them have space
for a few grass houses, with cocoanut trees, bananas and *kalo*
patches.   There are sixty-nine of these extraordinary chasms
within a distance of thirty miles !

I think we came through eleven, fording the streams in all
but two.   The descent into some of them is quite alarming.
You go down almost standing in your stirrups, at a right angle
with the horse's head, and up, grasping his mane to prevent
the saddle slipping.   He goes down like a goat, with his bare
feet, looking cautiously at each step, sometimes putting out a
foot and withdrawing it again in favour of better footing, and
sometimes gathering his four feet under him and sliding or
jumping.   The Mexican saddle has great advantages on these
tracks, which are nothing better than ledges cut on the sides
of precipices, for one goes up and down not only in perfect
security but without fatigue.   I am beginning to hope that I
am not too old, as I feared I was, to learn a new mode of
riding, for my companions rode at full speed over places where
I should have picked my way carefully at a foot-pace ; and
my horse followed them, galloping and stopping short at their
pleasure, and I successfully kept my seat, though not without
occasional fears of an ignominious downfall.   I even wish that
you could see me in my Rob Roy riding dress, with leather
belt and pouch, a *lei* of the orange seeds of the pandanus round
my throat, jingling Mexican spurs, blue saddle blanket, and
Rob Roy blanket strapped on behind the saddle !

This place is grandly situated 600 feet above a deep cove,
into which two beautiful gulches of great size run, with heavy
cascades, finer than Foyers at its best, and a native village is
picturesquely situated between the two.   The great white
rollers, whiter by contrast with the dark deep water, come into

the gulch just where we forded the river, and from the ford a passable road made for hauling sugar ascends to the house. The air is something absolutely delicious; and the murmur of the rollers and the deep boom of the cascades are very soothing There is little rise or fall in the cadence of the surf anywhere on the windward coast, but one even sound, loud or soft, like that made by a train in a tunnel.

We were kindly welcomed, and were at once "made at home." Delicious phrase! the full meaning of which I am learning in Hawaii, where, though everything has the fascination of novelty, I have ceased to feel myself a stranger. This is a roomy, rambling frame-house, with a verandah, and the door, as is usual here, opens directly into the sitting-room. The stair by which I go to my room suggests possibilities, for it has been removed three inches from the wall by an earth-quake, which also brought down the tall chimney of the boiling-house. Close by there are small, pretty frame-houses for the overseer, bookkeeper, sugar boiler, and machinist; a store, the factory, a pretty native church near the edge of the cliff, and quite a large native village below. It looks green and bright, and the atmosphere is perfect, with the cool air coming down from the mountains, and a soft breeze coming up from the blue dreamy ocean. Behind the house the uplands slope away to the colossal Mauna Kea. The actual, dense, impenetrable forest does not begin for a mile and a half from the coast, and its broad dark belt, extending to a height of 4000 feet, and beautifully broken, throws out into greater brightness the up-ward glades of grass and the fields of sugar-cane.

This is a very busy season, and as this is a large plantation there is an appearance of great animation. There are five or six saddled horses usually tethered below the house; and with overseers, white and coloured, natives riding at full gallop, and people coming on all sorts of errands, the hum of the crushing-mill, the rush of water in the flumes, and the grind of the waggons carrying cane, there is no end of stir.

The plantations in the Hilo district enjoy special advantages, for by turning some of the innumerable mountain streams into flumes the owners can bring a great part of their cane and all their wood for fuel down to the mills without other expense than the original cost of the woodwork. Mr. A. has 100 mules, but the greater part of their work is ploughing and hauling the kegs of sugar down to the cove, where in favourable weather they are put on board a schooner for Honolulu. This plantation employs 185 hands, native and Chinese, and turns out 600 tons of sugar a year. The natives are much liked as labourers, being docile and on the whole willing ; but native labour is hard to get, as the natives do not like to work for a term unless obliged, and a pernicious system of "advances' is practised. The labourers hire themselves to the planters, in the case of natives usually for a year, by a contract which has to be signed before a notary public. The wages are about eight dollars a month with food, or eleven dollars without food, and the planters supply houses and medical attendance. The Chinese are imported as coolies, and usually contract to work for five years. As a matter of policy no less than of humanity the "hands" are well treated ; for if a single instance of injustice were perpetrated on a plantation the factory might stand still the next year, for hardly a native would contract to serve again.

The Chinese are quiet and industrious, but smoke opium, and are much addicted to gaming. Many of them save money, and, when their term of service is over, set up stores, or grow vegetables for money. Each man employed has his horse, and on Saturday the hands form quite a cavalcade. Great tact, firmness, and knowledge of human nature are required in the manager of a plantation. The natives are at times disposed to shirk work without sufficient cause ; the native *lunas*, or overseers, are not always reasonable, the Chinamen and natives do not always agree, and quarrels and entanglements arise, and everything is referred to the decision of the manager, who, besides all things else, must know the exact amount of work which ought to be performed, both in the fields and factory, and see that it is done. Mr. A. is a keen, shrewd man of business, kind without being weak, and with an eye on every detail of his plantations. The requirements are endless. It reminds me very much of plantation life in Georgia in the old days of slavery. I never elsewhere heard of so many headaches, sore hands, and other trifling ailments. It is very amusing to see the attempts which the would-be invalids make to lengthen their brief, smiling faces into lugubriousness, and the sudden relaxation into naturalness when they are allowed a holiday. Mr. A. comes into the house constantly to consult his wife regarding the treatment of different ailments.

I have made a second tour through the factory, and am rather disgusted with sugar making. " All's well that ends

well," however, and the delicate crystalline result makes one
forget the initial stages of the manufacture. The cane, stripped
of its leaves, passes from the flumes under the rollers of the
crushing-mill, where it is subjected to a pressure of five or six
tons. One hundred pounds of cane under this process yield
up from sixty-five to seventy-five pounds of juice. This juice
passes, as a pale green cataract, into a trough, which conducts
it into a vat, where it is dosed with lime to neutralize its acid,
and is then run off into heated metal vessels. At this stage
the smell is abominable, and the turbid fluid with a thick scum
upon it is simply disgusting. After a preliminary heating and
skimming it is passed off into iron pans, several in a row, and
boiled and skimmed, and ladled from one to the other till it
reaches the last, which is nearest to the fire, and there it boils
with the greatest violence, seething and foaming, bringing all
the remaining scum to the surface. After the concentration
has proceeded far enough, the action of the heat is suspended,
and the reddish-brown, oily-looking liquid is drawn into the
vacuum-pan till it is about a third full; the concentration is
completed by boiling the juice in vacuo at a temperature of
150°, and even lower. As the boiling proceeds, the sugar-
boiler tests the contents of the pan by withdrawing a few
drops, and holding them up to the light on his finger ; and, by
certain minute changes in their condition, he judges when it is
time to add an additional quantity. When the pan is full, the
contents have thickened into the consistency of thick gruel by
the formation of minute crystals, and are then allowed to
descend into a heater, where they are kept warm till they
can be run into " forms" or tanks, where they are allowed to
granulate. The liquid, or molasses, which remains after the
first crystallization is returned to the vacuum pan and reboiled,
and this reboiling of the drainings is repeated two or three
times, with a gradually decreasing result in the quality and
quantity of the sugar. The last process, which is used to get rid
of the treacle, is a most beautiful one. The mass of sugar and
treacle is put into what are called "centrifugal pans," which are
drums about three feet in diameter and two feet high, which
make about 1000 revolutions a minute. These have false in-
teriors of wire gauze, and the mass is forced violently against
their sides by centrifugal action, and they let the treacle whirl
through, and retain the sugar crystals, which lie in a dry heap
in the centre.

The cane is being flumed in with great rapidity, and the

factory is working till late at night.   The cane from which the
juice has been expressed, called " trash," is dried and used as
fuel for the furnace which supplies the steam power.   The sugar
is packed in kegs, and a cooper and carpenter, as well as other
mechanics, are employed.

Sugar is now the great interest of the islands   Christian
missions and whaling have had their day, and now people talk
sugar.   Hawaii thrills to the news of a cent up or a cent down
in the American market.   All the interests of the kingdom are
threatened by this one, which, because it is grievously depressed and staggers under a heavy import duty in the
American market, is now clamorous in some quarters for
" annexation," and in others for a " reciprocity treaty," which
last means the cession of the Pearl River lagoon on Oahu,
with its adjacent shores, to America, for a Pacific naval station.
There are 200,000 acres of productive soil on the islands, of
which only a fifteenth is under cultivation, and of this large
area 150,000 is said to be specially adapted for sugar culture.
Hitherto, sugar growing has been a very disastrous speculation,
and few of the planters at present do more than keep their
heads above water.

Were labour plentiful and the duties removed, fortunes
might be made, for the soil yields on an average about three
times as much as that of the State of Louisiana.   Two and a
half tons to the acre is a common yield, five tons a frequent
one, and instances are known of the slowly matured cane of a
high altitude yielding as much as seven tons !   The magnificent climate makes it a very easy crop to grow.   There is no
brief harvest time with its rush, hurry, and frantic demand for
labour, nor frost to render necessary the hasty cutting of an
immature crop.   The same number of hands is kept on all the
year round.   The planters can plant pretty much when they
please, or not plant at all for two or three years, the only
difference in the latter case being that the *rattoons* which
spring up after the cutting of the former crop are smaller in
bulk.   They can cut when they please, whether the cane be
tasselled or not, and they can plant, cut, and grind at one
time !

It is a beautiful crop in any stage of growth, especially in
the tasselled stage.   Every part of it is useful—the cane pre-
eminently—the leaves as food for horses and mules, and the
tassels for making hats.   Here and elsewhere there is a plate
of cut cane always within reach, and the children chew it in-

cessantly. I fear you will be tired of sugar, but I find it more interesting than the wool and mutton of Victoria and New Zealand, and it is a most important item of the wealth of this toy kingdom, which last year exported 16,995,402 lbs. of sugar and 192,105 gallons of molasses.* It is really difficult to tear myself from the subject, for I see the cane waving in the sun while I write, and hear the busy hum of the crushing-mill.

I. L. B.

* In 1875 the export of sugar reached a total of 25,080,182 lbs.

LETTER IX.

Ephy Austin—A Hawaiian *Ménage*—Diet and Dress—Fern-hunting--A Primeval Forest.

ONOMEA, HAWAII.

THIS is such a pleasant house and household, Mrs. A. is as bright as though she were not an invalid, and her room, except at meals, is the gathering-place of the family. The four boys are bright, intelligent beings, out of doors barefooted, all day, and with a passion for horses, of which their father possesses about thirty. The youngest, Ephy, is the brightest child for three years old that I ever saw, but absolutely crazy about horses and mules. He talks of little else, and is constantly asking me to draw horses on his slate. He is a merry, audacious little creature, but came in this evening quite subdued. The sun was setting gloriously behind the forest-covered slopes, flooding the violet distances with a haze of gold, and, in a low voice, he said, "I've seen God."

There is the usual Chinese cook, who cooks and waits and looks good-natured, and of course has his own horse, and his wife, a most minute Chinese woman, comes in and attends to the rooms and to Mrs. A., and sews and mends. She wears her native dress—a large, stiff, flat cane hat, like a tray, fastened firmly on or to her head ; a scanty, loose frock of blue denim down to her knees, wide trousers of the same down to her ankles, and slippers. Her hair is knotted up ; she always wears silver armlets, and would not be seen without the hat for anything. There is not a bell in this or any house on the islands, and the bother of servants is hardly known, for the Chinamen do their work like automatons, and disappear at sunset. In a land where there are no carpets, no fires, no dust, no hot water needed, no windows to open and shut—for they are always open—no further service is really required. It is a simple arcadian life, and people live more happily than any that I

have seen elsewhere. It is pleasant to be among people whose
faces are not soured by the east wind, or wrinkled by the
worrying effort to "keep up appearances," which deceive nobody; who have no formal visiting, but real sociability; who
regard the light manual labour of domestic life as a pleasure,
not a thing to be ashamed of; who are contented with their
circumstances, and have leisure to be kind, cultured, and agreeable; and who live so tastefully, though simply, that they can
at any time ask a passing stranger to occupy the simple guest
chamber, or share the simple meal, without any of the soul-
harassing preparations which often make the exercise of hospitality a thing of terror to people in the same circumstances
at home.

People will ask you, "What is the food?" We have everywhere bread and biscuit made of California flour, griddle
cakes with molasses, cracked wheat, butter, not very good,
sweet potatoes, boiled *kalo*, Irish potatoes, and *poi*. I have
not seen fish on any table except at the Honolulu Hotel, or
any meat but beef, which is hard and dry as compared with
ours. We have China or Japan tea, and island coffee. Honolulu is the only place in which intoxicants are allowed to be
sold; and I have not seen beer, wine, or spirits in any house.
Bananas are an important article of diet, and sliced guavas,
eaten with milk and sugar, are very good. The cooking is
always done in detached cook houses, in and on American
cooking-stoves.

As to clothing. I wear my flannel riding-dress for both riding
and walking, and a black silk at other times. The resident
ladies wear prints and silks, and the gentlemen black cloth or
dark tweed suits. Flannel is not required, neither are pug-
garees, or white hats, or sunshades at any season. The changes
of temperature are very slight, and there is no chill when the
sun goes down. The air is always like balm; the rain is tepid
and does not give cold; in summer it may be three or four
degrees warmer. Windows and doors stand open the whole
year. A blanket is agreeable at night, but not absolutely
necessary. It is a truly delightful climate and mode of living,
with such an abundance of air and sunshine. My health im-
proves daily, and I do not consider myself an invalid.

Between working, reading aloud, talking, riding, and "loafing,"
I have very little time for letter writing; but I must tell you of
a delightful fern-hunting expedition on the margin of the forest
that I took yesterday, accompanied by Mr. Thompson and the

two elder boys. We rode in the *mauka* direction, outside cane ready for cutting, with silvery tassels gleaming in the sun, till we reached the verge of the forest, where an old trail was nearly obliterated by a trailing matted grass four feet high, and thousands of woody ferns, which conceal streams, holes, and pitfalls. When further riding was impossible, we tethered our horses and proceeded on foot. We were then 1,500 feet above the sea by the aneroid barometer, and the increased coolness was perceptible. The mercury is about four degrees lower for each 1,000 feet of ascent—rather more than this indeed on the windward side of the islands. The forest would be quite impenetrable were it not for the remains of wood-hauling trails, which, though grown up to the height of my shoulders, are still passable.

Underneath the green maze, invisible streams, deep down, made sweet music, sweeter even than the gentle murmur of the cool breeze among the trees. The forest on the volcano track, which I thought so tropical and wonderful a short time ago, is nothing for beauty to compare with this " garden of God." I wish I could describe it, but cannot; and as you know only our pale, small-leaved trees, with their uniform green, I cannot say that it is like this or that. One might exhaust the whole vocabulary of wonderment upon it. The former cutting of some trees gives atmosphere, and the tumbled nature of the ground shows everything to the best advantage. There were openings over which huge candle-nuts, with their pea-green and silver foliage, spread their giant arms, and the light played through their branches on an infinite variety of ferns. There were groves of bananas and plantains with shiny leaves 8 feet long, like enormous hart's-tongue, the bright-leaved *noni*, the dark-leaved *koa*, the mahogany of the Pacific ; the great glossy-leaved Eugenia—a forest tree as large as our largest elms ; the small-leaved *ohia*, its rose-crimson flowers making a glory in the forests, and its young shoots of carmine red vying with the colouring of the New England fall ; and the *lauhala* drooped its formal plumes, which creak in the faintest breeze ; and the superb breadfruit hung its untempting fruit, and spreading guavas displayed their ripe yellow treasures, and there were trees that had surrendered their own lives to a conquering army of vigorous parasites which had clothed their skeletons with an unapproachable and indistinguishable beauty, and over trees and parasites the tender tendrils of great mauve morning glories trailed and wreathed themselves, and the strong, strangling stems of the *ié* wound themselves round the tall *ohias,* which supported their quaint, yucca-like spikes of leaves fifty feet from the ground.

There were some superb plants of the glossy, tropical-looking bird's-nest fern, or *Asplenium Nidus,* which makes its home on the stems and branches of trees, and brightens the forest with its great shining fronds. I got a specimen from a *koa* tree. The plant had nine fronds, each one measuring from 4 feet 1 inch to 4 feet 7 inches in length, and from 7 to 9 inches in breadth. There were some very fine tree-ferns (*Cibotium Chamissoi ?*), two of which being accessible, we measured, and found them 17 and 20 feet high, their fronds 8 feet long, and their stems 4 feet 10 inches in circumference 3 feet from the ground. They showed the most various shades of green, from the dark tint of the mature frond, to the pale pea green of those which were just uncurling themselves. I managed to get up into a tree for the first time in my life to secure specimens of two beautiful parasitic ferns (*Polypodium tamariscinum* and *P. Hymenophylloides ?*). I saw for the first time, too, a Lygodium and the large, climbing potato-fern (*Polypodium spectrum*), very like a yam in the distance, and the *Vittaria elongata,* whose long grassy fronds adorn almost every tree. The beautiful *Microlepia tenuifolia* abounded, and there were a few plants of the loveliest fern I ever saw (*Trichomanes meifolium*), in specimens of which I indulged sparingly, and almost grudgingly, for it seemed unfitting that a form of such perfect beauty should be mummied in a herbarium. There was one fern in profusion, with from 90 to 130 pair of pinnæ on each frond; and the fronds, though often exceeding 5 feet in length, were only 2 inches broad (*Nephrolepis pectinata*). There were many prostrate trees, which nature has entirely covered with choice ferns, specially the rough stem of the tree-fern. I counted seventeen varieties on one trunk, and on the whole obtained thirty-five specimens for my collection.

The forest soon became completely impenetrable, the beautiful *Gleichenia Hawaiiensis* forming an impassable network over all the undergrowth. And, indeed, without this it would have been risky to make further explorations, for often masses of matted vegetation sustained us temporarily over streams six or eight feet below, whose musical tinkle alone warned us of our peril. I shall never again see anything so beautiful as this fringe of the impassable timber belt. I enjoyed it more than anything I have yet seen; it was intoxicating, my eyes were "satisfied with seeing." It was a dream, a rapture, this maze of form and colour, this entangled luxuriance, this bewildering beauty, through which we caught glimpses of a heavenly sky above, while far away, below glade and lawn, shimmered in surpassing loveliness the cool blue of the Pacific. To me, with my hatred of reptiles and insects, it is not the least among the charms of Hawaii, that these glorious entanglements, and cool, damp depths of a redundant vegetation give shelter to nothing of unseemly shape and venomous proboscis or fang. Here, in cool, dreamy, sunny Onomea, there are no horrid, drumming, stabbing, mosquitos as at Honolulu, to remind me of what I forget sometimes, that I am not in Eden.

I. L. B.

NOTE.—Throughout these letters the botanical names given are only those which are current on the Islands. Those specimens of ferns which survived the rough usage which befell them, are to be seen in the Herbarium of the Botanical Garden at Oxford, and have been arranged by my cousin, Professor Lawson.

LETTER X.

WAIPIO VALLEY, HAWAII.

THERE is something fearful in the isolation of this valley, open at one end to the sea, and walled in on all others by *palis* or precipices, from 1,000 to 2,000 feet in height, over the easiest of which hangs the dizzy track, which after trailing over the country for sixty difficult miles, connects Waipio with the little world of Hilo. The evening is very sombre, and darkness comes on early between these high walls. I am in a native house in which not a word of English is spoken, and Deborah, among her own people, has returned with zest to the exclusive use of her own tongue. This is more solitary than solitude, and tired as I am with riding and roughing it, I must console myself with writing to you. The natives, after staring and giggling for some time, took this letter out of my hand, with many exclamations, which, Deborah tells me, are at the rapidity and minuteness of my writing. I told them the letter was to my sister, and they asked if I had your picture. They are delighted with it, and it is going round a large circle assembled without. They see very few foreign women here, and are surprised that I have not brought a foreign man with me.

There was quite a bustle of small preparations before we left Onomea. Deborah was much excited, and I was not less so, for it is such a complete novelty to take a five days' ride alone with natives. D. is a very nice, native girl of seventeen, who speaks English tolerably, having been brought up by Mr. and Mrs. Austin. She was lately married to a white man employed on the plantation. Mr. A. most kindly lent me a favourite mule, but declined to state that she would not kick, or buck, or turn obstinate, or lie down in the water, all which performances are characteristic of mules. She has, however, as he expected, behaved as the most righteous of her species.

Our equipment was a matter for some consideration, as I had no waterproof; but eventually I wore my flannel riding dress, and carried my plaid in front of the saddle. My saddle-bags, which were behind, contained besides our changes of clothes, a jar of Liebig's essence of beef, some potted beef, a tin of butter, a tin of biscuits, a tin of sardines, a small loaf, and some roast yams. Deborah looked very *piquante* in a bloomer dress of dark blue, with masses of shining hair in natural ringlets falling over the collar, mixing with her *lei* of red rose-buds. She rode a powerful horse, of which she has much need, as this is the most severe road on horses on Hawaii, and it takes a really good animal to come to Waipio and go back to Hilo.

We got away at seven in bright sunshine, and D.'s husband accompanied us the first mile to see that our girths and gear were all right. It was very slippery, but my mule deftly gathered her feet under her, and slid when she could not walk. From Onomea to the place where we expected to find the guide, we kept going up and down the steep sides of ravines, and scrambling through torrents till we reached a deep and most picturesque gulch, with a primitive school-house at the bottom, and some grass-houses clustering under palms and *papayas*, a valley scene of endless ease and perpetual afternoon. Here we found that D.'s uncle, who was to have been our guide, could not go, because his horse was not strong enough, but her cousin volunteered his escort, and went away to catch his horse, while we tethered ours and went into the school-house.

This reminded me somewhat of the very poorest schools connected with the Edinburgh Ladies' Highland School Association, but the teacher had a remarkable paucity of clothing, and he seemed to have the charge of his baby, which, much clothed, and indeed much muffled, lay on the bench beside him. For there were benches, and a desk, and even a black-board and primers down in the deep wild gulch, where the music of living waters, and the thunderous roll of the Pacific, accompanied the children's tuneless voices as they sang an Hawaiian hymn. I shall remember nothing of the scholars but rows of gleaming white teeth, and splendid brown eyes. I thought both teacher and children very apathetic. There were lamentably few, though the pretty rigidly enforced law, which compels all children between the ages of six and fifteen to attend school for forty weeks of the year, had probably gathered

together all the children of the district. They all wore coloured
chemises and *leis* of flowers. Outside, some natives presented
us with some ripe *papayas.*

Mounting again, we were joined by two native women, who
were travelling the greater part of the way hither, and this
made it more cheerful for D. The elder one had nothing on
her head but her wild black hair, and she wore a black *holoku*,
a *lei* of the orange seeds of the pandanus, orange trousers and
big spurs strapped on her bare feet. A child of four, bundled
up in a black poncho, rode on a blanket behind the saddle,
and was tied to the woman's waist, by an orange shawl. The
younger woman, who was very pretty, wore a sailor's hat, *leis*
of crimson *ohia* blossoms round her hat and throat, a black
holoku, a crimson poncho, and one spur, and held up a green
umbrella whenever it rained.

We were shortly joined by Kaluna, the cousin, on an old,
big, wall-eyed, bare-tailed, raw-boned horse, whose wall-eyes
contrived to express mingled suspicion and fear, while a flabby,
pendant, lower lip, conveyed the impression of complete abject-
ness. He looked like some human beings who would be
vicious if they dared, but the vice had been beaten out of him
long ago, and only the fear remained. He has a raw suppu-
rating sore under the saddle, glueing the blanket to his lean
back, and crouches when he is mounted. Both legs on one
side look shorter than on the other, giving a crooked look to
himself and his rider, and his bare feet are worn thin as if he
had been on lava. I rode him for a mile yesterday, and when
he attempted a convulsive canter, with three short steps and a
stumble in it, his abbreviated off-legs made me feel as if I were
rolling over on one side. Kaluna beats him the whole time
with a heavy stick; but except when he strikes him most bar-
barously about his eyes and nose, he only cringes, without
quickening his pace. When I rode him mercifully the true
hound nature came out. The sufferings of this wretched animal
have been the great drawback on this journey. I have now
bribed Kaluna with as much as the horse is worth to give him
a month's rest, and long before that time I hope the owl-hawks
will be picking his bones.

The horse has come before the rider, but Kaluna is no non-
entity. He is a very handsome youth of sixteen, with eyes
which are remarkable, even in this land of splendid eyes, a
straight nose, a very fine mouth, and beautiful teeth, a mass of
wavy, almost curly hair, and a complexion not so brown as to

conceal the mantling of the bright southern blood in his cheeks.
His figure is lithe, athletic, and as pliable as if he were an in-
vertebrate animal, capable of unlimited doublings up and con-
tortions, to which his thin white shirt and blue cotton trousers
are no impediment. He is almost a complete savage; his
movements are impulsive and uncontrolled, and his handsome
face looks as if it belonged to a half-tamed creature out of the
woods. He talks loud, laughs incessantly, croons a monotonous
chant, which sounds almost as heathenish as tom-toms, throws
himself out of his saddle, hanging on by one foot, lingers behind
to gather fruits, and then comes tearing up, beating his horse
over the ears and nose, with a fearful yell and a prolonged
sound like *har-r-rouche*, striking my mule and threatening to
overturn me as he passes me on the narrow track. He is the
most thoroughly careless and irresponsible being I ever saw,
reckless about the horses, reckless about himself, without any
manners or any obvious sense of right and propriety. In his
mouth this musical tongue becomes as harsh as the speech of a
cockatoo or parrot. His manner is familiar. He rides up to
me, pokes his head under my hat, and says, interrogatively,
" Cold !" by which I understand that the poor boy is shivering
himself. In eating he plunges his hand into my bowl of fowl,
or snatches half my biscuit. Yet I daresay he means well, and
I am thoroughly amused with him, except when he maltreats
his horse.

It is a very strange life going about with natives, whose
ideas, as shown by their habits, are, to say the least of it, very
peculiar. Deborah speaks English fairly, having been brought
up by white people, and is a very nice girl. But were she one
of our own race I should not suppose her to be more than
eleven years old, and she does not seem able to understand my
ideas on any subject, though I can be very much interested
and amused with hearing hers.

We had a perfect day until the middle of the afternoon. The
dimpling Pacific was never more than a mile from us as we
kept the narrow track in the long green grass, and on our left
the blunt, snow-patched peaks of Mauna Kea rose from the
girdle of forest, looking so delusively near that I fancied a two-
hours' climb would take us to his lofty summit. The track for
twenty-six miles is just in and out of gulches, from 100 to 800
feet in depth, all opening on the sea, which sweeps into them
in three booming rollers. The candle-nut or *kukui* (*aleurites
triloba*) tree, which on the whole predominates, has leaves of a

rich, deep green when mature, which contrast beautifully with
the flaky, silvery look of the younger foliage. Some of the
shallower gulches are filled exclusively with this tree, which in
growing up to the light to within 100 feet of the top, presents
a mass and density of leafage quite unique, giving the gulch
the appearance as if billows of green had rolled in and solidified
there. Each gulch has some specialty of ferns and trees, and
in such a distance as sixty miles they vary considerably with
the variations of soil, climate, and temperature. But everywhere the rocks, trees, and soil are covered and crowded with
the most exquisite ferns and mosses, from the great tree-fern,
whose bright fronds light up the darker foliage, to the lovely
maiden-hair and graceful selaginellas which are mirrored in
pools of sparkling water. Everywhere, too, the great blue
morning glory opened to a heaven not bluer than itself.

The descent into the gulches is always solemn. You canter
along a bright breezy upland, and are suddenly arrested by a
precipice, and from the depths of a forest-draped abyss a low
plash or murmur rises, or a deep bass sound, significant of
water which must be crossed, and one reluctantly leaves the
upper air to plunge into heavy shadow, and each experience
increases one's apprehensions concerning the next. Though in
some gulches the *kukui* preponderates, in others the *lauhala*
whose aërial roots support it in otherwise impossible positions,
and in others the sombre *ohia*, yet there were some grand clefts
in which nature has mingled her treasures impartially, and out
of cool depths of ferns rose the feathery coco-palm, the glorious
breadfruit, with its green melon-like fruit, the large *ohia*, ideal
in its beauty,—the most gorgeous flowering tree I have ever
seen, with spikes of rose-crimson blossoms borne on the old
wood, blazing among its shining many-tinted leafage,—the tall
papaya with its fantastic crown, the profuse, gigantic plantain,
and innumerable other trees, shrubs, and lianas, in the beauty
and bounteousness of an endless spring. Imagine my surprise
on seeing at the bottom of one gulch, a grove of good-sized,
dark-leaved, very handsome trees, with an abundance of smooth,
round, green fruit upon them, and on reaching them finding
that they were orange trees, their great size, far exceeding that
of the largest at Valencia, having prevented me from recognizing them earlier! In another, some large shrubs with oval,
shining, dark leaves, much crimped at the edges, bright green
berries along the stalks, and masses of pure white flowers lying
flat, like snow on evergreens, turned out to be coffee! The

guava with its obtuse smooth leaves, sweet, white blossoms on
solitary, axillary stalks, and yellow fruit was universal.   The
novelty of the fruit, foliage, and vegetation is an intense delight
to me.   I should like to see how the rigid aspect of a coniferous
tree, of which there is not one indigenous to the islands, would
look by contrast. We passed through a long thicket of sumach,
an exotic from North America, which still retains its old habit
of shedding its leaves, and its grey, wintry, desolate-looking
branches reminded me that there are less favoured parts of the
world, and that you are among mist, cold, murk, slush, gales,
leaflessness, and all the dismal concomitants of an English
winter.

It is wonderful that people should have thought of crossing
these gulches on anything with four legs.   Formerly, that is,
within the last thirty years, the precipices could only be
ascended by climbing with the utmost care, and descended by
being lowered with ropes from crag to crag, and from tree to
tree, when hanging on by the hands became impracticable to
even the most experienced mountaineer.   In this last fashion
Mr. Coan and Mr. Lyons were let down to preach the gospel
to the people of the then populous valleys.   But within recent
years, narrow tracks, allowing one horse to pass another, have
been cut along the sides of these precipices, without any
windings to make them easier, and only deviating enough from
the perpendicular to allow of their descent by the sure-footed
native-born animals.   Most of them are worn by water and
animals' feet, broken, rugged, jagged, with steps of rock sometimes three feet high, produced by breakage here and there.
Up and down these the animals slip, jump, and scramble, some
of them standing still until severely spurred, or driven by some
one from behind.   Then there are softer descents, slippery
with damp, and perilous in heavy rains, down which they slide
dexterously, gathering all their legs under them.   On a few of
these tracks a false step means death, but the vegetation which
clothes the *pali* below, blinds one to the risk.   I don't think
anything would induce me to go up a swinging zigzag—up a
terrible *pali* opposite to me as I write, the sides of which are
quite undraped.

All the gulches for the first twenty-four miles contain running
water.   The great Hakalau gulch which we crossed early yesterday, has a river with a smooth bed as wide as the Thames at Eton.
Some have only small quiet streams, which pass gently through
ferny grottoes.   Others have fierce, strong torrents dashing

between abrupt walls of rock, among immense boulders into deep abysses, and cast themselves over precipice after precipice into the ocean. Probably, many of these are the courses of fire torrents, whose jagged masses of *a-a* have since been worn smooth, and channelled into holes by the action of water. A few are crossed on narrow bridges, but the majority are forded, if that quiet conventional term can be applied to the violent flounderings by which the horses bring one through. The transparency deceives them, and however deep the water is, they always try to lift their fore feet out of it, which gives them a disagreeable rolling motion. Mr. Brigham in his valuable monograph on the Hawaiian volcanoes quoted below,* appears as much impressed with these gulches as I am.

We lunched in one glorious valley, and Kaluna made drinking cups which held fully a pint, out of the beautiful leaves of the *Arum esculentum.* Towards afternoon turbid-looking clouds lowered over the sea, and by the time we reached the worst *pali* of all, the south side of Laupahoehoe, they burst on us in torrents of rain accompanied by strong wind. This terrible precipice takes one entirely by surprise. Kaluna, who rode first, disappeared so suddenly that I thought he had gone over. It is merely a dangerous broken ledge, and besides that it looks as if there were only foothold for a goat, one is dizzied by the sight of the foaming ocean immediately below, and, when we actually reached the bottom, there was only a narrow strip of shingle between the stupendous cliff and the resounding surges, which came up as if bent on destruction. The path by which we descended looked a mere thread on the side of the precipice. I don't know what the word beetling means, but if it means anything bad, I will certainly apply it to that *pali.*

A number of disastrous-looking native houses are clustered

---

* "The road from Hilo to Laupahoehoe, a distance of thirty miles, runs somewhat inland, and is one of the most remarkable in the world. Ravines, 1,800 or 2,000 feet deep, and less than a mile wide, extend far up the slopes of Mauna Kea. Streams, liable to sudden and tremendous freshets, must be traversed on a path of indescribable steepness, winding zig-zag up and down the beautifully wooded slopes or precipices, which are ornamented with cascades of every conceivable form. Few strangers, when they come to the worst precipices, dare to ride down, but such is the nature of the rough steps, that a horse or mule will pass them with less difficulty than a man on foot who is unused to climbing. No less than sixty-five streams must be crossed in a distance of thirty miles."—*Brigham* "*On the Hawaiian Volcanoes.*"

under some very tall palms in the open part of the gulch, but
it is a most wretched situation ; the roar of the surf is deafening, the scanty supply of water is brackish, there are rumours
that leprosy is rife, and the people are said to be the poorest
on Hawaii. We were warned that we could not spend a night
comfortably there, so wet, tired, and stiff, we rode on other six
miles to the house of a native called Bola-Bola, where we had
been instructed to remain. The rain was heavy and ceaseless,
and the trail had become so slippery that our progress was
much retarded. It was a most unpropitious-looking evening,
and I began to feel the painful stiffness arising from prolonged
fatigue in saturated clothes. I indulged in various imagina-
tions as we rode up the long ascent leading to Bola-Bola's,
but this time they were not of sofas and tea, and I never
aspired to anything beyond drying my clothes by a good
fire, for at Hilo some people had shrugged their shoulders, and
others had laughed mysteriously at the idea of our sleeping
there, and some had said it was one of the worst of native
houses.

A single glance was enough. It was a dilapidated frame-
house, altogether forlorn, standing unsheltered on a slope of
the mountain, with one or two yet more forlorn grass-piggeries,
which I supposed might be the cook house, and eating-house
near it.

A prolonged *har-r-r-rouche* from Kaluna brought out a man
with a female horde behind him, all shuffling into clothes as we
approached, and we stiffly dismounted from the wet saddles in
which we had sat for ten hours, and stiffly hobbled up into the
littered verandah, the water dripping from our clothes, and
squeezing out of our boots at every step. Inside there was
one room about 18 × 14 feet, which looked as if the people
had just arrived and had thrown down their goods promiscuously. There were mats on the floor not over clean, and
half the room was littered and piled with mats rolled up,
boxes, bamboos, saddles, blankets, lassos, cocoanuts, *kalo* roots,
bananas, quilts, pans, calabashes, bundles of hard *poi* in *ti*
leaves, bones, cats, fowls, clothes. A frightful old woman,
looking like a relic of the old heathen days, with bristling grey
hair cut short, her body tattooed all over, and no clothing but
a ragged blanket huddled round her shoulders ; a girl about
twelve, with torrents of shining hair, and a piece of bright
green calico thrown round her, and two very good-looking
young women in rose-coloured chemises, one of them holding

a baby, were squatting and lying on the mats, one over
another, like a heap of savages.

When the man found that we were going to stay all night he
bestirred himself, dragged some of the things to one side, and
put down a shake-down of *pulu* (the silky covering of the
fronds of one species of tree-fern), with a sheet over it, and a
gay quilt of orange and red cotton. There was a thin printed
muslin curtain to divide off one half of the room, a usual
arrangement in native houses. He then helped to unsaddle
the horses, and the confusion of the room was increased by a
heap of our wet saddles, blankets, and gear. All this time the
women lay on the floor and stared at us.

Rheumatism seemed impending, for the air up there was
chilly, and I said to Deborah that I must make some change in
my dress, and she signed to Kaluna, who sprang at my soaked
boots and pulled them off, and my stockings too, with a savage
alacrity which left it doubtful for a moment whether he had not
also pulled off my feet ! I had no means of making any
further change except putting on a wrapper over my wet
clothes.

Meanwhile the man killed and boiled a fowl, and boiled
some sweet potato, and when these untempting viands, and a
calabash of *poi* were put before us, we sat round them and
eat ; I with my knife, the others with their fingers. There
was coffee in a dirty bowl. The females had arranged a
row of pillows on their mat, and all lay face downwards, with
their chins resting upon them, staring at us with their great
brown eyes, and talking and laughing incessantly. They had
low sensual faces, like some low order of animal. When our
meal was over, the man threw them the relics, and they soon
picked the bones clean. It surprised me that after such a
badly served meal the man brought a bowl of water for our
hands, and something intended for a towel.

By this time it was dark, and a stone, deeply hollowed at
the top, was produced, containing beef fat and a piece of rag
for a wick, which burned with a strong flaring light. The
women gathered themselves up and sat round a large calabash
of *poi*, conveying the sour paste to their mouths with an
inimitable twist of the fingers, laying their heads back and
closing their eyes with a look of animal satisfaction. When
they had eaten they lay down as before, with their chins on
their pillows, and again the row of great brown eyes confronted
me. Deborah, Kaluna, and the women talked incessantly in

loud shrill voices till Kaluna uttered the word *auwé* with a long
groaning intonation, apparently signifying weariness, divested
himself of his clothes, and laid down on a mat alongside our
shake-down, upon which we let down the dividing curtain and
wrapped ourselves up as warmly as possible.

I was uneasy about Deborah who has had a cough for some
time, and consequently took the outside place under the window
which was broken, and presently a large cat jumped through the
hole and down upon me, followed by another and another, till
five wild cats had effected an entrance, making me a stepping-
stone to ulterior proceedings. Had there been a sixth I think I
could not have borne the infliction quietly. Strips of jerked
beef were hanging from the rafters, and by the light which was
still burning I watched the cats climb up stealthily, seize on
some of these, descend, and disappear through the window,
making me a stepping-stone as before, but with all their craft
they let some of the strips fall, which awoke Deborah, and next
I saw Kaluna's magnificent eyes peering at us under the
curtain. Then the natives got up, and smoked and eat more
poi at intervals, and talked, and Kaluna and Deborah quar-
relled, jokingly, about the time of night she told me, and the
moon through the rain-clouds occasionally gave us delusive
hopes of dawn, and I kept moving my place to get out of the
drip from the roof, and so the night passed. I was amused
all the time, though I should have preferred sleep to such
nocturnal diversions. It was so new, and so odd, to be the
only white person among eleven natives in a lonely house, and
yet to be as secure from danger and annoyance as in our own
home.

At last a pale dawn did appear, but the rain was still coming
down heavily, and our poor animals were standing dismally
with their heads down and their tails turned towards the wind.
Yesterday evening I took a change of clothes out of the damp
saddle bags, and put them into what I hoped was a dry place,
but they were soaked, wetter even than those in which I had
been sleeping, and my boots and Deborah's were so stiff, that
we gladly availed ourselves of Kaluna's most willing services.
The mode of washing was peculiar : he held a calabash with
about half-a-pint of water in it, while we bathed our faces and
hands, and all the natives looked on and tittered. This was
apparently his idea of politeness, for no persuasion would induce him to put the bowl down on the mat, and Deborah
evidently thought it was proper respect. We had a repetition

of the same viands as the night before for breakfast, and, as
before, the women lay with their chins on their pillows and
stared at us.

The rain ceased almost as soon as we started, and though it
has not been a bright day, it has been very pleasant. There
are no large gulches on to-day's journey. The track is mostly
through long grass, over undulating uplands, with park-like
clumps of trees, and thickets of guava and the exotic sumach.
Different ferns, flowers, and vegetation, with much less
luxuriance and little water, denoted a drier climate and a
different soil.

We moved on in single file at a jog-trot wherever the road
admitted of it, meeting mounted natives now and then, which
led to a delay for the exchange of *nuhou ;* and twice we had to
turn into the thicket to avoid what here seems to be considered
a danger. There are many large herds of semi-wild bullocks
on the mountains, branded cattle, as distinguished from the
wild or unbranded, and when they are wanted for food, a number
of experienced *vaccheros* on strong, shod horses go up, and
drive forty or fifty of them down. We met such a drove bound
for Hilo, with one or two men in front and others at the sides
and behind, uttering loud shouts. The bullocks are nearly
mad with being hunted and driven, and at times rush like a
living tornado, tearing up the earth with their horns. As soon
as the galloping riders are seen and the crooked-horned
beasts, you retire behind a screen. There must be some tradition of some one having been knocked down and hurt, for
reckless as the natives are said to be, they are careful about
this, and we were warned several times by travellers whom we
met, that there were "bullocks ahead." The law provides that
the *vaccheros* shall station one of their number at the head of a
gulch to give notice when cattle are to pass through.

We jogged on again till we met a native who told us that we
were quite close to our destination ; but there were no signs of
it, for we were still on the lofty uplands, and the only prominent
objects were huge headlands confronting the sea. I got off to
walk, as my mule seemed footsore, but had not gone many
yards when we came suddenly to the verge of a *pali*, about
1,000 feet deep, with a narrow, fertile valley, and a yet higher
pali on the other side, both abutting perpendicularly on the
sea. I should think the valley is not more than three miles
long, and it is walled in by high, inaccessible mountains. It is
in fact, a gulch on a greatly enlarged scale. The prospect below

us was very charming, a fertile region perfectly level, protected from the sea by sandhills, watered by a winding stream, and bright with fishponds, meadow lands, *kalo* patches, orange and coffee groves, figs, breadfruit, and palms. There were a number of grass-houses, and a native church with a spire, and another up the valley testified to the energy and aggressiveness of Rome. We saw all this from the moment we reached the *pali;* and it enlarged, and the detail grew upon us with every yard of the laborious descent of broken, craggy track, which is the only mode of access to the valley from the outer world. I got down on foot with difficulty; a difficulty much increased by the long rowels of my spurs, which caught on the rocks and entangled my dress, the simple expedient of taking them off not having occurred to me !

A neat frame-house, with large stones between it and the river, was our destination. It belongs to a native named Halemanu, a great man in the district, for, besides being a member of the legislature, he is deputy sheriff. He is a man of property, also; and though he cannot speak a word of English, he is well educated in Hawaiian, and writes an excellent hand. I brought a letter of introduction to him from Mr. Severance, and we were at once received with every hospitality, our horses cared for, and ourselves luxuriously lodged. We walked up the valley before dark to get a view of a cascade, and found supper ready on our return. This is such luxury after last night. There is a very light, bright sitting-room, with papered walls, and manilla matting on the floor, a round centre table with books and a photograph album upon it, two rocking-chairs, an office-desk, another table and chairs, and a Canadian lounge. I can't imagine in what way this furniture was brought here. Our bedroom opens from this, and it actually has a four-post bedstead with mosquito bars, a lounge and two chairs, and the floor is covered with native matting. The washing apparatus is rather an anomaly, for it consists of a basin and crash towel placed in the verandah, in full view of fifteen people. The natives all bathe in the river.

Halemanu has a cook house and native cook, and an eating-room, where I was surprised to find everything in foreign style —chairs, a table with a snow white cover, and table napkins, knives, forks, and even saltcellars. I asked him to eat with us, and he used a knife and fork quite correctly, never, for instance, putting the knife into his mouth. I was amused to see him afterwards, sitting on a mat among his family and dependants, helping himself to *poi* from a calabash with his fingers. He gave us for supper delicious river fish fried, boiled *kalo*, and Waipio coffee with boiled milk.

It is very annoying only to be able to converse with this man through an interpreter; and Deborah, as is natural, is rather unwilling to be troubled to speak English, now that she is among her own people. After supper we sat by candlelight in the parlour, and he showed me his photograph album. At eight he took a large Bible, put on glasses, and read a chapter in Hawaiian; after which he knelt and prayed with profound reverence of manner and tone. Towards the end I recognized the Hawaiian words for " Our Father." * Here in Waipio there is something pathetic in the idea of this Fatherhood, which is wider than the ties of kin and race. Even here not one is a stranger, an alien, a foreigner! And this man, so civilized and Christianized, only now in middle life, was, he said, " a big boy when the first teachers came," and may very likely have witnessed horrors in the *heiau*, or temple, close by, of which little is left now.

This bedroom is thoroughly comfortable. Kaluna wanted to sleep on the lounge here, probably because he is afraid of *akuas*, or spirits, but we have exiled him to a blanket on the parlour lounge.

I. L. B.

---

* The Lord's Prayer in Hawaiian runs thus :—E ko mako Makua i-loko o ka Lani, e hoanoia Kou Inoa E hiki mai Kou auhuni e malamaia Kou Makemake ma ka-nei honua e like me ia i malamaia ma ka Lani e haawi mai i a makau i ai no keia la e kala mai i ko makou lawehalaana me makou e kala nei i ka poe i lawehala mai i a makou mai alakai i a makou i ka hoowalewaleia mai ata a hookapele i a makou mai ka ino no ka mea Nou ke Aupuni a me ka Mana a me ka hoonaniia a man loa 'ku. Amene.

LETTER X.—*continued.*

The Waipio Fall — "Bessie Twinker" — William Wallace—**Cities of Refuge**—Human Sacrifices—Legendary Tyrants.

WE were thoroughly rested this morning, and very glad of a fine day for a visit to the great cascade, which is rarely seen by foreigners. My mule was slightly galled with the girth, and having a strong fellow feeling with Elisha's servant, "Alas, master, for it was borrowed!" I have bought for $20 a pretty, light, half-broken bay mare, which I rode to-day and liked much.

After breakfast, which was a repetition of last night's supper, we three, with Halemanu's daughter as guide, left on horseback for the waterfall, though the natives tried to dissuade us by saying that stones came down, and it was dangerous ; also that people could not go in their clothes, there was so much wading. In deference to this last opinion, D. rode without boots, and I without stockings. We rode through the beautiful valley till we reached a deep gorge turning off from it, which opens out into a nearly circular chasm with walls 2,000 feet in height, where we tethered our horses. A short time after leaving them, D. said, "She says we can't go further in our clothes," but when the natives saw me plunge boldly into the river in my riding dress, which is really not unlike a fashionable, Newport bathing suit, they thought better of it. It was a thoroughly rough tramp, wading ten times through the river, which was sometimes up to our knees, and sometimes to our waists, and besides the fighting among slippery rocks in rushing water, we had to crawl and slide up and down wet, mossy masses of dislodged rock, to push with eyes shut through wet jungles of Indian shot, guava, and a thorny vine, and sometimes to climb from tree to tree at a considerable height. When, after an hour's fighting we arrived in sight of the cascade, but not of the basin into which it falls, our pretty guide declined to go further, saying that the

wind was rising and that stones would fall and kill us ; but
being incredulous on this point, I left them, and with great
difficulty and many bruises, got up the river to its exit from the
basin, and there, being unable to climb the rocks on either
side, stood up to my throat in the still, tepid water till the
scene became real to me.

I do not care for any waterfall but Niagara, nor do I care in
itself for this one, for though its first leap is 200 feet and its
second 1,600, it is so frittered away and dissipated in spray,
owing to the very magnitude of its descent, that there is no
volume of water within sight to create mass or sound. But no
words can paint the majesty of the surroundings, the caverned,
precipitous walls of rock coming down in one black plunge
from the blue sky above to the dark abyss of water below, the
sullen, shuddering sound with which pieces of rock came
hurtling down among the trees, the thin tinkle of the water as
it falls, the full rush of the river, the feathery growth of ferns,
gigantic below, but so diminished by the height above, as only
to show their presence by the green tinge upon the rocks, while
in addition to the gloom produced by the stupendous height
of the cliffs, there is a cool, green darkness of dense forest, and
mighty trees of strange tropical forms glass themselves in the
black mirror of the basin. For one moment a ray of sunshine
turned the upper part of the spray into a rainbow, and never
to my eyes had the bow of promise looked so heavenly as
when it spanned the black, solemn, tree-shadowed abyss, whose
deep, still waters only catch a sunbeam on five days of the
year.

I found the natives regaling themselves on *papaya*, and on
live fresh-water shrimps, which they find in great numbers in
the river. I remembered that white people at home, calling
themselves civilized, eat live, or at least raw, oysters, but the
sight of these active, squirming shrimps struggling between the
white teeth of my associates was yet more repulsive.

We finished our adventurous expedition with limbs much
bruised, as well as torn and scratched, and before we emerged
from the chasm saw a rock dislodged, which came crashing
down not far from us, carrying away an *ohia*. It is a gruesome
and dowie den, but well worth a visit.

We mounted again, and rode as far as we could up the
valley, fording the river in deep water several times, and coming
down the other side. The coffee trees in full blossom were
very beautiful, and they, as well as the oranges, have escaped

the blight which has fallen upon both in other parts of the island. In addition to the usual tropical productions, there were some very fine fig trees and thickets of the castor-oil plant, a very handsome shrub, when, as here, it grows to a height of from 10 to 22 feet. The natives, having been joined by some Waipio women, rode at full gallop over all sorts of ground, and I enjoyed the speed of my mare without any apprehension of being thrown off. We rode among most extensive *kalo* plantations, and large artificial fish-ponds, in which hundreds of gold-fish were gleaming, and came back by the sea shore, green with the maritime convolvulus, and the smooth-bottomed river, which the Waipio folk use as a road. Canoes glide along it, brown-skinned men wade down it floating bundles of *kalo* after them, and strings of laden horses and mules follow each other along its still waters. I hear that in another and nearly unapproachable valley, a river serves the same purpose. While we were riding up it, a great gust lifted off its surface in fine spray, and almost blew us from our horses. Hawaii has no hurricanes, but at some hours of the day Waipio is subject to terrific gusts, which really justify the people in their objection to visiting the cascade. Some time ago, in one of these, this house was lifted up, carried 20 feet, and deposited in its present position.

Supper was ready for us—*kalo*, yams, spatchcock, *poi*, coffee, rolls, and Oregon kippered salmon ; and when I told Halemanu that the spatchcock and salmon reminded me of home, he was quite pleased, and said he would provide the same for breakfast to-morrow.

The owner of the mare, which I have named "Bessie Twinker," had willingly sold her to me, though I told him I could not pay him for her until I reached Onomea. I do not know what had caused my credit to suffer during my absence, but D., after talking long with him this evening, said to me, " He says he can't let you have the horse, because when you've taken it away, he thinks you will never send him the money." I told her indignantly to tell him that English women never cheated people, a broad and totally unsustainable assertion, which had the effect of satisfying the poor fellow.

After Halemanu, Deborah, Kaluna, and a number of natives had eaten their *poi*, Halemanu brought in a very handsome silver candlestick, and expressed a wish that Deborah should interpret for us. He asked a great many sensible questions about England, specially about the state of the poor, the extent of the franchise, and the influence of religion. When he heard that I had spent some years in Scotland, he said, " Do you know Mr. Wallace ? " I was quite puzzled, and tried to recall any man of that name who I had heard of as having visited Hawaii, when a happy flash of comprehension made me aware of his meaning, and I replied that he died long before I knew Scotland, and indeed before I was born ; but that the Scotch held his memory in great veneration, and were putting up a monument to him. But for the mistake as to dates, he seemed to have the usual notions as to the exploits of Wallace. He deplores most deeply the dwindling of his people, and his manner became very sad about it. D. said, " He's very un-happy ; he says, soon there will be no more Kanakas." He told me that this beautiful valley was once very populous, and even forty years ago, when Mr. Ellis visited it, there were 1,300 people here. Now probably there are not more than 200.

Here was the *Puhonua*, or place of refuge for all this part of the island. This, and the very complete one of Honaunau, on the other side of Hawaii, were the Hawaiian " Cities of Refuge." Could any tradition of the Mosaic ordinance on this subject have travelled hither ? These two sanctuaries were absolutely inviolable. The gates stood perpetually open, and though the fugitive was liable to be pursued to their very threshold, he had no sooner crossed it than he was safe from king, chief, or avenger. These gates were wide, and some faced the sea, and others the mountains. Hither the murderer, the manslayer, the *tabu*-breaker fled, repaired to the presence of the idol, and thanked it for aiding him to reach the place of security. After a certain time the fugitives were allowed to return to their families, and none dared to injure those to whom the high gods had granted their protection.

In time of war, tall spears, from which white flags were un-furled, were placed at each end of the enclosure, and until the proclamation of peace invited the vanquished to enter. These flags were fixed a short distance outside the walls, and no pur-suing warrior, even in the hot flush of victory, could pursue his routed foe one foot beyond. Within was the sacred pale of *pahu tabu*, and anyone attempting to strike his victim there would have been put to death by the priests and their adherents. In war time the children, old people, and many of the women of the neighbouring districts, were received within the enclosure, where they awaited the issue of the conflict in security, and were safe from violence in the event of defeat. These *puhonuas* contain pieces of stone weighing from 2 to 3 tons, raised 6 feet from the ground, and the walls, narrowing gradually towards the top, are 15 feet wide at the base and 12 feet high. They are truly grand monuments of humanity in the midst of the barbarous institutions of heathenism, and it shows a considerable degree of enlightenment, that even rebels in arms and fugitives from invading armies were safe, if they reached the sacred refuge, for the priests of *Keawe* knew no distinctions of party.

In dreadful contrast to this place of mercy, there were some very large *heiaus* (or temples) here, on whose hideous altars eighty human sacrifices are said to have been offered at one time. One of the legends told me concerning this lovely valley is, that King Umi, having vanquished the kings of the six divisions of Hawaii, was sacrificing captives in one of these *heiaus*, when the voice of his god, *Kuahilo* was heard from the clouds, demanding more slaughter. Fresh human blood streamed from the altars, but the insatiable demon continued to call for more, till Umi had sacrificed all the captives and all his own men but one, whom he at first refused to give up, as he was a great favourite, but *Kuahilo* thundered from heaven, till the favourite warrior was slain, and only the king and the sacrificing priest remained.

This valley of the "vanquished waters" abounds in legends. Some of these are about a cruel monster, King Hooku, who lived here, and whose memory, so far as he is remembered, is much execrated. It is told of him that if a man were said to have a handsome head, he sent some of his warriors to behead him, and then hacked and otherwise disfigured the face for a diversion. On one occasion he ordered a man's arm to be cut off and brought to him, simply because it was said to be more beautifully tattooed than his own. It is sixty-four years since the last human sacrifice was exposed on the Waipio altars, but there are several old people here who must have been at least thirty when Hawaii threw off idolatry for ever. Halemanu has again closed the evening with the simple worship of the true God.

I. L. B.

LETTER XI.

HILO, HAWAII.

THERE is a rumour that the king is coming as the guest of Admiral Pennock in the *Benicia*. If it turns out to be true, it will turn our quiet life upside down.

We met with fearful adventures in the swollen gulches between Laupahoehoe and Onomea. It is difficult to begin my letter with the plain prose of our departure from Waipio, which we accomplished on the morning after I last wrote. On rising after a sound sleep, I found that my potted beef, which I had carefully hung from a nail the night before, had been almost carried away by small ants. These ants swarm in every house on low altitudes. They assemble in legions as if by magic, and by their orderly activity carry away all that they do not devour, of all eatables which have not been placed on tables which have rags dipped in a solution of corrosive sublimate wound round their legs.

We breakfasted by lamplight, and because I had said that some of the viands reminded me of home, our kind host had provided them at that early hour. He absolutely refused to be paid anything for the accommodation of our party, and said he should be ashamed of himself if he took anything from a lady travelling without a husband.

It was a perfect morning. The full moon hung over the enclosing *palis*, gleaming on coffee and breadfruit groves, and on the surface of the river, which was just quivering under a soft sea breeze. The dew was heavy, smoke curled idly from native houses, the east was flushing with the dawn, and the valley looked the picture of perfect peace. A number of natives assembled to see us start, and they all shook hands with us, exchanging *alohas*, and presenting us with *leis* of roses and *ohias*. D. looked very pretty with a red hibiscus blossom

in her shining hair. You would have been amused to see me
shaking hands with men dressed only in *malos*, or in the
short blue shirt reaching to the waist, much worn by them
when at work.

I rode mv mare with some pride of proprietorship, and our
baggage for a time was packed on the mule, and we started up
the tremendous *pali* at the tail of a string of twenty mules and
horses laden with *kalo*. This was in the form of *paiai*, or hard
food, which is composed, as I think I mentioned before, of the
root baked and pounded, but without water. It is put up in
bundles wrapped in *ti* leaves, of from twenty to thirty pounds
each, secured with cocoanut fibre, in which state it will keep
for months, and much of the large quantity raised in Waipio is
exported to the plantations, the Waimea ranches, and the neighbouring districts. A square mile of *kalo*, it is estimated, would
feed 15,000 Hawaiians for a year.

It was a beautiful view from the top of the *pali*. The white
moon was setting, the earliest sunlight was lighting up the dewy
depths of the lonely valley, reddening with a rich rose red the
huge headland which forms one of its sentinels; heavy snow
had fallen during the night on Mauna Kea, and his great ragged
dome, snow-covered down to the forests, was blushing like an
Alpine peak at the touch of the early sun. It ripened into a
splendid joyous day, which redeemed the sweeping uplands of
Hamakua from the dreariness which I had thought belonged
to them. There was a fresh sea-breeze, and the sun, though
unclouded, was not too hot. We halted for an early lunch at
the clean grass-house we had stopped at before, and later in
the afternoon at that of the woman with whom we had ridden
from Hakalau, who received us very cordially, and regaled us
with *poi* and pork.

In order to avoid the amenities of Bola Bola's we rode thirty-
four miles, and towards evening descended the tremendous
steep, which leads to the surf-deafened village of Laupahochoe.
Halemanu had given me a note of introduction to a widow
named Honolulu, which Deborah said began thus, "As I know
that you have the only clean house in L," and on presenting it we
were made very welcome. Besides the widow, a very redundant
beauty, there were her two brothers and two male cousins, and
all bestirred themselves in our service, the men in killing and
cooking the supper, and the woman in preparing the beds. It
was quite a large room, with doors at the end and side, and
fully a third was curtained off by a calico curtain, with a

gorgeous Crétonne pattern upon it. I was delighted to see a four-post bed, with mosquito bars, and a clean *pulu* mattrass, with a linen sheet over it, covered with a beautiful quilt with a quaint arabesque pattern on a white ground running round it, and a wreath of green leaves in the centre. The native women exercise the utmost ingenuity in the patterns and colours of these quilts. Some of them are quite works of art. The materials, which are plain and printed cottons, cost about $8, and a complete quilt is worth from $18 to $50. The widow took six small pillows, daintily covered with silk, out of a chest, the uses of which were not obvious, as two large pillows were already on the bed. It was astonishing to see a native house so handsomely furnished in so poor a place. The mats on the floor were numerous and very fine. There were two tables, several chairs, a bureau with a swinging mirror upon it, a basin, crash towels, a caraffe and a kerosene lamp. It is all very well to be able to rough it, and yet better to enjoy doing so, but such luxuries add much to one's contentment after eleven hours in the saddle.

Honolulu wore a green chemise at first, but when supper was ready she put a Macgregor tartan *holoku* over it. The men were very active, and cooked the fowl in about the same time that it takes to pluck one at home. They spread the finest mat I have seen in the centre of the floor as a tablecloth, and put down on it bowls containing the fowl and sweet potatoes, and the unfailing calabash of *poi*. Tea, coffee, and milk were not procurable, and as the water is slimy and brackish, I offered a boy a dime to get me a cocoanut, and presently eight great, misshapen things were rolled down at the door. The outside is a smooth buff rind, underneath which is a fibrous covering, enormously strong and about an inch thick, which when stripped off reveals the nut as we see it, but of a very pale colour. Those we opened were quite young, and each contained nearly three tumblers of almost effervescent, very sweet, slightly acidulated, perfectly limpid water, with a strong flavour of cocoanut. It is a delicious beverage. The meat was so thin and soft that it could have been spooned out like the white of an egg if we had had any spoons. We all sat cross-legged round our meal, and all Laupahoehoe crowded into the room and verandah with the most persistent, unwinking, gimlet-ing stare I ever saw. It was really unpleasant, not only to hear a Babel of talking, of which, judging from the constant repetition of the words *wahine haole*, I was the subject, but to

have to eat under the focussed stare of twenty pair of eyes.
My folding camp-knife appears an object of great interest, and
it was handed round, inside and outside the house. When I
retired about seven, the assemblage was still in full session.

The stars were then bright, but when I woke the next
morning a strong breeze was blowing, the surf was roaring so
loud as almost to drown human voices, and rolling up in
gigantic surges, and to judge from appearances, the rain, which
was falling in torrents, had been falling for some hours. There
was much buzzing among the natives regarding our prospects
for the day. I shall always think from their tone and manner,
and the frequent repetition of the names of the three worst
gulches, that the older men tried to dissuade us from going;
but Deborah, who was very anxious to be at home by Sunday,
said that the verdict was that if we started at once for our ride
of twenty-three miles we might reach Onomea before the freshet
came on. This might have been the case had it not been for
Kaluna. Not only was his horse worn out, but nothing would
induce him to lead the mule, and she went off on foraging expeditions continually, which further detained us. Kaluna had
grown quite polite in his savage way. He always insisted on
putting on and taking off my boots, carried me once through
the Waipio river, helped me to pack the saddle-bags, and even
offered to brush my hair! He frequently brought me guavas
on the road, saying, "eat," and often rode up, saying interrogatively, "tired?" "cold?" D. told me that he was very
tired, and I was very sorry for him, for he was so thinly and
poorly dressed, and the natives are not strong enough to bear
exposure to cold as we can, and a temperature at 68° is cold
to them. But he was quite incorrigible, and thrashed his horse
to the last.

We breakfasted on fowl, *poi*, and cocoanut milk, in presence
of even a larger number of spectators than the night before,
one of them a very old man looking savagely picturesque,
with a red blanket tied round his waist, leaving his lean
chest and arms, which were elaborately tattooed, completely
exposed.

The mule had been slightly chafed by the gear, and in my
anxiety about a borrowed animal, of which Mr. Austin makes
a great joke, I put my saddle-bags on my own mare in an evil
hour, and not only these, but some fine cocoanuts, tied up in
a waterproof which had long ago proved its worthlessness. It
was a grotesquely miserable picture. The house is not far

from the beach, and the surf, beyond which a heavy mist hung, was coming in with such a tremendous sound that we had to shout at the top of our voices in order to be heard. The sides of the great gulch rose like prison walls, cascades which had no existence the previous night hurled themselves from the summit of the cliffs directly into the sea, the rain, which fell in sheets, not drops, covered the ground to the depth of two or three inches, and dripped from the wretched, shivering horses, which stood huddled together with their tails between their legs. My thin flannel suit was wet through even before we mounted. I dispensed with stockings, as I was told that wearing them in rain chills and stiffens the limbs. D., about whom I was anxious, as well as about the mule, had a really waterproof cloak, and I am glad to say has quite lost the cough from which she suffered before our expedition. She does not care about rain any more than I do.

We soon reached the top of the worst and dizziest of all the *palis*, and then splashed on, mile after mile, down sliding banks, and along rocky tracks, from which the soil had been completely carried, the rain falling all the time. In some places several feet of soil had been carried away, and we passed through water-rents, the sides of which were as high as our horses' heads, where the ground had been level a few days before. By noon the aspect of things became so bad that I wished we had a white man with us, as I was uneasy about some of the deepest gulches. When four hours' journey from Onomea, Kaluna's horse broke down, and he left us to get another, and we rode a mile out of our way to visit Deborah's grandparents.

Her uncle carried us across some water to their cook-house, where, happily, a *kalo* baking had just been accomplished in a hole in the ground, lined with stones, among which the embers were still warm. In this very small hut, in which a man could hardly stand upright, there were five men only dressed in *malos*, four women, two of them very old, much tattooed, and huddled up in blankets, two children, five pertinaciously sociable dogs, two cats, and heaps of things of different kinds. The natives are most gregarious, always visiting each other, and living in each other's houses, and so hospitable that no Hawaiian, however poor, will refuse to share his last mouthful of *poi* with a stranger of his own race. These people looked very poor, but probably were not really so, as they had a nice grass-house, with very fine mats, within a few yards.

A man went out, cut off the head of a fowl, singed it in the flame, cut it into pieces, put it into a pot to boil, and before our feet were warm the bird was cooked, and we ate it out of the pot with some baked *kalo*. D. took me out to see some mango trees, and a pond filled with gold fish, which she said had been hers when she was a child. She seemed very fond of her relatives, among whom she looked like a fairy princess; and I think they admired her very much, and treated her with some deference. The object of our visit was to procure a *lé* of birds' feathers which they had been making for her, and for which I am sure 300 birds must have been sacrificed. It was a very beautiful as well as costly ornament,* and most ingeniously packed for travelling by being laid at full length within a slender cylinder of bamboo.

We rode on again, somewhat unwillingly on my part, for though I thought my apprehensions might be cowardly and ignorant, yet D. was but a child, and had the attractive wilfulness of childhood, and she was, I saw, determined to get back to her husband, and the devotion and affection of the young wife were so pleasant to see, that I had not the heart to offer serious opposition to her wishes, especially as I knew that I might be exaggerating the possible peril. I gathered, however, from what she said, that her people wanted us to remain until Monday, especially as none of them could go with us, their horses being at some distance. I thought it a sign of difficulties ahead, that on one of the most frequented tracks in Hawaii, we had not met a single traveller, though it was Saturday, a special travelling day.

We crossed one gulch in which the water was strong, and up to our horses' bodies, and came upon the incorrigible Kaluna, who, instead of catching his horse, was recounting his adventures to a circle of natives, but promised to follow us soon. D. then said that the next gulch was rather a bad one, and that we must not wait for Kaluna, but ride fast, and try to get

* A small bird, Melithreptes Pacifica, inhabits the mountainous regions of Hawaii, and has under each wing a single feather, one inch long, of a bright canary yellow. The birds are caught by means of a viscid substance smeared on poles. Formerly they were strictly *tabu*. It is of these feathers that the *mamo* or war-cloak of Kamehameha I., now used on state occasions by the Hawaiian kings, is composed. This priceless mantle is four feet long, eleven and a half feet wide at the bottom, and its formation occupied nine successive reigns. It is one of the costliest of royal ornaments, if the labour spent upon it is estimated, and the feathers of which it is made have been valued at a dollar and a half for five.

through it. When we reached the *pali* above it, we heard the roaring of a torrent, and when we descended to its brink it looked truly bad, but D. rode in, and I waited on the margin. She got safely across, but when she was near the opposite side her large horse plunged, slipped, and scrambled in a most unpleasant way, and she screamed something to me which I could not hear. Then I went in, and

> " At the first plunge the horse sank low,
>   And the water broke o'er the saddle bow : "

but the brave animal struggled through, with the water up to the top of her back, till she reached the place where D.'s horse had looked so insecure. In another moment she and I rolled backwards into deep water, as if she had slipped from a submerged rock. I saw her fore feet pawing the air, and then only her head was above water. I struck her hard with my spurs, she snorted, clawed, made a desperate struggle, regained her footing, got into shallow water, and landed safely. It was a small but not an agreeable adventure.

We went on again, the track now really dangerous from denudation and slipperiness. The rain came down, if possible, yet more heavily, and coursed fiercely down each *pali* track. Hundreds of cascades leapt from the cliffs, bringing down stones with a rattling sound. We crossed a bridge over one gulch, where the water was thundering down in such volume that it seemed as if it must rend the hard basalt of the *palis*. Then we reached the lofty top of the great Hakalau gulch, the largest of all, with the double river, and the ocean close to the ford. Mingling with the deep reverberations of the surf, I heard the sharp, crisp rush of a river, and of "a river that has no bridge."

The dense foliage, and the exigencies of the steep track, which had become very difficult, owing to the washing away of the soil, prevented me from seeing anything till I got down. I found Deborah speaking to a native, who was gesticulating very emphatically, and pointing up the river. The roar was deafening, and the sight terrific. Where there were two shallow streams a week ago, with a house and good-sized piece of ground above their confluence, there was now one spinning, rushing, chafing, foaming river, twice as wide as the Clyde at Glasgow, the land was submerged, and, if I remember correctly, the house only stood above the flood. And, most fearful to look upon, the ocean, in three huge breakers, had come quite in, and its mountains of white surge looked fearfully near the only possible crossing. I entreated D. not to go on. She said we could not go back, that the last gulch was already impassable, that between the two there was no house in which we could sleep, that the river had a good bottom, that the man thought if our horses were strong we could cross now, but not later, &c. In short, she overbore all opposition, and plunged in, calling to me, "Spur, spur, all the time."

Just as I went in, I took my knife and cut open the cloak which contained the cocoanuts. Deborah's horse I knew was strong, and shod, but my unshod and untried mare, what of her? My soul and senses literally reeled among the dizzy horrors of the wide, wild tide, but with an effort I regained sense and self-possession, for we were in, and there was no turning. D., ahead, screeched to me what I could not hear; she said afterwards it was "spur, spur, and keep up the river;" the native was shrieking in Hawaiian from the hinder shore, and waving to the right, but the torrents of rain, the crash of the breakers, and the rush and hurry of the river confused both sight and hearing. I saw D.'s great horse carried off his legs, my mare, too, was swimming, and shortly afterwards, between swimming, struggling, and floundering, we reached what had been the junction of the two rivers, where there was foothold, and the water was only up to the seats of the saddles.

Remember, we were both sitting nearly up to our waists in water, and it was only by screaming that our voices were heard above the din, and to return or go on seemed equally perilous. Under these critical circumstances the following colloquy took place, on my side, with teeth chattering, and on hers with a sudden forgetfulness of English, produced by her first sense of the imminent danger we were in.

Self.—"My mare is so tired, and so heavily weighted, we shall be drowned, or I shall."

Deborah (with more reason on her side).—"But can't go back, we no stay here, water higher all minutes, spur horse, think we come through."

Self.—"But if we go on there is broader, deeper water between us and the shore ; your husband would not like you to run such a risk."

Deborah—"Think we get through ; if horses give out, we let go ; I swim and save you."

Even under these circumstances a gleam of the ludicrous

shot through me at the idea of this small fragile being bearing
up my weight among the breakers. I attempted to shift my
saddle-bags upon her powerful horse, but being full of water
and under water, the attempt failed, and as we spoke both our
horses were carried off their vantage ground into deep water.

With wilder fury the river rushed by, its waters whirled
dizzily, and, in spite of spurring and lifting with the rein, the
horses were swept seawards. I saw Deborah's horse spin
round, and thought woefully of the possible fate of the bright
young wife, almost a bride; only the horses' heads and our
own heads and shoulders were above water; the surf was
thundering on our left, and we were drifting towards it "broad-
side on." When I saw the young girl's face of horror I felt
increased presence of mind, and raising my voice to a shriek,
and telling her to do as I did, I lifted and turned my mare
with the rein, so that her chest and not her side should receive
the force of the river, and the brave animal, as if seeing what she
should do, struck out desperately. It was a horrible suspense.
Were we stemming the torrent, or was it sweeping us back that
very short distance which lay between us and the mountainous
breakers? I constantly spurred my mare, guiding her slightly
to the left, the side grew nearer, and after exhausting struggles,
Deborah's horse touched ground, and her voice came faintly
towards me like a voice in a dream, still calling "Spur, spur."
My mare touched ground twice, and was carried off again
before she fairly got to land some yards nearer the sea than
the bridle track.

I then put our saddle-bags on Deborah's horse. It was one
of the worst and steepest of the *palis* that we had to ascend;
but I can't remember anything about the road except that we
had to leap some place which we could not cross otherwise.
Deborah, then thoroughly alive to a sense of risk, said that
there was only one more bad gulch to cross before we reached
Onomea, but it was the most dangerous of all, and we could
not get across, she feared, but we might go and look at it.
I only remember the extreme solitude of the region, and
scrambling and sliding down a most precipitous *pali*, hearing a
roar like cataract upon cataract, and coming suddenly down
upon a sublime and picturesque scene, with only standing
room, and that knee-deep in water, between a savage torrent
and the cliff. This gulch, called the Scotchman's gulch, I am
told, because a Scotchman was drowned there, must be at its
crossing three-quarters of a mile inland, and three hundred feet

above the sea. In going to Waipio, on noticing the deep
holes and enormous boulders, some of them higher than a
man on horseback, I had thought what a fearful place it would
be if it were ever full; but my imagination had not reached
the reality.   One huge, compressed, impetuous torrent, leaping
in creamy foam, boiling in creamy eddies, rioting in deep,
black chasms, roared and thundered over the whole in rapids
of the most tempestuous kind, leaping down to the ocean in
three grand, broad cataracts, the nearest of them not more than
40 feet from the crossing.   Imagine the Moriston at the Falls,
four times as wide and fifty times as furious, walled in by precipices, and with a miniature Niagara above and below, and you
have a feeble illustration of it.

Portions of two or three rocks only could be seen, and on
one of these, about 12 feet from the shore, a nude native,
beautifully tattooed, with a lasso in his hands, was standing
nearly up to his knees in foam ; and about a third of the way
from the other side, another native in deeper water, steadying
himself by a pole.   A young woman on horseback, whose near
relative was dangerously ill at Hilo, was jammed under the
cliff, and the men were going to get her across.   Deborah, to
my dismay, said that if she got safely over we would go too, as
these natives were very skilful.   I asked if she thought her
husband would let her cross, and she said " No."   I asked her
if she were frightened, and she said "Yes ;" but she wished so
to get home, and her face was as pale as a brown face can be.
I only hope the man will prove worthy of her affectionate
devotion.

Here, though people say it is a most perilous gulch, I was
not afraid for her life or mine, with the amphibious natives to
help us; but I was sorely afraid of being bruised, and scared,
and of breaking the horses' legs, and I said I would not cross,
but would sleep among the trees ; but the tumult drowned our
voices, though the Hawaiians by screeching could make themselves understood.   The nearest man then approached the
shore, put the lasso round the nose of the woman's horse, and
dragged it into the torrent; and it was exciting to see a horse
creeping from rock to rock in a cataract with alarming possibilities in every direction.   But beasts may well be bold, as
they have not "the foreknowledge of death."   When the nearest
native had got the horse as far as he could, he threw the lasso
to the man who was steadying himself with the pole, and urged
the horse on.   There was a deep chasm between the two into

which the animal fell, as he tried to leap from one rock to another. I saw for a moment only a woman's head and shoulders, a horse's head, a commotion of foam, a native tugging at the lasso, and then a violent scramble on to a rock, and a plunging and floundering through deep water to shore.

Then Deborah said she would go, that her horse was a better and stronger one ; and the same process was repeated with the same slip into the chasm, only with the variation that for a second she went out of sight altogether. It was a terribly interesting and exciting spectacle with sublime accompaniments. Though I had no fear of absolute danger, yet my mare was tired, and I had made up my mind to remain on that side till the flood abated ; but I could not make the natives understand that I wished to turn, and while I was screaming " No, no," and trying to withdraw my stiffened limbs from the stirrups, the noose was put round the mare's nose, and she went in. It was horrible to know that into the chasm as the others went I too must go, and in the mare went with a blind plunge. With violent plunging and struggling she got her fore feet on the rock, but just as she was jumping up to it altogether she slipped back snorting into the hole, and the water went over my eyes. I struck her with my spurs, the men screeched and shouted, the hinder man jumped in, they both tugged at the lasso, and slipping and struggling, the animal gained the rock, and plunged through deep water to shore, the water covering that rock with a rush of foam, being fully two feet deep.

Kaluna came up just after we had crossed, undressed, made his clothes into a bundle, and got over amphibiously, leaping, swimming, and diving, looking like a water-god, with the horse and mule after him. His dexterity was a beautiful sight; but on looking back I wondered how human beings ever devised to cross such a flood. We got over just in time. Some travellers who reached Laupahoehoe shortly after we left, more experienced than we were, suffered a two days' detention rather than incur a similar risk. Several mules and horses, they say, have had their legs broken in crossing this gulch by getting them fast between the rocks.

Shortly after this, Deborah uttered a delighted exclamation, and her pretty face lighted up, and I saw her husband spurring along the top of the next *pali*, and he presently joined us, and I exchanged my tired mare for his fresh, powerful horse. He knew that a freshet was imminent, and believing that we should never leave Laupahoehoe, he was setting off, provided with tackle for getting himself across, intending to join us, and remain with us till the rivers fell. The presence of a responsible white man seemed a rest at once. We had several more gulches to cross, but none of them were dangerous; and we rode the last seven miles at a great pace, though the mire and water were often up to the horses' knees, and came up to Onomea at full gallop, with spirit and strength enough for riding other twenty miles. Dry clothing, hot baths, and good tea followed delightfully upon our drowning ride. I remained over Sunday at Onomea, and yesterday rode here with a native in heavy rain, and received a warm welcome. Our adventures are a nine days' wonder, and every one says that if we had had a white man or an experienced native with us, we should never have been allowed to attempt the perilous ride. I feel very thankful that we are living to tell of it, and that Deborah is not only not worse but considerably better. E—— will expect some reflections; but none were suggested at the time, and I will not now invent what I ought to have thought and felt.

Due honour must be given to the Mexican saddle. Had I been on a side-saddle, and encumbered with a riding-habit, I should have been drowned. I feel able now to ride anywhere and any distance upon it, while Miss Karpe, who began by being much stronger than I was, has never recovered from the volcano ride, and seems quite ill.

Last night Kilauea must have been tremendously active. At ten P.M., from the upper verandah, we saw the whole western sky fitfully illuminated, and the glare reddened the snow which is lying on Mauna Loa, an effect of fire on ice which can rarely be seen.

L. L. B.

LETTER XII.

" The High Priest of Pélé "—Missionary Hardships—A Renowned Baptism —The " Revival " — A Tidal Wave—Kapiolani's Heroism—Lava Flows and Earthquakes.

HILO, *February* 22.

My sojourn here is very pleasant, owing to the kindness and sociability of the people. I think that so much culture and such a variety of refined tastes can seldom be found in so small a community. There have been pleasant little gatherings for sewing, while some gentlemen read aloud, fern-printing in the verandah, microscopic and musical evenings, little social luncheons, and on Sunday evenings what is colloquially termed " a sing," at this most social house. One of the things I have specially enjoyed has been spending an afternoon at the Rev. Titus Coan's. He is not only one of the most venerable of the remaining missionaries, but such an authority on the Hawaiian volcanoes as to entitle him to be designated " the high-priest of Pélé !" In his modest, quiet way he told thrilling stories of the old missionary days.

As you know, the islands cast off idolatry in 1819, but it was not till 1835 that Mr. and Mrs. Coan arrived in Hilo, where Mr. and Mrs. Lyman had been toiling for some time, and had produced a marked change on the social condition of the people. Mr. C. was a fervid speaker, and physically very robust, and when he had mastered the language, he undertook much of the travelling and touring, and Mr. Lyman took charge of the home mission station, and the boarding and industrial school which he still indefatigably superintends. There were 15,000 natives then in the district, and its extremes were 100 miles apart. Portions of it could only be reached with peril to limbs and even life. Horses were only regarded as wild animals in those days, and Mr. C. traversed on foot the district I have just returned from, not lazily riding down the gulch sides, but climbing, or being let down by ropes from tree to tree, and

from crag to crag. In times of rain like last week, when it was
impossible to ford the rivers, he sometimes swam across, with
a rope to prevent him from being carried away, through others
he rode on the broad shoulders of a willing native, while a
company of strong men locked hands and stretched themselves
across the torrent, between him and the cataract, to prevent
him from being carried over in case his bearer should fall.
This experience was often repeated three or four times a day.
His smallest weekly number of sermons was six or seven, and
the largest from twenty-five to thirty. He often travelled in
drowning rain, crossed dangerous streams, climbed slippery
precipices, and frequently preached in wind and rain with all
his garments saturated. On every occasion he received aid
from the natives, who were so kind and friendly, that when he
used to sleep in the woods at night, he hung his watch on a
tree, knowing that it was perfectly safe from pilfering or curious
touch. Indeed the Christian teachers seem to have been regarded as *tabu.*

Before the end of that year, Mr. Coan had made the circuit
of Hawaii, a foot and canoe trip of 300 miles, in which he
nearly suffered canoe-wreck twice. In all, he has admitted
into the Christian church by baptism, 12,000 persons, besides
4,000 infants. He gave a most interesting account of one
great baptism. The greatest care was previously taken in selecting, teaching, watching, and examining the candidates. Those
from the distant villages came and spent several months here
for preliminary instruction. Many of these were converts of
two years' standing, a larger class had been on the list for more
than a year, and a smaller one for a lesser period. The
accepted candidates were announced by name several weeks
previously, and friends and enemies everywhere were called
upon to testify all that they knew about them. On the first
Sunday in July, 1838, 1705 persons, formerly heathens, were
baptised. They were seated close together on the earth-floor
in rows, with just space between for one to walk, and Mr.
Lyman and Mr. Coan, passing through them, sprinkled every
bowed head, after which Mr. C. admitted the weeping hundreds
into the fellowship of the Universal Church by pronouncing
the words, " I baptise you all in the Name of the Father, and
of the Son, and of the Holy Ghost." After this, 2400 converts
received the Holy Communion. I give Mr. C.'s own words
concerning those who partook of it, " who truly and earnestly
repented of their sins, and steadfastly purposed to lead new

lives." "The old and decrepit, the lame, the blind, the
maimed, the withered, the paralytic, and those afflicted with
divers diseases and torments; those with eyes, noses, lips, and
limbs consumed; with features distorted, and figures depraved
and loathsome: these came hobbling upon their staves, or led
and borne by others to the table of the Lord. Among the
throng you would have seen the hoary priest of idolatry, with
hands but recently washed from the blood of human victims,
together with thieves, adulterers, highway robbers, murderers,
and mothers whose hands reeked with the blood of their own
children. It seemed like one of the crowds the Saviour
gathered, and over which he pronounced the words of healing."

Though the people cast off idolatry in 1819 before the
arrival of the missionaries, they were very indifferent to Christian teaching until 1837, the year before the great baptism,
when a great religious stir began, and for four years affected all
the islands. I wish you could have heard Mr. C. and Mrs.
Lyman tell of that stirring time, when nearly all the large
population of the Hilo and Puna districts turned out to hear
the Gospel, and how the young people went up into the mountains and carried the news of the love of God and the good
life to come to the sick and old, who were afterwards baptized,
when often the only water which could be obtained for the
rite was that which dripped sparingly from the roofs of caves.
The Hawaiian notions of a future state, where any existed,
were peculiarly vague and dismal, and Mr. Ellis says that the
greater part of the people seemed to regard the tidings of *ora
loa ia Jesu* (endless life by Jesus) as the most joyful news they
had ever heard, " breaking upon them," to use their own phrase,
" like light in the morning." " Will my spirit never die, and
can this poor weak body live again?" an old chieftess exclaimed,
and this delighted surprise seemed the general feeling of the
natives. From less difficult distances the sick and lame were
brought on litters and on the backs of men, and the infirm
often crawled to the trail by which the missionary was to
pass, that they might hear of this good news which had come
to Hawaii-nei.

There were but these two preachers for the 15,000 people
scattered for 100 miles, who were all ravenous to hear, and
impatient of the tardy modes of evangelization. " If we die,"
said they, " let us die in the light." So this strange thing fell
out, that whole villages from miles away gathered to the mission
station. Two-thirds of the population of the district came in,

and within the radius of a mile the grass and banana houses clustered as thick as they could stand. Beautiful Hilo in a short time swelled from a population of 1000 to 10,000 ; and at any hour of the day or night the sound of the conch shell brought together from 3000 to 6000 worshippers. This vast camp-meeting continued for two years, but there was no disorder, and a decent quiet ruled throughout the strangely extemporized city. A new morality, a new social order, new notions on nearly all subjects, had to be inculcated as well as a new religion. Mrs. C. and Mrs. L. daily assembled the women and children, and taught them the habits and industries of civilization, to attend to their persons, to braid hats, and to wear and make clothes.

During this time, on November 7, 1837, one of the striking phenomena which make the islands remarkable occurred. The crescent sand-beach, said to be the most beautiful in the Pacific, the fringe of palms, the far-reaching groves behind, and the great ocean, slept in summer calm, as they sleep to-day. Four sermons, as usual, had been preached to audiences of 6000 people. There had been a funeral, the natives say, though Mr. C. does not remember it, and his text had been " Be ye also ready," and larger throngs than usual had followed the preachers to their homes. The fatiguing day was over, the natives were singing hymns in the still evening air, and Mr. C. "had gathered his family for prayers " in the very room in which he told me this story, when they were startled by " a sound as if a heavy mountain had fallen on the beach." There was at once a fearful cry, wailing, and indescribable confusion. The quiet ocean had risen in a moment in a gigantic wave, which, rushing in with the speed of a racehorse, and uplifting itself over the shore, swept everything into promiscuous ruin ; men, women, children, dogs, houses, food, canoes, clothing, floated wildly on the flood, and hundreds of people were struggling among the billows in the midst of their earthly all. Some were dashed on the shore, some were saved by friends who hurried to their aid, some were carried out to sea by the retiring water, and some stout swimmers sank exhausted ; yet the loss of life was not nearly so great as it would have been among a less amphibious people. Mr. C. described the roaring of the ocean, the cries of distress, the shrieks of the perishing, the frantic rush of hundreds to the shore, and the desolation of the whole neighbourhood of the beach, as forming a scene of the most thrilling and awful interest.

You will remember that I wrote from Kilauea regarding the terror which the Goddess of the Crater inspired, and her high-priest was necessarily a very awful personage. The particular high-priest of whom Mr. Coan told me was 6 feet 5 inches in height, and his sister, who was co-ordinate with him in authority, had a scarcely inferior altitude. His chief business was to keep Pélé appeased. He lived on the shore, but often went up to Kilauea with sacrifices. If a human victim were needed, he had only to point to a native, and the unfortunate wretch was at once strangled. He was not only the embodiment of heathen piety, but of heathen crime. Robbery was his pastime. His temper was so fierce and so uncurbed that no native dared even to tread on his shadow. More than once he had killed a man for the sake of food and clothes not worth fifty cents. He was a thoroughly wicked savage. Curiosity attracted him into one of the Hilo meetings, and the bad giant fell under the resistless, mysterious influence which was metamorphosing thousands of Hawaiians. " I have been deceived," he said, " I have deceived others, I have lived in darkness, and did not know the true God. I worshipped what was no God. I renounce it all. The true God has come. He speaks. I bow down to Him. I wish to be His son." The priestess, his sister, came soon after-wards, and they remained here several months for instruction. They were then about seventy years old, but they imbibed the New Testament spirit so thoroughly that they became as gentle, loving, and quiet as little children. After a long proba-tionary period they were baptized, and after several years of pious and lowly living, they passed gently and trustfully away.

The old church which was the scene of these earlier assem-blages came down with a crash after a night of heavy rain, the large timbers, which were planted in the moist earth after the fashion of the country to support the framework, having become too rotten to bear the weight of the saturated thatch. Without a day's loss of time the people began a new church. All were volunteers, some to remove from the wreck of the old building such timbers as might still be of service; some to quarry stone for a foundation, an extravagance never before dreamed of by an islander; some to bring sand in gourd-shells upon their heads, or laboriously gathered in the folds of bark-cloth aprons; some to bring lime from the coral reefs 20 feet under water; whilst the majority hurried to the forest belt, miles away on the mountain side, to fell the straightest and tallest trees. Then 50 or 100 men (for in that day horses and oxen were known only as wild beasts of the wilderness) attached hawsers to the butt ends of logs, and dragged them away through bush and brake, through broken ground and river beds, till they deposited them on the site of the new church. The wild, monotonous chant, as the men hauled in the timber, lives in the memories of the missionaries' children, who say that it seemed to them as if the preparations for Solomon's temple could not have exceeded the accumulations of the islanders !

I think that the greater number of the converts of those four years must have died ere this. In 1867 the old church at Hilo was divided into seven congregations, six of them with native pastors. To meet the wants of the widely-scattered people fifteen churches have been built, holding from 500 up to 1000. The present Hilo church, a very pretty wooden one, cost about $14,000. All these have been erected mainly by native money and labour. Probably the native Christians on Hawaii are not much better or worse than Christian communities elsewhere, but they seem a singularly generous people. Besides liberally sustaining their own clergy, the Hilo Christians have contributed altogether $100,000 for religious purposes. Mr. Coan's native congregation, sorely dwindled as it is, raises over $1200 annually for foreign missions ; and twelve of its members have gone as missionaries to the islands of Southern Polynesia.

Poor people ! It would be unfair to judge of them as we may legitimately be judged of, who inherit the influences of ten centuries of Christianity. They have only just emerged from a bloody and sensual heathenism, and to the instincts and volatility of these dark Polynesian races, the restraining influences of the Gospel are far more severe than to our cold, unimpulsive northern natures. The greatest of their disadvantages has been that some of the vilest of the whites who roam the Pacific had settled on the islands before the arrival of the Christian teachers, dragging the people down to even lower depths of depravity than those of heathenism, and that there are still resident foreigners who corrupt and destroy them.

I must tell you a story which the venerable Mrs. Lyman told me yesterday. In 1825, five years after the first missionaries landed, Kapiolani, a female *alii* of high rank, while living at Kaiwaaloa (where Captain Cook was murdered), became a Christian. Grieving for her people, most of whom still feared to anger Pélé, she announced that it was her intention to visit Kilauea, and dare the fearful goddess to do her worst. Her husband and many others tried to dissuade her, but she was resolute, and taking with her a large retinue, she took a journey of one hundred miles, mostly on foot, over the rugged lava, till she arrived near the crater. There a priestess of Pélé met her, threatened her with the displeasure of the goddess if she persisted in her hostile errand, and prophesied that she and her followers would perish miserably. Then, as now, *ohelo* berries grew profusely round the terminal wall of Kilauea, and there, as elsewhere, were sacred to Pélé, no one daring to eat of them till he had first offered some of them to the divinity. It was usual on arriving at the crater to break a branch covered with berries, and turning the face to the pit of fire, to throw half the branch over the precipice, saying, "Pélé, here are your *ohelos.* I offer some to you, some I also eat," after which the natives partook of them freely. Kapiolani gathered and eat them without this formula, after which she and her company of eighty persons descended to the black edge of Hale-mau-mau. There, in full view of the fiery pit, she thus addressed her followers :—"*Jehovah is my God. He kindled these fires. I fear not Pélé. If I perish by the anger of Pélé, then you may fear the power of Pélé ; but if I trust in Jehovah, and he should save me from the wrath of Pélé, when I break through her tabus, then you must fear and serve the Lord Jehovah. All the gods of Hawaii are vain ! Great is Jehovah's goodness in sending teachers to turn us from these vanities to the living God and the way of righteousness !* " Then they sang a hymn. I can fancy the strange procession winding its backward way over the cracked, hot, lava sea, the robust belief of the princess hardly sustaining the limping faith of her followers, whose fears would not be laid to rest until they reached the crater's rim without any signs of the pursuit of an avenging deity. It was more sublime than Elijah's appeal on the soft, green slopes of Carmel, but the popular belief in the Goddess of the Volcano survived this flagrant instance of her incapacity, and only died out many years afterwards.

Besides these interesting reminiscences, I have been hearing most thrilling stories from Mrs. Lyman and Mr. Coan of volcanoes, earthquakes, and tidal waves. Told by eye-witnesses, and on the very spot where the incidents occurred, they make a profound, and, I fear, an incommunicable impression. I look on these venerable people as I should on people who had seen the Deluge, or the burial of Pompeii, and wonder that they eat and dress and live like other mortals ! For they have

felt the perpetual shudder of earthquakes, and their eyes, which
look so calm and kind, have seen the inflowing of huge tidal
waves, the dull red glow of lava streams, and the leaping of fire
cataracts into deep-lying pools, burning them dry in a night
time. There were years in which there was no day in which
the smoke of underground furnaces was out of their sight, or
night which was not lurid with flames. Once they traced a
river of lava burrowing its way 1500 feet below the surface,
and saw it emerge, break over a precipice, and fall hissing
into the ocean. Once from their highest mountain a pillar of
fire 200 feet in diameter lifted itself for three weeks 1000 feet
into the air, making night day, for a hundred miles round, and
leaving as its monument a cone a mile in circumference. We
see a clothed and finished earth ; they see the building of an
island, layer on layer, hill on hill, the naked and deformed
product of the melting, forging, and welding, which go on
perpetually in the crater of Kilauea.

   I could fill many sheets with what I have heard, but must
content myself with telling you very little. In 1855 the fourth
recorded eruption of Mauna Loa occurred. The lava flowed
directly Hilo-wards, and for several months, spreading through
the dense forests which belt the mountain, crept slowly shorewards, threatening this beautiful portion of Hawaii with the
fate of the Cities of the Plain. Mr. C. made several visits to
the eruption, and on each return the simple people asked him
how much longer it would last. For five months they watched
the inundation, which came a little nearer every day. Should
they fly or not ? Would their beautiful homes become a waste
of jagged lava and black sand, like the neighbouring district of
Puna, once as fair as Hilo?" Such questions suggested themselves as they nightly watched the nearing glare, till the fiery
waves met with obstacles which piled them up in hillocks,
eight miles from Hilo, and the suspense was over. Only
gigantic causes can account for the gigantic phenomena of this
lava-flow. The eruption travelled forty miles in a straight line,
or sixty, including sinuosities. It was from one to three miles
broad, and from five to two hundred feet deep, according to
the contours of the mountain slopes over which it flowed. It
lasted for thirteen months, pouring out a torrent of lava which
covered nearly 300 square miles of land, and whose volume
was estimated at thirty-eight thousand millions of cubic feet !
In 1859 lava fountains 400 feet in height, and with a nearly
equal diameter, played on the summit of Mauna Loa. This

eruption ran fifty miles to the sea in eight days, but the flow
lasted much longer, and added a new promontory to Hawaii.

These magnificent overflows, however threatening, had done
little damage to cultivated regions, and none to human life;
and people began to think that the volcano was reformed.
But in 1868 terrors occurred which are without precedent in
island history. While Mrs. L. was giving me the narrative in
her graphic but simple way, and the sweet wind rustled through
the palms, and brought the rich scent of the ginger plant into
the shaded room, she seemed to be telling me a tale of another
world. On March 27, five years ago, a series of earthquakes
began, and became more startling from day to day; until their
succession became so rapid that "the island quivered like the
lid of a boiling pot nearly all the time between the heavier
shocks. The trembling was like that of a ship struck by a
heavy wave." Then the terminal crater of Mauna Loa (Mokuaweoweo) sent up columns of smoke, steam, and red light,
and it was shortly seen that the southern slope of its dome had
been rent, and that four separate rivers of molten stone were
pouring out of as many rents, and were flowing down the
mountain sides in diverging lines. Suddenly the rivers were
arrested, and the blue mountain dome appeared against the
still, blue sky without an indication of fire, steam, or smoke.
Hilo was much agitated by the sudden lull. No one was
deceived into security, for it was certain that the fires must
make themselves felt.

The earthquakes became nearly continuous; scarcely an
appreciable interval occurred between them; "the throbbing,
jerking, and quivering motions grew more positive, intense,
and sharp; they were vertical, rotary, lateral, and undulating," producing nausea, vertigo, and vomiting. Late in the
afternoon of a lovely day, April 2, the climax came. "The
crust of the earth rose and sank like the sea in a storm."
Rocks were rent, mountains fell, buildings and their contents
were shattered, trees swayed like reeds, animals were scared,
and ran about demented; men thought the judgment had
come. The earth opened in thousands of places, the roads in
Hilo cracked open, horses and their riders, and people afoot
were thrown violently to the ground; "it seemed as if the
rocky ribs of the mountains, and the granite walls and pillars
of the earth were breaking up." At Kilauea the shocks were
as frequent as the ticking of a watch. In Kau, south of Hilo,
they counted 300 shocks on that direful day; and Mrs. L.'s

son, who was in that district at the time, says that the earth
swayed to and fro, north and south, then east and west, then
round and round, up and down, in every imaginable direction,
everything crashing about them, "and the trees thrashing as if
torn by a strong rushing wind." He and others sat on the
ground bracing themselves with hands and feet to avoid being
rolled over. They saw an avalanche of red earth, which they
supposed to be lava, burst from the mountain side, throwing
rocks high into the air, swallowing up houses, trees, men, and
animals; and travelling three miles in as many minutes,
burying a hamlet, with thirty-one inhabitants and 500 head of
cattle. The people of the valleys fled to the mountains, which
themselves were splitting in all directions, and collecting on an
elevated spot, with the earth reeling under them, they spent
the night of April 2 in prayer and singing. Looking towards
the shore, they saw it sink, and at the same moment, a
wave, whose height was estimated at from forty to sixty feet,
hurled itself upon the coast, and receded five times, destroying
whole villages, and even strong stone houses, with a touch, and
engulfing for ever forty-six people who had lingered too near
the shore.

Still the earthquakes continued, and still the volcano gave no
sign. The nerves of many people gave way in these fearful
days. Some tried to get away to Honolulu, others kept
horses saddled on which to fly, they knew not whither. The
hourly question was, "What of the volcano?" People put
their ears to the quivering ground, and heard, or thought they
heard, the surgings of the imprisoned lava sea rending its way
among the ribs of the earth.

Five days after the destructive earthquake of April 2, the
ground south of Hilo burst open with a crash and roar which
at once answered all questions concerning the volcano. The
molten river, after travelling underground for twenty miles,
emerged through a fissure two miles in length with a tremendous force and volume. It was in a pleasant pastoral
region, supposed to be at rest for ever, at the top of a grass-
covered plateau sprinkled with native and foreign houses, and
rich in herds of cattle. Four huge fountains boiled up with
terrific fury, throwing crimson lava, and rocks weighing many
tons, to a height of from 500 to 1000 feet. Mr. Whitney, of
Honolulu, who was near the spot, says :—" From these great
fountains to the sea flowed a rapid stream of red lava, rolling,
rushing, and tumbling, like a swollen river, bearing along in its

current large rocks that made the lava foam as it dashed down the precipice and through the valley into the sea, surging and roaring throughout its length like a cataract, with a power and fury perfectly indescribable. It was nothing else than a *river of fire* from 200 to 800 feet wide and twenty deep, with a *speed varying from ten to twenty-five miles an hour !*" This same intelligent observer noticed as a peculiarity of the spouting that the lava was ejected by a *rotary motion,* and in the air both lava and stones always rotated *towards the south.* At Kilauea I noticed that the lava was ejected in a southerly direction. From the scene of these fire fountains, whose united length was about a mile, the river in its rush to the sea divided itself into four streams, between which it shut up men and beasts. One stream hurried to the sea in four hours, but the others took two days to travel ten miles. The aggregate width was a mile and a half. Where it entered the sea it extended the coast-line half a mile, but this worthless accession to Hawaiian acreage was dearly purchased by the loss, for ages at least, of 4000 acres of valuable pasture land, and a much larger quantity of magnificent forest. The whole south-east shore of Hawaii sank from four to six feet, which involved the destruction of several hamlets and the beautiful fringe of cocoa-nut trees. Though the region was very thinly peopled, 200 houses and 100 lives were sacrificed in this week of horrors, and from the reeling mountains, the uplifted ocean, and the fiery inundation, the terrified survivors fled into Hilo, each with a tale of woe and loss. The number of shocks of earthquake counted was 2000 in two weeks, an average of 140 a day; but on the other side of the island the number was incalculable.

I. L. B.

LETTER XIII.

A Royal Landing—The Royal Procession—Puna Woods—Lunalilo—The *Hookupu* — Loyal Enthusiasm — The Gift-bearers—The Gifts—The King's Speech.

HILO, HAWAII, *February.*

THE quiet, dreamy, afternoon existence of Hilo is disturbed. Two days ago an official intimation was received that the American Government had placed the U. S. ironclad "Benicia" at the disposal of King Lunalilo for a cruise round Hawaii, and that he would arrive here the following morning with Admiral Pennock and the U. S. generals Scholfield and Alexander.

Now this monarchy is no longer an old-time chieftaincy, made up of calabashes and *poi,* feather-cloaks, *kahilis,* and a little fuss, but has a civilized constitutional king, the equal of Queen Victoria, a civil list, &c., and though Lunalilo comes here trying to be a private individual and to rest from *Hookupus,* state entertainments, and privy councils, he brings with him a royal chamberlain and an adjutant-general in attendance. So the good people of Hilo have been decorating their houses anew with ferns and flowers, furbishing up their clothes, and holding mysterious consultations regarding etiquette and entertainments, just as if royalty were about to drop down in similar fashion on Bude or Tobermory. There were amusing attempts to bring about a practical reconciliation between the free-and-easiness of Republican notions and the respect due to a sovereign who reigns by "the will of the people" as well as by "the grace of God," but eventually the tact of the king made everything go smoothly.

At eight yesterday morning the "Benicia" anchored inside the reef, and Hilo blossomed into a most striking display of bunting; the Hawaiian colours, eight blue, red and white stripes, with the English union in the corner, and the flaunting flag of America being predominant. My heart warmed towards our own flag as the soft breeze lifted its rich folds among the glories of the tropical trees. Indeed, bunting to my mind never looked so well as when floating and fainting among cocoa-nut palms and all the shining greenery of Hilo, in the sunshine of a radiant morning. It was bright and warm, but the cool bulk of Mauna Kea, literally covered with snow, looked down as winter upon summer. Natives galloped in from all quarters, brightly dressed, wreathed, and garlanded, delighted in their hearts at the attention paid to their sovereign by a great foreign power, though they had been very averse to this journey, from a strange but prevalent idea that once on board a U.S. ship the king would be kidnapped and conveyed to America.

Lieut.-Governor Lyman and Mr. Severance, the sheriff, went out to the "Benicia," and the king landed at ten o'clock, being "graciously pleased" to accept the Governor's house as his residence during his visit. The American officers, naval and military, were received by the same loud, hospitable old whaling captain who entertained the Duke of Edinburgh some years ago here, and to judge from the hilarious sounds which came down the road from his house, they had what they would call "a good time." I had seen Lunalilo in state at Honolulu, but it was much more interesting to see him here, and this royalty is interesting in itself, as a thing on sufferance, standing be-tween this helpless nationality and its absorption by America. The king is a very fine-looking man of thirty-eight, tall, well formed, broad-chested, with his head well set on his shoulders, and his feet and hands small. His appearance is decidedly commanding and aristocratic : he is certainly handsome even according to our notions. He has a fine open brow, significant at once of brains and straightforwardness, a straight, propor-tionate nose, and a good mouth. The slight tendency to Poly-nesian overfulness about his lips is concealed by a well-shaped moustache. He wears whiskers cut in the English fashion. His eyes are large, dark-brown of course, and equally of course, he has a superb set of teeth. Owing to a slight fulness of the lower eyelid, which Queen Emma also has, his eyes have a singularly melancholy expression, very alien, I believe, to his character. He is remarkably gentlemanly looking, and has the grace of movement which seems usual with Hawaiians. When he landed he wore a dark morning suit and a black felt hat.

As soon as he stepped on shore, the natives, who were in crowds on the beach, cheered, yelled, and waved their hats

THE MOUNTAIN MAUNA KEA FROM HILO.

and handkerchiefs, and then a procession was formed, or rather formed itself, to escort him to the governor's house. A rabble of children ran in front, then came the king, over whom the natives had thrown some beautiful garlands of *ohia* and *mailé* (*Alyxia olivæformis*), with the governor on one side and the sheriff on the other, the chamberlain and adjutant-general walking behind. Then a native staggering under the weight of an enormous Hawaiian flag, the Hilo band, with my friend Upa beating the big drum, and an irregular rabble (*i. e.* unorganised crowd) of men, women, and children, going at a trot to keep up with the king's rapid strides. The crowd was unwilling to disperse even when he entered the house, and he came out and made a short speech, the gist of which was that he was delighted to see his native subjects, and would hold a reception for them on the ensuing Monday, when we shall see a most interesting sight, a native crowd gathered from all Southern Hawaii for a *hookupu*, an old custom, signifying the bringing of gift-offerings to a king or chief.

In the afternoon Dr. Wetmore and I rode to the beautiful Puna woods on a botanising excursion. We were galloping down to the beach round a sharp corner, when we had to pull our horses almost on their haunches to avoid knocking over the king, the American admiral, the captain of the "Benicia," nine of their officers, and the two generals. When I saw the politely veiled stare of the white men it occurred to me that probably it was the first time that they had seen a white woman riding cavalier fashion ! We had a delicious gallop over the sands to the Waiakea river, which we crossed, and came upon one of the vast lava-flows of ages since, over which we had to ride carefully, as the *pahoehoe* lies in rivers, coils, tortuosities, and holes partially concealed by a luxuriant growth of ferns and convolvuli. The country is thickly sprinkled with cocoa-nut and breadfruit trees, which merge into the dense, dark, glorious forest, which tenderly hides out of sight hideous, broken lava, on which one cannot venture six feet from the track without the risk of breaking one's limbs. All these tropical forests are absolutely impenetrable, except to axe and billhook, and after a trail has been laboriously opened, it needs to be cut once or twice a year, so rapid is the growth of vegetation. This one, through the Puna woods, only admits of one person at a time. It was really rapturously lovely. Through the trees we saw the soft steel-blue of the summer sky : not a leaf stirred, not a bird sang, a hush had fallen on

insect life, the quiet was perfect, even the ring of our horses'
hoofs on the lava was a discord.   There was a slight coolness
in the air and a fresh mossy smell.   It only required some
suggestion of decay, and the rustle of a fallen leaf now and
then, to make it an exact reproduction of a fine day in our
English October.   The forest was enlivened by many natives
bound for Hilo, driving horses loaded with cocoanuts, breadfruit, live fowls, *poi* and *kalo*, while others with difficulty urged
garlanded pigs in the same direction, all as presents for the
king.   We brought back some very scarce parasitic ferns.

HILO, *February* 24.

I rode over by myself to Onomea on Saturday to get a little
rest from the excitements of Hilo.   A gentleman lent me a
strong, showy mare to go out on, telling me that she was frisky
and must be held while I mounted ; but before my feet were
fairly in the stirrups, she shook herself from the Chinaman who
held her, and danced away.   I rode her five miles before she
quieted down.   She pranced, jumped, danced, and fretted on
the edge of precipices, was furious at the scow and fords, and
seemed demented with good spirits.   Onomea looked glorious,
and its serenity was most refreshing.   I rode into Hilo the
next day in time for morning service, and the mare, after a
good gallop, subsided into a staidness of demeanour befitting
the day.   Just as I was leaving, they asked me to take the
news to the sheriff that a man had been killed a few hours
before.   He was riding into Hilo with a child behind him, and
they went over by no means one of the worst of the *palis.*
The man and horse were killed, but the child was unhurt, and
his wailing among the deep ferns attracted the attention of
passers-by to the disaster.   The natives ride over these dangerous *palis* so carelessly, and on such tired, starved horses,
that accidents are not infrequent.   Hilo had never looked
so lovely to me as in the pure, bright calm of this Sunday
morning.

The verandahs of all the native houses were crowded with
strangers, who had come in to share in the jubilations attending
the king's visit.   At the risk of emulating "Jenkins," or the
"Court Newsman," I must tell you that Lunalilo, who is by
no means an habitual church-goer, attended Mr. Coan's native
church in the morning, and the foreign church at night, when
the choir sang a very fine anthem.   I don't wish to write about

his faults, which have doubtless been rumoured in the English papers. It is hoped that his new responsibilities will assist him to conquer them, else I fear he may go the way of several of the Hawaiian kings. He has begun his reign with marked good sense in selecting as his advisers confessedly the best men in his kingdom, and all his public actions since his election have shown both tact and good feeling. If sons, as is often asserted, take their intellects from their mothers, he should be decidedly superior, for his mother, Kekauluohi, a chieftainess of the highest rank, and one of the queens of Kamehameha II., who died in London, was in 1839 chosen for her abilities by Kamehameha III., as his *kuhina nui*, or premier, an officer recognised under the old system of Hawaiian government as second only in authority to the king, and without whose signature even his act was not legal. As Kaahumanu II. she continued to hold this important position until her death in 1845.

But the present king does not come of the direct line of the Hawaiian kings, but of a far older family. His father is a commoner, but Hawaiian rank is inherited through the mother. He received a good English education at the school which the missionaries established for the sons of chiefs, and was noted as a very bright scholar, with an early developed taste for literature and poetry. His disposition is said to be most amiable and genial, and his affability endeared him especially to his own countrymen, by whom he was called *alii lokomaikai*, "the kind chief." In spite of his high rank, which gave him precedence of all others on the islands, he was ignored by two previous governments, and often complained that he was never allowed any opportunity of becoming acquainted with public affairs, or of learning whether he possessed any capacity for business. Thus, without experience, but with noble and liberal instincts, and the highest and most patriotic aspirations for the welfare and improvement of his " weak little kingdom," he was unexpectedly called to the throne about three months ago, amidst such an enthusiasm as had never before been witnessed on Hawaii-nei, as the unanimous choice of the people. He called on Mr. Coan the day of his arrival; and when the flute band of Mr. Lyman's school serenaded him, he made the youths a kind address, in which he said he had been taught as they were, and hoped hereafter to profit by the instruction he had received.

This has been a great day in Hilo. The old native custom

of *hookupu* was revived, and it has been a most interesting spectacle. I don't think I ever enjoyed sight-seeing so much. The weather has been splendid, which was most fortunate, for many of the natives came in from distances of from sixty to eighty miles. From early daylight they trooped in on their half broken steeds, and by ten o'clock there were fully a thousand horses tethered on the grass by the sea. Almost every house displayed flags, and the court-house, where the reception was to take place, was most tastefully decorated. It is a very pretty two-storied frame building, with deep double verandahs, and stands on a large lawn of fine *mainienie* grass,* with roads on three sides. Long before ten, crowds had gathered outside the low walls of the lawn, natives and foreigners galloped in all directions, boats and canoes enlivened the bay, bands played, and the foreigners, on this occasion rather a disregarded minority, assembled in holiday dress in the upper verandah of the court-house. Hawaiian flags on tall bamboos decorated the little gateways which gave admission to the lawn, an enormous standard on the government flagstaff could be seen for miles, and the stars and stripes waved from the neighbouring plantations and from several houses in Hilo. At ten punctually, Lunalilo, Governor Lyman, the sheriff of Hawaii, the royal chamberlain, and the adjutant-general, walked up to the court-house, and the king took his place, standing in the lower verandah with his suite about him. All the foreigners were either on the upper balcony, or on the stairs leading to it, on which, to get the best possible view of the spectacle, I stood for three mortal hours. The attendant gentlemen were well dressed, but wore "shocking bad hats;" and the king wore a sort of shooting suit, a short brown cut-away coat, an ash-coloured waistcoat and ash-coloured trousers with a blue stripe. He stood bareheaded. He dressed in this style in order that the natives might attend the reception in every-day dress, and not run the risk of spoiling their best clothes by Hilo torrents. The dress of the king and his attendants was almost concealed by wreaths of *ohia* blossoms and festoons of *mailé,* some of them two yards long, which had been thrown over them, and which bestowed a fantastic glamour on the otherwise prosaic inelegance of their European dress. But indeed the spectacle, as a whole, was altogether poetical, as it was an ebullition of natural, national, human feeling, in which the heart had the

---

* Cynodon Dactylon (?)

first place. I very soon ceased to notice the incongruous elements, which were supplied chiefly by the Americans present. There were Republicans by birth and nature, destitute of traditions of loyalty or reverence for aught on earth; who bore on their faces not only republicanism, but that quintessence of puritan republicanism which hails from New England; and these were subjects of a foreign king, nay, several were office-holders who had taken the oath of allegiance, and from whose lips " His Majesty, Your Majesty," flowed far more copiously than from ours which are " to the manner born."

On the king's appearance, the cheering was tremendous,—regular British cheering, well led, succeeded by that which is not British, " three cheers and a tiger," but it was " Hi, hi, hi, hullah !" Every hat was off, every handkerchief in air, tears in many eyes, enthusiasm universal, for the people were come to welcome the king of their choice; the prospective restorer of the Constitution " trampled upon " by Kamehameha V., " the kind chief," who was making them welcome to his presence after the fashion of their old feudal lords. When the cheering had subsided, the eighty boys of Missionary Lyman's School, who, dressed in white linen with crimson *leis*, were grouped in a hollow square round the flagstaff, sang the Hawaiian national anthem, the music of which is the same as ours. More cheering and enthusiasm, and then the natives came through the gate across the lawn, and up to the verandah where the king stood, in one continuous procession, till 2,400 Hawaiians had enjoyed one moment of infinite and ever to be remembered satisfaction in the royal presence. Every now and then the white, pale-eyed, unpicturesque face of a foreigner passed by, but these were few, and the foreign school children were received by themselves after Mr. Lyman's boys. The Americans have introduced the villanous custom of shaking hands at these receptions, borrowing it, I suppose, from a presidential reception at Washington; and after the king had gone through this ceremony with each native, the present was deposited in front of the verandah, and the gratified giver took his place on the grass. Not a man, woman, or child came empty handed. Every face beamed with pride, wonder, and complacency, for here was a sovereign for whom cannon roared, and yards were manned, of their own colour, who called them his brethren.

The variety of costume was infinite. All the women wore the native dress, the sack or *holoku*, many of which were black,

blue, green, or bright rose colour, some were bright yellow, a
few were pure white, and others were a mixture of orange and
scarlet. Some wore very pretty hats made from cane-tops, and
trimmed with hibiscus blossoms or passion-flowers ; others wore
bright-coloured handkerchiefs, knotted lightly round their flowing hair, or wreaths of the *Microlepia tenuifolia.* Many had
tied bandanas in a graceful knot over the left shoulder. All
wore two, three, four, or even six beautiful *leis*, besides long
festoons of the fragrant *mailé.* *Leis* of the crimson *ohia*
blossoms were universal ; but besides these there were *leis* of
small red and white double roses, *pohas,** yellow amaranth,
sugar cane tassels like frosted silver, the orange pandanus, the
delicious gardenia, and a very few of orange blossoms, and
the great granadilla or passion-flower. Few if any of the
women wore shoes, and none of the children had anything on
their heads.

A string of 200 Chinamen passed by, "plantation hands,"
with boyish faces, and cunning, almond-shaped eyes. They
were dressed in loose, blue, denim trousers with shirts of the
same, fastening at the side over them, their front hair closely
shaven, and the rest gathered into pigtails, which were wound
several times round their heads. These all deposited money
in the adjutant-general's hand. The dress of the Hawaiian
men was more varied and singular than that of the women,
every kind of dress and undress, with *leis* of *ohia* and garlands
of *mailé* covering all deficiencies. The poor things came up
with pathetic innocence, many of them with nothing on but
an old shirt, and cotton trousers rolled up to the knees. Some
had red shirts and blue trousers, others considered that a shirt
was an effective outer garment. Some wore highly ornamental,
dandified shirts, and trousers tucked into high, rusty, mud-
covered boots. A few young men were in white straw hats,
white shirts, and white trousers, with crimson *leis* round their
hats and throats. Some had diggers' scarves round their waists ;
but the most effective costume was sported by a few old men,
who had tied crash towels over their shoulders.

It was often amusing and pathetic at once to see them come
up. Obviously, when the critical moment arrived, they were
as anxious to do the right thing as a *débutante* is to back her
train successfully out of the royal presence at St. James's. Some
were so agitated at last as to require much coaching from the

* Physalis Peruviana.

governor as to how to present their gifts and shake hands. Some half dropped down on their knees, others passionately and with tears kissed the king's hand, or grasped it convulsively in both their own; while a few were so embarrassed by the presents they were carrying that they had no hands at all to shake, and the sovereign good-naturedly clapped them on the shoulders. Some of them, in shaking hands, adroitly slipped coins into the king's palm, so as to make sure that he received their loving tribute. There had been a *hui*, or native meeting, which had passed resolutions, afterwards presented to Lunalilo, setting forth that whereas he received a great deal of money in revenue from the *haoles*, they, his native people, would feel that he did not love them if he would not receive from their own hands contributions in silver for his support. So, in order not to wound their feelings, he accepted these rather troublesome cash donations.

One woman, sorely afflicted with quaking palsy, dragged herself slowly along. One hand hung by her side helpless, and the other grasped a live fowl so tightly that she could not loosen it to shake hands, whereupon the king raised the helpless arm, which called forth much cheering. There was one poor cripple who had only the use of his arms. His knees were doubled under him, and he trailed his body along the ground. He had dragged himself two miles "to lie for a moment at the king's feet," and even his poor arms carried a gift. He looked hardly like a human shape, as his desire was realised; and, I doubt not, would have been content then and there to die. There were ancient men, tattooed all over, who had passed their first youth when the idols were cast away, and who remembered the old days of tyranny when it was an offence, punishable with death, for a man to let his shadow fall on the king; and when none of "the swinish multitude" had any rights which they could sustain against their chiefs. These came up bewildered, trembling, almost falling on their knees, hardly daring to raise their eyes to the king's kind, encouraging face, and bathed his hand with tears while they kissed it. Numbers of little children were led up by their parents; there were babies in arms, and younglings carried on parents' backs, and the king stooped and shook hands with all, and even pulled out the babies' hands from under their mufflings and the old people wept, and cheers rent the air.

Next in interest to this procession of beaming faces, and the blaze of colour, was the sight of the presents, and the un-

grudging generosity with which they were brought. Many of
the women presented live fowls tied by the legs, which were
deposited, one upon another, till they formed a fainting, palpitating heap under the hot sun. Some of the men brought
decorated hogs tied by one leg, which squealed so persistently
in the presence of royalty, that they were removed to the rear.
Hundreds carried nets of sweet potatoes, eggs, and *kalo*,
artistically arranged. Men staggered along in couples with
bamboos between them, supporting clusters of bananas weighing nearly a hundredweight. Others brought yams, cocoanuts,
oranges, onions, pumpkins, early pineapples, and even the
great, delicious fruit of the large passion-flower. A few maidens
presented the king with bouquets of choice flowers, and costly
leis of the yellow feathers of the *Melithreptes Pacifica.* There
were fully two tons of *kalo* and sweet potatoes in front of the
court house, hundreds of fowls, and piles of bananas, eggs, and
cocoanuts. The *hookupu* was a beautiful sight, all the more so
that not one of that radiant, loving, gift-offering throng came in
quest of office, or for any other thing that he could obtain.
It was just the old-time spirit of reverence for the man who
typifies rule, blended with the extreme of personal devotion to
the prince whom a united people had placed upon the throne.
The feeling was genuine and pathetic in its intensity. It is
said that the natives like their king better, because he was
truly, "above all," the last of a proud and imperious house,
which, in virtue of a pedigree of centuries, looked down upon
the nobility of the Kamehamehas.

When the last gift was deposited, the lawn in front of the
court-house was one densely-packed, variegated mass of excited,
buzzing Hawaiians. While the king was taking a short rest,
two ancient and hideous females, who looked like heathen
priestesses, chanted a monotonous and heathenish-sounding
chant or *mêlê*, in eulogy of some ancient idolater. It just
served to remind me that this attractive crowd was but one
generation removed from slaughter-loving gods and human
sacrifices.

The king and his suite re-appeared in the upper balcony,
where all the foreigners were assembled, including the two
venerable missionaries and a French priest of benign aspect,
and his appearance was the signal for a fresh outburst of enthusiasm. Advancing to the front, he made an extemporaneous
speech, of which the following is a literal translation :—

"To all present I tender my warmest *aloha.* This day, on which you are gathered to pay your respects to me, I will remember to the day of my death. (Cheers.) I am filled with love to you all, fellow-citizens (*makaainana*), who have come here on this occasion, and for all the people, because by your unanimous choice I have been made your King, a young sovereign, to reign over you, and to fill the very distinguished office which I now occupy. (Cheers.) You are parents to me, and I will be your Father. (Tremendous cheering.) Formerly, in the days of our departed ancestors, you were not permitted to approach them; they and you were kept apart; but now we meet and associate together. (Cheers). I urge you all to persevere in the right, to forsake the ignorant ways of the olden time. There is but one God, whom it is our duty to obey. Let us forsake every kind of idolatry.

"In the year 1820 Rev. Messrs. Bingham, Thurston, and others came to these Islands and proclaimed the Word of God. It is their teachings which have enabled you to be what you are to-day. Now they have all gone to that spirit land, and only Mrs. Thurston remains. We are greatly indebted to them. (Cheers.) There are also among us here (alluding to Revs. Coan and Lyman) old and grey-haired fathers, whose examples we should endeavour to imitate, and obey their teachings.

"I am very glad to see the young men of the present time so well instructed in knowledge—perhaps some of them are your children. You must persevere in your search of wisdom and in habits of morality. Do not be indolent. (Cheers.) Those who have striven hard after knowledge and good character, are the ones who deserve and shall receive places of trust hereafter under the government.

"At the present time I have four foreigners as my ministerial advisers. But if, among these young men now standing before me, and under this flag, there are any who shall qualify themselves to fill these positions, then I will select them to fill their places. (Loud cheers.) *Aloha* to you all."

His manner as a speaker was extremely good, with sufficient gesticulation for the emphasis of particular points. The address was frequently interrupted by applause, and when at its conclusion he bowed gracefully to the crowd and said, "My *aloha* to you all," the cheering and enthusiasm were absolutely unbounded. And so the great *hookupu* ended, and the assemblage broke up into knots to discuss the royal speech and the day's doings.

I. L. B.

LETTER XIV.

HILO, HAWAII.

THE king "signified his intention to honour Mr. and Mrs.
Severance with his company" on the evening of the day after
the reception, and this involved a regular party and supper.
You can hardly imagine the difficulties connected with "refreshments," where few, if any, of the materials which we consider
necessary for dishes suitable for such occasions can be procured at the stores, and even milk and butter are scarce com-
modities. I had won a reputation as a cook by making a
much appreciated Bengal curry, and an English "roly-poly"
pudding, and when I offered my services, Mrs. S. kindly
accepted them, and she and I, with the Chinese cook and a
Chinese prisoner to assist us, have been cooking for a day and
a half. I wanted to make a gigantic trifle, a dish not known
here, and we hunted every store, hoping to find almonds and
raspberry jam among the "assorted notions," but in vain ;
however, grated cocoanut supplied the place of the first, and
a kind friend sent a pot of the last. The Chinamen were very
diverting. The cook looked on, and laughed constantly, and
perhaps was a little jealous : at all events when he thought we
had spoilt some cakes in the oven, he capered into Mrs. S.'s
room, gesticulating, and exclaiming satirically, " Lu, Lu ! cakes
so good, cakes so fine ! " No intoxicants were to be used on
the occasion, Hilo notions being rigid on this subject ; but I
hope it was not a crime that I clandestinely used two glasses of
sherry, without which my trifle would have been a failure. We
worked hard, and made trifle, sponge cake, pound cake, spiced
cake, dozens of cocoanut cakes and drops, custards, and sand-
wiches of potted meat, and enjoyed our preparations so much
that we found it hard to exchange kitchen for social duties,
and go to " Father Lyman," who entertained the king and a
number of Hilo folk in the evening.

Their rooms, not very large, were quite full. When the king entered, the company received him standing, and the flute band in the verandah played the national anthem, and afterwards at intervals during the evening sang some Hawaiian songs of the king's composition. I was presented to him, and as he is very courteous to strangers, he talked to me a good deal. He is a gentlemanly, courteous, unassuming man, hardly assuming enough in fact, and apparently very intelligent and well read. I was exceedingly pleased with him. He spoke a good deal of Queen Emma's reception in England, and of her raptures with Venice, and some other cities of the continent. He said he had the greatest desire to visit some parts of Europe, Great Britain specially, because he thought that by coming in contact with some of our leading statesmen, he might gain a more accurate knowledge than he possessed of the principles of constitutional government. He said he hoped that in two years Hawaii-nei would be so settled as to allow of his travelling, and that in the meantime he was studying French with a view to enjoying the continent.

He asked a great many questions regarding things at home, specially concerning the limitation of the power of the Crown. He cannot reconcile the theoretical right of the sovereign to choose his advisers with his practically submitting to receive them from a Parliamentary majority. He seemed to find a difficulty in understanding that the sovereign's right to refuse his assent to a Bill which had passed both Houses was by no means the same thing in practice as the possession of a veto. He said that in his reading of our constitutional history, the power of the sovereign seemed almost absolute, while if he understood facts rightly, the throne was more of an "ornament," or "figure-head," than a power at all. He asked me if it were true that Republican feeling was spreading very much in England, and if I thought that the monarchy would survive the present sovereign, on whose prudence and exalted virtues he seemed to think it rested. He said he thought his little kingdom had aped the style of the great monarchies too much, and that he should like to abolish a good many high sounding titles, sinecure offices, the household troops, and some of the "imitation pomp" of his court. He said he had never enjoyed anything so much since his accession as the *hookupu* of the morning, and asked me what I thought of it. I was glad to be able to answer truthfully that I had never seen a state pageant or ceremonial that I had enjoyed half so much, or that had impressed me so favourably. He has a very musical voice, a natural nobility and refinement of manner, and obvious tact and good feeling, rather, I should think, the result of amiable and gentlemanly instincts than of training or consideration, all which combine to make him interesting, altogether apart from his position as a Polynesian sovereign.

Where there are no servants, a party involves the hosts and their friends in the bustle of personal preparation, but all worked with a will, and by sunset the decorations were completed. All the Chinese lamps in Hilo were hung in the front verandah, and seats were placed in the front and side verandahs, on which the drawing-room opens by four doors, so there was plenty of room, though there were thirty people. The side verandah was enclosed by a drapery of flags, and the whole was tastefully decorated with festoons and wreaths of ferns. The king arrived early with his attendants, and was received by the host and hostess, and like a perfectly civilized guest, he handed Mrs. S. into the room. The great wish of the genial entertainers was to prevent stiffness and give the king a really social evening, so the "chair game," magical music, and a refined kind of blind man's buff, better suited to the occasion, but less "jolly" than the old riotous game, were shortly introduced. Lunalilo only looked on at first, and then entered into the games with a heartiness and zest which showed that he at least enjoyed the evening. Supper was served at nine. Several nests of Japanese tables had been borrowed, and these, dispersed about the room and verandah, broke up the guests into little social knots. Three Hilo ladies and I were the waitresses, and I was pleased to see that the good things were thoroughly appreciated, and that the trifle was universally popular. After supper there was a little dancing, and as few of the Hilo people knew any dance correctly, it was very amusing for the on-lookers. There was a great deal of promenading in the verandah, and a great deal of talking and merriment, which were enjoyed by a crowd of natives who stood the whole evening outside the garden fence. I don't think that any of the Hilo people are so unhappy as to possess an evening dress, and the pretty morning dresses of the ladies, and the thick boots, easy morning coats, and black ties of the gentlemen, gave a jolly "break-down" look to the affair, which would have been deemed inadmissible in less civilized society.

Some of my photographs of some of our eminent literary

and scientific men were lying on the table, and the king in looking at them showed a surprising amount of knowledge of what they had written or done, quite entitling him to unite in Dean Stanley's "Communion of Educated Men." I had previously asked him for his signature for my autograph collection, and he said he had composed a stanza for me which he thought I might like to have in addition. He called with it on the following afternoon, apologising for his dress, a short jacket and blue trowsers, stuffed into boots plastered with mud up to the knees. I was surprised when he asked me if the lines were correctly spelt, for he speaks English remarkably well. They are simply a kind wish, unaffectedly expressed.

"HILO, HAWAII, *Feb.* 26.

> "Whereso'er thou may'st roam,
> Whereso'er thou mak'st thy home,
> May God thy footsteps guide,
> Watch o'er thee and provide.
> This is my earnest prayer for thee,
> Welcome, stranger, from over the sea.
>
> "LUNALILO R."

It startles one sometimes to hear American vulgarisms uttered in his harmonious tones. The American admiral and generals had just arrived from the volcano, stiff, sore, bruised, jaded, "done," and the king said, "I guess the Admiral's about used up." He is really remarkably attractive, but I observe a look of irresolution about his mouth, indicative of a facility of disposition capable of being turned to the worst account. I think from what I have heard that the Hawaiian kings have fallen victims rather to unscrupulous foreigners, than to their own bad instincts.

My last day has been taken up with farewell visits, and I finish this on board the "Kilauea." Miss Karpe and I had to ride two miles, to a point at which it was possible to embark without risk, a heavy surf having for three weeks rendered it impossible for loaded boats to communicate with the shore at Hilo. My clothes were soaked when we reached the rocks, and Upa, very wet, carried us into a wet whale-boat, with water up to our ancles, which brought us over a heavy, sickening swell into this steamer, which is dirty as well as wet. I told Upa to lead my mare, and ride his own horse, but the

last I saw of him was on the mare's back, racing a troop of
natives along the beach.*

I. L. B.

* This was almost his last exploit. A few days later the sheriff had
the painful duty of committing him as a leper to the leper settlement on
Molokai. He was a leading spirit among the Hilo natives, and his joyous
nature will be missed by everyone. He has left a wife and some beautiful
children, who, it is feared, will eventually share his fate.

LETTER XV.

WAIMEA, HAWAII.

THERE is no limit to the oddities of the steam-ship " Kilauea." She lay rolling on the Hilo swell for two hours, and two hours after we sailed her machinery broke down, and we lay-to for five hours, in what they here call a heavy gale and sea. It was a miserable night. No privacy: the saloon both hot and wet, almost every one sick. I lay in my berth in my soaked clothes watching the proceedings of a gigantic cock-roach, and listening, not without amusement, to the awful groans of a Chinaman, and a "rough customer" from Cali-fornia, who occupied the next berths.

In the middle of the night the water came in great dashes through the skylight upon the table, and soon the saloon was afloat to the depth of from four to six inches. When the " Kilauea " rolled, and the water splashed in simultaneously, we were treated to vigorous "douches," which soon saturated the pillows, mattresses, and our clothing. One sea put out the lamp, and a ship's lantern, making "darkness visible," was swung in its stead. In an English ship there would have been a great fuss and a great flying about of stewards, on pretence of mending matters, but when the passengers shouted for our good steward, the serene creature came in with a melancholy smile on his face, said nothing, but quietly sat down on the transom, with his bare feet in the water, contemplating it with a comic air of helplessness. Breakfast, of course, could not be served, but a plate was put at one end of the table for the silent old Scotch captain, who tucked up his feet and sat with his oilskins and sou'-wester on, while the charming steward, with trousers rolled up to his knees, waded about, pacifying us by bringing us excellent curry as we sat on the edges of our berths, and putting on a sweetly apologetic manner, as if penitent for the gross misbehaviour of the ship. Such a man would reconcile me to far greater discomfort than that of the " Kilauea." I wonder if he is ever unamiable, or tired, or perturbed?

The next day was fine, and we were all much on deck to dry our clothes in the sun. The southern and leeward coasts of Hawaii as far as Kaawaloa are not much more attractive than coal-fields. Contrasted with the shining shores of Hilo, they are as dust and ashes; long reaches of black lava and miles of clinkers marking the courses of lava-flows, whose black desolation and deformity nature, as yet, has done almost nothing to clothe. Cocoa-nut trees usually, however, fringe the shore, but were it not for the wonderful colour of the ocean, like liquid, transparent turquoise, revealing the coral forests shelving down into purple depths, and the exciting proximity of sharks, it would have been wearisome. After leaving the bay where Captain Cook met his death, we passed through a fleet of twenty-seven canoes, each one hollowed out of the trunk of a single tree, from fifteen to twenty-five feet long, about twenty inches deep, hardly wide enough for a fat man, and pointed at both ends. On one side there is an outrigger formed of two long, bent sticks, to the outer ends of which is bound a curved beam of light wood, which skims along the surface of the water, rendering the canoe secure from an upset on that side, while the weight of the outrigger makes an upset on the other very unlikely. In calms they are paddled, and shoot over the water with great rapidity, but whenever there is any breeze a small sprit-sail is used. They are said to be able to stand very rough water, but they are singularly precarious and irresponsible looking contrivances, and for these, as well as for all other seas, I should much prefer a staunch whale-boat. We sailed for some hours along a lava coast, streamless, rainless, verdureless, blazing under the fierce light of a tropical sun, and some time after noon anchored in the scorching bay of Kawaihae.

A foreign store, a number of native houses, a great *heiau*, or heathen temple on a height, a fringe of cocoa-nut palms, and a background of blazing hills, flaring with varieties of red, hardly toned down by any attempt at vegetation, a crystalline atmosphere palpitating with heat, deep, rippleless, clear water, with coral groves below, and a view of the three great Hawaiian mountains, are the salient features of this outlet of

Hawaiian commerce.   But ah ! how soft and mild a blue the
sky was, looking inland, where, for the first time, I saw far
aloft, above solid masses of white cloud, sky hung, strangely
uplifted, the great volcanic domes of Mauna Kea, Mauna Loa,
and Hualalai, looking as if they had all passed into an endless
repose.

Shortly before we arrived I found that the sailing of the
San Francisco steamer is put off for a week, so I took advantage of a kind invitation I received some time ago to visit
Waimea, and go from thence to Waimanu, a wonderful valley
beyond Waipio, very little visited by foreigners.   A gentleman
and lady rode up here with me, and I got a horse on the beach
with a native bullock saddle on him, an uncouth contrivance of
wood not covered with hide, and a strong lassoing horn.   The
great wooden stirrups could not be shortened, but I soon found
myself able, in true savage fashion, to gallop up and down hill
without any.

The chief object of interest on this ride is the great *heiau*,
which stands on a bare, steep hill above the sea, not easy of
access.   It was the last heathen temple built on Hawaii.   On
entering the huge pile, which stood gaunt and desolate in the
thin red air, the story of the old bloody heathenism of the
islands returned to my memory.   The entrance is by a narrow
passage between two high walls, and it was by this that the
sacrificing priests dragged the human victims into the presence
of Tairi, a hideous wooden idol, crowned with a helmet, and
covered with red feathers, the favourite war-god of Kamehameha the Great, by whom this temple was built, before he
proceeded to the conquest of Oahu.

The shape is an irregular parallelogram, 224 feet long, and
100 wide.   At each end, and on the *mauka* side, the walls,
which are very solid and compact, though built of lava stones
without mortar, are twenty feet high, and twelve feet wide at
the bottom, but narrow gradually towards the top, where they
are finished with a course of smooth stones six feet broad.   On
the sea side, the wall, which has been partly thrown down, was
not more than six or seven feet high, and there were paved
platforms for the accommodation of the *alii*, or chiefs, and the
people in their orders.   The upper terrace is spacious, and
paved with flat smooth stones which were brought from a considerable distance, the greater part of the population of the
island having been employed on the building.   At the south
end there was an inner court, where the principal idol stood,

surrounded by a number of inferior deities, for the Hawaiians had "gods many, and lords many." Here also was the *anu*, a lofty frame of wickerwork, shaped like an obelisk, hollow, and five feet square at its base. Within this, the priest, who was the oracle of the god, stood, and of him the king used to inquire concerning war or peace, or any affair of national importance. It appears that the tones of the oracular voice were more distinct than the meaning of the utterances. However, the supposed answers were generally acted upon.

On the outside of this inner court was the *lélé*, or altar, on which human and other sacrifices were offered. On the day of the dedication of the temple to Tairi, vast offerings of fruit, dogs, and hogs were presented, and eleven human beings were immolated on the altar. These victims were taken from among captives, or those who had broken *Tabu*, or had rendered themselves obnoxious to the chiefs, and were often blind, maimed, or crippled persons. Sometimes they were dispatched at a distance with a stone or club, and their bodies were dragged along the narrow passage up which I walked shuddering; but oftener they were bound and taken alive into the *heiau* to be slain in the outer court. The priests, in slaying these sacrifices, were careful to mangle the bodies as little as possible. From two to twenty were offered at once. They were laid in a row with their faces downwards on the altar before the idol, to which they were presented in a kind of prayer by the priest, and, if offerings of hogs were presented at the same time, these were piled upon them, and the whole mass was left to putrefy.

The only dwellings within the *heiau* were those of the priests, and the "sacred house" of the king, in which he resided during the seasons of strict *Tabu*. A doleful place this *heiau* is, haunted not only by the memories of almost unimaginable terrors, but by the sore thought that generations of Hawaiians lived and died in the unutterable darkness of this ignorant worship, passing in long procession from these grim rites into the presence of the Father whose infinite compassions they had never known.

Every hundred feet of ascent from the rainless, fervid beach of Kawaihae increased the freshness of the temperature, and rendered exercise more delightful. From the fringe of palms along the coast to the damp hills north of Waimea, a distance of ten miles, there is not a tree or stream, though the scorched earth is deeply scored by the rush of fierce temporary torrents.

Hitherto, I have only travelled over the green coast which
faces the trade winds, where clouds gather and shed their
rains, and this desert, which occupies a great part of leeward
Hawaii, displeases me. It lies burning in the fierce splendours
of a zone, which, until now, I had forgotten was the torrid
zone, unwatered and unfruitful, red and desolate under the
sun. The island is here only twenty-two miles wide, and
strong winds sweep across it, whirling up its surface in great
brown clouds, so that the uplands in part appear a smoking
plain, backed by naked volcanic cones. No water, no grass,
no ferns. Some thornless thistles, a little brush of sapless-
looking indigo, and some species of compositæ struggle for a
doleful existence. There is nothing tropical about it but the
intense heat. The red soil becomes suffused with a green
tinge ten miles from the beach, and at the summit of the ascent the desert blends with this beautiful Waimea plain, one
of the most marked features of Hawaii. The air became damp
and cool; miles of fine, smooth, green grass stretched out
before us ; high hills, broken, pinnacled, wooded, and cleft
with deep ravines, rose on our left ; we heard the dash and
music of falling water : to the north it was like the Munster
Thal, to the south altogether volcanic. The tropics had
vanished. There were frame houses sheltered from the winds
by artificial screens of mulberry trees, and from the incursions
of cattle by rough walls of lava stones five feet high ; a mission
and court house, a native church, much too large for the
shrunken population, and other indications of an inhabited
region. Except for the woods which clothe the hills, the
characteristic of the scenery is baldness.

On clambering over the wall which surrounds my host's
kraal of dwellings, I heard in the dusk strange, sweet voices
crying rudely and emphatically, " Who are you ? What do you
want ? " and was relieved to find that the somewhat inhospit-
able interrogation only proceeded from two Australian mag-
pies. Mr. S—— is a Tasmanian, married to a young half-white
lady : and her native mother and seven or eight dark girls are
here, besides a number of natives and Chinese, and half
Chinese, who are employed about the place. Sheep are the
source of my host's wealth. He has 25,000 at three stations
on Mauna Kea, and, at an altitude of 6000 feet they
flourish, and are free from some of the maladies to which
they are liable elsewhere. Though there are only three or four
sheep owners on the islands, they exported 288,526 lbs. of

wool in 1872.* Mr. S—— has also 1000 head of cattle and 50 horses.

The industry of Waimea is cattle raising, and some feeble attempts are being made to improve the degenerate island breed by the importation of a few short-horn cows from New Zealand. These plains afford magnificent pasturage as well as galloping ground. They are a very great thoroughfare. The island, which is an equilateral triangle, about 300 miles in "circuit," can only be crossed here. Elsewhere, an impenetrable forest belt, and an impassable volcanic wilderness, compel travellers to take the burning track of adamant which snakes round the southern coast, when they are minded to go from one side of Hawaii to the other. Waimea also has the singular distinction of a road from the beach, which is traversed on great occasions by two or three oxen and mule teams, and very rarely by a more ambitious conveyance. There are few hours of day or night in which the tremulous *thud* of shoeless horses galloping on grass is not heard in Waimea.

The altitude of this great table-land is 2500 feet, and the air is never too hot, the temperature averaging 64° Fahrenheit. There is mist or rain on most days of the year for a short time, and the mornings and evenings are clear and cool. The long sweeping curves of the three great Hawaiian mountains spring from this level. The huge bulk of Mauna Kea without shoulders or spurs, rises directly from the Waimea level on the south to the altitude of 14,000 feet, and his base is thickly clustered with tufa-cones of a bright red colour, from 300 to 1000 feet in height. Considerably further back, indeed forty miles away, the smooth dome of Mauna Loa appears very serene now, but only thirteen years ago the light was so brilliant, from one of its tremendous eruptions, that here it was possible to read a newspaper by it, and during its height candles were unnecessary in the evenings ! Nearer the coast, and about thirty miles from here, is the less conspicuous dome of the dead volcano of Hualalai. If all Hawaii, south of Waimea, were submerged to a depth of 8000 feet, three nearly equi-distant, dome-shaped volcanic islands would remain, the highest of which would have an altitude of 6000 feet. To the south of these plains violent volcanic action is everywhere apparent, not only in tufa-cones, but in tracts of ashes, scoriæ, and volcanic sand. Near the centre there are some very curious caves, possibly "lava-bubbles," which were used by the

* In 1875 the export of wool had increased to 465,469 lbs.

natives as places of sepulture. The Kohala hills, picturesque, wooded, and abrupt, bound Waimea on the north, with exquisite grassy slopes, and bring down an abundance of water to the plain, but owing to the lightness of the soil and the evaporation produced by the tremendous winds, the moisture disappears within two miles of the hills, and an area of rich soil, ten miles by twelve, which, if irrigated, would be invaluable, is nothing but a worthless dusty desert, perpetually encroaching on the grass. As soon as the plains slope towards the east, the vegetation of the tropics reappears, and the face of the country is densely covered with a swampy and impenetrable bush hardly at all explored, which shades the sources of the streams which fall into the Waipio and Waimanu Valleys, and is supposed to contain water enough to irrigate the Saharas of leeward Hawaii.

The climate of the plain is most invigorating. If there were waggon roads and obtainable comforts, Waimea, with its cool, equable temperature, might become the great health resort of invalids from the Pacific coast. But Hawaii is not a place for the sick or old ; for, if people cannot ride on horseback, they can have neither society nor change. Mr. Lyons, one of the most famous of the early missionaries, still clings to this place, where he has worked for forty years. He is an Hawaiian poet; and, besides translating some of our best hymns, has composed enough to make up the greater part of a bulky volume, which is said to be of great merit. He says that the language lends itself very readily to rhythmical expression. He was indefatigable in his youth, and was four times let down the *pali* by ropes to preach in the Waimanu Valley. Neither he nor his wife can mount a horse now, and it is very dreary for them, as the population has receded and dwindled from about them. Their house is made lively, however, by some bright little native girls, who board with them, and receive an English and industrial education.

The moral atmosphere of Waimea has never been a wholesome one. The region was very early settled by a class of what may be truly termed "mean whites," the "beachcombers" and riff-raff of the Pacific. They lived infamous lives, and added their own to the indigenous vices of the islands, turning the district into a perfect sink of iniquity, in which they were known by such befitting *aliases* as " Jake the Devil," &c. The coming of the missionaries, and the settlement of moral, orderly whites on Hawaii, have slowly created

a public opinion averse to flagrant immorality, and the out-
rageous license of former years would now meet with legal
penalties. Many of the old settlers are dead, and others have
drifted to regions beyond restraining influences, but still "the
Waimea crowd" is not considered up to the mark. Most of
the present set of foreigners are Englishmen who have
married native women. It was in such quarters as this that
the great antagonistic influence to the complete Christianiza-
tion of the natives was created, and it is from such suspicious
sources that the aspersions on missionary work are usually
derived.

Waimea has its own beauty—the grand breezy plain, the
gigantic sweep of the mountain curves, the incessant changes
of colour, and the morning view of Mauna Kea, with the pure
snow on its ragged dome, rose-flushed in the early sunlight.
I don't agree with Disraeli that "happiness is atmosphere;"
yet constant sunshine, and a climate which never threatens
one with discomfort or ills, certainly conduce to equable
cheerfulness.

I am quite interested with a native lady here, the first I have
met with who has been able to express her ideas in English.
She is extremely shrewd and intelligent, very satirical, and a
great mimic. She very cleverly burlesques the way in which
white people express their admiration of scenery, and, in fact,
ridicules admiration of scenery for itself. She evidently thinks
us a sour, morose, worrying, forlorn race. "We," she said,
"are always happy; we never grieve long about anything;
when any one dies we break our hearts for some days, and
then we are happy again. We are happy all day long, not like
white people, happy one moment, gloomy another: we've no
cares, the days are too short. What are *haoles* always unhappy
about?" Perhaps she expresses the general feeling of her
careless, pleasure-loving, mirth-loving people, who, whatever
commands they disobey, fulfil the one, "Take no thought for
the morrow." The fabrication of the beautiful quilts I before
wrote of is a favourite occupation of native women, and they
make all their own and their husbands' clothes ; but making
leis, going into the woods to collect materials for them, talking,
riding, bathing, visiting, and otherwise amusing themselves,
take up the greater part of their time. Perhaps if we white
women always wore *holokus* of one shape, we should have
fewer gloomy moments !

                                                    I. L. B

LETTER XVI.

A Grass Lodge—Alone Among "Savages"—A Dizzy Pali—Out of the World—Elysium—A Lapse into Savagery—A Troubled Night—The Waimanu Valley—A Silent World—A *Pilikia*.

WAIMANU VALLEY, HAWAII.

I AM sitting at the door of a grass lodge, at the end of all things, for no one can pass further by land than this huge, lonely cleft. About thirty natives are sittting about me, all

Ordinary Female Costume.

staring, laughing, and chattering, and I am the only white person in the region. We have all had a meal, sitting round a large calabash of *poi* and a fowl, which was killed in my honour, and roasted in one of their stone ovens. I have for-

gotten my knife, and have had to help myself after the primitive fashion of aborigines, not without some fear, for some of
them I am sure are in an advanced state of leprosy. The
brown tattooed limbs of one man are stretched across the mat,
the others are sitting cross-legged, making *lauhala leis.* One
man is making fishing-lines of a beautifully white and marvel-
lously tenacious fibre, obtained from an Hawaiian " flax " plant
(possibly *Urtica argentea*), very different from the New Zealand
Phormium tenax. Nearly all the people of the valley are outside, having come to see the *wahine haole:* only one white
woman, and she a resident of Hawaii, having been seen in
Waimanu before. I am really alone, miles of mountain and
gulch lie between me and the nearest whites. This is a wonderful place : a ravine about three miles long and three-quarters
of a mile wide, without an obvious means of ingress, being
walled in by precipices from 2000 to 4000 feet high. Five
cascades dive from the *palis* at its head, and unite to form a
placid river about up to a horse's body here, and deep enough
for a horse to swim in a little below. Dense forests of various
shades of green fill up the greater part of the valley, concealing
the basins into which the cascades leap, and the grey basalt of
the *palis* is mostly hidden by greenery. At the open end, two
bald bluffs, one of them 2000 feet in height, confront the
Pacific, and its loud booming surf comes up to within one
hundred yards of the house where I am writing, but is banked
off by a heaped-up barrier of colossal shingle.

Hot and silent, a sunset world of an endless afternoon, it
seems a palpable and living dream. And a few of these people,
I understand, have dreamed away their lives here, never having
been beyond their valley, at least by land. But it is a dream
of ceaseless speech and rippling laughter. They are the
merriest people I have yet seen, and doubtless their isolated
life is dear to them.

I wish I could sketch this most picturesque scene. In the
verandah, which is formed of mats, two handsome youths, and
five women in green, red, and orange chemises, all with *leis* of
ferns round their hair, are reclining on the ground. Outside of
this there is a pavement of large lava stones, and groups in all
colours, wreathed and garlanded, including some much disfigured
old people, crouching in red and yellow blankets, are sitting
and lying there. Some are fondling small dogs ; and a number
of large ones, with a whole tribe of amicable cats, are picking
bones. Surf-boards, paddles, saddles, lassos, spurs, gear, and

bundles of *ti* leaves are lying about. Thirteen horses are
tethered outside, some of which brought the riders who escorted
me triumphantly from the head of the valley. The foreheads
of the precipices opposite are reddening in the sunset, and
between them and me horses and children are constantly swimming across the broad, still stream which divides the village
into two parts; and now and then a man in a *malo*, and children who have come up the river swimming, with their clothes
in one hand, increase the assemblage.

All are intently watching me, but are as kind and good-
natured as possible; and my guide from Waipio is discoursing
to them about me. He knows a little abrupt, disjointed, almost
unintelligible English, and comes up every now and then with
an interrogation in his manner, "Father? mother? married?
watch? How came?" "You" appears beyond his efforts.
"*Kilauea? Lunalilo?*" Then he goes back and orates
rapidly, gesticulating emphatically. A very handsome, pleasant-
looking man, with a red sash round his waist, who, I understand from signs, is the schoolmaster, emerged from the throng,
and sat down beside me; but his English appears limited to
these words, "How old?" When I told him by counting on
my fingers he laughed heartily, and said, "Too old," and he
told the others, and they all laughed. I have photographs of
Queen Victoria and Mr. Coan in my writing-book, and when I
exhibited them they crowded round me clapping their hands,
and screaming with delight when they recognized Mr. Coan.
The king's handwriting was then handed round amidst reverent
"ahs" and "ohs," or what sounded like them. This letter was
also passed round and examined lengthwise, sidewise, and upside down. They shrieked with satirical laughter when I
pressed some fragile ferns in my blotting-book. The natives
think it quite idiotic in us to attach any value to "withered
leaves." My inkstand with its double-spring lids has been a
great amusement. Each one opened both, and shut them
again, and a chorus of "*maikai, maikai,*" (good) ran round the
circle. They seem so simple and good that at last I have
trusted them with my watch, which excites unbounded admiration, probably because of its small size. It is now on its travels;
but I am not the least anxious about it. A man pointed to
a hut some distance on the other side of the river, and appeared
interrogative, and on my replying affirmatively, he mounted a
horse and carried off the watch in the direction indicated. Mr.
Ellis came to this valley in a canoe, and he mentions that when

he preached, the natives, who seemed to be very indifferent to the general truths of Christianity, became very deeply interested when they heard of *Ora loa ia Jesu* (endless life by Jesus). While I was up the valley the poor people made a wonderful bed of seven fine mats, one over the other, on one side of the house, and screened it off with a flaring muslin curtain; but on the other side there are ten pillows in a row, so that I wonder how many are to occupy the den during the night. I am now writing inside the house, with a hollowed stone with some beef fat with a wick in it, for a light, and two youths seem delegated to attend upon me. One holds my ink, and if I look up, the other rushes for something that I am supposed to want. They insist on thinking that I am cold because my clothes are wet, and have thrown over me several folds of *tapa*, made from the inner bark of the *wauti* or cloth plant (*Broussonetia papyrifera*). They brought me a *kalo* leaf containing a number of living freshwater shrimps, and were quite surprised when I did not eat them.

WAIPIO, *March 5th.*

It seems fully a week since I left Waimea yesterday morning, so many new experiences have been crowded into the time. I will try to sketch my expedition while my old friend Halemanu is preparing dinner. The morning opened gloriously. The broad Waimea plains were flooded with red and gold, and the snowy crest of Mauna Kea was cloudless. We breakfasted by lamp light (the days of course are short in this latitude), and were away before six. My host kindly provided me with a very fine horse and some provisions in a leather wallet, and with another white man and a native accompanied me as far as this valley, where they had some business. The morning deepened into gorgeousness. A blue mist hung in heavy folds round the violet bases of the mountains, which rose white and sharp into the rose-flushed sky ; the dew lay blue and sparkling on the short crisp grass; the air was absolutely pure, and with a suspicion of frost in it. It was all very fair, and the horses enjoyed the morning freshness, and danced and champed their bits as though they disliked being reined in. We rode over level, grass-covered ground, till we reached the Hamakua bush, fringed with dead trees, and full of *ohias* and immense fern trees, some of them with a double tier of fronds, far larger and finer than any that I saw in New Zealand. There are herds of wild goats, cattle, and pigs on the island. and they roam through-

out this region, trampling, grubbing, and rending, grinding
the bark of the old trees and eating up the young ones.
This ravaging is threatening at no distant date to destroy the
beauty and alter the climate of the mountainous region of
Hawaii.   The cattle are a hideous breed—all bones, hide, and
horns.

We were at the top of the Waipio *pali* at eight, and our bare-
footed horses, used to the soft pastures of Waimea, refused to
carry us down its rocky steep, so we had to walk.   I admired
this lonely valley far more than before.   It was full of infinite
depths of blue—blue smoke in lazy spirals curled upwards ; it
was eloquent in a morning silence that I felt reluctant to break.
Against its dewy greenness the beach shone like coarse gold,
and its slow, silver river lingered lovingly, as though loth to
leave it, and be merged in the reckless, loud-tongued Pacific.
Across the valley, the track I was to take climbed up in thready
zigzags, and disappeared round a bold headland.   It was
worth a second visit just to get a glimpse of such a vision of
peace.

Halemanu, with hospitable alacrity, soon made breakfast
ready, after which Mr. S., having arranged for my further
journey, left me here, and for the first time I found myself
alone among natives ignorant of English.   For the Waimanu
trip it is essential to have a horse bred in the Waimanu Valley
and used to its dizzy *palis*, and such a horse was procured, and
a handsome native, called Hananui, as guide.   We were away
by ten, and galloped across the valley till we came to the
nearly perpendicular *pali* on the other side.   The sight of this
air-hung trail from Halemanu's house has turned back several
travellers who were bent on the trip, but I had been told that
it was quite safe on a Waimanu horse ; and keeping under my
fears as best I could, I let Hananui precede me, and began the
ascent, which is visible from here for an hour.   The *pali* is as
nearly perpendicular as can be.   Not a bush or fern, hardly a
tuft of any green thing, clothes its bare, scathed sides.   It
terminates precipitously on the sea at a height of 2000 feet.
Along this shelving wall, something like a sheep track, from
thirty to forty-six inches broad, goes up in great swinging zigzags, sometimes as broken steps of rock breast high, at others
as a smooth ledge with hardly foothold, in three places carried
away by heavy rains—altogether the most frightful track that
imagination can conceive.   It was most unpleasant to see the
guide's horse straining and scrambling, looking every now and

then as if about to fall over backwards. My horse went up wisely and nobly, but slipping, jumping, scrambling, and sending stones over the ledge, now and then hanging for a second by his fore feet. The higher we went the narrower and worse it grew. The girth was loose, so as not to impede the horse's respiration, the broad cinch which usually passes under the body having been fastened round his chest, and yet it was once or twice necessary to run the risk of losing my balance by taking my left foot out of the stirrup to press it against the horse's neck to prevent it from being crushed, while my right hung over the precipice. We came to a place where the path had been carried away, leaving a declivity of loose sand and gravel. You can hardly realize how difficult it was to dismount, when there was no margin outside the horse. I somehow slid under him, being careful not to turn the saddle, and getting hold of his hind leg, screwed myself round carefully behind him. It was alarming to see these sure-footed creatures struggle and slide in the deep gravel as though they must go over, and not less so to find myself sliding, though I was grasping my horse's tail.

Between the summit and Waimanu, a distance of ten miles, there are nine gulches, two of them about 900 feet deep, all very beautiful, owing to the broken ground, the luxuriant vegetation, and the bright streams, but the *kona*, or south wind, was blowing, bringing up the hot breath of the equatorial belt, and the sun was perfectly unclouded, so that the heat of the gorges was intense. They succeed each other occasionally with very great rapidity. Between two of the deepest and steepest there is a ridge not more than fifty yards wide.

Soon after noon we simultaneously stopped our horses. The Waimanu Valley lay 2500 feet (it is said) below us, and the trail struck off into space. It was a scene of loneliness to which Waipio seems the world. In a second the eye took in the twenty grass lodges of its inhabitants, the five cascades which dive into the dense forests of its upper end, its river like a silver ribbon, and its meadows of living green. In ten seconds a bird could have spanned the ravine and feasted on its loveliness, but we could only tip over the dizzy ridge that overhangs the valley, and laboriously descend into its heat and silence. The track is as steep and broken as that which goes up from hence, but not nearly so narrow, and without its elements of terror, for *kukuis*, *lauhalas*, *ohias*, and *ti* trees, with a lavish growth of ferns and trailers, grow luxuriantly in every damp

rift of rock, and screen from view the precipices of the *pali.*
The valley looks as if it could only be reached in a long day's
travel, so very far it is below, but the steepness of the track
makes it accessible in an hour from the summit. As we descended, houses and a church which had looked like toys at
first, dilated on our sight, the silver ribbon became a stream,
the specks on the meadows turned into horses, the white, wavy
line on the Pacific beach turned into a curling wave, and lower
still, I saw people, who had seen us coming down, hastily
shuffling into clothes.

There were four houses huddled between the *pali* and the
river, and six or eight, with a church and schoolhouse on the
other side ; and between these and the ocean a steep, narrow
beach, composed of large stones worn as round and smooth as
cannon balls, on which the surf roars the whole year round.
The *pali* which walls in the valley on the other side is inaccessible. The school children and a great part of the population
had assembled in front of the house which I described before.
There was a sort of dyke of rough lava stones round it, difficult
to climb, but the natives, though they are very kind, did not,
on this or any similar occasion, offer me any help, which
neglect, I suppose, arises from the fact that the native women
never need help, as they are as strong, fearless, and active as
the men, and rival them in swimming and other athletic sports.
An old man, clothed only with his dark skin, was pounding
baked *kalo* for *poi*, in front of the house ; a woman with flowers
in her hair, but apparently not otherwise clothed, was wading
up to her waist in the river, pushing before her a light trumpet-
shaped basket used for catching shrimps, and the other women
wore the usual bright-coloured chemises.

I wanted to make the most of the six hours of daylight left,
and we remounted our horses and rode for some distance up
the river, which is the highway of the valley, all the children
swimming on our right and left, each holding up a bundle of
clothes with one hand, and two canoes paddled behind us.
The river is still and clear, with a smooth bottom, but comes
halfway up a horse's body, and riders take their feet out of the
stirrups, bring them to a level with the saddle, lean slightly
back, and hold them against the horse's neck. Equestrians
following this fashion, canoes gliding, children and dogs swimming, were a most amusing picture. Several of the children
swim to and from school every day. I was anxious to get rid
of this voluntary escort, and we took a gallop over the springy

grass till we reached some very pretty grass houses, under the
shade of the most magnificent bread-fruit trees on Hawaii, loaded
with fruit. There were orange trees in blossom, and coffee
trees with masses of sweet white flowers lying among their
flaky branches like snow, and the unfailing cocoa-nut rising out
of banana groves, and clusters of gardenia smothering the red
hibiscus. Here Hananui adopted a showman's air ; he made
me feel as if I were one of Barnum's placarded monsters. I
had nothing to do but sit on my horse and be stared at. I felt
that my bleached face was unpleasing, that my eyes and hair
were faded, and that I had a great deal to answer for in the
way of colour and attire. From the way in which he asked me
unintelligible questions, I gathered that the people were cate-
chizing him about me, and that he was romancing largely at
my expense. They brought me some bananas and cocoa-nut
milk, which were most refreshing.

Beyond the houses the valley became a jungle of Indian shot
(*Canna indica*), eight or nine feet high, guavas and *ohias*, with
an entangled undergrowth of ferns rather difficult to pene-
trate, and soon Hananui, whose soul was hankering after the
delights of society, stopped, saying, " *Lios* (horses) no go."
" We'll try," I replied, and rode on first. He sat on his horse
laughing immoderately, and then followed me. I see that in
travelling with natives it is essential to have a definite plan of
action in one's own mind, and to verge on self-assertion in
carrying it out. We fought our way a little further, and then
he went out of sight altogether in the jungle, his horse having
floundered up to his girths in soft ground, on which we dismounted and tethered the horses. H. had never been any
further, and as I failed to make him understand that I desired
to visit the home of the five cascades, I had to reverse our
positions and act as guide. We crept along the side of a
torrent among exquisite trees, moss, and ferns, till we came to
a place where it divided. There were three horses tethered
there, some wearing apparel lying on the rocks, and some
human footprints along one of the streams, which decided me
in favour of the other. H. remonstrated by signs, as doubtless he espied an opportunity for much gossip in the other
direction, but on my appearing persistent, he again laughed and
followed me.

From this point it was one perfect, rapturous, intoxicating,
supreme vision of beauty, and I felt, as I now believe, that at
last I had reached a scene on which foreign eyes had never

looked. The glories of the tropical forest closed us in with their depth, colour, and redundancy. Here the operations of nature are rapid and decisive. A rainfall of eleven feet in a year and a hothouse temperature force every plant into cease- less activity, and make short work of decay. Leafage, blossom, fruitage, are simultaneous and perennial. The river, about as broad as the Cam at Cambridge, leaped along, clear like amber, pausing to rest awhile in deep bright pools, where fish were sporting above the golden sand, a sparkling, rushing, terrorless stream, " without mysteries or agonies," broken by rocks, green with mosses and fragile ferns, and in whose un- chilled waters, not more than three feet deep, wading was both safe and pleasant. It was not possible to creep along its margin, the forest was so dense and tangled, so we waded the whole way, and wherever the water ran fiercely my unshod guide helped me. One varied, glorious maze of vegetation came down to it, and every green thing leant lovingly towards it, or stooped to touch it, and over its whole magic length was arched and interlaced the magnificent large-leaved *ohia*, whose millions of spikes of rose-crimson blossoms lit up the whole arcade, and the light of the afternoon sun slanted and trickled through them, dancing in the mirthful water, turning its far- down sands to gold, and brightening the many-shaded greens of candlenut and breadfruit. It shone on majestic fern-trees, on the fragile *Polypodium tamariscinum*, which clung trem- blingly to the branches of the *ohia*, on the beautiful lygodium, which adorned the uncouth trunk of the breadfruit ; on shining banana leaves and glossy, trailing yams ; on gigantic lianas, which, climbing to the tops of the largest trees, descended in vast festoons, passing from tree to tree, and interlacing the forest with a living network ; and on lycopodiums of every kind, from those which wrapped the rocks in feathery green to others hardly distinguishable from ferns. But there were twi- light depths too, where no sunlight penetrated the leafy gloom, damp and cool : dreamy shades, in which the music of the water was all too sweet, and the loveliness too entrancing, creating that sadness, hardly " akin to pain," which is latent in all intense enjoyment. Here and there a tree had fallen across the river, from which grew upwards and trailed downwards, fairy-like, semi-transparent mosses and ferns, all glittering with moisture and sunshine, and now and then a scarlet tropic bird heightened the effect by the flash of his plumage.

After an hour of wading we emerged into broad sunny daylight at the home of the five cascades, which fall from a semi-
circular precipice into three basins. It is not, however,
possible to pass from one to the other. This great gulf is a
grand sight, with its dark deep basin from which it seemed so
far to look up to the heavenly blue, and the water falling
calmly and unhurriedly, amidst innumerable rainbows, from a
height of 3000 feet. The sides were draped with ferns
flourishing under the spray, and at the base the rock was very
deeply caverned. I enjoyed a delicious bath, relying on sun
and wind to dry my clothes, and then reluctantly waded down
the river. At its confluence with another stream, still arched
by *ohias*, a man and two women appeared rising out of the
water, like a vision of the elder world in the days of Fauns,
and Naiads, and Hamadryads. The water was up to their
waists, and *leis* of *ohia* blossoms and ferns, and masses of
unbound hair fantastically wreathed with moss, fell over their
faultless forms, and their rich brown skin gleamed in the
slant sunshine. They were catching shrimps with trumpet-
shaped baskets, perhaps rather a prosaic occupation. They
joined us, and we waded down together to the place where they
had left their horses. The women slipped into their *holokus*,
and the man insisted on my riding his barebacked horse to the
place where we had left our own, and then we all galloped over
the soft grass.

Waimanu had turned out to meet us about thirty people on
horseback, all of whom shook hands with me, and some of
them threw over me garlands of *ohia*, pandanus, and hibiscus.
Where our cavalcade entered the river, a number of children
and dogs and three canoes awaited us, and thus escorted I
returned triumphantly to the house. The procession on the
river of paddling canoes, swimming children and dogs, and
more than thirty riders, with their feet tucked up round their
horses' necks, all escorting a "pale face," was grotesque and
enchanting, and I revelled in this lapse into savagery, and enjoyed heartily the kindliness and goodwill of this unsophisticated
people.

When darkness spread over the valley, clear voices ascended
in a weird recitative, the room filled up with people, pipes
circulated freely, *poi* was again produced, and calabashes of
cocoa-nut milk. The *mêlées* were long, and I crept within my
curtain and lay down, but the drowsiness which legitimately
came over me after riding thirty miles and wading two, was

broken in upon by two monstrous cockroaches really as large as mice, with fierce-looking antennæ and prominent eyes, both of which mounted guard on my pillow. On rising to drive them away, I found to my dismay that they were but the leaders of a host, which only made a temporary retreat, rustling over the mat and dried grass with the crisp tread of mice, and scaring away sleep for some hours. Worse than these were the mosquitos, also an imported nuisance, which stabbed and stung without any preliminary droning; and the heat was worse still, for thirteen human beings were lying on the floor and the door was shut. Had I known that two of these were lepers, I should have felt far from comfortable. As it was, I got up soon after midnight, and cautiously stepping among the sleeping forms, went out of doors. Everything favoured reflection, but I think the topics to which my mind most frequently reverted were my own absolute security—a lone white woman among " savages," and the civilizing influence which Christianity has exercised, so that even in this isolated valley, gouged out of a mountainous coast, there was nothing disagreeable or improper to be seen. The night was very still, but the sea was moaning ; the river rippled very gently as it brushed past the reeds ; there was a hardly perceptible vibration in the atmosphere, which suggested falling water and quivering leaves; and the air was full of a heavy, drowsy fragrance, the breath of orange flowers, perhaps, and of the night-blowing Cereus, which had opened its ivory urn to the moon. I should have liked to stay out all night in the vague, delicious moonlight, but the dew was heavy, and moreover I had not any boots on, so I reluctantly returned to the grass house, which was stifling with heat and smells of cocoa-nut oil, tobacco, and the rancid smoke from beef fat.

Before sunrise this morning my horse was saddled, and a number of natives had assembled. Hananui had disappeared, but the man who lent me his bare-backed horse yesterday was ready to act as guide. My boots could not then be found, so I adopted the native fashion of riding with bare feet. We again rode up the river in that slow and solemn fashion in which horses walk in water, galloped over a stretch of grass, crossed a bright stream several times, and then entered a dense jungle of Indian shot, plantains, and sadlerias, with breadfruit, *kukui*, and *ohia* rising out of it. There were thousands of plantains, a fruit resembling the banana, but that it requires cooking. The Indian shot, the yellow-blossomed variety, was of a gigantic size. Its hard, black seeds put into a bladder furnish the *chic-chac*, which in many places is used as an accompaniment to the utterly abominable and heathenish tom-tom. Here guavas as large as oranges and as yellow as lemons ripened and fell unheeded. Sometimes deep down we heard the rush of water, and Paalau got down and groped for it on his hands and knees; sometimes we heard a noise as of hip-popotami, but nothing could be seen but the tips of ears, as a herd of happy, unbroken horses, scared by our approach, crashed away through the jungle. Clear rapid streams, fern-fringed, sometimes offered us a few yards of highway, but the jungle ever grew more dense, the forest trees larger, the lianas more tangled, the streams more sunk and rocky, and though the horses shut their eyes and boldly pushed through the tangle, we were fairly foiled when within half a mile from the head of the valley. I thoroughly appreciated the unsightly leather guards which are here used to cover the stirrups and feet, as without them I could not have ridden ten yards. We were so hemmed in that it was difficult to dismount, but I bound some wild *kalo* leaves round my feet, and managed to get over some broken rock to a knoll, from which I obtained a superb view of the wonderful cleft. *Palis* 3000 feet in height walled in its head with a complete inaccessibility. It lay in cool dewy shadow till the sudden sun flushed its precipices with pink, and a broad bar of light revealed the great chasm in which it terminates, while far off its portals opened upon the red eastern sky. This little, lonely world had become so very dear to me, that I found it hard to leave it.

There was some stir near the sea, for a man was about to build a grass house, and they were preparing a stone pavement for it. Thirty people sat on the ground in a line from the beach, and passed stones from hand to hand, as men pass buckets at a fire. It seemed a very attractive occupation, and I could hardly get Hananui to leave it. The natives are most gregarious and social in their habits. They assemble together for everything that has to be made or done, and the occupations and amusements are shared by both sexes. In old days it is said that a king of Hawaii assembled most of the adults of the then populous island, and formed a human chain three miles long to pass up stones for the building of the great *Heiau* in Kona. It is said that this valley had 2000 inhabitants forty years ago, but they have dwindled to 117. The former estimate is probably not an excessive one, for nearly the whole valley is suitable for the culture of *kalo*, and a square mile of *kalo* will feed 15,000 natives for a year.

Two women were shrimping in the river, the children were swimming to school, blue smoke curled up into the still air, *kalo* was baking among the stones, and a group of women sat sewing and making *leis* on the ground. The Waimanu day had begun; and it was odd to think that through the long summer years days dawned like this, and that the people of the valley grew grey and old in shrimping and sewing and *kalo* baking. All Waimanu shook hands with me, the kindly " *Aloha* " filled the air, and the women threw garlands over us both. I could hardly induce my host to accept a dollar and a half for my entertainment. From the dizzy summit of the *pali*, where the sun was high and hot, I looked my last on the dark, cool valley, slumbering in an endless calm, the deepest, greenest, quaintest cleft on all the island.

The sun was fierce and bright, the ocean had a metallic glint, the hot breath of the *kona* was scorching. My hands, swollen from mosquito bites, could not be stuffed into my gloves, and inflamed under the sun, and my wet boots baked and stiffened on my feet. Hananui plaited a crown of leaves for my hot head, which I found a great relief. I was still minded to linger, for one side of each glorious gulch was cool with shadow and dripping with dew. The blue morning glories were yet unwilted, rivulets dropped down into ferny grottoes and lingered there, rose *ohia* blossoms lighted shady places, orange flowers gleamed like stars amidst the dense leafage, and the crimped-leaved coffee shrubs were white with their mimic snow. It was my last tropical dream, and I was rudely roused by finding myself on the unsightly verge of the great bluff on the north side of this valley, which plunges to the sea with an uncompromising perpendicular dip of 2000 feet, and carries on its dizzy brow a shelving trail not more than two feet wide !

I felt that I must go back and live and die in Waimanu rather than descend that scathed steep, and being stupid with terror flung myself from my horse, forgetting that it was much safer to trust to his four feet than to my two, and to an animal without " nerves," dizziness, or " the fore-knowledge of death," than to my palsied, cowardly self. I had intended to go into details of the horrible descent, but the " *pilikia* " is over now, and Halemanu claps me on the shoulder with an approving smile, ejaculating, " *Maikai, maikai* " (good).   Besides, my returning senses inform me that I have not tasted food since yesterday, and some delicious river fishes are smoking on the table.   .   .   .   .   .   .

I. L. B.

LETTER XVII.

Beautiful Lahaina !—The Leper Island—Sister Phœbe—A Family School
—Gentle Discipline—Local Difficulties.

. . . I HAVE been spending the day at Lahaina on Maui, on my way from Kawaihae to Honolulu. Lahaina is thoroughly beautiful and tropical looking, with its white latticed houses peeping out from under coco palms, breadfruit, candlenut, tamarinds, mangoes, bananas, and oranges, with the brilliant green of a narrow strip of sugar-cane for a background, and above, the flushed mountains of Eeka, riven here and there by cool green chasms, rise to a height of 6000 feet. Beautiful Lahaina ! It is an oasis in a dazzling desert, straggling for nearly two miles along the shore, but compressed into a width of half a mile. It was a great missionary centre, as well as a great whaling station, but the whalers have deserted it, and missions are represented now only by the seminary of La-hainaluna on the hillside. An old palace, the remains of a fort, a custom-house, and a native church are the most conspicuous buildings. The stores and dwellings of the foreign residents are scattered along the shore, and the light frame house, with its green verandah, buried amid gorgeous exotics and shaded by candlenut and breadfruit, looks as seemly and in keeping as in far-off Massachusetts, under hickory and elm. The grass houses of the natives cluster along the waters' edge, or in lanes dark with mangoes and bananas, and fragrant with gardenia fringing the cane-fields. These, with adobe houses and walls, the flush of the soil, the gaudy dresses of the natives, the masses of brilliant exotics, the intense blue of the sea, and the dry blaze of the tropical heat, give a decided individuality to the capital of Maui. The heat of Lahaina is a dry, robust, bracing, joyous heat. The mercury stood at 80°, the usual temperature of the " flare " or sea level on the leeward side of the islands ; but I strolled through the cane-fields and along the glaring beach without suffering the least inconvenience from the sun, and found the unusual precaution of a white umbrella perfectly needless.

The beach is formed of pure white broken coral; the sea is blue with the calm, pure blue of turquoise, but crystalline in its purity, and breaks for ever over the environing coral reef with a low deep music. Blue water stretched to the far horizon, the sky was blazing blue, the leafage was almost dazzling to the eye, the mountainous island of Molokai floated like a great blue morning glory on the yet bluer sea; a sweet, soft breeze rustled through the palms, lazy ripples plashed lightly on the sand; humanity basked, flower-clad, in sunny indolence; everything was redundant, fervid, beautiful. How can I make you realize the glorious, bountiful, sun-steeped tropics under our cold grey skies, and amidst our pale, monotonous, lustreless greens?

Yet Molokai is only enchanting in the distance, for its blue petals enfold 400 lepers doomed to endless isolation, and 300 more are shortly to be weeded out and sent thither. In to-day's paper appeared the painful notice, "All lepers are required to report themselves to the Government health officer within fourteen days from this date for inspection, and final banishment to Molokai." It is hoped that leprosy may be "stamped out" by these stringent measures, but the leprous taint must be strong in many families, and the social, gregarious natives smoke each other's pipes and wear each other's clothes, and either from fatalism or ignorance have disregarded all precautions regarding this woful disease; and now that measures are being taken for the isolation of lepers, they are concealing them under mats and in caves and woods. This forlorn malady, called here Chinese leprosy, in the cases that I have seen, confers nothing of the white, scaly look attributed to Syrian leprosy; but the face is red, puffed, bloated, and shining, and the eyes glazed, and I am told that in its advanced stage the swollen limbs decay and drop off. It is a fresh item of the infinite curse which has come upon this race, and with Molokai in sight the Hesperides vanished, and I ceased to believe that the Fortunate Islands exist here or elsewhere on this weary earth.

My destination was the industrial training and boarding school for girls, taught and superintended by two English ladies of Miss Sellon's sisterhood, Sisters Mary Clara and Phœbe; and I found it buried under the shade of the finest candlenut trees I have yet seen. A rude wooden cross in front is a touching and fitting emblem of the Saviour, for whom these pious women have sacrificed friends, sympathy, and the social intercourse and amenities which are within daily reach of our workers at home. The large house, which is either plastered stone or adobe, contains the dormitories, visitors' room, and oratory, and three houses at the back, all densely shaded, are used as schoolroom, cook-house, laundry, and refectory. There is a playground under some fine tamarind trees, and an adobe wall encloses, without secluding, the whole. The visitors' room is about twelve feet by eight feet, very bare, with a deal table and three chairs in it, but it was vacant, and I crossed to the large, shady, airy schoolroom, where I found the senior sister engaged in teaching, while the junior was busy in the cook-house. These ladies in eight years have never left Lahaina. Other people may think it necessary to leave its broiling heat, and seek health and recreation on the mountains, but their work has left them no leisure, and their zeal no desire, for a holiday. A very solid, careful English education is given here, as well as a thorough training in all housewifely arts, and in the more important matters of modest dress and deportment, and propriety in language. There are thirty-seven boarders, native and half-native, and mixed native and Chinese, between the ages of four and eighteen. They provide their own clothes, beds, and bedding, and I think pay forty dollars a year. The capitation grant from Government for two years was 2325 dollars. Sister Phœbe was my cicerone, and I owe her one of the pleasantest days I have spent on the islands. The elder Sister is in middle life, but though fragile-looking, has a pure complexion and a lovely countenance; the younger is scarcely middle-aged, one of the brightest, bonniest, sweetest-looking women I ever saw, with fun dancing in her eyes and round the corners of her mouth; yet the regnant expression on both faces was serenity, as though they had attained to "the love which looketh kindly, and the wisdom which looketh soberly on all things."

I never saw such a mirthful-looking set of girls. Some were cooking the dinner, some ironing, others reading English aloud; but each occupation seemed a pastime, and whenever they spoke to the Sisters they clung about them as if they were their mothers. I heard them read the Bible and an historical lesson, as well as play on a piano and sing, and they wrote some very difficult passages from dictation without any errors, and in a flowing, legible handwriting that I am disposed to envy. Their

accent and intonation were pleasing, and there was a briskness
and emulation about their style of answering questions, rarely
found in country schools with us, significant of intelligence and
good teaching. All but the younger girls spoke English as
fluently as Hawaiian. I cannot convey a notion of the blithe-
ness and independence of manner of these children. To say
that they were free and easy would be wrong; it was rather the
manner of very frolicksome daughters to very indulgent mothers
or aunts. It was a family manner rather than a school manner,
and the rule is obviously one of love. The Sisters are very
wise in adapting their discipline to the native character and
circumstances. The rigidity which is customary in similar institutions at home would be out of place, as well as fatal here,
and would ultimately lead to a rebound of a most injurious
description. Strict obedience is of course required, but the
rules are few and lenient, and there is no more pressure of discipline than in a well-ordered family. The native amusements
generally are objectionable, but Hawaiians are a dancing
people, and will dance, or else indulge in less innocent pas-
times; so the Sisters have taught them various English dances,
and I never saw anything prettier or more graceful than their
style of dancing. There is no uniform dress. The girls
wear pretty print frocks, made in the English style, and several
of them wore the hibiscus in their shining hair. Some of the
elder girls were beautiful in face as well as graceful in figure,
but there was a snaky undulation about their movements which
I never saw among Europeans. All looked bubbling over with
fun and frolic, and there was a refinement and intelligence
about their expression which contrasted favourably with that of
the ordinary female face on the islands.

There are two dormitories, excellently ventilated, with a
four-post bed, with mosquito-bars, for each girl, and the beds
were covered with those brilliant-coloured quilts in which the
natives delight, and in which they exercise considerable ingenuity as well as individuality of taste. One Sister sleeps in
each dormitory, and these highly-educated and refined women
have no place of retirement except a very plain oratory; and
having taken the vow of poverty, they have of course no possessions, none of the books, pictures, and knick-knacks wherewith others adorn their surroundings. Their whole lives, with
the exception of the time passed in the oratory, are spent with
the girls, and in visiting the afflicted at their homes, and this
through eight blazing years, with the mercury always at 80°.

The Hawaiian women have no notions of virtue as we understand it, and if there is to be any future for this race it must come through a higher morality. Consequently the removal of these girls from evil and impure surroundings, the placing them under the happiest influences in favour of purity and goodness, the forming and fostering of industrious and housewifely habits, and the raising them in their occupations and amusements above those which are natural to their race, are in themselves a noble, and in some degree, a hopeful work, but it admits of neither pause nor relaxation. Those who carry it on are truly "the lowest in the meanest task," for they have undertaken not only the superintendence of menial work (so called), but the work itself, in teaching by example and instruction the womanly industries of home. They have no society, until lately no regular Liturgical worship, and of necessity a very infrequent celebration of the Holy Communion; and they have undergone the trial which arose very naturally out of the ecclesiastical relations of the American missionaries, of being regarded as enemies, or at least dangerous interlopers, by the excellent men who had long resided on the islands as Christian teachers, and with whose views on such matters as dress and recreation their own are somewhat at variance. In the first instance, the habit they wore, their designations, the presence of Miss Sellon, the fame of whose Ritualistic tendencies had reached the islands, and their manifest connection with a section of the English Church which is regarded here with peculiar disfavour, roused a strongly antagonistic feeling regarding their work and the drift of their religious teaching. They are not connected with the " Honolulu Mission." *

I. L. B.

* It gives me pleasure to add that the Sisters have lived down this very natural distrust, and that in a subsequent residence of five months on the islands, I only heard one opinion, and that of the most favourable kind, regarding the Lahaina School, and the excellence and wisdom of the manner in which it is conducted. I have been told by many who on most points are quite out of sympathy with the Sisters, not only that their work is recognized as a most valuable agency, but that their influence has come to be regarded as among the chiefest of the blessings of Lahaina.

LETTER XVIII.

HAWAIIAN HOTEL, HONOLULU, *March 20th.*

OAHU, with its grey pinnacles, deep valleys, cool chasms,
ruddy headlands, and volcanic cones, all clothed in green by
the recent rains, looked unspeakably lovely as we landed by
sunrise in a rose-flushed atmosphere, and Honolulu, shady,
dew-bathed, and brilliant with flowers, deserved its name,
"The Paradise of the Pacific." The hotel is pleasant, and
Mrs. D.'s presence makes it sweet and home-like; but in a
very few days I have lost much of the health I gained on
Hawaii, and the "Rolling Moses" and the Rocky Mountains
can hardly come too soon. For Honolulu is truly a metropolis,
gay, hospitable, and restless, and this hotel centralizes the rest-
lessness. Visiting begins at breakfast time, when it ends I
know not, and receiving and making visits, court festivities,
entertainments given by the commissioners of the great powers,
riding parties, picnics, verandah parties, "sociables," and
luncheon and evening parties on board the ships of war, succeed each other with frightful rapidity. This is all on the surface, but beneath and better than this is a kindness which
leaves no stranger to a sense of loneliness, no want uncared
for, and no sorrow unalleviated. This, more than its beauty
and its glorious climate, makes Honolulu "Paradise" for the
many who arrive here sick and friendless. I notice that the
people are very intimate with each other, and generally address
each other by their Christian names. Very many are the descendants of the clerical and secular members of the mission,
and these, besides being naturally intimate, are further drawn
and held together by a society called "The Cousins' Society,"
the objects of which are admirable. The people take an intense interest in each other, and love each other unusually.
Possibly they hate each other as cordially when occasion offers.

It is a charming town, and the society is delightful. I wish I
were well enough to enjoy it.

For people in the early stages of consumption this climate is
perfect, owing to its equability, as also for bronchial affections.
Unlike the health resorts of the Mediterranean, Algeria, Ma-
deira, and Florida, where great summer heats or an unhealthy
season compel half-cured invalids to depart in the spring, to
return the next winter with fresh colds to begin the half-cure
process again, people can live here until they are completely
cured, as the climate is never unhealthy, and never too hot.
Though the regular trades, which blow for nine months of the
year, have not yet set in, and the mercury stands at 80°, there
is no sultriness; a sea breeze and a mountain breeze fan the
town, and the purple nights, when the stars hang out like
lamps, and the moon gives a light which is almost golden, are
cool and delicious. Roughly computed, the annual mean
temperature is 75° 55′, with a divergence in either direction of
only 7° 55′. As a general rule the temperature is cooler by four
degrees for every thousand feet of altitude, so that people can
choose their climate to suit themselves without leaving the
islands.

I am gradually learning a little of the topography of this
island and of Honolulu, but the last is very intricate. The appearance of Oahu from the sea is deceptive. It looks hardly
larger than Arran, but it is really forty-six miles long by twenty-
five broad, and is 530 square miles in extent. Diamond Hill,
or Leahi, is the most prominent object south of the town, beyond the palm groves of Waikiki. It is red and arid, except
when, as now, it is verdure-tinged by recent rains. Its height
is 760 feet, and its crater nearly as deep, but its cone is rapidly
diminishing. Some years ago, when the enormous quantity of
thirty-six inches of rain fell in one week, the degradation of
both exterior and interior was something incredible, and the
same process is being carried on slowly or rapidly at all times.
The Punchbowl, immediately behind Honolulu, is a crater of
the same kind, but of yet more brilliant colouring: so red is it
indeed, that one might suppose that its fires had just died out.
In 1786 an observer noted it as being composed of high peaks;
but atmospheric influences have reduced it to the appearance of
a single wasting tufa cone, similar to those which stud the
northern slopes of Mauna Kea. There are a number of shore
craters on the island, and six groups of tufa cones, but from
the disintegration of the lava, and the great depth of the soil

in many places, it is supposed that volcanic action ceased earlier than on Maui or Hawaii. The shores are mostly fringed with coral reefs, often half a mile in width, composed of cemented coral fragments, shells, sand, and a growing species of zoophyte. The ancient reefs are elevated thirty, forty, and even 100 feet in some places, forming barriers which have changed lagoons into solid ground. Honolulu was a bay or lagoon, protected from the sea by a coral reef a mile wide ; but the elevation of this reef twenty-five feet has furnished a site for the capital, by converting the bay into a low but beautifully situated plain.

The mountainous range behind is a rocky wall with outlying ridges, valleys of great size cutting the mountain to its core on either side, until the culminating peaks of Waiolani and Kona-huanui, 4000 feet above the sea, seem as if rent in twain to form the Nuuanu Valley. The windward side of this range is fertile, and is dotted over with rice and sugar plantations, but the leeward side has not a trace of the redundancy of the tropics, and this very barrenness gives a unique charm to the exotic beauty of Honolulu.

It is daily a fresh pleasure to stroll along the shady streets and revel among palms and bananas, to see clusters of the granadilla and night-blowing Cereus mixed with the double blue pea, tumbling over walls and fences, while the vermilion flowers of the *Ponciana Regia,* like spikes of red coral, and the flaring magenta Bougainvillea (which is not a flower at all, but an audacious freak of terminal leaves) light up the shade, and the purple-leaved Dracæna which we grow in pots for dinner-table ornament, is as common as a weed.

Besides this hotel, and the handsome but exaggerated and inappropriate Government buildings not yet finished, there are few " imposing edifices" here. The tasteful but temporary English Cathedral, the Kaiwaiaho Church, diminished once to suit a dwindled population, but already too large again; the prison, a clean, roomy building, empty in the daytime, because the convicts are sent out to labour on roads and public works; the Queen's Hospital for Curables, for which Queen Emma and her husband became mendicants in Honolulu; the Court House, a staring, unshaded building; and the Iolani Palace, almost exhaust the category. Of this last, little can be said, except that it is appropriate and proportioned to a kingdom of 56,000 souls, which is more than can be said of the income of the king, the salaries of the ministers, and some other things.

It stands in pleasure-grounds of about an acre in extent, with a fine avenue running through them, and is approached by a flight of steps which leads to a tolerably spacious hall, decorated in the European style. Portraits of Louis Philippe and his queen, presented by themselves, and of the late Admiral Thomas, adorn the walls. The Hawaiians have a profound respect for this officer's memory, as it was through him that the sovereignty of the islands was promptly restored to the native rulers, after the infamous affair of its cession to England, as represented by Lord George Paulet. There are also some ornamental vases and miniature copies of some of Thorwaldsen's works. The throne-room takes up the left wing of the palace. This unfortunately resembles a rather dreary drawing-room in London or New York, and has no distinctive features except a decorated chair, which is the Hawaiian throne. There is an Hawaiian crown also, neither grand nor costly, but this I have not seen. At present the palace is only used for state receptions and entertainments, for the king is living at his private residence of Haemoeipio, not far off.

Miss W. kindly introduced me to Queen Emma, or Kalele onalani, the widowed queen of Kamehameha IV., whom you will remember as having visited England a few years ago, when she received great attention. She has one-fourth of English blood in her veins, but her complexion is fully as dark as if she were of unmixed Hawaiian descent, and her features, though refined by education and circumstances, are also Hawaiian ; but she is a very pretty, as well as a very graceful woman. She was brought up by Dr. Rooke, an English physician here, and though educated at the American school for the children of chiefs, is very English in her leanings and sympathies, an attached member of the English Church, and an ardent supporter of the " Honolulu Mission." Socially she is very popular, and her exceeding kindness and benevolence, with her strongly national feeling as an Hawaiian, make her much beloved by the natives.

The winter palace, as her town house is called, is a large, shady abode, like an old-fashioned New England house externally, but with two deep verandahs, and the entrance is on the upper one. The lower floor seemed given up to attendants and offices, and a native woman was ironing clothes under a tree. Upstairs, the house is like a tasteful, English country house, with a pleasant English look, as if its furniture and ornaments had been gradually accumulating during a series of years, and

possessed individual histories and reminiscences, rather than as
if they had been ordered together as "plenishings" from
stores.   Indeed, it is the most English-looking house I have
seen since I left home, except Bishopscourt at Melbourne.   If
there were a bell I did not see it; and we did not ring, for the
queen received us at the door of the drawing-room, which was
open.   I had seen her before in European dress, driving a pair
of showy black horses in a stylish English phaeton; but on
this occasion she was not receiving visitors formally, and was
indulging in wearing the native *holoku*, and her black wavy hair
was left to its own devices.   She is rather below the middle
height, very young-looking for her age, which is thirty-seven,
and very graceful in her movements.   Her manner is indeed
very fascinating from a combination of unconscious dignity
with ladylike simplicity.   Her expression is sweet and gentle,
with the same look of sadness about her eyes that the king has,
but she has a brightness and archness of expression which give
a great charm to her appearance.   She has sorrowed much :
first, for the death, at the age of four, of her only child, the
Prince of Hawaii, who when dying was baptized into the
English Church by the name of Albert Edward, Queen Victoria
and the Prince of Wales being his sponsors; and secondly, for
the premature death of her husband, to whom she was much
attached.   She speaks English beautifully, only hesitating now
and then for the most correct form of expression.   She spoke a
good deal and with great pleasure of England ; and described
Venice and the emotions it excited in her so admirably, that I
should like to have heard her describe all Europe.

A few days afterwards I went to a garden party at her
house.   It was a very pretty sight, and the "everybody" of
Honolulu was there to the number of 250.   I must describe it
for the benefit of ——, who persists in thinking that coloured
royalty must necessarily be grotesque.   People arrived shortly
before sunset, and was received by Queen Emma, who sat on
the lawn, with her attendants about her, very simply dressed in
black silk.   The king, at whose entrance the band played the
national anthem, stood on another lawn, where presentations
were made by the chamberlain ; and those who were already
acquainted with him had an opportunity for a few minutes'
conversation.   He was dressed in a well-made black morning
suit, and wore the ribbon and star of the Austrian order of
Francis Joseph.   His simplicity was atoned for by the super-
lative splendour of his suite ; the governor of Oahu, and the

high chief Kalakaua, who was a rival candidate for the throne,
being conspicuously resplendent. The basis of the costume
appeared to be the Windsor uniform, but it was smothered with
epaulettes, cordons, and lace; and each dignitary has a uniform
peculiar to his office, so that the display of gold lace was prodigious. The chiefs are so raised above the common people in
height, size, and general nobility of aspect, that many have
supposed them to be of a different race; and the *alii* who
represented the dwindled order that night were certainly superb
enough in appearance to justify the supposition. Beside their
splendour and stateliness, the forty officers of the English and
American war-ships, though all in full-dress uniform, looked
decidedly insignificant; and I doubt not that the natives who
were assembled outside the garden railings in crowds were not
behind me in making invidious comparisons.

Chairs and benches were placed under the beautiful trees,
and people grouped themselves on these, and promenaded,
flirted, talked politics and gossip, or listened to the royal band,
which played at intervals, and played well. The dress of the
ladies, whether white or coloured, was both pretty and appropriate. Most of the younger women were in white, and wore
natural flowers in their hair; and many of the elder ladies wore
black or coloured silks, with lace and trains. There were
several beautiful *leis* of the gardenia, which filled all the garden
with their delicious odour. Tea and ices were handed round
on Sèvres china by footmen and pages in appropriate liveries.
What a wonderful leap from calabashes and *poi, malos* and *paus,*
to this correct and tasteful civilization ! As soon as the brief,
amber twilight of the tropics was over, the garden was suddenly
illuminated by myriads of Chinese lanterns, and the effect was
bewitching. The upper suite of rooms was thrown open for
those who preferred dancing under cover; but I think that the
greater part of the assemblage chose the shady walks and
purple night. Supper was served at eleven, and the party broke
up soon afterwards; but I must confess that, charming as it
was, I left before eight, for society makes heavier demands on
my strength than the rough, open-air life of Hawaii.

The dwindling of the race is a most pathetic subject. Here
is a sovereign chosen amidst an outburst of popular enthusiasm,
with a cabinet, a legislature, and a costly and elaborate governing machinery, sufficient in Yankee phrase to " run " an empire
of several millions, and here are only 49,000 native Hawaiians ;
and if the decrease be not arrested, in a quarter of a century

there will not be an Hawaiian to govern. The chiefs, or *alii*, are a nearly extinct order; and, with a few exceptions, those who remain are childless. In riding through Hawaii I came

A Hawaiian Lady.

everywhere upon traces of a once numerous population, where the hill slopes are now only a wilderness of guava scrub, and upon churches and school-houses all too large, while in some hamlets the voices of young children were altogether wanting. This nation, with its elaborate governmental machinery, its churches and institutions, has to me the mournful aspect of a shrivelled and wizened old man dressed in clothing much too big, the garments of his once athletic and vigorous youth. Nor can I divest myself of the idea that the laughing, flower-clad hordes of riders who make the town gay with their presence, are but like butterflies fluttering out their short lives in the sunshine,

> ". . . a wreck and residue,
> Whose only business is to perish."

The statistics on this subject are perfectly appalling. If we reduce Captain Cook's estimate of the native population by one-fourth it was 300,000 in 1779. In 1872 it was only 49,000. The first official census was in 1832, when the native population was 130,000. This makes the decrease 80,000 in forty years, or at the rate of 2000 a year, and fixes the period for the final extinction of the race in 1897, if that rate were to continue. It is a pity, for many reasons, that it is dying out. It has shown a singular aptitude for politics and civilization, and it would have been interesting to watch the development of a strictly Polynesian monarchy starting under passably fair conditions. Whites have conveyed to these shores slow but infallible destruction on the one hand, and on the other the knowledge of the life that is to come; and the rival influences of blessing and cursing have now been fifty years at work, producing results with which most reading people are familiar.

I have not heard the subject spoken of, but I should think that the decrease in the population must cause the burden of taxation to press heavily on that which remains. Kings, cabinet ministers, an army, a police, a national debt, a supreme court, and common schools, are costly luxuries or necessaries. The civil list is ludicrously out of proportion to the resources of the islands, and the heads of the four departments—Foreign Relations, Interior, Finance, and Law (Attorney-General)—receive $5000 a year each ! * Expenses and salaries have been increasing for the last thirty years. For schools alone every man between twenty-one and sixty pays a tax of two dollars annually, and there is an additional general tax for the same purpose. I suppose that there is not a better educated country in the world. Education is compulsory ; and besides the primary schools, there are a number of academies, all under Government supervision, and there are 324 teachers, or one for

* These salaries have since been cut down to $4000, and the present Legislature (1876) is contemplating a further reduction.

every twenty-seven children.   There is a Board of Education,
and Kamakau, its president, reported to the last biennial session of the legislature that out of 8931 children between the
ages of six and fifteen, 8287 were actually attending school!
Among other direct taxes, every quadruped that can be called
a horse, above two years old, pays a dollar a year, and every
dog a dollar and a half.   Does not all this sound painfully
civilized?   If the influence of the tropics has betrayed me into
rhapsody and ecstacy in earlier letters, these dry details will
turn the scale in favour of prosaic sobriety!

I have said little about Honolulu, except of its tropical
beauty.   It does not look as if it had "seen better days."   Its
wharves are well cared for, and its streets and roads are very
clean.   The retail stores are generally to be found in two long
streets which run inland, and in a splay street which crosses
both.   The upper storekeepers, with a few exceptions, are
Americans, but one street is nearly given up to Chinamen's
stores, and one of the wealthiest and most honourable merchants in the town is a Chinaman.   There is an ice factory,
and icecream is included in the daily bill of fare here, and iced
water is supplied without limit, but lately the machinery has
only worked in spasms, and the absence of ice is regarded as a
local calamity, though the water supplied from the water-
works is both cool and pure.   There are two good photo-
graphers and two booksellers.   I don't think that plate glass fronts
are yet to be seen.   Many of the storekeepers employ native
"assistants;" but the natives show little aptitude for mercantile
affairs, or indeed for the "splendid science" of money-making
generally, and in this respect contrast with the Chinamen, who,
having come here as coolies, have contrived to secure a large
share of the small traffic of the islands.   Most things are ex-
pensive, but they are good.   I have seen little of such decided
rubbish as is to be found in the cheap stores of London and
Edinburgh, except in tawdry artificial flowers.   Good black
silks are to be bought, and are as essential to the equipment of
a lady as at home.   Saddles are to be had at most of the
stores, from the elaborate Mexican and Californian saddle,
worth from 30 to 50 dollars, to a worthless imitation of the
English saddle, dear at five.   Boots and shoes, perhaps because in this climate they are a mere luxury, are frightfully dear,
and so are books, writing paper, and stationery generally; a
sheet of Bristol board, which we buy at home for 6*d.*, being
half a dollar here.   But it is quite a pleasure to make pur-

chases in the stores.   There is so much cordiality and courtesy
that, as at this hotel, the bill recedes into the background,
and the purchaser feels the indebted party.

The money is extremely puzzling.   These islands, like California, have repudiated greenbacks, and the only paper cur-
rency is a small number of treasury notes for large amounts.
The coin in circulation is gold and silver, but gold is scarce,
which is an inconvenience to people who have to carry a large
amount of money about with them.   The coinage is nominally
that of the United States, but the dollars are Mexican, or French
5 franc pieces, and people speak of " *rials,*" which have no existence here, and of " bits," a Californian slang term for $12\frac{1}{2}$
cents, a coin which to my knowledge does not exist anywhere.
A dime, or 10 cents, is the lowest coin I have seen, and copper
is not in circulation.   An envelope, a penny bottle of ink, a
pencil, a spool of thread, cost 10 cents each; postage-stamps cost
2 cents each for inter-island postage, but one must buy five of
them, and dimes slip away quickly and imperceptibly.   There
is a loss on English money, as half-a-crown only passes for a
half-dollar, sixpence for a dime, and so forth ; indeed, the
average loss seems to be about twopence in the shilling.

There are four newspapers : the *Honolulu Gazette,* the *Pacific
Commercial Advertiser, Ka Nupepa Kuokoa* (the " Independent
Press "), and a lately started spasmodic sheet, partly in English
and partly in Hawaiian, the *Nuhou* (News).*   The two first
are moral and respectable, but indulge in the American sins of
personalities and mutual vituperation.   The *Nuhou* is scurrilous
and diverting, and appears " run " with a special object, which
I have not as yet succeeded in unravelling from its pungent but
not always intelligible pages.   I think perhaps the writing in
each paper has something of the American tendency to hysteria
and convulsions, though these maladies are mild as compared
with the " real thing " in the *Alta California,* which is largely
taken here.   Besides these there are monthly sheets called *The
Friend,* the oldest paper in the Pacific, edited by good " Father
Damon," and the *Church Messenger,* edited by Bishop Willis,
partly devotional and partly devoted to the Honolulu Mission.
All our popular American and English literature is read here,
and I have hardly seen a table without " Scribner's " or " Harper's Monthly," or " Good Words."

I have lived far too much in America to feel myself a

---

* The *Nuhou* has since expired.

stranger where, as here, American influence and customs are
dominant; but the English who are in Honolulu just now, *in
transitu* from New Zealand, complain bitterly of its "Yan-
keeism," and are very far from being at home, and I doubt not
that Mr. M——, whom you will see, will not confirm my
favourable description. It is quite true that the islands are
Americanized, and with the exception of the Finance Minister,
who is a Scotchman, Americans "run" the Government and
fill the Chief Justiceship and other high offices of State. It is,
however, perfectly fair, for Americans have civilized and Christianized Hawaii-nei, and we have done little except make an
unjust and afterwards disavowed seizure of the islands.

On looking over this letter I find it an *olla podrida* of tropical
glories, royal festivities, finance matters, and odds and ends in
general. I dare say you will find it dull after my letters from
Hawaii, but there are others who will prefer its prosaic details
to Kilauea and Waimanu; and I confess that, amidst the
general lusciousness of tropical life, I myself enjoy the dryness
and tartness of statistics, and hard, uncoloured facts.

                                                    I. L. B.

LETTER XIX.

Hawaiian Women—The Honolulu Market—Annexation and Reciprocity
—A Probable Future—The "Rolling Moses."

HAWAIIAN HOTEL, HONOLULU.

MY latest news of you is five months old, and though I have
not the slightest expectation that I shall hear from you, I go up
to the roof to look out for the "Rolling Moses" with more
impatience and anxiety than those whose business journeys are
being delayed by her non-arrival. If such an unlikely thing
were to happen as that she were to bring a letter, I should be
much tempted to stay five months longer on the islands rather
than try the climate of Colorado, for I have come to feel at
home, people are so very genial, and suggest so many plans for
my future enjoyment, the islands in their physical and social
aspects are so novel and interesting, and the climate is unrivalled and restorative.

Honolulu has not yet lost the charm of novelty for me. I
am never satiated with its exotic beauties, and the sight of a
kaleidoscopic whirl of native riders is always fascinating. The
passion for riding, in a people who only learned equitation in
the last generation, is most curious. It is very curious, too, to
see women incessantly enjoying and amusing themselves in
riding, swimming, and making *leis*. They have few home ties
in the shape of children, and I fear make them fewer still by
neglecting them for the sake of riding and frolic, and man
seems rather the helpmeet than the "oppressor" of woman;
though I believe that the women have abandoned that right of
choosing their husbands, which, it is said, that they exercised
in the old days. Used to the down-trodden look and harassed,
care-worn faces of the over-worked women of the same class at
home and in the colonies, the laughing, careless faces of the
Hawaiian women have the effect upon me of a perpetual marvel.
But the expression generally has little of the courteousness,

innocence, and childishness of the negro physiognomy. The Hawaiians are a handsome people, scornful and sarcastic-looking even with their mirthfulness; and those who know them say

Natives of Honolulu.

that they are always quizzing and mimicking the *haoles*, and that they give every one a nickname founded on some personal peculiarity.

The women are free from our tasteless perversity as to colour and ornament, and have an instinct of the becoming. At first the *holoku*, which is only a full, yoke nightgown, is not attractive, but I admire it heartily now, and the sagacity of those who devised it. It conceals awkwardness, and befits grace of movement: it is fit for the climate, is equally adapted for walking and riding, and has that general appropriateness which is desirable in costume. The women have a most peculiar walk, with a swinging motion from the hip at each step, in which the shoulder sympathises. I never saw anything at all like it. It has neither the delicate shuffle of the Frenchwoman, the robust,

decided jerk of the Englishwoman, the stately glide of the
Spaniard, or the stealthiness of the squaw ; and I should know
a Hawaiian woman by it in any part of the world. A majestic
wahine with small, bare feet, a grand, swinging, deliberate gait,
hibiscus blossoms in her flowing hair, and a *lé* of yellow flowers
falling over her *holoku*, marching through these streets, has a
tragic grandeur of appearance, which makes the diminutive,
fair-skinned *haole*, tottering along hesitatingly in high-heeled
shoes, look grotesque by comparison.

On Saturday, our kind host took Mrs. D. and myself to the
market, where we saw the natives in all their glory. The
women, in squads of a dozen at a time, their Pa-ús streaming
behind them, were cantering up and down the streets, and men
and women were thronging into the market-place ; a brilliant,
laughing, joking crowd, their jaunty hats trimmed with fresh
flowers, and *leis* of the crimson *ohia* and orange *lauhala* falling
over their costumes, which were white, green, black, scarlet,
blue, and every other colour that can be dyed or imagined.
The market is a straggling, open space, with a number of
shabby stalls partially surrounding it, but really we could not
see the place for the people. There must have been 2000
there.

Some of the stalls were piled up with wonderful fish, crimson,
green, rose, blue, opaline—fish that have spent their lives in
coral groves under the warm, bright water. Some of them had
wonderful shapes too, and there was one that riveted my attention and fascinated me. It was, I thought at first, a heap,
composed of a dog fish, some limpets, and a multitude of water
snakes, and other abominable forms ; but my eyes slowly informed me of the fact, which I took in reluctantly and with
extreme disgust, that the whole formed one living monster, a
revolting compound of a large paunch with eyes, and a multitude of nervy, snaky, out reaching, twining, grasping, tentacular
arms, several feet in length, I should think, if extended, but
then lying in a crowded undulating heap ; the creature was
dying, and the iridescence was passing over what seemed to be
its body in waves of colour, such as glorify the last hour of the
dolphin. But not the colours of the rainbow could glorify this
hideous, abominable form, which ought to be left to riot in
ocean depths, with its loathsome kindred. You have read " *Les
Travailleurs du Mer*," and can imagine with what feelings I
looked upon a living Devil-fish ! The monster is much esteemed
by the natives as an article of food, and indeed is generally

relished. I have seen it on foreign tables, salted, under the name of squid.*

We passed on to beautiful creatures, the *kihi-kihi*, or sea-cock, with alternate black and yellow transverse bands on his body; the *hinalea*, like a glorified mullet, with bright green, longitudinal bands on a dark shining head, a purple body of different shapes, and a blue spotted tail with a yellow tip. The *ohua* too, a pink scaled fish, shaped like a trout; the *opukai*, beautifully striped and mottled; the mullet and flying fish as common here as mackerel at home; the *hala*, a fine pink-fleshed fish, the albicore, the bonita, the *manini* striped black and white, and many others. There was an abundance of *opilu* or limpets, also the *pipi*, a small oyster found among the coral; the *ula*, as large as a clawless lobster, but more beautiful and variegated; and turtles which were cheap and plentiful. Then there were purple-spiked sea urchins, black-spiked sea eggs or *wana*, and *ina* or eggs without spikes, and many other curiosities of the bright Pacific. It was odd to see the pearly teeth of a native meeting in some bright-coloured fish, while the tail hung out of his mouth, for they eat fish raw, and some of them were obviously at the height of epicurean enjoyment. Seaweed and fresh-water weed are much relished by Hawaiians, and there were four or five kinds for sale, all included in the term *limu*. Some of this was baked, and put up in balls weighing one pound each. There were packages of baked fish, and dried fish, and of many other things which looked uncleanly and disgusting; but no matter what the package was, the leaf of the *Ti* tree was invariably the wrapping, tied round with sennet, the coarse fibre obtained from the husk of the cocoa-nut. Fish, here, averages about ten cents. per pound, and is dearer than meat; but in many parts of the islands it is cheap and abundant.

There is a ferment going on in this kingdom, mainly got up by the sugar planters and the interests dependent on them, and two political lectures have lately been given in the large hall of the hotel in advocacy of their views; one, on annexation, by Mr. Phillips, who has something of the oratorical gift of his cousin, Wendell Phillips; and the other, on a reciprocal treaty, by Mr. Carter. Both were crowded by ladies and gentlemen,

---

* This monster is a cephalopod of the order *Dibranchiata*, and has eight flexible arms, each crowded with 120 pair of suckers, and two longer feelers about six feet in length, differing considerably from the others in form.

and the first was most enthusiastically received. Mrs. D. and I usually spend our evenings in writing and working in the verandah, or in each other's rooms; but I have become so interested in the affairs of this little state, that in spite of the mosquitos, I attended both lectures, but was not warmed into sympathy with the views of either speaker.

I daresay that some of my friends here would quarrel with my conclusions, but I will briefly give the *data* on which they are based. The census of 1872 gives the native population at 49,044 souls; of whom, 700 are lepers; and it is *decreasing* at the rate of from 1200 to 2000 a year, while the excess of native males over females on the islands is 3216. The foreign population is 5366, and it is *increasing* at the rate of 200 a year; and the number of half-castes of all nations has *increased* at the rate of 140 a year. The Chinese, who came here originally as plantation coolies, outnumber all the other nationalities together, excluding the Americans; but the Americans constitute the ruling and the monied class. Sugar is the reigning interest on the islands, and it is almost entirely in American hands. It is burdened here by the difficulty of procuring labour, and at San Francisco by a heavy import duty. There are thirty-five plantations on the islands, and there is room for fifty more. The profit, as it is, is hardly worth mentioning, and few of the planters do more than keep their heads above water. Plantations which cost $50,000 have been sold for $15,000; and others which cost $150,000 have been sold for $40,000. If the islands were annexed, and the duty taken off, many of these struggling planters would clear $50,000 a year and upwards. So, no wonder that Mr. Phillips's lecture was received with enthusiastic plaudits. It focussed all the clamour I have heard on Hawaii and elsewhere, exalted the " almighty dollar," and was savoury with the odour of coming prosperity. But he went far, very far; he has aroused a cry among the natives *" Hawaii for the Hawaiians,"* which, very likely, may breed mischief; for I am very sure that this brief civilization has not quenched the " red fire " of race; and his hint regarding the judicious disposal of the king in the event of annexation, was felt by many of the more sober whites to be highly impolitic.

The reciprocity treaty, very lucidly advocated by Mr. Carter, and which means the cession of a lagoon with a portion of circumjacent territory on this island, to the United States, for a Pacific naval station, meets with more general favour as a safer measure; but the natives are indisposed to bribe the Great

Republic to remit the sugar duties by the surrender of a square
inch of Hawaiian soil; and, from a British point of view, I
heartily sympathise with them.*   Foreign, *i.e.* American feeling
is running high upon the subject. People say that things are
so bad that something must be done, and it remains to be seen
whether natives or foreigners can exercise the strongest pressure
on the king.   I was unfavourably impressed in both lectures
by the way in which the natives and their interests were
quietly ignored, or as quietly subordinated to the sugar
interest.

It is never safe to forecast destiny; yet it seems most probable that sooner or later in this century the closing catastrophe
must come.   The more thoughtful among the natives acquiesce
helplessly and patiently in their advancing fate; but the less
intelligent, as I had some opportunity of hearing at Hilo, are
becoming restive and irritable, and may drift into something
worse if the knowledge of the annexationist views of the
foreigners is diffused among them.   Things are preparing for
change, and I think that the Americans will be wise in their
generation if they let them ripen for many years to come.
Lunalilo has a broken constitution, and probably will not live
long.   Kalakaua will probably succeed him, and "after him the
deluge," unless he leaves a suitable successor, for there are no
more chiefs with pre-eminent claims to the throne.   The feeling among the people is changing, the feudal instinct is disappearing, the old despotic line of the Kamehamehas is extinct;
and king-making by paper ballots, introduced a few months
ago, is an approximation to president-making, with the canvas-
sing, stumping, and wrangling, incidental to such a contested
election.   Annexation, or peaceful absorption, is the "manifest
destiny" of the islands, with the probable result lately most
wittily prophesied by Mark Twain in the *New York Tribune,*
but it is impious and impolitic to hasten it.   Much as I like
America, I shrink from the day when her universal political
corruption and her unrivalled political immorality shall be
naturalised on Hawaii-nei. . . . Sunday evening.   The "Roll-

---

* The native feeling on this subject proved strong 'enough to coerce
Lunalilo and the Cabinet, and the idea of ceding Pearl River was abandoned.   In 1875 King Kalakaua and Chancellor Allen visited Washington,
and a Reciprocity Treaty with America was negociated on the simple
principle of Free Trade.   It has not yet come into operation, however, as
the United States revenue laws, necessary to make it effective, have not
been enacted, and the Hawaiian planters are still in a state of suspense.—
I. L. B. 1876.

ing Moses" is in, and Sabbatic quiet has given place to general excitement. People thought they heard her steaming in at 4 a.m., and got up in great agitation. Her guns fired during morning service, and I doubt whether I or any other person heard another word of the sermon. The first batch of letters for the hotel came, but none for me; the second, none for me; and I had gone to my room in despair, when some one tossed a large package in at my verandah door, and to my infinite joy I found that one of my benign fellow-passengers in the *Nevada,* had taken the responsibility of getting my letters at San Francisco and forwarding them here. I don't know how to be grateful enough to the good man. With such late and good news, everything seems bright; and I have at once decided to take the first schooner for the leeward group, and remain four months longer on the islands.

L. L. B.

LETTER XX.

KOLOA, KAUAI, *March 23rd.*

I AM spending a few days on some quaint old mission pre-mises, and the "guest house," where I am lodged, is an adobe house, with walls two feet thick, and a very thick grass roof comes down six feet all round to shade the windows. It is itself shaded by date palms and algarobas, and is surrounded by hibiscus, oleanders, and the *datura arborea* (?), which at night fill the air with sweetness. I am the only guest, and the solitude of the guest house in which I am writing is most refreshing to tired nerves. There is not a sound but the rust-ling of trees.

The first event to record is that the trade winds have set in, and though they may yet yield once or twice to the *kona*, they will soon be firmly established for nine months. They are not soft airs as I supposed, but riotous, rollicking breezes, which keep up a constant clamour, blowing the trees about, slamming doors, taking liberties with papers, making themselves heard and felt everywhere, flecking the blue Pacific with foam, lower-ing the mercury three degrees, bringing new health and vigour with them,—wholesome, cheery, frolicsome north-easters. They brought me here from Oahu in eighteen hours, for which I thank them heartily.

You will think me a Sybarite for howling about those eighteen hours of running to leeward, when the residents of Kauai, if they have to go to Honolulu in the intervals between the quarterly trips of the *Kilauea*, have to spend from three to nine days in beating to windward. These inter-island voyages of extreme detention, rolling on a lazy swell in tropical heat, or beating for days against the strong trades without shelter from the sun, and without anything that could be called accommoda-tion, were among the inevitable hardships to which the missionaries' wives and children were exposed in every migration for nearly forty years.

When I reached the wharf at Honolulu the sight of the *Jenny*, the small sixty-ton schooner by which I was to travel, nearly made me give up this pleasant plan, so small she looked, and so cumbered with natives and their accompaniments of mats, dogs, and calabashes of *poi*. But she is clean, and as sweet as a boat can be which carries through the tropics cattle, hides, sugar, and molasses. She is very low in the water, her deck is the real "fisherman's walk, two steps and overboard ;" and on this occasion was occupied solely by natives. The Attorney-General and Mrs. Judd were to have been my fellow voyagers, but my disappointment at their non-appearance was considerably mitigated by the fact that there was not stowage room for more than one white passenger ! Mrs. Dexter pitied me heartily, for it made her quite ill to look down the cabin hatch; but I convinced her that no inconveniences are legitimate subjects for sympathy which are endured in the pursuit of pleasure. There was just room on deck for me to sit on a box, and the obliging, gentlemanly master, who, with his son and myself, were the only whites on board, sat on the taffrail.

The *Jenny* spread her white duck sails, glided gracefully away from the wharf, and bounded through the coral reef; the red sunlight faded, the stars came out, the Honolulu light went down in the distance, and in two hours the little craft was out of sight of land on the broad, crisp Pacific. It was so chilly, that after admiring as long as I could, I dived into the cabin, a mere den, with a table, and a berth on each side, in one of which I lay down, and the other was alternately occupied by the captain and his son. But limited as I thought it, boards have been placed across on some occasions, and eleven whites have been packed into a space six feet by eight ! The heat and suffocation were nearly intolerable, the black flies swarmed, the mosquitos were countless and vicious, the fleas agile beyond anything, and the cockroaches gigantic. Some of the finer cargo was in the cabin, and large rats, only too visible by the light of a swinging lamp, were assailing it, and one with a portentous tail ran over my berth more than once, producing a *stampede* among the cockroaches each time. I have seldom spent a more miserable night, though there was the extreme satisfaction of knowing that every inch of canvas was drawing.

Towards morning the short jerking motion of a ship close hauled, made me know that we were standing in for the land, and at daylight we anchored in Koloa Roads. The view is a pleasant one. The rains have been abundant, and the land, which here rises rather gradually from the sea, is dotted with houses, abounds in signs of cultivation, and then spreads up into a rolling country between precipitous ranges of mountains. The hills look something like those of Oahu, but their wonderful greenness denotes a cooler climate and more copious rains, also their slopes and valleys are densely wooded, and Kauai obviously has its characteristic features, one of which must certainly be a superabundance of that most unsightly cactus, the prickly pear, to which the motto *nemo me impune lacessit* most literally applies.

I had not time to tell you before that this trip to Kauai was hastily arranged for me by several of my Honolulu friends, some of whom gave me letters of introduction, while others wrote forewarning their friends of my arrival. I am often reminded of Hazael's question, "Is thy servant a dog that he should do this thing?" There is no inn or boarding house on the island, and I had hitherto believed that I could not be concussed into following the usual custom whereby a traveller throws himself on the hospitality of the residents. Yet, under the influence of Honolulu persuasions, I am doing this very thing, but with an amount of *mauvaise honte* and trepidation, which I will not voluntarily undergo again.

My first introduction was to Mrs. Smith, wife of a secular member of the Mission, and it requested her to find means of forwarding me a distance of twenty-three miles. Her son was at the landing with a buggy, a most unpleasant index of the existence of carriage roads, and brought me here ; and Mrs. Smith most courteously met me at the door. When I presented my letter I felt like a thief detected in a first offence, but I was at once made welcome, and my kind hosts insist on my remaining with them for some days. Their house is a pretty old-fashioned looking tropical dwelling, much shaded by exotics, and the parlour is homelike with new books. There are two sons and two daughters at home, all, as well as their parents, interesting themselves assiduously in the welfare of the natives. Six bright-looking native girls are receiving an industrial training in the house. Yesterday being Sunday, the young people taught a Sunday school twice, besides attending the native church, an act of respect to Divine service in Hawaiian which always has an influence on the native attendance.

We have had some beautiful rides in the neighbourhood. It is a wild, lonely, picturesque coast, and the Pacific moans along it, casting itself on it in heavy surges, with a singularly dreary sound. There are some very fine specimens of the phenomena called "blow-holes" on the shore, not like the "spouting cave" at Iona, however. We spent a long time in. watching the action of one, though not the finest. At half tide this "spouting horn" throws up a column of water over sixty feet in height from a very small orifice, and the effect of the compressed air rushing through a crevice near it, sometimes with groans and shrieks, and at others with a hollow roar like the warning fog-horn on a coast, is magnificent, when, as to-day, there is a heavy swell on the coast.

Kauai is much out of the island world, owing to the infrequent visits of the *Kilauea*, but really it is only twelve hours by steam from the capital. Strangers visit it seldom, as it has no active volcano like Hawaii, or colossal crater like Maui, or anything sensational of any kind. It is called the "Garden Island," and has no great wastes of black lava and red ash like its neighbours. It is queerly shaped, almost circular, with a diameter of from twenty-eight to thirty miles, and its area is about 500 square miles. Waialeale, its highest mountain, is about 6000 feet high, but little is known of it, for it is swampy and dangerous, and a part of it is a forest-covered and little explored table-land, terminating on the sea in a range of perpendicular precipices 2000 feet in depth, so steep, it is said, that a wild cat could not get round them. Owing to these, and the virtual inaccessibility of a large region behind them, no one can travel round the island by land, and small as it is, very little seems to be known of portions of its area.

Kauai has apparently two centres of formation, and its mountains are thickly dotted with craters. The age and density of the vegetation within and without those in this Koloa district, indicate a very long cessation from volcanic action. It is truly an oddly contrived island. An elevated rolling region, park-like, liberally ornamented with clumps of *ohia, lauhala, hau,* (hibiscus) and *koa,* and intersected with gullies full of large eugenias, lies outside the mountain spurs behind Koloa. It is only the tropical trees, specially the *lauhala* or "screw pine," the whimsical shapes of outlying ridges, which now and then

lie like the leaves in a book, and the strange forms of extinct
craters, which distinguish it from some of our most beautiful
park scenery, such as Windsor Great Park or Belvoir. It is a
soft tranquil beauty, and a tolerable road which owes little
enough to art, increases the likeness to the sweet home
scenery of England. In this part of the island the ground
seems devoid of stones, and the grass is as fine and smooth as
a race course.

The latest traces of volcanic action are found here. From
the Koloa Ridge to, and into the sea, a barren uneven surface of *pahoehoe* extends, often bulged up in immense bubbles,
some of which have partially burst, leaving caverns, one of
which, near the shore, is paved with the ancient coral reef!

The valleys of Kauai are long, and widen to the sea, and
their dark rich soil is often ten feet deep. On the windward
side the rivers are very numerous and picturesque. Between
the strong winds and the lightness of the soil, I should think
that like some parts of the Highlands, " it would take a shower
every day." The leeward side, quite close to the sea, is flushed
and nearly barren, but there is very little of this desert region.
Kauai is less legible in its formation than the other islands.
Its mountains, from their impenetrable forests, dangerous
breaks, and swampiness, are difficult of access, and its ridges
are said to be more utterly irregular, its lavas more decomposed, and its natural sections more completely smothered
under a profuse vegetation than those of any other island in
the tropical Pacific. Geologists suppose, from the degradation of its ridges, and the absence of any recent volcanic products, that it is the oldest of the group, but so far as I have
read, none of them venture to conjecture how many ages it has
taken to convert its hard basalt into the rich soil which now
sustains trees of enormous size. If this theory be correct, the
volcanoes must have gone on dying out from west to east, and
from north to south, till only *Kilauea* remains, and its ener-
gies appear to be declining. The central mountain of this
island is built of a heavy ferruginous basalt, but the shore
ridges contain less iron, are more porous, and vary in
their structure from a compact phonolite, to a ponderous
basalt.

The population of Kauai is a widely scattered one of 4900,
and as it is an out of the world region the people are probably
better, and less sophisticated. They are accounted rustics, or
" pagans," in the classical sense, elsewhere. Horses are good

and very cheap, and the natives of both sexes are most expert riders. Among their feats, are picking up small coins from the ground while going at full gallop, or while riding at the same speed wringing off the heads of unfortunate fowls, whose bodies are buried in the earth.

There are very few foreigners, and they appear on the whole a good set, and very friendly among each other. Many of them are actively interested in promoting the improvement of the natives, but it is uphill work, and ill-rewarded, at least on earth. The four sugar plantations employ a good deal of Chinese labour, and I fear that the Chinamen are stealthily tempting the Hawaiians to smoke opium.

All the world over, however far behind aborigines are in the useful arts, they exercise a singular ingenuity in devising means for intoxicating and stupefying themselves. On these islands distillation is illegal, and a foreigner is liable to conviction and punishment for giving spirits to a native Hawaiian, yet the natives contrive to distil very intoxicating drinks, specially from the root of the *ti* tree, and as the spirit is unrectified it is both fiery and unwholesome. Licences to sell spirits are confined to the capital. In spite of the notoriously bad effect of alcohol in the tropics, people drink hard, and the number of deaths which can be distinctly traced to spirit drinking is startling.

The prohibition on selling liquor to natives is the subject of incessant discussions and "interpellations" in the national legislature. Probably all the natives agree in regarding it as a badge of the "inferiority of colour;" but I have been told generally that the most intelligent and thoughtful among them are in favour of its continuance, on the ground that if additional facilities for drinking were afforded, the decrease in the population would be accelerated. In the printed "Parliamentary Proceedings," I see that petitions are constantly presented praying that the distillation of spirits may be declared free, while a few are in favour of "total prohibition." Another prayer is "that Hawaiians may have the same privileges as white people in buying and drinking spirituous liquors."

A bill to repeal the invidious distinction was brought into the legislature not long since; but the influence of the descendants of the missionaries and of an influential part of the white community is so strongly against spirit drinking, as well as against the sale of drink to the natives, that the law remains on the Statute-book.

The tune in which it was discussed is well indicated by the language of Kalakaua, Lunalilo's rival : " The restrictions imposed by this law do the people no good, but rather harm ; for instead of inculcating the principles of honour, they teach them to steal behind the bar, the stable, and the closet, where they may be sheltered from the eyes of the law.   The heavy licence imposed on the liquor dealers, and the prohibition against selling to the natives are an infringement of our civil rights, binding not only the purchaser but the dealer against acquiring and possessing property.   Then, Mr. President, I ask, where lies virtue, where lies justice ?   Not in those that bind the liberty of this people, by refusing them the privilege that they now crave, of drinking spirituous liquors without restriction.   Will you by persisting that this law remain in force make us a nation of hypocrites ? or will you repeal it, that honour and virtue may for once be yours, O Hawaii."   A committee of the Assembly, in reporting on the question of the prohibition of the sale of intoxicants to anybody, through its chairman, Mr. Carter, stated, " Experience teaches that such prohibition could not be enforced without a strong public sentiment to indorse it, and such a sentiment does not prevail in this community, as is evidenced by the fact that the sale of intoxicating drinks to natives is largely practised in defiance of law and the executive, and that the manufacture of intoxicating drinks, though prohibited, is carried on in every district of the kingdom."   So the most important question agitated in every country ruled or colonised by Anglo-Saxons, is also here astir.

I was led to this digression by seeing, for the first time, some very fine plants of the *Piper methysticum.*   This is *awa,* truly a " plant of renown " throughout Polynesia.   Strange tales are told of it.   It is said to produce profound sleep, with visions more enchanting than those of opium or hasheesh, and that its repetition, instead of being deleterious, is harmless and even wholesome.   Its sale is prohibited, except on the production of evidence that it has been prescribed as a drug.   Nevertheless no law on the islands is so grossly violated.   It is easy to *give* it, and easy to grow it, or dig it up in the woods, so that, in spite of the legal restrictions, it is used to an enormous extent.   It was proposed absolutely to prohibit the sale of it though the sum paid for the licence is no inconsiderable item in the revenue of a kingdom, which, like many others, is experiencing the difficulty of " making both ends meet ; " but the

committee which sat upon the subject reported "that such
prohibition is not practicable, unless its growth and cultivation
are prevented. So long as public sentiment permits the open
violation of the existing laws regulating its sale without rebuke,
so long will it be of little use to attempt prohibition." One
cannot be a day on the islands without hearing wonderful
stories about *awa;* and its use is defended by some who are
strongly opposed to the use as well as abuse of intoxicants.
People who like "The Earl and the Doctor" delight themselves in the strongly sensuous element which pervades Polynesian life, delight themselves too, in contemplating the
preparation and results of the *awa* beverage ; but both are to
me extremely disgusting, and I cannot believe that any drink,
which stupefies the senses, and deprives a human being of the
power to exercise reason and will, is anything but hurtful to the
moral nature.

While passing the Navigator group, one of my fellow-
passengers, who had been for some time in Tutuila, described the preparation of *awa* poetically, the root "being
masticated by the pearly teeth of flower-clad maidens ;" but
I was an accidental witness of a nocturnal "*awa* drinking"
on Hawaii, and saw nothing but very plain prose. I feel as if
I must approach the subject mysteriously. I had no time to
tell you of the circumstance when it occurred, when also I
was completely ignorant that it was an illegal affair ; and now
with a sort of "guilty knowledge" I tremble to relate what I
saw, and to divulge that though I could not touch the beverage,
I tasted the root, which has an acrid, pungent taste, something
like horse-radish, with an aromatic flavour in addition, and I
can imagine that the acquired taste for it must, like other
acquired tastes, be perfectly irresistible, even without the
additional gratification of the results which follow its exercise.

In the particular instance which I saw, two girls who were
not beautiful, and an old man who would have been hideous
but for a set of sound, regular teeth, were sitting on the ground
masticating the *awa* root, the process being contemplated with
extreme interest by a number of adults. When, by careful
chewing, they had reduced the root to a pulpy consistence,
they tossed it into a large calabash, and relieved their mouths
of superfluous saliva before preparing a fresh mouthful. This
went on till a considerable quantity was provided, and then
water was added, and the mass was kneaded and stirred with
the hands till it looked like soap suds. It was then strained ;

and after more water had been added it was poured into cocoa-
nut calabashes, and handed round.   Its appearance eventually
was like weak, frothy coffee and milk.   The appearance of
purely animal gratification on the faces of those who drank it,
instead of being poetic, was of the low, gross earth.   Heads
thrown back, lips parted with a feeble, sensual smile, eyes hazy
and unfocussed, arms folded on the breast, and the mental
faculties numbed and sliding out of reach.

Those who drink it pass through the stage of idiocy into a
deep sleep, which it is said can be reproduced once without
an extra dose, by bathing in cold water.   Confirmed *awa*
drinkers might be mistaken for lepers, for they are covered
with whitish scales, and have inflamed eyes and a leathery skin,
for the epidermis is thickened and whitened, and eventually
peels off.   The habit has been adopted by not a few whites,
especially on Hawaii, though, of course, to a certain extent
clandestinely.   *Awa* is taken also as a medicine, and was
supposed to be a certain cure for corpulence.

The root and base of the stem are the parts used, and it is
best when these are fresh.   It seems to exercise a powerful
fascination, and to be loved and glorified as whisky is in
Scotland, and wine in southern Europe.   In some of the other
islands of Polynesia, on festive occasions, when the chewed
root is placed in the calabash, and the water is poured on, the
whole assemblage sings appropriate songs in its praise ; and
this is kept up until the decoction has been strained to its
dregs.   But here, as the using it as a beverage is an illicit process, a great mystery attends it.   It is said that *awa* drinking
is again on the increase, and with the illicit distillation of
unwholesome spirits, the illicit sale of imported spirits and the
opium smoking, the consumption of stimulants and narcotics
on the islands is very considerable.*

To turn from drink to climate.   It is strange that with such
a heavy rainfall, dwellings built on the ground and never dried
by fires should be so perfectly free from damp as they are.   On
seeing the houses here and in Honolulu, buried away in dense
foliage, my first thought was, " how lovely in summer, but how
unendurably damp in winter," forgetting that I arrived in the
nominal winter, and that it is really summer all the year.   Lest
you should think that I am exaggerating the charms of the

---

* According to the revenue returns for the biennial period ending March
31, 1874, the revenue derived from *awa* was over $9000, and that from
opium over $46,000.

climate, I copy a sentence from a speech made by Kame-hameha IV., at the opening of an Hawaiian agricultural society :—

"Who ever heard of winter on our shores? Where among us shall we find the numberless drawbacks which, in less favoured countries, the labourer has to contend with? They have no place in our beautiful group, which rests like a water lily on the swelling bosom of the Pacific. The heaven is tranquil above our heads, and the sun keeps his jealous eye upon us every day, while his rays are so tempered that they never wither prematurely what they have warmed into life."* The kindness of my hosts is quite overwhelming. They will not hear of my buying a horse, but insist on my taking away with me the one which I have been riding since I came, the best I have ridden on the islands, surefooted, fast, easy, and ambitious. I have complete sympathy with the passion which the natives have for riding. Horses are abundant and cheap on Kauai: a fairly good one can be bought for $20. I think every child possesses one. Indeed the horses seem to out-number the people.

The eight native girls who are being trained and educated here as a "family school" have their horses, and go out to ride as English children go for a romp into a play-ground. Yesterday Mrs. S. said, "Now, girls, get the horses," and soon two little creatures of eight and ten came galloping up on two spirited animals. They had not only caught and bridled them, but had put on the complicated Mexican saddles as securely as if men had done it ; and I got a lesson from them in making the Mexican knot with the thong which secures the cinch, which will make me independent henceforward.

These children can all speak English, and their remarks are most original and amusing. They have not a particle of

---

* The following paragraph from Dr. Rupert Anderson's sober-minded book on the Sandwich Islands fully bears out the king's remarks :—" The islands all lie within the range of the trade winds, which blow with great regularity nine months of the year, and on the leeward side, where their course is obstructed by mountains, there are regular land and sea breezes. The weather at all seasons is delightful, the sky usually cloudless, the atmosphere clear and bracing. Nothing can exceed the soft brilliancy of the moonlight nights. Thunderstorms are rare and light in their nature. Hurricanes are unknown. The general temperature is the nearest in the world to that point regarded by physiologists as most conducive to health and longevity. By ascending the mountains any desirable degree of temperature may be obtained."

respect of manner, as we understand it, but seem very docile. They are naïve and fascinating in their manners, and the most joyous children I ever saw. When they are not at their lessons, or household occupations, they are dancing on stilts, acting plays of their own invention, riding or bathing, and they laugh all day long. Mrs. S. has trained nearly seventy since she has been here. If there were nothing else they see family life in a pure and happy form, which must in itself be a moral training, and by dint of untiring watchfulness they are kept aloof from the corrupt native associations. Indeed they are not allowed to have any intercourse with natives, for, according to one of the missionaries who has spent many years on the islands: " None know or can conceive without personal observation the nameless taint that pervades the whole garrulous talk and gregarious life of all heathen peoples, and above which our poor Hawaiian friends have not yet risen." Of this universal impurity of speech every one speaks in the strongest terms, and careful white parents not only seclude their children in early years from unrestrained intercourse with the natives, but prevent them from acquiring the Hawaiian tongue. In this respect the training of native girls involves a degree of patient watchfulness which must at times press heavily on those who undertake it, as the carefulness of years might fail of its result, if it were intermitted for one afternoon.

I. L. B.

LETTER XXI.

MAKAUELI, KAUAI.

AFTER my letters from Hawaii, and their narratives of
volcanoes, freshets, and out of the world valleys, you will think
my present letters dull, so I must begin this one pleasantly,
by telling you that though I have no stirring adventures to
relate, I am enjoying myself and improving again in health,
and that the people are hospitable, genial, and cultivated, and
that Kauai, though altogether different from Hawaii, has an
extreme beauty altogether its own, which wins one's love, though
it does not startle one into admiration like that of the Hawaiian
gulches. Is it because that, though the magic of novelty is
over it, there is a perpetual undercurrent of home resemblance?
The dash of its musical waters might be in Cumberland; its
swelling uplands, with their clumps of tree, might be in Kent;
and then again, steep, broken, wooded ridges, with glades of
grass, suggest the Val Moutiers; and broader sweeps of mountain outline, the finest scenery of the Alleghanies.

But yet the very things which have a certain tenderness of
familiarity, are in a foreign setting. The great expanse of
restful sea, so faintly blue all day, and so faintly red in the late
afternoon, is like no other ocean in its unutterable peace; and
this joyous, riotous trade-wind, which rustles the trees all day,
and falls asleep at night, and cools the air, seems to come from
some widely different laboratory than that in which our vicious
east winds, and damp west winds, and piercing north winds,
and suffocating south winds are concocted. Here one cannot
ride "into the teeth of a north-easter," for such the trade-wind
really is, without feeling at once invigorated, and wrapped in

an atmosphere of balm. It is not here so tropical looking as
in Hawaii, and though there are not the frightful volcanic
wildernesses which make a thirsty solitude in the centre of that
island, neither are there those bursts of tropical luxuriance
which make every gulch an epitome of Paradise : I really cannot define the difference, for here, as there, palms glass themselves in still waters, bananas flourish, and the forests are green
with ferns.

We took three days for our journey of twenty-three miles from
Koloa, the we, consisting of Mrs. ——, the widow of an early
missionary teacher, venerable in years and character, a native
boy of ten years old, her squire, a second Kaluna, without
Kaluna's good qualities, and myself. Mrs. —— is not a bold
horsewoman, and preferred to keep to a foot's pace, which
fretted my ambitious animal, whose innocent antics alarmed her
in turn. We only rode seven miles the first day, through a
park-like region, very like Western Wisconsin, and just like
what I expected and failed to find in New Zealand. Grass-
land much tumbled about, the turf very fine and green, dotted
over with clumps and single trees, with picturesque, rocky
hills, deeply cleft by water-courses were on our right, and on
our left the green slopes blended with the flushed, stony soil
near the sea, on which indigo and various compositæ are the
chief vegetation. It was hot, but among the hills on our right,
cool clouds were coming down in frequent showers, and the
white foam of cascades gleamed among the *ohias*, whose dark
foliage at a distance has almost the look of pine woods.

Our first halting place was one of the prettiest places I ever
saw, a buff frame-house, with a deep verandah festooned with
passion flowers, two or three guest houses, also bright with
trailers, scattered about under the trees near it, a pretty
garden, a background of grey, rocky hills cool with woods
and ravines, and over all the vicinity, that air of exquisite
trimness which is artificially produced in England, but is
natural here.

Kaluna the Second soon showed symptoms of being troublesome. The native servants were away, and he was dull, and
for that I pitied him. He asked leave to go back to Koloa for
a " sleeping tapa," which was refused, and either out of spite
or carelessness, instead of fastening the horses into the pasture,
he let them go, and the following morning when we were ready
for our journey they were lost. Then he borrowed a horse,
and late in the afternoon returned with the four animals,

all white with foam and dust, and this escapade detained
us another night. Subsequently, after disobeying orders, he
lost his horse, which was a borrowed one, deserted his mistress,
and absconded !

The slopes over which we travelled were red, hot, and stony,
cleft in one place however, by a green, fertile valley, full of
rice and *kalo* patches, and native houses, with a broad river,
the Hanapépé, flowing quietly down the middle, which we
forded near the sea, where it was half-way up my horse's sides.
After plodding all day over stony soil in the changeless sunshine, as the shadows lengthened, we turned directly up
towards the mountains and began a two hours' ascent. It was
delicious. They were so cool, so green, so varied, their grey
pinnacles so splintered, their precipices so abrupt, their ravines
so dark and deep, and their lower slopes covered with the
greenest and finest grass ; then dark *ohias* rose singly, then in
twos and threes, and finally mixed in dense forest masses, with
the pea-green of the *kukui.*

It became yet lovelier as the track wound through deep
wooded ravines, or snaked along the narrow tops of spine-
like ridges ; the air became cooler, damper, and more like
elixir, till at a height of 1500 feet we came upon Makaueli,
ideally situated upon an unequalled natural plateau, a house of
patriarchial size for the islands, with a verandah festooned with
roses, fuchsias, the water lemon, and other passion flowers, and
with a large guest-house attached. It stands on a natural
lawn, with abrupt slopes, sprinkled with orange trees burdened
with fruit, *ohias*, and hibiscus. From the back verandah the
forest-covered mountains rise, and in front a deep ravine
widens to the grassy slopes below and the lonely Pacific,—as
I write, a golden sea, on which the island of Niihau, eighteen
miles distant, floats like an amethyst.

The solitude is perfect. Except the " quarters " at the back,
I think there is not a house, native or foreign, within six miles,
though there are several hundred natives on the property.
Birds sing in the morning, and the trees rustle throughout the
day ; but in the cool evenings the air is perfectly still, and the
trickle of a stream is the only sound.

The house has the striking novelty of a chimney, and there
is a fire all day long in the dining-room.

I must now say a little about my hosts and try to give you
some idea of them. I heard their history from Mr. Damon,
and thought it too strange to be altogether true until it was

confirmed by themselves.* The venerable lady at the head of the house emigrated from Scotland to New Zealand many years ago, where her husband was unfortunately drowned, and she being left to bring up a large family, and manage a large property, was equally successful with both. Her great ambition was to keep her family together, something on the old patriarchal system ; and when her children grew up, and it seemed as if even their very extensive New Zealand property was not large enough for them, she sold it, and embarking her family and movable possessions on board a clipper-ship, owned and commanded by one of her sons-in-law, they sailed through the Pacific in search of a home where they could remain together.

They were strongly tempted by Tahiti, but some reasons having decided them against it, they sailed northwards and put into Honolulu. Mr. Damon, who was seaman's chaplain, on going down to the wharf one day, was surprised to find their trim barque, with this large family party on board, with a beautiful and brilliant old lady at his head, books, pictures, work, and all that could add refinement to a floating home, about them, and cattle and sheep of valuable breeds in pens on deck. They then sailed for British Columbia, but were much disappointed with it, and in three months they reappeared at Honolulu, much at a loss regarding their future prospects.

The island of Niihau was then for sale, and in a very short time they purchased it of Kamehameha V. for a ridiculously low price, and taking their wooden houses with them, established themselves for seven years. It is truly isolated, both by a heavy surf and a disagreeable sea-passage, and they afterwards bought this beautiful and extensive property, made a road, and built the house. Only the second son and his wife live now on Niihau, where they are the only white residents among 350 natives. It has an area of 70,000 acres, and could sustain a far larger number of sheep than the 20,000 now upon it. It is said that the transfer of the island involved some hardships, owing to a number of the natives having neglected to legalise their claims to their *kuleanas,* but the present possessors have made themselves thoroughly acquainted with the language, and take the warmest interest in the island

---

* These circumstances are well-known throughout the islands, and with the omission of some personal details, there is nothing which may not be known by a larger public.

population. Niihau is famous for its very fine mats, and for
necklaces of shells six yards long, as well as for the extreme
beauty and variety of the shells which are found there.

The household here consists first and foremost of its head,
Mrs. ――, a lady of the old Scotch type, very talented, bright,
humorous, charming, with a definite character which impresses
its force upon everybody ; beautiful in her old age, disdaining
that servile conformity to prevailing fashion which makes many
old people at once ugly and contemptible : speaking English
with a slight, old-fashioned, refined Scotch accent, which gives
naïveté to everything she says ; up to the latest novelty in
theology and politics : devoted to her children and grandchildren, the life of the family, and though upwards of seventy,
the first to rise, and the last to retire in the house. She was
away when I came, but some days afterwards rode up on horseback, in a large, drawn silk bonnet, which she rarely lays aside,
as light in her figure and step as a young girl, looking as if she
had walked out of an old picture, or one of Dean Ramsay's
books.

Then there are her eldest son, a bachelor, two widowed
daughters with six children between them, three of whom are
grown up young men, and a tutor, a young Prussian officer,
who was on Maximilian's staff up to the time of the Queretaro
disaster, and is still suffering from Mexican barbarities. The
remaining daughter is married to a Norwegian gentleman, who
owns and resides on the next property. So the family is
together, and the property is large enough to give scope to the
grandchildren as they require it.

They are thoroughly Hawaiianised. The young people all
speak Hawaiian as easily as English, and the three young men,
who are superb young fellows, about six feet high, not only
emulate the natives in feats of horsemanship, such as throwing
the lasso, and picking up a coin while going at full gallop,
but are surf-board riders, an art which it has been said to be
impossible for foreigners to acquire.

The natives on Niihau and in this part of Kauai, call
Mrs. ―― "Mama." Their rent seems to consist in giving
one or more days' service in a month, so it is a revival of
the old feudality. In order to patronise native labour, my
hosts dispense with a Chinese, and employ a native cook,
and native women come in and profess to do some of the
housework, but it is a very troublesome arrangement, and
ends in the ladies doing all the finer cooking, and superin-

tending the coarser, setting the table, trimming the lamps, cutting out and "fixing" all the needlework, besides planning the indoor and outdoor work which the natives are supposed to do. Having related their proficiency in domestic duties, must add that they are splendid horsewomen, one of them an excellent shot, and the other has enough practical knowledge of seamanship, as well as navigation, to enable her to take a ship round the world ! It is a busy life, owing to the large number of natives daily employed, and the necessity of looking after the native *lunas*, or overseers. Dr. Smith at Koloa, twenty-two miles off, is the only doctor on the island, and the natives resort to this house in great numbers for advice and medicine in their many ailments. It is much such a life as people lead at Raasay, Applecross, or some other remote Highland place, only that people who come to visit here, unless they ride twenty-two miles, must come to the coast in the *Jenny* instead of being conveyed by one of David Hutcheson's luxurious steamers.

We were sitting in the library one morning when Mr. M., of Timaru, N.Z., rode up with an introduction, and was of course cordially welcomed. He goes on to England, where you will doubtless cross-question him concerning my statements. During his visit a large party of us made a delightful expedition to the Hanapépé Falls, one of the "lions" of Kauai. It is often considered too "rough" for ladies, and when Mrs. —— and I said we were going, I saw Mr. M. look as if he thought we should be a dependent nuisance ; I was amused afterwards with his surprise at Mrs. ——'s courageous horsemanship, and at his obvious confusion as to whether he should help us, which question he wisely decided in the negative.

If "happiness is atmosphere," we were happy. The day was brilliant, and as cool as early June at home, but the sweet, joyous trade-wind could not be brewed elsewhere than on the Pacific. The scenery was glorious, and mountains, trees, frolicsome water, and scarlet birds, all rioted as if in conscious happiness. Existence was a luxury, and reckless riding a mere outcome of the animal spirits of horses and riders, and the *thud* of the shoeless feet as the horses galloped over the soft grass was sweeter than music. I could hardly hold my horse at all, and down hills as steep as the east side of Arthur's Seat, over knife-like ridges too narrow for two to ride abreast, and along side-tracks only a foot wide, we rode at full gallop, till we pulled up at the top of a descent of 2,000 feet with a broad, rapid river at its feet, emerging from between colossal walls of rock to girdle a natural lawn of the bright *manienie* grass. There had been a "drive" of horses, and numbers of these, with their picturesque saddles, were picketed there, while their yet more picturesque, scarlet-shirted riders lounged in the sun.

It was a difficult two hours' ride, from thence to the Falls, worthy of Hawaii, and since my adventures in the Hilo gulches I cannot cross running water without feeling an amount of nervousness which I can conceal, but cannot reason myself out of. In going and returning, we forded the broad, rugged river twenty-six times, always in water up to my horse's girths, and the bottom was so rocky and full of holes, and the torrent so impetuous, that the animals floundered badly and evidently disliked the whole affair. Once it had been possible to ride along the edge, but the river had torn away what there was of margin in a freshet, so that we had to cross perpetually, to attain the rough, boulder-strewn strips which lay between the cliffs and itself. Sometimes we rode over roundish boulders like those on the top of Ben Cruachan, or like those of the landing at Iona, and most of those under the rush of the bright, foaming water were covered with a silky, green weed, on which the horses slipped alarmingly. My companions always took the lead, and by the time that each of their horses had struggled, slipped, and floundered in and out of holes, and breasted and leapt up steep banks, I was ready to echo Mr. M.'s exclamation regarding Mrs. ——, "I never saw such riding; I never saw ladies with such nerve." I certainly never saw people encounter such difficulties for the sake of scenery. Generally, a fall would be regarded as practically inaccessible which could only be approached in such a way.

I will not inflict another description of similar scenery upon you, but this, though perhaps exceeding all others in beauty, is not only a type, perhaps the finest type, of a species of *cañon* very common on these islands, but is also so interesting geologically that you must tolerate a very few words upon it.

The valley for two or three miles from the sea is nearly level, very fertile, and walled in by *palis* 250 feet high, much grooved vertically, and presenting fine layers of conglomerate and grey basalt; and the Hanapépé winds quietly through the region which it fertilises, a stream several hundred feet wide, with a soft, smooth bottom. But four miles inland the bed becomes rugged and declivitous, and the mountain walls close in, forming a most magnificent *cañon* from 1000 to 2500 feet deep. Other *cañons* of nearly equal beauty descend to swell the Hanapépé with their clear, cool, tributaries, and there are "meetings of the waters" worthier of verse than those of Avoca. The walls are broken and highly fantastic, narrowing here, receding there, their strangely-arched recesses festooned with the feathery trichomanes, their clustering columns and broken buttresses suggesting some old-world minster, and their stately tiers of columnar basalt rising one above another in barren grey into the far-off blue sky. The river in carving out the gorge so grandly has most energetically removed all rubbish, and even the tributaries of the lateral *cañons* do not accumulate any "wash" in the main bed. The walls as a rule rise clear from the stream, which, besides its lateral tributaries, receives other contributions in the form of water-falls, which hurl themselves into it from the cliffs in one leap.

After ascending it for four miles all further progress was barred by a *pali* which curves round from the right, and closes the chasm with a perpendicular wall, over which the Hana-pépé precipitates itself from a height of 326 feet, forming the Koula Falls. At the summit is a very fine entablature of curved columnar basalt, resembling the clam shell cave at Staffa, and two high, sharp, and impending peaks on the other side form a stately gateway for a stream which enters from another and broader valley; but it is but one among many small cascades, which round the arc of the falls flash out in foam among the dark foliage, and contribute their tiny warble to the diapason of the waterfall. It rewards one well for penetrating the deep gash which has been made into the earth. It seemed so very far away from all buzzing, frivolous, or vexing things, in the cool, dark abyss into which only the noon-day sun penetrates. All beautiful things which love damp; all exquisite, tender ferns and mosses; all shade-loving parasites flourish there in perennial beauty. And high above in the sunshine, the pea-green candle-nut struggles with the dark *ohia* for precarious roothold on rocky ledges, and dense masses of Eugenia, aflame with crimson flowers, and bananas, and all the leafy wealth born of heat and damp fill up the clefts which fissure the *pali*. Every now and then some scarlet tropic bird flashed across the shadow, but it was á very lifeless and silent scene.   The arches, buttresses, and columns suggest a temple, and the deep tone of the fall is as organ music.   It is all beauty, solemnity, and worship.

It was sad to leave it and to think how very few eyes can ever feast themselves on its beauty.   We came back again into gladness and sunshine, and to the vulgar necessity of eating, which the natives ministered to by presenting us with a substantial meal of stewed fowls and sweet potatoes at the nearest cabin.   There must have been something intoxicating in the air, for we rode wildly and recklessly, galloping down steep hills (which on principle I object to), and putting our horses to their utmost speed.   Mine ran off with me several times, and once nearly upset Mr. M.'s horse, as he probably will tell you.

The natives annoy me everywhere by their inhumanity to their horses.   To-day I became an object of derision to them for hunting for sow-thistles, and bringing back a large bundle of them to my excellent animal.   They starve their horses from mere carelessness or laziness, spur them mercilessly, when the jaded, famished things almost drop from exhaustion, ride them with great sores under the saddles, and with their bodies deeply cut with the rough girths ; and though horses are not regarded as more essential in any part of the world, they neglect and maltreat them in every way, and laugh scornfully if one shows any consideration for them.   Except for short shopping distances in Honolulu, I have never seen a native man or woman walking.   They think walking a degradation, and I have seen men take the trouble to mount horses to go 100 yards.

Afterwards we made a three days' expedition into the heart of the nearer mountainous district, attended by seven mounted natives.   Mr. K., from whose house we started, has the finest mango grove on the islands.   It is a fine foliaged tree, but is everywhere covered with a black blight, which gives the groves the appearance of being in mourning, as the tough, glutinous film covers all the older leaves.   The mango is an exotic fruit, and people think a great deal of it, and send boxes of mangoes as presents to their friends.   It is yellow, with a reddish bloom, something like a magnum bonum plum, three times magnified.   The only way of eating it in comfort is to have a tub of water beside you.   It should be eaten in private by any one who wants to retain the admiration of his friends.   It

has an immense stone, and a disproportionately small pulp. I
think it tastes strongly of turpentine at first, but this is a
heresy.

Beyond Waielva and its mango groves there is a very curious
sand bank about 60 feet high, formed by wind and currents,
and of a steep, uniform angle from top to bottom. It is very
coarse sand, composed of shells, coral, and lava. When two
handfuls are slapped together, a sound like the barking of a
dog ensues, hence its name, the Barking Sands. It is a
common amusement with strangers to slide their horses down
the steep incline, which produces a sound like subterranean thunder, which terrifies unaccustomed animals. Besides
this phenomenon, the mirage is often seen on the dry, hot
soil, and so perfectly, too, that strangers have been known
to attempt to ride round the large lake which they saw before
them.

Pleasant as our mountain trip was, both in itself, and as a
specimen of the way in which foreigners recreate themselves
on the islands, I was glad to get back to the broad Waimea,
on which long shadows of palms reposed themselves in the
slant sunshine, and in the short red twilight to arrive at this
breezy height, and be welcomed by a blazing fire.

Mrs. ——, in speaking of the mode of living here, was
telling me that on a recent visit to England she felt depressed
the whole time by what appeared to her " the scarcity " in the
country. I never knew the meaning of the Old Testament
blessing of "plenty" and "bread to the full" till I was in
abundant Victoria, and it is much the same here. At home
we know nothing of this, which was one of the chiefest of
the blessings promised in the Old Testament. Its *genialising*
effect is very obvious. A man feels more practically independent, possibly, when he can say to all his friends, " Drop in to
dinner whenever you like," than if he possessed the franchise
six times over ; and people can indulge in hospitality and
exercise the franchise, too, here, for meat is only twopence a
pound, and bananas can be got for the gathering. The ever-
increasing cost of food with us, and the ever-increasing love of
display, wither up all those kindly instincts which find expres
sion in housing and feeding both friends and strangers.

I. L. B.

LETTER XXII.

LIHUE, KAUAI.

I RODE from Makaueli to Dr. Smith's, at Koloa, with two native attendants, a *luna* to sustain my dignity, and an inferior native to carry my carpet-bag. Horses are ridden with curb-bits here, and I had only brought a light snaffle, and my horse ran away with me again on the road, and when he stopped at last, these men rode alongside of me, mimicking me, throwing themselves back with their feet forwards, tugging at their bridles, and shrieking with laughter, exclaiming *Maikai! Maikai!* (good).

I remained several days at Koloa, and would gladly have accepted the hospitable invitation to stay as many weeks, but for a cowardly objection to "beating to windward" in the *Jenny.* One day, the girls asked me to go with them to the forests and return by moonlight, but they only spoke of them as the haunts of ferns, because they supposed that I should think nothing of them after the forests of Australia and New Zealand! They were not like the tropical woods of Hawaii, and owe more to the exceeding picturesqueness of the natural scenery. Hawaii is all domes and humps, Kauai all peaks and sierras. There were deep ravines, along which bright, fern-shrouded streams brawled among wild bananas, overarched by Eugenias, with their gory blossoms : walls of peaks, and broken precipices, grey ridges rising out of the blue forest gloom, high mountains with mists wreathing their spiky summits, for a background : gleams of a distant silver sea : and the nearer, many-tinted woods were not matted together in jungle fashion, but festooned and adorned with numberless lianas, and even the prostrate trunks of fallen trees took on new beauty from the exquisite ferns which covered them. Long cathedral aisles stretched away in far-off vistas, and so perfect at times was the Gothic illusion, that I found myself listening for anthems and the roll of organs. So cool and moist it was, and triumphantly redundant in vagaries of form and greenery, it was a forest of forests, and it became a necessity to return the next day, and the next; and I think if I had remained at Koloa I should have been returning still !

This place is outside the beauty, among cane-fields, and is much swept by the trade winds. Mr. Rice, my host, is the son of an esteemed missionary, and he and his wife take a deep interest in the natives. When he brought her here as a bride a few months ago, the natives were so delighted that he had married an island lady who could speak Hawaiian, that they gave them an *ahaaina*, or native feast, on a grand scale. The food was cooked in Polynesian style, by being wrapped up in greens called *luau*, and baked underground. There were two bullocks, nineteen hogs, a hundred fowls, any quantity of *poi* and fruit, and innumerable native dishes. Five hundred natives, profusely decorated with *leis* of flowers and *mailé*, were there, and each brought a gift for the bride. After the feast they chaunted *mélés* in praise of Mr. Rice, and Mrs. Rice played to them on her piano, an instrument which they had not seen before, and sang songs to them in Hawaiian. Mr. and Mrs. R. teach in and superintend a native Sunday-school, and have enlisted twenty native teachers, and in order to keep up the interest and promote cordial feeling, they and the other teachers meet once a month for a regular teachers' meeting, taking the houses in rotation. Refreshments are served afterwards, and they say that nothing can be more agreeable than the good feeling at the meetings, and the tact and graceful hospitality which prevail at the subsequent entertainments.

The Hawaiians are a most pleasant people to foreigners, but many of their ways are altogether aggravating. Unlike the Chinamen, they seldom do a thing right twice. In my experience, they have almost never saddled and bridled my horse quite correctly. Either a strap has been left unbuckled, or the blanket has been wrinkled under the saddle. They are too easy to care much about anything. If any serious loss arises to themselves or others through their carelessness, they shrug their shoulders, and say, "What does it matter?" Any

A FOREST STREAM IN KAUAI.

trouble is just a *pilikia*. They can't help it. If they lose your horse from neglecting to tether it, they only laugh when they find you are wanting to proceed on your journey. Time, they think, is nothing to any one. "What's the use of being in a hurry?" Their neglect of their children, a cause from which a large proportion of the few that are born perish, is a part of this universal carelessness. The crime of infanticide, which formerly prevailed to a horrible extent, has long been extinct; but the love of pleasure and the dislike of trouble which partially actuated it, are apparently still stronger among the women than the maternal instinct, and they do not take the trouble necessary to rear their infants. They give their children away, too, to a great extent, and I have heard of instances in which children have been so passed from hand to hand, that they are quite ignorant of their real parents. It is an odd caprice in some cases, that women who have given away their own children are passionately attached to those whom they have received as presents, but I have nowhere seen such tenderness lavished upon infants as upon the pet dogs that the women carry about with them. Though they are so deficient in adhesiveness to family ties, that wives seek other husbands, and even children desert their parents for adoptive homes, the tie of race is intensely strong, and they are remarkably affectionate to each other, sharing with each other food, clothing, and all that they possess. There are no paupers among them but the lunatics and the lepers, and vagrancy is unknown. Happily on these sunny shores no man or woman can be tempted into sin by want.

With all their faults, and their intolerable carelessness, all the foreigners like them, partly from the absolute security which they enjoy among them. They are so thoroughly good-natured, mirthful, and friendly, and so ready to enter heart and soul into all *haole* diversions, that the islands would be dreary indeed if the dwindling race became extinct.

Among the many misfortunes of the islands, it has been a fortunate thing that the missionaries' families have turned out so well, and that there is no ground for the common reproach that good men's sons turn out reprobates.

The Americans show their usual practical sagacity in missionary matters. In 1853, when these islands were nominally Christianised, and a native ministry consisting of fifty-six pastors had been established, the American Board of Missions, which had expended during thirty-five years nine hundred and three

thousand dollars in Christianising the group, and had sent out
149 male and female missionaries, resolved that it should not
receive any further aid either in men or money.

In the early days, the King and chiefs had bestowed lands
upon the Mission, on which substantial mission premises had
been erected, and on withdrawing from the islands, the Board
wisely made over these lands to the Mission families as free-
hold property. The result has been that, instead of a universal
migration of the young people to America, numbers of them
have been attached to Hawaiian soil. The establishment at
an early date of Punahou College, at which for a small sum
both boys and girls receive a first-class English education, also
contributed to retain them on the islands, and numbers of the
young men entered into sugar-growing, cattle-raising, store-
keeping, and other businesses here. At Honolulu and Hilo a
large proportion of the residents of the upper class are missionaries' children; most of the respectable foreigners on
Kauai are either belonging to, or intimately connected with,
the Mission families; and they are profusely scattered through
Maui and Hawaii in various capacities, and are bound to each
other by ties of extreme intimacy and friendliness, as well as
by marriage and affinity. This "clan" has given society
what it much wants—a sound moral core, and in spite of all
disadvantageous influences, has successfully upheld a public
opinion in favour of religion and virtue. The members of it
possess the moral backbone of New England, and its solid
good qualities, a thorough knowledge of the language and
habits of the natives, a hereditary interest in them, a solid
education, and in many cases much general culture.

In former letters I have mentioned Mr. Coan and Mr. Lyons
as missionaries. I must correct this, as there have been no
actual missionaries on the islands for twenty years. When
the Board withdrew its support, many of the missionaries returned to America; some, especially among the secular
members, went into other positions on the group, while the
two first-mentioned and two or three besides, remained as
pastors of native congregations.

I venture to think that the Board has been premature in
transferring the islands to a native pastorate at such a very
early stage of their Christianity. Such a pastorate must be too
feeble to uphold a robust Christian standard of living. As an
adjunct it would be essential to the stability of native Christianity, but it is not possible that it can be trusted as the sole

depository of doctrine and discipline, and even were it all it ought to be, it would lack the power to repress the lax morality which is ruining the nation. Probably each year will render the overhaste of this course more apparent, and it is likely that some other mode of upholding pure Christianity will have to be adopted, when the venerable men who now sustain and guide the native pastors by their influence shall have been gathered to their rest.

I. L. B.

LETTER XXIII.

LIHUE, KAUAI, *April* 17.

BEFORE leaving Kauai I must tell you of a solitary expedition I have just made to the lovely valley of Hanalei. It was only a three days' "frolic," but an essentially "good time." Mr. Rice provided me with a horse and a very pleasing native guide. I did not leave till two in the afternoon, as I only intended to ride fifteen miles, and, as the custom is, ask for a night's lodging at a settler's house. However, as I drew near Mr. B.'s ranch, I felt my false courage oozing out of the tips of my fingers, and as I rode up to the door, certain obnoxious colonial words, such as "sundowners," and "bummers," occurred to me, and I felt myself a "sundowner" when the host came out and asked me to dismount. He said he was sorry his wife was away, but he would do his best for me in her absence, and took me down to a room where a very rough-looking man was tenderly nursing a baby a year old, which was badly burned or scalded, and which began to cry violently at my entrance, and required the united efforts of the two bereaved men to pacify it. I took it while they went to make some tea, and it kicked, roared, and fought until they came back. By that time I had prepared a neat little speech, saying that I was not the least tired, and would only trouble them for a glass of water; and, having covered my cowardice successfully, I went on, having been urged by the hospitable ranchman to be sure to stay for the night at his father-in-law's house, a few miles further on. I saw that the wishes of the native went in the same direction, but after this experience I assured myself that I had not the necessary nerve for this species of mendicancy, and went on as fast as the horse could

gallop wherever the ground admitted of it, the scenery becoming more magnificent as the dark, frowning mountains of
Hanalei loomed through the gathering twilight.

But they were fifteen miles off, and on the way we came to a
broad, beautiful ravine, through which a wide, deep river glided
into the breakers. I had received some warnings about this,
but it was supposed that we could cross in a ferry scow, of
which, however, I only found the bones. The guide and the
people at the ferryman's house talked long without result, but
eventually, by many signs, I contrived to get them to take
me over in a crazy punt, half full of water, and the horses
swam across. Before we reached the top of the ravine, the last
redness of twilight had died from off the melancholy ocean,
the black forms of mountains looked huge in the darkness, and
the wind sighed so eerily through the creeking *lauhalas*, as to add
much to the effect. It became so very dark that I could only
just see my horse's ears, and we found ourselves occasionally
in odd predicaments, such as getting into crevices, or dipping
off from steep banks; and it was in dense darkness that we
arrived above what appeared to be a valley with twinkling
lights, lying at the foot of a precipice, and walled in on all sides
but one by lofty mountains. It was rather queer, diving over
the wooded *pali* on a narrow track, with nothing in sight but
the white jacket of the native, who had already indicated that
he was at the end of his resources regarding the way, but just
as a river gleamed alarmingly through the gloom, a horseman
on a powerful horse brushed through the wood, and on being
challenged in Hawaiian replied in educated English, and very
politely turned with me, and escorted me over a disagreeable ferry in a scow without rails, and to my destination, two
miles beyond.

Yesterday, when I left, the morning was brilliant, and after
ascending the *pali*, I stayed for some time on an eminence
which commands the valley, presented by Mr. Wyllie to Lady
Franklin, in compliment to her admiration of its loveliness.
Hanalei has been likened by some to Paradise, and by others
to the Vale of Kaschmir. Everyone who sees it raves about
it. " See Hanalei and die," is the feeling of the islanders, and
certainly I was not disappointed, nor should I be with Paradise
itself were it even a shade less fair ! It has every element of
beauty, and in the bright sunshine, with the dark shadows on
the mountains, the waterfalls streaking their wooded sides, the
river rushing under *kukuis* and *ohias*, and then lingering lovingly

amidst lively greenery, it looked as if the curse had never
lighted there.

Its mouth, where it opens on the Pacific, is from two to three
miles wide, but the boundary mountains gradually approach
each other, so that five miles from the sea a narrow gorge of
wonderful beauty alone remains. The crystal Hanalei flows
placidly to the sea for the last three or four miles, tired by its
impetuous rush from the mountains, and mirrors on its breast
hundreds of acres of cane, growing on a plantation formerly
belonging to Mr. Wyllie, an enterprising Ayrshire man, and one
of the ablest and most disinterested foreigners who ever administered Hawaiian affairs. Westward of the valley there is
a region of mountains, slashed by deep ravines. The upper
ridges are densely timbered, and many of the *ohias* have a circumference of twenty-five feet, three feet from the ground. It
was sad to turn away for ever from the loveliness of Hanalei,
even though by taking another route, which involved a ride of
forty miles, I passed through and in view of, most entrancing
picturesqueness. Indeed, for mere loveliness, I think that part
of Kauai exceeds anything that I have seen.

The atmosphere and scenery were so glorious that it was
possible to think of nothing all day, but just allow oneself pas-
sively to drink in sensations of exquisite pleasure. I wish all
the hard-worked people at home, who lead joyless lives in sun-
less alleys, could just have one such day, and enjoy it as I did,
that they might know how fair God's earth is, and how fairer His
Paradise must be, if even from this we cannot conceive "of
the things which He hath prepared for them that love Him."
I never before felt so sad for those whose lives are passed
amidst unpropitious surroundings, or so thankful for my own
capacity of enjoying nature.

Just as we were coming up out of a deep river, a native
riding about six feet from me was caught in a quicksand. He
jumped off, but the horse sank half way up its body. I wanted
to stay and see it extricated, for its struggles only sank it
deeper, but the natives shrugged their shoulders, and said in
Hawaiian, " only a horse," and something they always say when
anything happens, equivalent to " What's the odds?" It was
a joyously-exciting day, and I was galloping down a grass hill
at a pace which I should not have assumed had white people
been with me, when a native rode up to me and said twice
over, "*maikai! paniola,*" and laughed heartily. When my
native came up, he pointed to me and again said, "*paniola;*"

and afterwards we were joined by two women, to whom my
guide spoke of me as *paniola;* and on coming to the top of a
hill they put their horses into a gallop, and we all rode down
at a tremendous, and, as I should once have thought, a break-
neck speed, when one of the women patted me on the shoulder,
exclaiming, "*maikai! maikai! paniola.*" I thought they said
"*spaniola*," taking me for a Spaniard, but on reaching Lihue,
and asking the meaning of the word, Mrs. Rice said, " Oh,
lassoing cattle, and all that kind of thing." I was disposed to
accept the inference as a compliment; but when I told Mrs. R.
that the word had been applied to myself, she laughed very
much, and said she would have toned down its meaning had
she known that!

We rode through forests lighted up by crimson flowers,
through mountain valleys greener than Alpine meadows, descended steep *palis*, and forded deep, strong rivers, pausing at
the beautiful Wailua Falls, which leap in a broad sheet of foam
and a heavy body of water into a dark basin, walled in by
cliffs so hard that even the ferns and mosses which revel in
damp, fail to find roothold in the naked rock. Both above and
below, this river passes through a majestic *cañon*, and its neighbourhood abounds in small cones, some with crateriform cavities at the top, some broken down, and others, apparently of
great age, wooded to their summits. A singular ridge, called
Mauna Kalalea, runs along this part of the island, picturesque
beyond anything, and, from its abruptness and peculiar formation, it deceives the eye into judging it to be as high as the
gigantic domes of Hawaii. Its peaks are needle-like, or else
blunt projections of columnar basalt, rising ofttimes as terraces. At a beautiful village called Anahola the ridge terminates abruptly, and its highest portion is so thin that a large
patch of sky can be seen through a hole which has been worn
in it.

I reached Lihue by daylight, having established my reputation as a *paniola* by riding forty miles in 7½ hours, " very good
time " for the islands. I hope to return here in August, as my
hospitable friends will not allow me to leave on any other condition. The kindness I have received on Kauai is quite over-
whelming, and I shall remember its refined and virtuous homes
as long as its loveliness and delicious climate.

I. L. B.

HAWAIIAN HOTEL, HONOLULU, *April 23rd.*

I have nothing new to add.   Mr. Dexter is so far recovered
that I fear I shall not find my friends here on my return.
People are in the usual fever about the mail, and I must close
this.

L. L. B.

LETTER XXIV.

The Princess Keelikolani—The Paradise of Maui—An Island Sahara—
The Dead Volcano of Haleakala—Cloud Scenery—Maui Hospitality.

ULUPALAKUA, MAUI, *May 12th.*

IT is three weeks since I left the Hawaiian Hotel and its
green mist of algarobas, but my pleasant visits in this island
do not furnish much that will interest you. There was great
excitement on the wharf at Honolulu the evening I left. It
was crowded with natives, the king's band was playing, old
hags were chanting *melés*, and several of the royal family, and
of the "upper ten thousand" were there, taking leave of the
Governess of Hawaii, the Princess Keelikolani, the late king's
half-sister. The throng and excitement were so great, that we
were outside the reef before I got a good view of this lady, the
largest and the richest woman on the islands. Her size and
appearance are most unfortunate, but she is said to be good and
kind. She was dressed in a very common black *holoku*, with a
red bandana round her throat, round which she wore a *lé* of
immense oleanders, as well as round her hair, which was cut
short. She had a large retinue, and her female attendants all
wore *leis* of oleander. They spread very fine mats on the deck,
under *pulu* beds, covered with gorgeous quilts, on which the
Princess and her suite slept, and in the morning the beds were
removed, breakfast was spread on the mats, and she, some of
her attendants, and two or three white men who received in-
vitations, sat on the deck round it. It was a far less attractive
meal than that which the serene steward served below. The
calabashes, which contained the pale pink *poi*, were of highly
polished *kou* wood, but there were no foreign refinements. The
other dishes were several kinds of raw fish, dried devil-fish,
boiled *kalo*, sweet potatoes, bananas, and cocoa-nut milk.

I had a very uncomfortable night on a mattress on the deck,
which was overcrowded with natives, and some of the native

women and two foreigners had got a whisky bottle, and behaved disgracefully. We went round by the Leper Island.

I landed at Maaleia, on the leeward side of the sandy isthmus which unites East and West Maui, got a good horse, and, with Mr. G——, rode across to the residence of " Father Alexander," at Wailuku, a flourishing district of sugar plantations. Mr. and Mrs. Alexander were among the early missionaries, and still live on the mission premises. Several of their sons are settled on the island in the sugar business, and it was to the Heiku plantation, fifteen miles off, of which Mr. S. Alexander is manager, that I went on the following day, still escorted by Mr. G——. Here we heard that captains of schooners which had arrived from Hawaii, report that a light is visible on the terminal crater of Mauna Loa, 14,000 feet above the sea, that Kilauea, the flank crater, is unusually active, and that several severe shocks of earthquake have been felt. This is exciting news.

Behind Wailuku is the Iao valley, up which I rode with two island friends, and spent a day of overflowing, satisfied admiration. At Iao people may throw away pen and pencil in equal despair. The trail leads down a gorge dark with forest trees, which then opens out into an amphitheatre, walled in by precipices, from three to six thousand feet high, misty with a thousand waterfalls, plumed with *kukuis*, and feathery with ferns. A green-clad needle of stone, one thousand feet in height, the last refuge of an army routed when the Wailuku (waters of destruction) ran red with blood, keeps guard over the valley. Other needles there are ; and mimic ruins of bastions, ramparts, and towers came and passed mysteriously : and the shining fronts of turrets gleamed through trailing mists, changing into drifting visions of things that came and went in sunshine and shadow, mountains raising battered peaks into a cloudless sky, green crags moist with ferns, and mists of water that could not fall, but frittered themselves away on slopes of maidenhair, and depths of forest and ferns through which bright streams warble through the summer years. Clouds boiling up from below drifted at times across the mountain fronts, or lay like snow masses in the unsunned chasms : and over the grey crags and piled up pinnacles, and glorified green of the marvellous vision, lay a veil of thin blue haze, steeping the whole in a serenity which seemed hardly to belong to earth.

The track from Wailuku to Heiku is over a Sahara in miniature, a dreary expanse of sand and shifting sandhills, with a

rare, dismal growth of thornless thistles and indigo, and a tremendous surf thunders on the margin. Trackless, glaring,
choking, a guide is absolutely necessary to a stranger, for the
footprints or wheel-marks of one moment are obliterated the
next. I crossed the isthmus three times, and the third time
was quite as incapable of shaping my course across it as the
first, and though I had recklessly declined a guide, was only
too thankful for the one who was forced upon me. It is a
hateful ride, yet anything so hideous and aggressively odious is
a salutary experience in a land of so much beauty. Sand, sand,
sand ! Sand-hills, smooth and red ; sand-plains, rippled, white,
and glaring ; sand drifts shifting ; sand clouds whirling ; sand
in your eyes, nose, and mouth ; sand stinging your face like
pin points ; sand hiding even your horse's ears ; sand rippling
like waves, hissing like spin-drift, malignant, venomous ! You
can only open one eye at a time for a wink at where you
are going. Looking down upon it from Heiku, you can see
nothing all day but the dense brown clouds of a perpetual
sand-storm.

My charming hostess and her husband made Heiku so
fascinating, that I only quitted it hoping to return. The object
which usually attracts strangers to Maui is the great dead
volcano of Haleakala, "The house of the sun," and I was
fortunate in all the circumstances of my ascent. My host at
Heiku provided me with a horse and native attendant, and I
rode over the evening before to the house of his brother, Mr.
J. Alexander, who accompanied me, and his intelligent and
cultured society was one of the pleasures of the day.

People usually go up in the afternoon, camp near the summit,
light a fire, are devoured by fleas, roast and freeze alternately
till morning, and get up to see the grand spectacle of the sunrise, but I think our plan preferable, of leaving at two in the
morning. The moon had set. It was densely dark, and it was
raining on one side of the road, though quite fine on the other.
By the lamplight which streamed from our early breakfast table,
I only saw wet mules and horses, laden with gear for a mountain
ascent, a trim little Japanese, who darted about helping, my
native, who was picturesquely dressed in a Mexican poncho,
Mr. Alexander, who wore something which made him unrecog-
nisable ; and myself, a tatterdemalion figure, wearing a much-
worn green topcoat of his over my riding suit, and a tartan
shawl arranged so as to fall nearly to my feet. Then we went
forth into the darkness. The road soon degenerated into a

wood road, then into a bridle track, then into a mere trail
ascending all the way ; and at dawn, when the rain was over,
we found ourselves more than half-way up the mountain, amidst
rocks, scoriæ, tussocks, *ohelos,* a few common compositæ, and a
few coarse ferns and woody plants, which became coarser and
scantier the higher we went up, but never wholly ceased ; for,
at the very summit, 10,200 feet high, there are some tufts of
grass, and stunted specimens of a common asplenium in clefts.
Many people suffer from mountain sickness on this ascent, but
I suffered from nothing but the excruciating cold, which be-
numbed my limbs and penetrated to my bones ; and though I
dismounted several times and tried to walk, uphill exercise was
impossible in the rarefied air.   The atmosphere was but one
degree below the freezing-point, but at that height, a brisk
breeze on soaked clothes was scarcely bearable.

The sunrise turned the densely packed clouds below into
great rosy masses, which broke now and then, showing a vivid
blue sea, and patches of velvety green.   At seven, after toiling
over a last steep bit, among scoriæ, and some very scanty and
unlovely vegetation, we reached what was said to be the summit,
where a ragged wall of rock shut out the forward view.   Dis-
mounting on some cinders, we stepped into a gap, and from
thence looked down into the most gigantic crater on the earth.
I confess that with the living fires of Kilauea in my memory, I
was at first disappointed with the deadness of a volcano of
whose activity there are no traditions extant.   Though during
the hours which followed, its majesty and wonderment grew
upon me, yet a careful study of the admirable map of the crater,
a comparison of the heights of the very considerable cones
which are buried within it, and the attempt to realize the figures
which represent its circumference, area, and depth, not only
give a far better idea of it than any verbal description, but
impress its singular sublimity and magnitude upon one far more
forcibly than a single visit to the actual crater.

I mentioned in one of my first letters that East Maui, that
part of the island which lies east of the isthmus of perpetual
dust-storms, consists of a mountain dome 10,000 feet in height,
with a monstrous base.   Its slopes are very regular, varying
from eight to ten degrees.   Its lava-beds differ from those of
Kauai and Oahu in being lighter in colour, less cellular, and
more impervious to water.   The windward side of the mountain
is gashed and slashed by streams, which in their violence have
excavated large pot-holes, which serve as reservoirs, and it is

covered to a height of over 2000 feet by a luxuriant growth of timber. On the leeward side, several black and very fresh-looking streams of lava run into the sea, and the whole coast for some height above the shore shows most vigorous volcanic action. Elsewhere the rock is red and broken, and lateral cones abound near the base.

The ascent from Makawao, though it is over rather a desolate tract of land, has in its lower stages such a dismal growth of pining *koa* and spurious sandal-wood, and in its upper ones so much *ohelo* scrub, with grass and common aspleniums quite up to the top, that as one sits lazily on one's sure-footed horse, the fact that one is ascending a huge volcano is not forced upon one by any overmastering sterility and nakedness. Somehow, one expects to pass through some ulterior stage of blackness up to the summit. It is no such thing ; and the great surprise of Haleakala to me was, that when according to calculation there should have been a summit, an abyss of vast dimensions opened below. The mountain top has been in fact blown off, and one is totally powerless to imagine what the forces must have been which rent it asunder.

The crater was clear of fog and clouds, and lighted in every part by the risen sun. The whole, with its contents, can be seen at a single glance, though its girdling precipices are nine-teen miles in extent. Its huge, irregular floor is 2000 feet below; New York might be hidden away within it, with abundant room to spare ; and more than one of the numerous sub-sidiary cones which uplift themselves solitary or in clusters through the area, attain the height of Arthur's Seat at Edinburgh. On the north and east are the Koolau and Kaupo Gaps, as deep as the crater, through which oceans of lava found their way to the sea. It looks as if the volcanic forces, content with rending the mountain top in twain, had then passed into an endless repose.

The crater appears to be composed of a hard grey clink-stone, much fissured ; but lower down the mountain, the rock is softer, and has a bluish tinge. The internal cones are of very regular shape, and most of them look as if their fires had only just gone out, with their sides fiercely red, and their central cavities lined with layers of black ash. They are all composed of cinders of light specific gravity, and much of the ash is tinged with the hydrated oxide of iron. Very few of the usual volcanic products are present.* Small quantities of

* According to Mr. Brigham, the products of the Hawaiian volcanoes

sulphur, in a very impure form, exist here and there, but there
are no sulphur or steam-cracks, or hot springs, on any part of
the mountain. With its cold ashes and dead force, it is a most
tremendous spectacle of the power of fire.

Some previous travellers had generously left some faggots on
the summit, and we made a large fire for warmth, and I rolled
my blanket round me, and sat with my feet among the hot
embers, but all to no purpose. The wind was strong and keen,
and the fierce splendour of the tropic sun conveyed no heat.
Mr. A. went away investigating, the native rolled himself in his
poncho and fell asleep by the fire, and I divided the time
between glimpses into the awful desolation of the crater,
snatched between the icy gusts of wind, and the enjoyment of
the wonderful cloud scenery which to everybody is a great
charm of the view from Haleakala. The day was perfect ; for
first we had an inimitable view of the crater and all that could
be seen from the mountain-top, and then an equally inimitable
view of Cloudland. There was the gaunt, hideous, desolate
abyss, with its fiery cones, its rivers and surges of black lava
and grey ash crossing and mingling all over the area, mixed with
splotches of colour and coils of satin rock, its walls dark and
frowning, everywhere riven and splintered, and clouds perpetually drifting in through the great gaps, and filling up the whole
crater with white, swirling masses, which in a few minutes
melted away in the sunshine, leaving it all as sharply definite
as before. Before noon clouds surrounded the whole mountain,
not in the vague, flocculent, meaningless masses one usually
sees, but in Arctic oceans, where lofty icebergs, floes and pack,
lay piled on each other, glistening with the frost of a Polar
winter ; then alps on alps, and peaks of well remembered
ranges gleaming above glaciers, and the semblance of forests
in deep ravines loaded with new fallen snow. Snow-drifts,
avalanches, oceans held in bondage of eternal ice, and all this
massed together, shifting, breaking, glistering, filling up the
broad channel which divides Maui from Hawaii, and far away
above the lonely masses, rose, in turquoise blue, like distant
islands, the lofty Hawaiian domes of Mauna Kea and Mauna
Loa, with snow on Mauna Kea yet more dazzling than the
clouds. There never was a stranger contrast than between the

are : native sulphur, pyrites, salt, sal ammoniac, hydrochloric acid,
hæmatite, sulphurous acid, sulphuric acid, quartz, crystals, palagonite,
feldspar, chrysolite, Thompsonite, gypsum, solfatarite, copperas, nitre,
Aarragonite, Labradorite, limonite.

hideous desolation of the crater below, and those blue and jewelled summits rising above the shifting clouds.

After some time the scene shifted, and through glacial rifts appeared as in a dream the Eeka mountains which enfold the Iao valley, broad fields of cane 8000 feet below, the flushed, palm-fringed coast, and the deep blue sea sleeping in perpetual calm. But according to the well-known fraud which isolated altitudes perpetrate upon the eye, it appeared as if we were looking *up* at our landscape, not down ; and no effort of the eye or imagination would put things at their proper levels.

But gradually the clouds massed themselves, the familiar earth disappeared, and we were "pinnacled in mid-heaven" in unutterable isolation blank forgotten units, in a white, wonderful, illuminated world, without permanence or solidity. Our voices sounded thin in the upper air. The keen, incisive wind that swept the summit, had no kinship with the soft breezes which were rustling the tasselled cane in the green fields of earth which had lately gleamed through the drift. It was a new world and without sympathy, a solitude which could be felt. Was it nearer God, I wonder, because so far from man and his little works and ways? At least they seemed little there, in presence of the tokens of a catastrophe which had not only blown off a mountain top, and scattered it over the island, but had disembowelled the mountain itself to a depth of 2000 feet.

Soon after noon we began to descend ; and in a hollow of the mountain, not far from the ragged edge of the crater, then filled up with billows of cloud, we came upon what we were searching for ; not, however, one or two, but thousands of silverswords, their cold, frosted silver gleam making the hill-side look like winter or moonlight. They can be preserved in their beauty by putting them under a glass shade, but it must be of monstrous dimensions, as the finer plants measure 2 ft. by 18 in. without the flower stalk. They exactly resemble the finest work in frosted silver, the curve of their globular mass of leaves is perfect, and one thinks of them rather as the base of an *épergne* for an imperial table, or as a prize at Ascot or Goodwood, than as anything organic. A particular altitude and temperature appear essential to them, and they are not found straggling above or below a given line.

We reached Makawao very tired, soon after dark, to be heartily congratulated on our successful ascent, and bearing no worse traces of it than lobster-coloured faces, badly blistered.

After accepting sundry hospitalities I rode over here, skirting the mountain at a height of 2000 feet, a most tedious ride, only enlivened by the blaze of nasturtiums in some of the shallow gulches. It is very pretty here, and I wish all invalids could revel in the sweet, changeless air. The name signifies "ripe bread-fruit of the gods." The plantation is 2000 feet above the sea, and is one of the finest on the islands; and owing to the slow maturity of the cane at so great a height, the yield is from five to six tons an acre. Water is very scarce; all that is used in the boiling-house and elsewhere has been carefully led into concrete tanks for storage, and even the walks in the proprietor's beautiful garden are laid with cement for the same purpose. He has planted many thousand Australian eucalyptus trees on the hill-side in the hope of procuring a larger rainfall, so that the neighbourhood has quite an exotic appearance. Below, the coast is black and volcanic-looking, jutting into the sea in naked lava promontories, which nature has done nothing to drape.

Maui is very "foreign" and civilised, and although it has a native population of over 12,000, the natives are much crowded on plantations, and one encounters little of native life. There is a large society composed of planters' and merchants' families, and the residents are profuse in their hospitality. It is not infrequently taken undue advantage of, and I have heard of planters compelled to feign excuses for leaving their houses, in order to get rid of unintroduced and obnoxious visitors, who have quartered themselves on them for weeks at a time. It is wonderful that their patient hospitality is not worn out, even though, as they say, they sometimes "entertain angels unawares."

I. L. B.

LETTER XXV.

KALAIEHA, HAWAII.

My departure from Ulupalakua illustrates some of the uncertainties of island travelling. On Monday night my things were
packed, and my trunk sent off to the landing; but at five on
Tuesday, Mr. Whipple came to my door to say that the
Kilauea was not in the Lahaina roads, and was probably laid
up for repairs. I was much disappointed, for the mild climate
had disagreed with me, and I was longing for the roystering
winds and unconventional life of windward Hawaii, and there
was not another steamer for three weeks.

However, some time afterwards, I was unpacking, and in the
midst of a floor littered with ferns, photographs, books, and
clothes, when Mrs. W. rushed in to say that the steamer was
just reaching the landing below, and that there was scarcely the
barest hope of catching her. Hopeless as the case seemed, we
crushed most of my things promiscuously into a carpet bag,
Mr. W. rode off with it, a horse was imperfectly saddled for me,
and I mounted him, with my bag, straps, spurs, and a package
of ferns in one hand, and my plaid over the saddle, while Mrs.
W. stuffed the rest of my possessions into a clothes-bag, and
the Chinaman ran away frantically to catch a horse on which
to ride down with them.

I galloped off after Mr. W., though people called to me that
I could not catch the boat, and that my horse would fall on
the steep, broken descent. My saddle slipped over his
shoulders, but he still sped down the hill with the rapid "rack-
ing" movement of a Narraganset pacer. First a new veil
blew away, next my plaid was missing, then I passed my trunk
on the ox-cart which should have been at the landing; but still,

though the heat was fierce, and the glare from the black lava blinding, I dashed heedlessly down, and in twenty minutes had ridden three miles down a descent of 2000 feet, to find the *Kilauea* puffing and smoking with her anchor up ; but I was in time, for her friendly clerk, knowing that I was coming, detained the scow. You will not wonder at my desperation when I tell you that half-way down, a person called to me, " Mauna Loa is in action ! "

While I was slipping off the saddle and bridle, Mr. W. arrived with the carpet-bag, yet more over-heated and shaking with exertion than I was, then the Chinaman with a bag of oddments, next a native who had picked up my plaid and ferns on the road, and another with my trunk, which he had rescued from the ox-cart ; so I only lost my veil and two brushes, which are irreplaceable here.

The quiet of the nine hours' trip in the *Kilauea* restored my equanimity, and prepared me to enjoy the delicious evening which followed. The silver waters of Kawaihae Bay reflected the full moon, the three great mountains of Hawaii were cloudless as I had not before seen them, all the asperity of the leeward shore was softened into beauty, and the long shadows of bending palms were as still and perfect as the palms themselves. And there was a new sight above the silver water, for the huge dome of Mauna Loa, forty miles away, was burning red and fitfully. Horses and a servant awaited me, and we were soon clattering over the hard sand by the shining sea, and up the ascent which leads to the windy table-lands of Waimea. The air was like new life. At a height of 500 feet we met the first whiff of the trades, the atmosphere grew cooler and cooler, the night-wind fresher, the moonlight whiter ; wider the sweeping uplands, redder the light of the burning mountain, till I wrapped my plaid about me, but still was chilled to the bone, and when the four hours' ride was over, soon after midnight, my limbs were stiff with tropical cold. And this, within 20° of the equator, and only 2500 feet above the fiery sea-shore, with its temperature of 80°, where Sydney Smith would certainly have desired to " take off his flesh, and sit in his bones ! "

I delight in Hawaii more than ever, with its unconventional life, great upland sweeps, unexplored forests, riotous breezes, and general atmosphere of freedom, airiness, and expansion. As I find that a lady can travel alone with perfect safety, I have many projects in view, but whatever I do or plan to do, I find my eyes always turning to the light on the top of Mauna Loa. I know that the ascent is not feasible for me, and that so far as I am concerned the mystery must remain unsolved; but that glory, nearly 14,000 feet aloft, rising, falling, "a pillar of cloud by day and a pillar of fire by night," uplifted in its awful loneliness above all human interests, has an intolerable fascination. As the twilight deepens, the light intensifies, and often as I watch it in the night, it seems to flare up and take the form of a fiery palm-tree. No one has ascended the mountain since the activity began a month ago; but the fire is believed to be in "the old traditional crater of Mokuaweoweo, in a region rarely visited by man."

A few days ago I was so fortunate as to make the acquaintance of Mr. W. L. Green (now Minister of Foreign Affairs), an English resident in Honolulu, a gentleman of wide scientific and literary culture,* one of whose objects in visiting Hawaii is the investigation of certain volcanic phenomena. He asked me to make the ascent of Mauna Kea with him, and we have satisfactorily accomplished it to-day.

The interior of the island, in which we have spent the last two days, is totally different, not only from the luxuriant windward slopes, but from the fiery leeward margin. The altitude of the central plateau is from 5000 to 6000 feet, there is not a single native dwelling on it, or even a trail across it, it is totally destitute of water, and sustains only a miserable scrub of *mamané*, stunted *ohias*, *pukeawe*, *ohelos*, a few compositæ, and some of the hardiest ferns. The transient residents of this sheep station, and those of another on Hualalai, thirty miles off, are the only human inhabitants of a region as large as Kent. Wild goats, wild geese (Bernicla sandvicensis), and the Melithreptes Pacifica, constitute its chief population. These geese are web-footed, though water does not exist. They build their nests in the grass, and lay two or three white eggs.

Our track from Waimea lay for the first few miles over light soil, destitute of any vegetation, across dry, glaring, rocky beds of streams, and round the bases of numerous tufa cones, from 200 to 1500 feet in height, with steep, smooth sides, composed of a very red ash. We crossed a flank of Mauna Kea at a height of 6000 feet, and a short descent brought us out upon

* Author of a recent book, "The Molten Globe."

this vast tableland, which lies between the bulbous domes of Mauna Kea, Mauna Loa, and Hualalai, the loneliest, saddest, dreariest expanse I ever saw.

The air was clear and the sun bright, yet nothing softened into beauty this formless desert of volcanic sand, stones, and lava, on which tufts of grass and a harsh scrub war with wind and drought for a loveless existence. Yet, such is the effect of atmosphere, that Mauna Loa, utterly destitute of vegetation, and with his sides scored and stained by the black lava-flows of ages, looked liked a sapphire streaked with lapis lazuli. Nearly blinded by scuds of sand, we rode for hours through the volcanic wilderness ; always the same rigid *mamané*, (Sophora Chrysophylla ?) the same withered grass, and the same thornless thistles, through which the strong wind swept with a desolate screech.

The trail, which dips 1000 feet, again ascends, the country becomes very wild, there are ancient craters of great height densely wooded, wooded ravines, the great bulk of Mauna Kea with his ragged crest towers above tumbled rocky regions, which look as if nature, disgusted with her work, had broken it to pieces in a passion ; there are living and dead trees, a steep elevation, and below, a broad river of most jagged and uneven *a-a*. The afternoon fog, which serves instead of rain, rolled up in dense masses, through which we heard the plaintive bleating of sheep, and among blasted trees and distorted rocks we came upon Kalaieha.

I have described the "foreign residences" elsewhere. Here is one of another type, in which a wealthy sheepowner's son, married to a very pretty native woman, leads for some months in the year, from choice, a life so rough, that most people would think it a hardship to lead it from necessity. There are two apartments, a loft and a "lean-to." The hospitable owners gave me their sleeping-room, which was divided from the "living-room" by a canvas partition. This last has a rude stone chimney split by an earthquake, holding fire enough to roast an ox. Round it the floor is paved with great rough stones. A fire of logs, fully three feet high, was burning, but there was a faulty draught, and it emitted a stinging smoke. I looked for something to sit upon, but there was nothing but a nigh bench, or chopping-block, and a fixed seat in the corner of the wall. The rest of the furniture consisted of a small table, some pots, a frying-pan, a tin dish and plates, a dipper, and some tin pannikins. Four or five rifles and "shot-guns,"

and a piece of raw meat, were hanging against the wall.   A
tin bowl was brought to me for washing, which served the
same purpose for every one.   The oil was exhausted, so re-
course was had to the native expedient of a jar of beef fat with
a wick in it.

We were most hospitably received, but the native wife, as is
usually the case, was too shy to eat with us, or even to appear
at all.   Our host is a superb young man, very frank and pre-
possessing looking, a thorough mountaineer, most expert with
the lasso and in hunting wild cattle.   The "station" consists
of a wool shed, a low grass hut, a hut with one side gone, a
bell-tent, and the more substantial cabin in which we are lodged.
Several saddled horses were tethered outside, and some natives
were shearing sheep, but the fog shut out whatever else there
might be of an outer world.   Every now and then a native came
in and sat on the floor to warm himself, but there were no mats
as in native houses.   It was intolerably cold.   I singed my
clothes by sitting in the chimney, but could not warm myself.
A fowl was stewed native fashion, and some rice was boiled,
and we had sheep's milk and some ice cold water, the drip, I
think, from a neighbouring cave, as running and standing water
are unknown.

There are 9000 sheep here, but they require hardly any
attendance except at shearing time, and dogs are not used in
herding them.   Indeed, labour is much dispensed with, as the
sheep are shorn unwashed, a great contrast to the elaborate washings of the flocks of the Australian Riverina.   They
come down at night of their own sagacity, in close converging
columns, sleep on the gravel about the station, and in the early
morning betake themselves to their feeding grounds on the
mountain.

Mauna Kea, and the forests which skirt his base, are the
resort of thousands of wild cattle, and there are many men
nearly as wild, who live half savage lives in the woods, gaining
their living by lassoing and shooting these animals for their
skins.   Wild black swine also abound.

The mist as usual disappeared at night, leaving a sky wonderful with stars, which burned blue and pale against the furnace
glare on the top of Mauna Loa, to which we are comparatively
near.   I woke at three from the hopeless cold, and before five
went out with Mr. Green to explore the adjacent lava.   The
atmosphere was perfectly pure, and suffused with rose-colour,
not a cloud-fleece hung round the mountain tops, hoar-frost

whitened the ground, the pure, white smoke of the volcano rose into the reddening sky, and the air was elixir. It has been said and written that there are no steam-cracks or similar traces of volcanic action on Mauna Kea, but in several fissures I noticed ferns growing belonging to an altitude 4000 feet lower, and on putting my arm down, found a heat which compelled me to withdraw it, and as the sun rose these cracks steamed in all directions.   There are caves full of ferns, lava bubbles in reality, crust over crust, each from twelve to eighteen inches thick, rolls of lava cooled in coils, and hideous *a-a* streams on which it is impossible to walk two yards without the risk of breaking one's limbs or cutting one's boots to pieces.

I will not weary you with the details of our mountain ascent. Our host provided ourselves and the native servant with three strong bullock-horses, and accompanied us himself. The first climb is through deep volcanic sand slashed by deep clefts, showing bands of red and black ash.   We saw no birds, but twice started a rout of wild black hogs, and once came upon a wild bull of large size with some cows and a calf, all so tired with tramping over the lava that they only managed to keep just out of our way.   They usually keep near the mountain top in the daytime for fear of the hunters, and come down at night to feed.   About 11,000 were shot and lassoed last year. Mr. S—— says that they don't need any water but that of the dew-drenched grass, and that horses reared on the mountains refuse to drink, and are scared by the sight of pools or running streams.   Unlike horses I saw at Waikiki, which shut their eyes and plunged their heads into water up to their ears, in search of a saltish weed which grows in the lagoons.

The actual forest, which is principally *koa*, ceases at a height of about 6000 feet, but a deplorable vegetation beginning with *mamané* scrub, and ending with withered wormwood and tufts of coarse grass, straggles up 3000 feet higher, and a scaly orange lichen is found in rare patches at a height of 11,000 feet.

The side of Mauna Kea towards Waimea is precipitous and inaccessible, but to our powerful mountain horses the ascent from Kalaieha presented no difficulty.

We rode on hour after hour in intense cold, till we reached a height where the last stain of lichen disappeared, and the desolation was complete and oppressive.   This area of tufa

cones, dark and grey basalt, clinkers, scoriæ, fine ash, and ferruginous basalt, is something gigantic. We were three hours
in ascending through it, and the eye could at no time take in
its limit, for the mountain which from any point of view below
appears as a well defined dome with a ragged top, has at the
summit the aspect of a ridge, or rather a number of ridges,
with between 20 and 30 definite peaks, varying in height
from 900 to 1400 feet. Among these cones are large plains of
clinkers and fine gravel, but no lava-streams, and at a height of
12,000 feet the sides of some of the valleys are filled up with
snow, of a purity so immaculate and a brilliancy so intense as
the fierce light of the tropical sun beat upon it, that I feared
snow-blindness. We ascended one of the smaller cones, which
was about 900 feet high, and found it contained a crater of
nearly the same depth, with a very even slope, and lined entirely with red ash, which at the bottom became so bright and
fiery-looking that it looked as if the fires, which have not burned
for ages, had only died out that morning.

After riding steadily for six hours, our horses, snorting and
panting, and plunging up to their knees in fine volcanic ash,
and halting, trembling and exhausted, every few feet, carried
us up the great tufa cone which crowns the summit of this vast,
fire-flushed, fire-created mountain, and we dismounted in deep
snow on the crest of the highest peak in the Pacific, 13,953 feet
above the sea. This summit is a group of six red tufa cones,
with very little apparent difference in their altitude, and with
deep valleys filled with red ash between them. The terminal
cone on which we were has no cavity, but most of those forming the group, as well as the thirty which I counted around
and below us, are truncated cones with craters within, and
with outer slopes, whose estimated angle is about 30°. On these
slopes the snow lay heavily. In coming up we had had a superb
view of Mauna Loa, but before we reached the top, the clouds
had congregated, and lay in glistening masses all round the
mountain about half way up, shutting out the smiling earth, and
leaving us alone with the view of the sublime desolation of the
volcano.

We only remained an hour on the top, and came down by a
very circuitous route, which took us round numerous cones,
and over miles of clinkers varying in size from a ton to a few
ounces, and past a lake the edges of which were frozen, and
which in itself is a curiosity, as no other part of the mountain
"holds water." Not far off is a cave, a lava-bubble, in which

the natives used to live when they came up here to quarry a very hard adjacent phonolite for their axes and other tools. While the others poked about, I was glad to make it a refuge from the piercing wind. Hundreds of unfinished axes lie round the cave entrance, and there is quite a large mound of unfinished chips.

This is a very interesting spot to Hawaiian antiquaries. They argue, from the amount of the chippings, that this mass of phonolite was quarried for ages by countless generations of men, and that the mountain top must have been upheaved, and the island inhabited, in a very remote past. The stones have not been worked since Captain Cook's day ; yet there is not a weather-stain upon them, and the air is so dry and rarified that meat will keep fresh for three months. I found a mass of crystals of the greenish volcanic glass, called olivine, imbedded in a piece of phonolite which looked as blue and fresh as if only quarried yesterday.

We travelled for miles through ashes and scoriæ, and then descended into a dense afternoon fog ; but Mr. S. is a practised mountaineer, and never faltered for a moment, and our horses made such good speed that late in the afternoon we were able to warm ourselves by a gallop, which brought us in here ravenous for supper before dark, having ridden for thirteen hours. I hope I have made it clear that the top of this dead volcano, whether cones or ravines, is deep soft ashes and sand.

To-morrow morning I intend to ride the thirty miles to Waimea with two native women, and the next day to go off on my adventurous expedition to Hilo, for which I have bought for $45 a big, strong, heavy horse, which I have named Kahélé. He has the poking head and unmistakable gait of a bullock-horse, but is said to be " a good traveller."

I. L. B.

LETTER XXVI.

Alone with Nature—A Light Equipment—Kahélé—A Garrulous
Assemblage—A Paralysed Village—Hilo.

"MY CAMP," HAWAIIAN SLOPES, *May* 21.

THIS is the height of enjoyment in travelling. I have just
encamped under a *lauhala* tree, with my saddle inverted for a
pillow, my horse tied by a long lariat to a guava bush, my gear,
saddle-bags, and rations for two days lying about, and my
saddle blanket drying in the sun. Overhead the sun blazes,
and casts no shadow; a few fleecy clouds hover near him, and
far below, the great expanse of the Pacific gleams in a deeper
blue than the sky. Far above, towers the rugged and snow-
patched, but no longer mysterious dome of Mauna Kea; while
everywhere, ravines, woods, waterfalls, and stretches of lawn-
like grass delight the eye. All green that I have ever seen, of
English lawns in June, or Alpine valleys, seems poor and
colourless as compared with the dazzling green of this sixty-five
miles. It is a joyous green, a glory. Whenever I look up
from my writing, I ask, Was there ever such green? Was there
ever such sunshine? Was there ever such an atmosphere?
Was there ever such an adventure? And Nature—for I have
no other companion, and wish for none—answers, "No." The
novelty is that I am alone, my conveyance my own horse; no
luggage to look after, for it is all in my saddle-bags; no guide
to bother, hurry, or hinder me; and with knowledge enough of
the country to stop when and where I please. A native guide,
besides being a considerable expense, is a great nuisance; and
as the trail is easy to find, and the rivers are low, I resolved
for once to taste the delights of perfect independence! This
is a blessed country, for a lady can travel everywhere in absolute security.

My goal is the volcano of Kilauea, with various diverging

expedition, involving a ride of about 350 miles; but my health has so wonderfully improved, that it is easier to me now to ride forty miles in a day than ten some months ago.

You have no idea of the preparations required for such a ride, and the importance which "littles" assume. Food for two days had to be taken, and all superfluous weight to be discarded, as every pound tells on a horse on a hard journey. My saddle-bags contain, besides "Sunday clothes," dress for any "gaieties" which Hilo may offer; but I circumscribed my stock of clothes as much as possible, having fallen into the rough-and-ready practice of washing them at night, and putting them on unironed in the morning. I carry besides, a canvas bag on the horn of my saddle, containing two days' provender, and a knife, horse-shoe nails, glycerine, thread, twine, leather thongs, with other little et ceteras, the lack of which might prove troublesome, a thermometer and aneroid in a leather case, and a plaid. I have discarded, owing to their weight, all the well-meant luxuries which were bestowed upon me, such as drinking cups, flasks, etnas, sandwich cases, knife cases, spoons, pocket mirrors, &c. The inside of a watchcase makes a sufficient mirror, and I make a cup from a *kalo* leaf. All cases are a mistake,—at least I think so, as I contemplate my light equipment with complacency.

Yesterday's dawn was the reddest I have seen on the mountains, and the day was all the dawn promised. A three-mile gallop down the dewy grass, and slackened speed through the bush, brought me once again to the breezy slopes of Hamakua, and the trail I travelled in February, with Deborah and Kaluna. Though as green then as now, it was the rainy season, a carnival of rain and mud. Somehow the summer does make a difference, even in a land without a winter. The temperature was perfect. It was dreamily lovely. No song of birds, or busy hum of insects, accompanied the rustle of the *lauhala* leaves and the low murmur of the surf. But there is no hot sleep of noon here—the delicious trades keep the air always wakeful.

When the gentleman who guided me through the bush left me on the side of a *pali*, I discovered that Kahélé, though strong, gentle, and sure-footed, possesses the odious fault known as balking, and expressed his aversion to ascend the other side in a most unmistakable manner. He swung round. put his head down, and no amount of spurring could get him to do anything but turn round and round, till the gentleman, who had left me, returned, beat him with a stick, and threw stones at him, till he got him started again.

I have tried coaxing him, but without result, and have had prolonged fights with him in nearly every gulch, and on the worst *pali* of all he refused for some time to breast a step, scrambled round and round in a most dangerous place, and slipped his hind legs quite over the edge before I could get nim on.

His sociability too is ridiculously annoying. Whenever he sees natives in the distance, he neighs, points his ears, holds up his heavy head, quickens his pace, and as soon as we meet them, swings round and joins them, and can only be extricated after a pitched battle. On a narrow bridge I met Kaluna on a good horse, improved in manners, appearance, and English, and at first he must have thought that I was singularly pleased to see him, by my turning round and joining him at once; but presently, seeing the true state of the case, he belaboured Kahélé with a heavy stick. The animal is very gentle and companionable, and I dislike to spur him ; besides, he seems insensible to it; so the last time I tried Rarey's plan, and bringing his head quite round, twisted the bridle round the horn of the saddle, so that he had to turn round and round for my pleasure, rather than to indulge his own temper, a process which will, I hope, conquer him mercifully.

But in consequence of these battles, and a halt which I made, as, now, for no other purpose than to enjoy my felicitous circumstances, the sun was sinking in a mist of gold behind Mauna Loa long before I reached the end of my day's journey. It was extremely lovely. A heavy dew was falling, odours of Eden rose from the earth, colours glowed in the sky, and the dewiest and richest green was all round. There were several gulches to cross after the sun had set, and a silence, which was almost audible, reigned in their leafy solitudes. It was quite dark when I reached the trail which dips over the great *pali* of Laupahoehoe, 700 feet in height. but I found myself riding carelessly down what I hardly dared to go up, carefully and in company, four months before. But whatever improvement time has made in my health and nerves, it has made none in this wretched, zoophyte village.

Leading Kahélé, I groped about till I found the house of the widow Honolulu, with whom I had lodged before, and presently all the natives assembled to stare at me. After rubbing my horse and feeding him on a large bundle of *ti* leaves that I

had secured on the road, I took my own meal as a spectacle.
Two old crones seized on my ankles, murmuring *lomi, lomi,*
and subjected them to the native process of shampooing.
They had unrestrained curiosity as to the beginning and end of
my journey. I said " *Waimea, Hamakua,*" when they all
chorused, " *Maikai;* " for a ride of forty miles was not bad
for a *wahine haole.* I said, " *Wai lio.*" (water for the horse),
when they signified that there was only some brackish stuff
unfit for drinking.

In spite of the garrulous assemblage, I was asleep before
eight, and never woke till I found myself in a blaze of sunshine
this morning, and in perfect solitude. I got myself some
breakfast, and then looked about the village for some inhabitants, but found none, except an unhappy Portuguese with one
leg, and an old man who looked like a leper, to whom I said
" *Ko*" (cane) " *lio*" (horse), exhibiting a rial at the same
time, on which he cut me a large bundle, and I sat on a stone
and watched Kahélé as he munched it for an hour and a
half.

It was very hot and serene down there between those *palis*
700 and 800 feet high. The huts of the village were all shut,
and not a creature stirred. The palms above my head looked
as if they had always been old, and there was no movement
among their golden plumes. The sea itself rolled shorewards
more silently and lazily than usual. An old dog slept in the
sunshine, and whenever I moved, by a great effort, opened one
eye. The man who cut the cane fell asleep on the grass.
Kahélé ate as slowly as if he had resolved to try my patience,
and be revenged on me for my conquest of him yesterday, and
his heavy munching was the only vital sound. I got up and
walked about to assure myself that I was awake, saddled and
bridled the horse, and mounted the great southward *pali,*
thankful to reach the breeze and the upper air in full possession
of my faculties, after the torpor and paralysis of the valley
below.

Never were waters so bright or stretches of upland lawns so
joyous as to-day, or the forest entanglements so entrancing.
The beautiful *Eugenia malaccensis* is now in full blossom, and
its stems and branches are blazing in all the gulches, with
bunches of rose-crimson stamens borne on short spikelets.

HILO, HAWAII, *May 24th.*

Once more I am in dear, beautiful Hilo. Death entered my Hawaiian "home" lately, and took "Baby Bell" away, and I miss her sweet angel-presence at every turn; but otherwise there are no changes, and I am very happy to be under the roof of these dear friends again, but indeed each tree, flower, and fern in Hilo is a friend. I would not even wish the straggling Pride of India, and over-abundant lantana, away from this fairest of the island Edens. I wish I could transport you here this moment from our sour easterly skies to this endless summer and endless sunshine, and shimmer of a peaceful sea, and an atmosphere whose influences are all cheering. Though from 13 to 16 feet of rain fall here in the year the air is not damp. Wet clothes hung up in the verandah even during rain, dry rapidly, and a substance so sensitive to damp as botanical paper does not mildew.

I met Deborah on horseback near Onomea, and she told me that the Austins were expecting me, and so I spent three days very pleasantly with them on my way here.

I. L. B.

The old *Kilauea* has just come in, and has brought the English mail, and a United States mail, an event which sets Hilo agog. Then for a few hours its still, drowsy life becomes galvanized, and people really persuade themselves that they have something to do, and all the foreigners write letters hastily, or add postscripts to those already written, and lose the mail, and rush down frantically to the beach to send their late letters by favour of the obliging purser. The mail to-day was an event to me, as it has brought your long-looked-for letters.

LETTER XXVII.

Puna, the Home of the Coco-palm—A Magical Spring—A Leper Exodus —"Bill Ragsdale "—Self-sacrifice of Father Damiens.

MR. AND MRS. SEVERANCE and I have just returned from a three days' expedition to Puna in the south of Hawaii, and I preferred their agreeable company even to solitude ! My sociable Kahélé was also pleased, and consequently behaved very well. We were compelled to ride for twenty-three miles in single file, owing to the extreme narrowness of the lava track, which has been literally hammered down in some places to make it passable even for shod horses. We were a party of four, and a very fat policeman on a very fat horse brought up the rear.

At some distance from Hilo there is a glorious burst of tropical forest, and then the track passes into green grass dotted over with clumps of the pandanus and the beautiful eugenia. In that hot, dry district the fruit was already ripe, and we quenched our thirst with it. The " native apple," as it is called, is of such a brilliant crimson colour as to be hardly less beautiful than the flowers. The rind is very thin, and the inside is white, juicy, and very slightly acidulated. We were always near the sea, and the surf kept bursting up behind the trees in great snowy drifts, and every opening gave us a glimpse of deep blue water. The coast the whole way is composed of great blocks of very hard, black lava, more or less elevated, upon which the surges break in perpetual thunder.

Suddenly the verdure ceased, and we emerged upon a hideous scene, one of the many lava flows from Kilauea, an irregular branching stream, about a mile broad. It is suggestive of fearful work on the part of nature, for here the volcano has not created but destroyed. The black, tumbled sea mocked the bright sunshine, all tossed, jagged, spiked, twirled, thrown heap on heap, broken, rifted, upheaved in great masses, burrowing in ravines of its own making, full of broken bubble caves, and torn by *a-a* streams. Close to the track, crystals of olivine lie in great profusion, and in a few of the crevices there are young plants of a fern which everywhere has the audacity to act as the herald of vegetation.

Beyond this desert the country is different in its features from the rest of the island, a green, smiling land of Beulah, varied by lines of craters covered within and without with vegetation. For thirty miles the track passes under the deep shade of coco palms, of which Puna is the true home ; and from under their feathery shadow, and from amidst the dark leafage of the breadfruit, gleamed the rose-crimson apples of the eugenia, and the golden balls of the guava. I have not before seen this exquisite palm to advantage, for those which fringe the coast have, as compared with these, a look of tattered, sombre, harassed antiquity. Here they stood in thousands, young as well as old, their fronds gigantic, their stems curving every way, and the golden light, which is peculiar to them, toned into a golden green. They were loaded with fruit in all stages, indeed it is produced in such abundance that thousands of nuts lie unheeded on the ground. Animals, including dogs and cats, revel in the meat, and in the scarcity of good water the milk is a useful substitute.

Late in the afternoon we reached our destination, a comfortable frame house, on one of those fine natural lawns in which Hawaii abounds. A shower at seven each morning keeps Puna always green. Our kind host, a German, married to a native woman, served our meals in a house made of grass and bamboo ; but the wife and children, as is usual in these cases, never appeared at table, and contented themselves with contemplating us at a great distance.

The next afternoon we rode to one of the natural curiosities of Puna, which gave me intense pleasure. It lies at the base of a cone crowned with a *heiau* and a clump of coco palms. Passing among bread-fruit and guavas into a palm grove of exquisite beauty, we came suddenly upon a lofty, wooded cliff of hard basalt, with ferns growing out of every crevice in its ragged but perpendicular sides. At its feet is a cleft about 60 feet long, 16 wide, and 18 deep, full of water at a temperature of 90°. This has an absolute transparency of a singular kind, and perpetrates wonderful optical illusions. Every thing

put into it is transformed. The rocks, broken timber, and old
cocoa-nuts which lie below it, are a frosted blue; the dusky
skins of natives are changed to alabaster; and as my companion, in a light print *holoku*, swam to and fro, her feet and
hands became like polished marble tinged with blue, and her
dress floated through the water as if woven of blue light.
Everything about this spring is far more striking and beautiful
than the colour in the Blue Grotto. It is heaven in the
water, a jewelled floor of marvels, "a sea of glass," "like unto
sapphire," a type, perhaps, of that on which the blessed stand
before the throne of God. Above, the feathery palms rose into
the crystalline blue, and made an amber light below, and all
fair and lovely things were mirrored in the wonderful waters.
The specific gravity must be much greater that that of ordinary
water, for it did not seem possible to sink, or even be thoroughly
immersed in it. The mercury in the air was 79°, but on coming
out of the water we felt quite chilly.

I like Puna. It is like nothing else, but something about it
made us feel as if we were dwelling in a castle of indolence. I
developed a capacity for doing nothing, which horrified me, and
except when we energised ourselves to go to the hot spring, my
companions and I were content to dream in the verandah, and
watch the lengthening shadows, and drink cocoa-nut milk, till
the abrupt exit of the sun startled us, and we saw the young
moon carrying the old one tenderly, and a fitful glare 60 miles
away, where the solemn fires of Mauna Loa are burning at a
height of nearly 14,000 feet.

HILO.

There are many "littles," but few "mickles" here. It is
among the last that two foreign gentlemen have successfully
accomplished the ascent of Mauna Loa, and the mystery of its
fires is solved. I write "successfully," as they went up and
down in safety, but they were involved in a series of *pilikias :*
girths, stirrup-leathers, and cruppers slipping and breaking, and
their sufferings on the summit from cold and mountain sickness
appear to have been nearly incapacitating. Although much
excited, they are collected enough to pronounce it "the most
sublime sight ever seen." They, as well as several natives who
have passed by Kilauea, report it as in full activity, which
bears against the assertion that the flank crater becomes quiet
when the summit crater is active.

Another and sadder " mickle " has been the departure of ten
lepers for Molokai. The *Kilauea*, with the Marshal, and Mr.
Wilder, who embodies the Board of Health, has just left the
bay, taking away forty lepers on this cruise ; and the relations
of those who have been taken from Hilo are still howling on the
beach.   When one hears the wailing, and sees the temporary
agony of the separated relatives, one longs for " the days of
the Son of Man," and that his healing touch, as of old in
Galilee, might cleanse these unfortunates.   Nine of the lepers
were sent on board from the temporary pest-house, but their
case, though deeply commiserated, has been overshadowed by
that of the talented half-white, " Bill Ragsdale," whom I mentioned in one of my earlier letters, and who is certainly the
most " notorious " man in Hilo. He has a remarkable gift of
eloquence, both in English and Hawaiian : a combination of
pathos, invective, and sarcasm ; and his manner, though the-
atrical, is considered perfect by his native admirers. His moral
character, however, has been very low, which makes the outburst of feeling at his fate the more remarkable.

Yesterday, he wrote a letter to Sheriff Severance, giving
himself up as a leper to be dealt with by the law, expressing
himself as ready to be expatriated to-day, but requesting that
he might not be put into the leper-house, and that he might go
on board the steamer alone.   The fact of his giving himself up
excited much sympathy, as, in his case, the signs of the malady
are hardly apparent, and he might have escaped suspicion for
some time.

He was riding about all this morning, taking leave of people,
and of the pleasant Hilo lanes, which he will never see again,
and just as the steamer was weighing anchor, walked down to
the shore as carefully dressed as usual, decorated with *leis* of
ohia and gardenia, and escorted by nearly the whole native
population. On my first landing here, the glee-club, singing
and flower-clad, went out to meet him ; now tears and sobs
accompanied him, and his countrymen and women clung to
him, kissing him to the last moment, whilst all the foreigners
shook hands as they offered him their good wishes.   He made
a short speech in native, urging quiet submission to the stringent
measures which government is taking in order to stamp out
leprosy, and then said a few words in English.   His last words,
as he stepped into the boat, were to all : " *Aloha*, may God
bless you, my brothers," and then the whale boat took him the
first stage towards his living grave.   He took a horse, a Bible,

and some legal books with him ; and, doubtless, in consideration of the prominent positions he has filled, specially that of
interpreter to the Legislature, unusual indulgence will be
granted to him.

At the weekly prayer meeting held this evening, the medical
officer gave a very pathetic account of his interview with him
this morning, in which he had feelingly requested the prayers of
the church.   It was with unusual fervour afterwards that prayer
was offered, not for him only, but for "all those who, living,
have this day been consigned to the oblivion of the grave, and
for the five hundred of our fellow-subjects now suffering on
Molokai." A noble instance of devotion has just been given
by Father Damiens, a Belgian priest, who has gone to spend
his life amidst the hideous scenes, and the sickness and death
of the ghastly valley of Kalawao.*

I. L. B.

* A chapter on Leprosy and the Leper Settlement is given at the close
of these Letters.

LETTER XXVIII.

HILO, *June 2nd.*

OFTEN since I finished my last letter has Hazael's reply to Elisha occurred to me, "Is thy servant a dog, that he should do this thing?" For in answer to people who have said, "I hope nothing will induce you to attempt the ascent of Mauna Loa," I always said, "Oh dear, no! I should never dream of it!" or, "Nothing would persuade me to think of it!"

This morning early, Mr. Green came in, on his way to Kilauea, to which I was to accompany him, and on my casually remarking that I envied him his further journey, he at once asked me to join him, and I joyfully accepted the invitation! For, indeed, my heart has been secretly set on going, and I have had to repeat to myself fifty times a day, "no, I must not think of it, for it is *impossible.*"

Mr. Green is going up well equipped with a tent, horses, a baggage mule, and a servant, and is confident of being able to get a guide and additional mules fifty miles from Hilo. I had to go to the Union School examination where the Hilo world was gathered, but I could think of nothing but the future; and I can hardly write sense, the prospect of the next week is so exciting, and the time for making preparations is so short. It is an adventurous trip anyhow, and the sufferings which our predecessors have undergone, from Commodore Wilkes downwards, make us anxious not to omit any precaution. The distance which has to be travelled through an uninhabited region, the height and total isolation of the summit, the uncertainty as to the state of the crater, and the duration of its

activity, with the possibility of total failure owing to fog or
strong wind, combine to make our ascent an experimental
trip.

The news of the project soon spread through the village,
and as the ascent has only once been performed by a woman,
the kindly people are profuse in offers of assistance, and in interest in the journey, and every one is congratulating me on
my good fortune in having Mr. Green for my travelling companion.   I have hunted all the beach stores through for such
essentials as will pack into small compass, and every one
said, "So you are going 'to the mountain;' I hope you'll
have a good time;" or, "I hope you'll have the luck to
get up."

Among the friends of my hosts all sorts of useful articles
were produced, a camp kettle, a camping blanket, a huge
Mexican poncho, a cardigan, capacious saddle-bags, &c.   Nor
was Kahélé forgotten, for the last contribution was a bag of
oats !   The greatest difficulty was about warm clothing, for in
this perfect climate, woollen underclothing is not necessary
as in many tropical countries, but it is absolutely essential
on yonder mountain, and till late in the afternoon the best intentions and the most energetic rummaging in old trunks failed
to produce it.   At last Mrs. ——, wife of an old Scotch
settler, bestowed upon me the invaluable loan of a stout
flannel shirt, and a pair of venerable worsted stockings, much
darned, knitted in Fifeshire a quarter of a century ago.   When
she brought them, the excellent lady exclaimed, "Oh,
what some people will do!" with an obvious personal
reference.

She tells us that her husband, who owns the ranch on the
mountain at which we are to stay the last night, has been
obliged to forbid any of his natives going up as guides, and
that she fears we shall not get a guide, as the native who went
up with Mr. Whyte suffered so dreadfully from mountain sickness, that they were obliged to help him down, and he declares
that he will not go up again.   Mr. Whyte tells us that he
suffered himself from vomiting and vertigo for fourteen hours,
and severely from thirst also, as the water froze in the canteens; but I am almost well now, and as my capacity for
"roughing it" has been severely tested, I hope to "get on"
much better.

A party made the ascent nine months ago, and the members of it also suffered severely, but I see no reason why

cautious people, who look well to their gear and clothing, and are prudent with regard to taking exercise at the top, should suffer anything worse than the inconveniences which are inseparable from nocturnal cold at a high elevation.

My preparations are completed to-night, the last good wishes have been spoken, and we intend to leave early to-morrow morning.

I. L. B.

```

# LETTER XXIX.*

A Second Visit to Kilauea—Remarkable Changes in Halemaumau—
Terrible Aspects of the Pit—Theory and Aspects of the "Blowing
Cones"—A Shock of Earthquake—A Mountain Ranch.

CRATER HOUSE, KILAUEA, *June 4th.*

ONCE more I write with the splendours of the quenchless
fires in sight, and the usual world seems twilight and common-
place by the fierce glare of Halemaumau, and the fitful glare of
the other and loftier flame, which is burning ten thousand feet
higher in lonely Mokua-weo-weo.

Mr. Green and I left Hilo soon after daylight this morning,
and made about "the worst time" ever made on the route.
We jogged on slowly and silently for thirty miles in Indian file,
through bursts of tropical beauty, over an ocean of fern-clad
*pahoehoe,* the air hot and stagnant, the horses lazy and indif-
ferent, till I was awoke from the kind of cautious doze into
which one falls on a sure-footed horse, by a decided cool-
ness in the atmosphere, and Kahélé broke into a lumbering
gallop, which he kept up till we reached this house, where, in
spite of the exercise, we are glad to get close to a large wood
fire. Although we are shivering, the mercury is at 57°, but in
this warm and equable climate, one's sensations are not signi-
ficant of the height of the thermometer.

It is very fascinating to be here on the crater's edge, and to
look across its three miles of blackness to the clouds of red
vapour which Halemaumau is sending up, and altogether ex-
citing to watch the lofty curve of Mauna Loa upheave itself
against the moon, while far and faint, we see, or think we see,
that solemn light, which ever since my landing at Kawaihae
has been so mysteriously attractive. It is three days off yet.

* I venture to present this journal letter just as it was written, trusting
that the interest which attaches to volcanic regions, will carry the reader
through the minuteness and multiplicity of the details.
```

Perhaps its spasmodic fires will die out, and we shall find only blackness. Perhaps anything, except our seeing it as it ought to be seen ! The practical difficulty about a guide increases, and Mr. Gilman cannot help us to solve it. And if it be so cold at 4000 feet, what will it be at 14,000?

KILAUEA, *June 5th.*

I have no room in my thoughts for anything but volcanoes, and it will be so for some days to come. We have been all day in the crater, in fact I left Mr. Green and his native there, and came up with the guide, sore, stiff, bruised, cut, singed, grimy, with my thick gloves shrivelled off by the touch of sulphurous acid, and my boots nearly burned off. But what are cuts, bruises, fatigue, and singed eyelashes, in comparison with the awful sublimities I have witnessed to-day? The activity of Kilauea on Jan. 31 was as child's play to its activity to-day: as a display of fireworks compared to the conflagration of a metropolis. *Then*, the sense of awe gave way speedily to that of admiration of the dancing fire fountains of a fiery lake; *now*, it was all terror, horror, and sublimity, blackness, suffocating gases, scorching heat, crashings, surgings, detonations; half seen fires, hideous, tortured, wallowing waves. I feel as if the terrors of Kilauea would haunt me all my life, and be the Nemesis of weak and tired hours.

We left early, and descended the terminal wall, still, as before, green with ferns, *ohias*, and sandalwood, and bright with clusters of turquoise berries, and the red fruit and waxy blossom of the *ohelo*. The lowest depression of the crater, which I described before as a level, fissured sea of iridescent lava, has been apparently partially flooded by a recent overflow from Halemaumau, and the same agency has filled up the larger rifts with great shining rolls of black lava, obnoxiously like boa-constrictors in a state of repletion. In crossing this central area for the second time, with a mind less distracted by the novelty of the surroundings, I observed considerable deposits of remarkably impure sulphur, as well as sulphates of lime and alum in the larger fissures. The presence of moisture was always apparent in connection with these formations. The solidified surges and convolutions in which the lava lies, the latter sometimes so beautifully formed as to look like coils of wire rope, are truly wonderful. Within the cracks there are extraordinary coloured growths, orange, grey, buff, like mineral lichens, but very hard and brittle.

The recent lava flow by which Halemaumau has considerably heightened its walls, has raised the hill by which you

Halemaumau, Jan. 31.

ascend to the brink of the pit to a height of fully five hundred feet from the basin, and this elevation is at present much more fiery and precarious than the former one. It is dead, but not cold, lets one through into cracks hot with corrosive acid, rings hollow everywhere, and its steep acclivities lie in waves, streams, coils, twists, and tortuosities of all kinds, the surface glazed and smoothish, and with a metallic lustre.

Somehow, I expected to find Kilauea as I had left it in January, though the volumes of dense white smoke which are now rolling up from it might have indicated a change; but after the toilsome, breathless climbing of the awful lava hill, with the crust becoming more brittle, and the footing hotter at each step, instead of laughing fire fountains tossing themselves in gory splendour above the rim, there was a hot, sulphurous, mephitic chaos, covering, who knows what, of horror?

So far as we could judge, the level of the lake had sunk to about 80 feet below the margin, and the lately formed precipice was overhanging it considerably. About seven feet back from the edge of the ledge, there was a fissure about eighteen inches

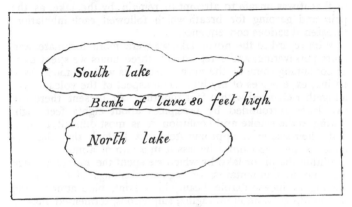

Outline of Halemaumau, June 4.

wide, emitting heavy fumes of sulphurous acid gas. Our visit seemed in vain, for on the risky verge of this crack we could only get momentary glimpses of wallowing fire, glaring lurid through dense masses of furious smoke which were rolling themselves round in the abyss as if driven by a hurricane.

After failing to get a better standpoint, we suffered so much from the gases, that we coasted the north, till we reached the south lake, one with the other on my former visit, but now separated by a solid lava barrier about three hundred feet broad, and eighty high. Here there was comparatively little smoke, and the whole mass of contained lava was ebullient and incandescent, its level marked the whole way round by a shelf or rim of molten lava, which adhered to the side, as ice often adheres to the margin of rapids, when the rest of the water is liberated and in motion. There was very little centri-petal action apparent. Though the mass was violently agitated it always took a southerly direction, and dashed itself with fearful violence against some lofty, undermined cliffs which formed its southern limit. The whole region vibrated with the shock of the fiery surges. To stand there was " to snatch a

fearful joy," out of a pain and terror which were unendurable.
For two or three minutes we kept going to the edge, seeing
the spectacle as with a flash, through half closed eyes, and
going back again; but a few trials, in which throats, nostrils,
and eyes were irritated to torture by the acid gases, convinced
us that it was unsafe to attempt to remain by the lake, as the
pain and gasping for breath which followed each inhalation,
threatened serious consequences.

With regard to the north lake we were more fortunate, and
more persevering, and I regard the three hours we spent by it
as containing some of the most solemn, as well as most fascinating, experiences of my life. The aspect of the volcano had
altogether changed within four months. At present there are
two lakes surrounded by precipices about eighty feet high.
Owing to the smoke and confusion it is most difficult to estimate their size even approximately, but I think that the diameter of the two cannot be less than a fifth of a mile.

Within the pit or lake by which we spent the morning, there
were no fiery mountains, or regular plashings of fiery waves
playing in indescribable beauty in a faint, blue atmosphere,
but lurid, gory, molten, raging, sulphurous, tormented masses
of matter, half seen through masses as restless, of lurid smoke.
Here, the violent action appeared centripetal, but with a southward tendency. Apparently, huge, bulging masses of a lurid-
coloured lava were wallowing the whole time one over another
in a central whirlpool, which occasionally flung up a wave of
fire thirty or forty feet. The greatest intensity of action was
always preceded by a dull, throbbing roar, as if the imprisoned
gases were seeking the vent which was afforded them by the
upward bulging of the wave and its bursting into spray. The
colour of the lava which appeared to be thrown upwards from
great depths, was more fiery and less gory than that nearer the
surface. Now and then, through rifts in the smoke, we saw a
convergence of the whole molten mass into the centre, which
rose wallowing and convulsed to a considerable height. The
awful sublimity of what we did see, was enhanced by the knowledge that it was only a thousandth part of what we did not see,
mere momentary glimpses of a terror and fearfulness which
otherwise could not have been borne.

A ledge, only three or four feet wide, hung over the lake,
and between that and the comparative *terra firma* of the old
lava, there was a fissure of unknown depth, emitting hot blasts
of pernicious gases. The guide would not venture on the out-

side ledge, but Mr. Green, in his scientific zeal, crossed the crack, telling me not to follow him, but presently, in his absorption with what he saw, called to me to come, and I jumped across, and this remained our perilous standpoint.*

Burned, singed, stifled, blinded, only able to stand on one foot at a time, jumping back across the fissure every two or three minutes to escape an unendurable whiff of heat and sulphurous stench, or when splitting sounds below threatened the disruption of the ledge : lured as often back by the fascination of the horrors below ; so we spent three hours.

There was every circumstance of awfulness to make the impression of the sight indelible. Sometimes, dense volumes of smoke hid everything, and yet, upwards, from out "their sulphurous canopy" fearful sounds arose, crashings, thunderings, detonations, and we never knew then whether the spray of some uplifted wave might not dash up to where we stood. At other times the smoke partially lifting, but still swirling in strong eddies, revealed a central whirlpool of fire, wallowing at unknown depths, to which the lava, from all parts of the lake, slid centrewards and downwards as into a vortex, where it mingled its waves with indescribable noise and fury, and then, breaking upwards, dashed itself to a great height in fierce, gory gouts and clots, while hell itself seemed opening at our feet. At times, again, bits of the lake skinned over with a skin of a wonderful silvery, satiny sheen, to be immediately devoured ; and as the lurid billows broke, they were mingled with bright patches as if of misplaced moonlight. Always changing, always suggesting force which nothing could repel, agony indescribable, mystery inscrutable, terror unutterable, a thing of eternal dread, revealed only in glimpses !

It is natural to think that St. John the Evangelist, in some Patmos vision, was transported to the brink of this "bottomless pit," and found in its blackness and turbulence of agony the fittest emblems of those tortures of remorse and memory, which we may well believe are the quenchless flames of the region of self-chosen exile from goodness and from God. As natural, too, that all Scripture phrases which typify the place of woe should recur to one with the force of a new interpretation, "Who can dwell with the everlasting burnings?" "The smoke

---

* Since then, the Austins of Onomea were standing on a similar ledge, when a sound as of a surge striking below, made them jump back hastily, and in another moment the projection split off and was engulfed in the fiery lake.

of their torment goeth up for ever and ever," "The place of
hell," "The bottomless pit," "The vengeance of eternal fire,"
"A lake of fire burning with brimstone." No sight can be so
fearful as this glimpse into the interior of the earth, where
fires are for ever wallowing with purposeless force and aimless
agony.

Beyond the lake there is a horrible region in which dense
volumes of smoke proceed from the upper ground, with loud
bellowings and detonations, and we took our perilous way in
that direction, over very hot lava which gave way constantly.
It is near this that the steady fires are situated which are visible
from this house at night. We came first upon a solitary
"blowing cone," beyond which there was a group of three or
four, but it is not from these that the smoke proceeds, but from
the extensive area beyond them, covered with smoke and steam
cracks, and smoking banks, which are probably formed of sulphur deposits. I visited only the solitary cone, for the footing
was so precarious, the sight so fearful, and the ebullitions of
gases so dangerous, that I did not dare to go near the others,
and do not wish ever to look upon their like again.

The one I saw was of beehive shape, about twelve feet high,
hollow inside, and its walls were about two feet thick. A part
of its imperfect top was blown off, and a piece of its side blown
out, and the side rent gave one a frightful view of its interior,
with the risk of having lava spat at one at intervals. The name
"Blowing Cone" is an apt one, if the theory of their construction be correct. It is supposed that when the surface of the
lava cools rapidly owing to enfeebled action below, the gases
force their way upwards through small vents, which then serve
as "blow holes" for the imprisoned fluid beneath. This,
rapidly cooling as it is ejected, forms a ring on the surface of
the crust, which, growing upwards by accretion, forms a
chimney, eventually nearly or quite closed at the top, so as to
form a cone. In this case the cone is about eighty feet above
the present level of the lake, and fully one hundred yards distant from its present verge.

The whole of the inside was red and molten, full of knobs,
and great fiery stalactites. Jets of lava at a white heat were
thrown up constantly, and frequently the rent in the side spat out
lava in clots, which cooled rapidly, and looked like drops of bottle-
green glass. The glimpses I got of the interior were necessarily
brief and intermittent. The blast or roar which came up from
below was more than deafening; it was stunning: and accom

panied with heavy subterranean rumblings and detonations. The chimney, so far as I could see, opened out gradually downwards to a great width, and appeared to be about forty feet deep; and at its base there was an abyss of lashing, tumbling, restless fire, emitting an ominous, surging sound, and breaking upwards with a fury which threatened to blow the cone and the crust on which it stands, into the air.

The heat was intense, and the stinging sulphurous gases, which were given forth in large quantities, most poisonous. The group of cones west of this one, was visited by Mr. Green; but he found it impossible to make any further explorations. He has seen nearly all the recent volcanic phenomena, but says that these cones present the most "infernal" appearance he has ever witnessed. We returned for a last look at Halemaumau, but the smoke was so dense, and the sulphur fumes so stifling, that, as in a fearful dream, we only heard the thunder of its hidden surges. I write thunder, and one speaks of the lashing of waves; but these are words pertaining to the familiar earth, and have no place in connection with Kilauea. The breaking lava has a voice all its own, full of compressed fury. Its sound, motion, and aspect are all infernal. *Hellish*, is the only fitting term.

We are dwelling on a cooled crust all over Southern Hawaii, the whole region is recent lava, and between this and the sea there are several distinct lines of craters thirty miles long, all of which at some time or other have vomited forth the innumerable lava streams which streak the whole country in the districts of Kau, Puna, and Hilo. In fact, Hawaii is a great slag. There is something very solemn in the position of this crater-house: with smoke and steam coming out of every pore of the ground, and in front the huge crater, which to-night lights all the sky. My second visit has produced a far deeper impression even than the first, and one of awe and terror solely.

Kilauea is altogether different from the European volcanoes which send lava and stones into the air in fierce, sudden spasms, and then subside into harmlessness. Ever changing, never resting, the force which stirs it never weakening, raging for ever with tossing and strength like the ocean: its labours unfinished, and possibly never to be finished, its very unexpectedness adds to its sublimity and terror, for until you reach the terminal wall of the crater, it looks by daylight but a smoking pit in the midst of a dreary stretch of waste land.

Last night I thought the Southern Cross out of place; to-night it seems essential, as Calvary over against Sinai. For Halemaumau involuntarily typifies the necessity which shall consume all evil: and the constellation, pale against its lurid light, the great love and yearning of the Father, " who spared not His own Son, but delivered Him up for us all," that, " as in Adam all die, even so in Christ shall all be made alive."

AINEPO, HAWAII, *June 5th.*

WE had a great fright last evening. We had been engaging mules, and talking over our plans with our half-Indian host, when he opened the door and exclaimed, " There's no light on Mauna Loa; the fire's gone out." We rushed out, and though the night was clear and frosty, the mountain curve rose against the sky without the accustomed wavering glow upon it. " I'm afraid you'll have your trouble for nothing," Mr. Gilman unsympathisingly remarked; " anyhow, its awfully cold up there," and rubbing his hands, reseated himself at the fire. Mr. G. and I stayed out till we were half-frozen, and I persuaded myself and him that there was a redder tinge than the moonlight above the summit, but the mountain has given no sign all day, so that I fear that I " evolved " the light out of my " inner consciousness."

Mr. Gilman was eloquent on the misfortunes of our predecessors, lent me a pair of woollen socks to put on over my gloves, told me privately that if anyone could succeed in getting a guide it would be Mr. Green, and dispatched us at eight this morning with a lurking smile at our "fool's errand," thinly veiled by warm wishes for our success. Mr. Reid has two ranches on the mountain, seven miles distant from each other, and was expected every hour at the crater-house on his way to Hilo, but it was not known from which he was coming, and as it appeared that our last hope of getting a guide lay in securing his goodwill, Mr. G., his servant, and pack-mule took the lower trail, and I, with a native, a string of mules, and a pack-horse, the upper. Our plans for intercepting the good man were well laid and successful, but turned out resultless.

This has been an irresistibly comical day, and it is just as well to have something amusing interjected between the sublimities of Kilauea, and whatever to-morrow may bring forth. When our cavalcades separated, I followed the guide on a blind trail into the little-known regions on the skirts of Mauna Loa.

We only travelled two miles an hour, and the mules kept getting up rows, kicking, and entangling their legs in the lariats, and one peculiarly malign animal dealt poor Kahélé a gratuitous kick on his nose, making it bleed.

It is a strange, unique country, without any beauty. The seaward view is over a great stretch of apparent table-land, spotted with craters, and split by cracks emitting smoke or steam. The whole region is black with streams of spiked and jagged lava, meandering over it, with charred stumps of trees rising out of them.

The trail, if such it could be called, wound among *koa* and sandalwood trees occasionally, but habitually we picked our way over waves, coils, and hummocks of *pahoehoe* surrounded by volcanic sand, and with only a few tufts of grass, abortive *ohelos*, and vigorous sow-thistles (much relished by Kahélé) growing in their crevices. Horrid cracks, 50 or 60 feet wide, probably made by earthquakes, abounded, and a black chasm of most infernal aspect dogged us on the left. It was all scrambling up and down. Sometimes there was long, ugly grass, a brownish green, coarse and tufty, for a mile or more. Sometimes clumps of wintry-looking, dead trees, sometimes clumps of attenuated living ones; but nothing to please the eye. We saw neither man nor beast the whole way, except a wild bull, which, tearing down the mountain side, crossed the trail just in front of us, causing a stampede among the mules, and it was fully an hour before they were all caught again.

The only other incident was an earthquake, the most severe, the men here tell me, that has been experienced for two years. One is prepared for any caprices on the part of the earth here, yet when there was a fearful internal throbbing and rumbling, and the trees and grass swayed rapidly, and great rocks and masses of soil were dislodged, and bounded down the hillside, and the earth reeled, and my poor horse staggered and stopped short, far from rising to the magnitude of the occasion, I thought I was attacked with vertigo, and grasped the horn of my saddle to save myself from falling. After a moment of profound stillness, there was again a subterranean sound like a train in a tunnel, and the earth reeled again with such violence, that I felt as if the horse and myself had gone over. Poor K. was nervous for some time afterwards. The motion was as violent as that of a large ship in a mid-Atlantic storm. There were four minor shocks within half an hour afterwards.

After crawling along for seven hours, and for the last two in a dripping fog, so dense that I had to keep within kicking range of the mules for fear of being lost, we heard the lowing of domestic cattle, and came to a place where felled trees, very difficult for the horses to cross, were lying. Then a rude boundary wall appeared, inside of which was a small, poor-looking grass house, consisting of one partially-divided room, with a small, ruinous-looking cook-house, a shed, and an unfinished frame-house near it. It looked, and is, a disconsolate conclusion of a wet day's ride. I rode into the corral, and found two or three very rough-looking whites and half-whites standing, and addressing one of them, I found he was Mr. Reid's manager there. I asked if they could give me a night's lodging, which seemed a diverting notion to them; and they said they could give me the rough accommodation they had, but it was hard even for them, till the new house was put up. They brought me into this very rough shelter, a draughty grass room, with a bench, table, and one chair in it. Two men came in, but not the native wife and family, and sat down to a calabash of *poi* and some strips of dried beef, food so coarse, that they apologised for not offering it to me. They said they had sent to the lower ranch for some flour, and in the meantime they gave me some milk in a broken bowl, their "nearest approach to a tumbler," they said. I was almost starving, for all our food was on the pack-mule. This is the place where we had been told that we could obtain tea, flour, beef, and fowls !

By some fatality my pen, ink, and knitting were on the pack-mule; it was very cold, the afternoon fog closed us in, and darkness came on prematurely, so that I felt a most absurd sense of *ennui*, and went over to the cook-house, where I found Gandle cooking, and his native wife, with a heap of children and dogs lying round the stove. I joined them till my clothes were dry, on which the man, who, in spite of his rough exterior, was really friendly and hospitable, remarked that he saw I was "one of the sort who knew how to take people as I found them."

This regular afternoon mist which sets in at a certain altitude, blotting out the sun and sky, and bringing the horizon within a few yards, makes me certain after all that the mists of rainless Eden were a phenomenon, the loss of which is not to be regretted.

Still the afternoon hung on, and I went back to the house feeling that the most desirable event which the future could produce would be—a meal. Now and then the men came in and talked for a while, and as the darkness and cold intensified, they brought in an arrangement extemporised out of what looked like a battered tin bath, half full of earth, with some lighted faggots at the top, which gave out a little warmth and much stinging smoke. Actual, undoubted, night came on without Mr. Green, of whose failure I felt certain, and without food, and being blinded by the smoke, I rolled myself in a blanket and fell asleep on the bench, only to wake in a great fright, believing that the volcano house was burning over my head, and that a venerable missionary was taking advantage of the confusion to rob my saddle-bags, which in truth one of the men was moving out of harm's way, having piled up the fire two feet high.

Presently a number of voices outside shouted *Haole!* and Mr. Green came in shaking the water from his waterproof, with the welcome words, " Everything's settled for to-morrow." Mr. Reid threw cold water on the ascent, and could give no help ; and Mr. G. being thus left to himself, after a great deal of trouble, has engaged as guide an active young goat-hunter, who, though he has never been to the top of the mountain, knows other parts of it so well that he is sure he can take us up. Mr. G. also brings an additional mule and pack-horse, so that our equipment is complete, except in the matter of cruppers, which we have been obliged to make for ourselves out of goats' hair rope, and old stockings. If Mr. G. has an eye for the picturesque, he must have been gratified as he came in from the fog and darkness into the grass room, with the flaring fire in the middle, the rifles gleaming on the wall, the two men in very rough clothing, and myself huddled up in a blanket sitting on the floor, where my friend was very glad to join us.

Mr. Green has brought nothing but tea from Kapapala, but Gandle has made some excellent rolls, besides feasting us on stewed fowl, dough nuts, and milk ! Little comfort is promised for to-night, as Gandle says, with a twinkle of kindly malice in his eye, that we shall not " get a wink of sleep, for the place swarms with fleas." They are a great pest of the colder regions of the islands, and, like all other nuisances, are said to have been imported ! Gandle and the other man have entertained us with the misfortunes of our predecessors, on which they seem to gloat with ill-omened satisfaction.

I. L. B.

LETTER XXIX.—*continued.*

Ascent of Mauna Loa—*Pahoehoe* and *a-a*—The Crater of Mokuaweoweo—The Great Fire-fountain — Our Camp—A Night Scene—An Alarming Ride.

KAPAPALA, *June 8th.*

THE fleas at Ainepo quite fulfilled Mr. Gandle's prognostications, and I was glad when the stars went out one by one, and a red, cloudless dawn broke over the mountain, accompanied by a heavy dew and a morning mist, which soon rolled itself up into rosy folds and disappeared, and there was a legitimate excuse for getting up. Our host provided us with flour, sugar, and dough nuts, and a hot breakfast, and our expedition, comprising two natives who knew not a word of English, Mr. G. who does not know very much more Hawaiian than I do, and myself, started at seven. We had four superb mules, and two good pack-horses, a large tent, and a plentiful supply of camping blankets. I put on all my own warm clothes, as well as most of those which had been lent to me, which gave me the squat, padded look of a puffin or Esquimaux, but all and more were needed long before we reached the top. The mules were beyond all praise. They went up the most severe ascent I have ever seen, climbing steadily for nine hours, without a touch of the spur, and after twenty-four hours of cold, thirst, and hunger, came down again as actively as cats. The pack-horses too were very good, but from the comparative clumsiness with which they move their feet they were severely cut.

We went off, as usual, in single file, the guide first, and Mr. G. last. The track was passably legible for some time, and wound through long grass and small *koa* trees, mixed with stunted *ohias* and a few common ferns. Half these *koa* trees are dead, and all, both living and dead, have their branches covered with a long hairy lichen, nearly white, making the dead forest in the slight mist look like a wood in England when covered with rime on a fine winter morning. The *koa* tree has a peculiarity of bearing two distinct species of leaves on the same twig, one like a curved willow leaf, the other that of an acacia.

After two hours' ascent we camped on the verge of the timber line, and fed our animals, while the two natives hewed firewood, and loaded the spare pack-horse with it. The sky was by that time cloudless, and the atmosphere brilliant, and both remained so until we reached the same place twenty-eight hours later, so that the weather favoured us in every respect, for there is " weather " on the mountain, rains, fogs, and wind storms. The grass only grows sparsely in tufts above this place, and though vegetation exists up to a height of 10,000 feet on this side, it consists, for the most part, of grey lichens, a little withered grass, and a hardy asplenium.

At this spot the real business of the ascent begins, and we tightened our girths, distributed the baggage as fairly as possible, and made all secure before remounting.

We soon entered on vast uplands of *pahoehoe* which ground away the animals' feet, a horrid waste, extending upwards for 7000 feet. For miles and miles, above and around, great billowy masses, tossed and twisted into an infinity of fantastic shapes, arrest and weary the eye, lava in all its forms, from a compact phonolite to the lightest pumice stone, the mere froth of the volcano. Recollect the vastness of this mountain. The whole south of this large island, down to and below the water's edge, is composed of its slopes. Its height is nearly three miles, and its base is 180 miles in circumference, so that Wales might be packed away within it, leaving room to spare. Yet its whole bulk, above a height of about 8000 feet, is one frightful desert, at once the creation and the prey of the mightiest force on earth.

Struggling, slipping, tumbling, jumping, ledge after ledge was surmounted, but still, upheaved against the glittering sky, rose new difficulties to be overcome. Immense bubbles have risen from the confused masses, and bursting, have yawned apart. Swift-running streams of more recent lava have cleft straight furrows through the older congealed surface. Massive flows have fallen in, exposing caverned depths of jagged outlines. Earthquakes have riven the mountain, splitting its sides and opening deep *crevasses*, which must be leapt or circumvented. Horrid streams of *a-a*, which, after rushing remorselessly over the kindlier lava, have heaped rugged pinnacles of brown scoriæ into impassable walls, have to be cautiously

skirted. Winding round the bases of tossed up, fissured hummocks of *pahoehoe*, leaping from one broken hummock to
another, clambering up acclivities so steep that the pack-horse
rolled backwards once, and my cat-like mule fell twice, moving
cautiously over crusts which rang hollow to the tread ; stepping
over deep cracks, which, perhaps, led down to the burning,
fathomless sea, traversing hilly lakes ruptured by earthquakes,
and split in cooling into a thousand fissures, painfully toiling
up the sides of mounds of scoriæ frothed with pumice-stone,
and again for miles surmounting rolling surfaces of billowy,
ropy lava—so passed the long day, under the tropic sun and
the deep blue sky.

Towards afternoon, clouds heaped themselves in snowy
masses, all radiance and beauty to us, all fog and gloom below,
girdling the whole mountain, and interposing their glittering
screen between us and the dark timber belt, the black,
smoking shores of Kau, and the blue shimmer of the Pacific.
From that time, for twenty-four hours, the lower world, and
"works and ways of busy men" were entirely shut out, and
we were alone with this trackless and inanimate region of
horror.

For the first time our guide hesitated as to the right track,
for the faint suspicion of white smoke, which had kept alive
our hope that the fire was still burning, had ceased to be
visible. We called a halt while he reconnoitred, tried to eat
some food, found that our pulses were beating 100 a minute,
bathed our heads, specially our temples, with snow, as we had
been advised to do by the oldest mountaineer on Hawaii, and
heaped on yet more clothing. In fact, I tied a double woollen
scarf over all my face but my eyes, and put on a French soldier's
overcoat, with cape and hood, which Mr. Green had brought
in case of emergency. The cold had become intense. We
had not wasted words at any time, and on remounting, preserved as profound a silence as if we were on a forlorn hope,
even the natives intermitting their ceaseless gabble.

Upwards still, in the cold bright air, coasting the edges of
deep cracks, climbing endless terraces, the mules panting
heavily, our breath coming as if from excoriated lungs,—so we
surmounted the highest ledge. But on reaching the apparent
summit we were to all appearance as far from the faint smoke
as ever, for this magnificent dome, whose base is sixty miles in
diameter, is crowned by a ghastly, volcanic table-land, cre-
viced, riven, and ashy, twenty-four miles in circumference. A

table-land, indeed, of dark grey lava, blotched by outbursts, and torn by streams of brown *a-a*, and full of hideous *crevasses* and fearful shapes, as if a hundred waves of lava had rolled themselves one on another, and had congealed in confused heaps.

Our guide took us a little wrong once, but soon recovered himself with much sagacity. "Wrong" on Mauna Loa means being arrested by an impassable *a-a* stream, and our last predecessors had nearly been stopped by getting into one in which they suffered severely.

These *a-a* streams are very deep, and when in a state of fusion move along in a mass twenty feet high sometimes, with very solid walls. Professor Alexander, of Honolulu, supposes them to be from the beginning less fluid than *pahoehoe*, and that they advance very slowly, being full of solid points, or centres of cooling : that *a-a*, in fact, *grains* like sugar. Its hardness is indescribable. It is an aggregate of upright, rugged, adamantine points, and at a distance, a river of it looks like a dark brown *Mer de Glace*.

At half-past four we reached the edge of an *a-a* stream, about as wide as the Ouse at Huntingdon Bridge, and it was obvious that somehow or other we must cross it : indeed, I know not if it be possible to reach the crater without passing through one or another of these obstacles.* I should have liked to have left the animals there, but it was represented as impossible to proceed on foot, and though this was a decided misrepresentation, Mr. Green plunged in. I had resolved that he should never have any bother in consequence of his kindness in taking me with him, and, indeed, everyone had enough to do in taking care of himself and his own beast, but I never found it harder to repress a cry for help. Not that I was in the least danger, but there was every risk of the beautiful mule being much hurt, or breaking her legs. The fear shown by the animals was pathetic ; they shrank back, cowered, trembled, breathed hard and heavily, and stumbled and plunged painfully. It was sickening to see their terror and suffering, the struggling and slipping into cracks, the blood and torture. The mules with their small legs and wonderful agility were more frightened than hurt, but the horses were splashed with blood up to their knees, and their poor eyes looked piteous.

* Professor George Forbes who ascended Mauna Loa in 1875, informs me that he reached the crater without passing through *a-a*.

We were then, as we knew, close to the edge of the crater, but the faint smoke wreath had disappeared, and there was nothing but the westering sun hanging like a ball over the black horizon of the desolate summit. We rode as far as a deep fissure filled with frozen snow, with a ledge beyond, threw ourselves from our mules, jumped the fissure, and more than 800 feet below yawned the inaccessible blackness and horror of the crater of Mokuaweoweo, six miles in circumference, and 11,000 feet long by 8000 wide. The mystery was solved, for at one end of the crater, in a deep gorge of its own, above the level of the rest of the area, there was the lonely fire, the reflection of which, for six weeks, has been seen for 100 miles.

Nearly opposite us, a thing of beauty, a fountain of pure, yellow fire, unlike the gory gleam of Kilauea, was regularly playing in several united but independent jets, throwing up its glorious incandescence, to a height, as we afterwards ascertained, of from 150 to 300 feet, and attaining at one time 600 ! You cannot imagine such a beautiful sight. The sunset gold was not purer than the living fire. The distance which we were from it, divested it of the inevitable horrors which surround it. It was all beauty. For the last two miles of the ascent, we had heard a distant, vibrating roar : there, at the crater's edge, it was a glorious sound, the roar of an ocean at dispeace, mingled with the hollow murmur of surf echoing in sea caves, booming on, rising and falling, like the thunder music of windward Hawaii.

We sat on the ledge outside the fissure for some time, and Mr. Green actually proposed to pitch the tent there, but I dissuaded him, on the ground that an earthquake might send the whole thing tumbling into the crater; nor was this a whimsical objection, for during the night there were two such falls, and after breakfast, another quite near us.

We had travelled for two days under a strong impression that the fires had died out, so you can imagine the sort of stupor of satisfaction with which we feasted on the glorious certainty. Yes, it was glorious, that far-off fire-fountain, and the lurid cracks in the slow-moving, black-crusted flood, which passed calmly down from the higher level to the grand area of the crater.

This area, over two miles long, and a mile and a half wide, with precipitous sides 800 feet deep, and a broad second shelf about 300 feet below the one we occupied, at that time ap-

peared a dark grey, tolerably level lake, with great black
blotches, and yellow and white stains, the whole much fissured.
No steam or smoke proceeded from any part of the level surface, and it had the unnaturally dead look which follows the
action of fire.   A ledge, or false beach, which must mark a
once higher level of the lava, skirts the lake, at an elevation of
thirty feet probably, and this fringed the area with various signs
of present volcanic action, steaming sulphur banks, and heavy
jets of smoke.   The other side, above the crater, has a ridgy,
broken look, giving the false impression of a mountainous
region beyond.   At this time the luminous fountain, and the
red cracks in the river of lava which proceeded from it, were
the only fires visible in the great area of blackness.   In former
days people have descended to the floor of the crater, but
owing to the breaking away of the accessible part of the precipice, a descent is not feasible, though I doubt not that a
man might even now get down, if he went up with suitable
tackle, and sufficient assistance.

The one disappointment was that this extraordinary fire-
fountain was not only 800 feet below us, but nearly three-
quarters of a mile from us, and that it was impossible to get
any nearer to it.   Those who have made the ascent before have
found themselves obliged either to camp on the very spot we
occupied, or a little below it.

The natives pitched the tent as near to the crater as was
safe, with one pole in a crack, and the other in the great fissure, which was filled to within three feet of the top with snow
and ice.   As the opening of the tent was on the crater side, we
could not get in or out without going down into this *crevasse.*
The tent walls were held down with stones to make it as snug
as possible, but *snug* is a word of the lower earth, and has no
meaning on that frozen mountain top.   The natural floor was
of rough slabs of lava, laid partly edgewise, so that a newly
macadamised road would have been as soft a bed.   The
natives spread the horse blankets over it, and I arranged the
camping blankets, made my own part of the tent as comfortable as possible by putting my inverted saddle down for a
pillow, put on my last reserve of warm clothing, took the food
out of the saddle bags, and then felt how impossible it was to
exert myself in the rarefied air, or even to upbraid Mr. Green
for having forgotten the tea, of which I had reminded him as
often as was consistent with politeness !

This discovery was not made till after we had boiled the

kettle, and my dismay was softened by remembering that as
water boils up there at 192°, our tea would have been worthless. In spite of my objection to stimulants, and in defiance
of the law against giving liquor to natives, I made a great tin
of brandy toddy, of which all partook, along with tinned salmon
and dough-nuts. Then the men piled faggots on the fire and
began their everlasting chatter, and Mr. Green and I, huddled
up in blankets, sat on the outer ledge in solemn silence, to
devote ourselves to the volcano.

The sun was just setting: the tooth-like peaks of Mauna
Kea, cold and snow slashed, which were blushing red, the next
minute turned ghastly against a chilly sky, and with the dis-
appearance of the sun it became severely cold ; yet we were
able to remain there till 9.30, the first people to whom such a
thing has been possible, so supremely favoured were we by the
absence of wind.

When the sun had set, and the brief, red glow of the tropics
had vanished, a new world came into being, and wonder after
wonder flashed forth from the previously lifeless crater. Everywhere through its vast expanse appeared glints of fire—fires
bright and steady, burning in rows like blast furnaces ; fires
lone and isolated, unwinking like planets, or twinkling like
stars ; rows of little fires marking the margin of the lowest
level of the crater ; fire molten in deep *crevasses ;* fire in wavy
lines ; fire, calm, stationary, and restful : an incandescent lake
two miles in length beneath a deceptive crust of darkness, and
whose depth one dare not fathom even in thought. Broad in
the glare, giving light enough to read by at a distance of three-
quarters of a mile, making the moon look as blue as an ordinary English sky, its golden gleam changed to a vivid rose
colour, lighting up the whole of the vast precipices of that
part of the crater with a rosy red, bringing out every detail
here, throwing cliffs and heights into huge, black masses there,
rising, falling, never intermitting, leaping in lofty jets with
glorious shapes like wheatsheaves, coruscating, reddening, the
most glorious thing beneath the moon was the fire-fountain of
Mokuaweoweo.

By day the cooled crust of the lake had looked black and
even sooty, with a fountain of molten gold playing upwards
from it ; by night it was all incandescent, with black blotches
of cooled scum upon it, which were perpetually being devoured.
The centre of the lake was at a white heat, and waves of white
hot lava appeared to be wallowing there as in a whirlpool, and

from this centre the fountain rose, solid at its base, which is estimated at 150 feet in diameter, but thinning and frittering as it rose into the air, and falling from the great altitude to which it attained, in fiery spray, which made a very distinct clatter on the fiery surface below. When one jet was about half high, another rose so as to keep up the action without intermission ; and in the lower part of the fountain two subsidiary curved jets of great volume continually crossed each other. So, " alone in its glory," perennial, self-born, springing up in sparkling light, the fire-fountain played on as the hours went by.

From the nearer margin of this incandescent lake there was a mighty but deliberate overflow, a " silent tide " of fire, passing to the lower level, glowing under and amidst its crust, with the brightness of metal passing from a surface. In the bank of partially cooled and crusted lava which appears to support the lake, there were rifts showing the molten lava within. In one place heavy, white vapour blew off in powerful jets from the edge of the lake, and elsewhere there were frequent jets and ebullitions of the same, but there was not a trace of vapour over the burning lake itself. The crusted large area, with its blowing cones, blotches and rifts of fire, was nearly all visible, and from the thickness and quietness of the crust it was obvious that the ocean of lava below was comparatively at rest, but a dark precipice concealed a part of the glowing and highly agitated lake, adding another mystery to its sublimity.

It is probable that the whole interior of this huge dome is fluid, for the eruptions from this summit crater do not proceed from its filling up and running over, but from the mountain sides being unable to bear the enormous pressure ; when they give way, high or low, and bursting, allow the fiery contents to escape. So, in 1855, the mountain side split open, and the lava gushed forth for thirteen months in a stream which ran for 60 miles, and flooded Hawaii for 300 square miles.*

From the camping ground, immense cracks parallel with the crater, extend for some distance, and the whole of the compact grey stone of the summit is much fissured. These cracks, like the one by which our tent was pitched, contain water resting on ice. It shows the extreme difference of climate on the two sides of Hawaii, that while vegetation straggles

---

* Since white men have inhabited the islands, there have been ten recorded eruptions from the craters of Mauna Loa, and one from Hualalai.

up to a height of 10,000 feet on the windward side in a few
miserable, blasted forms, it absolutely ceases at a height of
7000 feet on the leeward.

It was too cold to sit up all night; so by the "fire light" J
wrote the enclosed note to you with fingers nearly freezing or
the pen, and climbed into the tent.

It is possible that tent life in the East, or in the Rocky
Mountains, with beds, tables, travelling knick-knacks of all
descriptions, and servants who study their master's whims,
may be very charming; but my experience of it having been
of the make-shift and non-luxurious kind, is not delectable. A
wooden saddle, without stuffing, made a very fair pillow; but
the ridges of the lava were severe. I could not spare enough
blankets to soften them, and one particularly intractable point
persisted in making itself felt. I crowded on everything attain-
able, two pairs of gloves, with Mr. Gilman's socks over them,
and a thick plaid muffled up my face. Mr. Green and the
natives, buried in blankets, occupied the other part of the tent.
The phrase, "sleeping on the brink of a volcano," was literally true, for I fell asleep, and fear I might have been
prosaic enough to sleep all night, had it not been for fleas
which had come up in the camping blankets. When I woke,
it was light enough to see that the three muffled figures were
all asleep, instead of spending the night in shiverings and
vertigo, as it appears that others have done. Doubtless the
bathing of our heads several times with snow and ice-water had
been beneficial.

Circumstances were singular. It was a strange thing to
sleep on a lava-bed at a height of nearly 14,000 feet, far away
from the nearest dwelling, "in a region," as Mr. Jarves says,
"rarely visited by man," hearing all the time the roar, clash,
and thunder of the mightiest volcano in the world. It seemed
a wild dream, as that majestic sound moved on. There were
two loud reports, followed by a prolonged crash, occa-
sioned by parts of the crater walls giving way; vibrating
rumblings, as if of earthquakes; and then a louder surging
of the fiery ocean, and a series of most imposing detonations.
Creeping over the sleeping forms, which never stirred even
though I had to kneel upon one of the natives while I untied
the flap of the tent, I crept cautiously into the *crevasse* in which
the snow-water was then hard frozen, and out upon the projecting ledge. The four hours in which we had previously
watched the volcano had passed like one; but the lonely hours

which followed might have been two minutes or a year, for time was obliterated.

Coldly the Pole-star shivered above the frozen summit, and a blue moon, nearly full, withdrew her faded light into infinite space. The Southern Cross had set. Two peaks below the Pole-star, sharply defined against the sky, were the only signs of any other world than the world of fire and mystery around. It was light, broadly, vividly light; the sun himself, one would have thought, might look pale beside it. But such a light! The silver index of my thermometer, which had fallen to 23° Fahrenheit, was ruby red; that of the aneroid, which gave the height at 13,603 feet, was the same. The white duck of the tent was rosy, and all the crater walls and the dull-grey ridges which lie around were a vivid rose red.

All Hawaii was sleeping. Our Hilo friends looked out the last thing; saw the glare, and probably wondered how we were "getting on," high up among the stars. Mine were the only mortal eyes which saw what is perhaps the grandest spectacle on earth. Once or twice I felt so overwhelmed by the very sublimity of the loneliness, that I turned to the six animals, which stood shivering in the north wind, without any consciousness than that of cold, hunger, and thirst. It was some relief even to pity them, for pity was at least a human feeling, and a momentary rest from the thrill of the new sensations inspired by the circumstances. The moon herself looked a wan, unfamiliar thing—not the same moon which floods the palm and mango groves of Hilo with light and tenderness. And those palm and mango groves, and lighted homes, and seas, and ships, and cities, and faces of friends, and all familiar things, and the day before, and the years before, were as things in dreams, coming up out of a vanished past. And would there ever be another day, and would the earth ever be young and green again, and would men buy and sell and strive for gold, and should I ever with a human voice tell living human beings of the things of this midnight? How far it was from all the world, uplifted above love, hate, and storms of passion, and war, and wreck of thrones, and dissonant clash of human thought, serene in the eternal solitudes!

Things had changed, as they change hourly in craters. The previous loud detonations were probably connected with the evolutions of some "blowing cones," which were now very fierce, and throwing up lava at the comparatively dead end of the crater. Lone stars of fire broke out frequently through the blackened crust. The molten river, flowing from the in-candescent lake, had advanced and broadened considerably. That lake itself, whose diameter has been estimated at 800 feet, was rose-red and self-illuminated, and the increased noise was owing to the increased force of the fire-fountain, which was playing regularly at a height of 300 feet, with the cross fountains, like wheat-sheaves, at its lower part. These cross-fountains were the colour of a mixture of blood and fire, and the lower part of the perpendicular jets was the same; but as they rose and thinned, this colour passed into a vivid rose-red, and the spray and splashes were as rubies and flame mingled. For ever falling in fiery masses and fiery foam: accompanied by a thunder-music of its own: companioned only by the solemn stars: exhibiting no other token of its glories to man than the reflection of its fires on mist and smoke; it burns for the Creator's eye alone, for no foot of mortal can approach it.

Hours passed as I watched the indescribable glories of the fire-fountain, its beauty of form, and its radiant reflection on the precipices, 800 feet high, which wall it in, and listened to its surges beating, and the ebb and flow of its thunder-music. Then a change occurred. The jets, which for long had been playing at a height of 300 feet, suddenly became quite low, and for a few seconds appeared as cones of fire wallowing in a sea of light; then with a roar like the sound of gathering waters, nearly the whole surface of the lake was lifted up by the action of some powerful internal force, and its whole radiant mass, rose three times, in one glorious, upward burst, to a height, as estimated by the surrounding cliffs, of 600 feet, while the earth trembled, and the moon and stars withdrew abashed into far-off space. After this the fire-fountain played as before. The cold had become intense, 11° of frost; and I crept back into the tent: those words occurring to me with a new meaning, " dwelling in the light which no man can approach unto."

We remained in the tent till the sun had slightly warmed the air, and then attempted to prepare breakfast by the fire; but no one could eat anything, and the native from Waimea complained of severe headache, which shortly became ago-nizing, and he lay on the ground moaning, and completely prostrated by mountain sickness. I felt extreme lassitude, and exhaustion followed the slightest effort; but the use of snow to the head produced great relief. The water in our canteens

was hard frozen, and the keenness of the cold aggravated the
uncomfortable symptoms which accompany pulses at 110°.
The native guide was the only person capable of work, so we
were late in getting off, and rode four and a half hours to the
camping ground, only stopping once to tighten our girths. Not
a rope, strap, buckle, or any of our gear gave way, and though
I rode without a crupper, the breeching of a pack mule's saddle
kept mine steady.

The descent, to the riders, is far more trying than the ascent,
owing to the continued stretch of very steep declivity for
8000 feet; but our mules never tripped, and came into
Ainepo as if they had not travelled at all. The horses were
terribly cut, both again in the *a-a* stream, and on the descent.
It was sickening to follow them, for at first they left fragments
of hide and hair on the rocks, then flesh, and when there was
no more hide or flesh to come off their poor heels and fet
locks, blood dripped on every rock, and if they stood still for
a few moments, every hoof left a little puddle of gore. We had
all the enjoyment and they all the misery. I was much exhausted when we reached the camping-ground, but soon revived
under the influence of food; but the poor native, who was
really very ill, abandoned himself to wretchedness, and has only
recovered to-day.

The belt of cloud which was all radiance above, was all
drizzling fog below, and we reached Ainepo in a regular Scotch
mist. The ranchmen seemed rather grumpy at our successful ascent, which involved the failure of all their pro-
phecies, and, indeed, we were thoroughly unsatisfactory
travellers, arriving fresh and complacent, with neither adventures nor disasters to gladden people's hearts. We started for
this ranch seven miles further, soon after dark, and arrived
before nine, after the most successful ascent of Mauna Loa
ever made.

Without being a Sybarite, I certainly do prefer a comfortable
pulu bed to one of ridgy lava, and the fire which blazes on this
broad hearth to the camp-fire on the frozen top of the volcano.
The worthy ranchman expected us, and has treated us very
sumptuously, and even Kahélé is being regaled on Chinese
sorghum. The Sunday's rest, too, is a luxury, which I wonder
that travellers can ever forego. If one is always on the move,
even very vivid impressions are hunted out of the memory by
the last new thing. Though I am not unduly tired, even had
it not been Sunday, I should have liked a day in which to recall

and arrange my memories of Mauna Loa before the forty-eight miles' ride to Hilo.

This afternoon, we were sitting under the verandah talking volcanic talk, when there was a loud rumbling, and a smart shock of earthquake, and I have been twice interrupted in writing this letter by other shocks, in which all the frame-work of the house has yawned and closed again. They say that four years ago, at the time of the great "mud flow" which is close by, this house was moved several feet by an earthquake, and that all the cattle walls which surround it were thrown down. The ranchman tells us that on January 7th and 8th, 1873, there was a sudden and tremendous outburst of Mauna Loa. The ground, he says, throbbed and quivered for twenty miles ; a tremendous roaring, like that of a blast furnace, was heard for the same distance, and clouds of black smoke trailed out over the sea for thirty miles.

We have dismissed our guide with encomiums. His charge was $10 ; but Mr. Green would not allow me to share that, or any part of the expense, or pay anything, but $6 for my own mule. The guide is a goat-hunter, and the chase is very curiously pursued. The hunter catches sight of a flock of goats, and hunts them up the mountain, till, agile and fleet of foot as they are, he actually tires them out, and gets close enough to them to cut their throats for the sake of their skins. If I understand rightly, this young man has captured as many as seventy in a day.

CRATER HOUSE, KILAUEA, *June 9th.*

This morning Mr. Green left for Kona, and I for Kilauea ; the ranchman's native wife and her sister riding with me for several miles to put me on the right track. Kahélé's sociable instincts are so strong, that, before they left me, I dismounted, blindfolded him, and led him round and round several times, a process which so successfully confused his intellects, that he started off in this direction with more alacrity than usual. They certainly put me on a track which could not be mistaken, for it was a narrow, straight path, cut and hammered through a broad, horrible *a-a* stream, whose jagged spikes were the height of the horse. But beyond this lie ten miles of *pa hoehoe*, the lava-flows of ages, with only now and then the vestige of a trail.

Except the perilous crossing of the Hilo gulches in February, this is the most difficult ride I have had—eerie and impressive in every way. The loneliness was absolute. For several hours I saw no trace of human beings, except the very rare print of a shod horse's hoof. It is a region for ever " desolate and without inhabitant," trackless, waterless, silent, as if it had passed into the passionless calm of lunar solitudes. It is composed of rough hummocks of *pahoehoe*, rising out of a sandy desert. Only stunted *ohias*, loaded with crimson tufts, raise themselves out of cracks : twisted, tortured growths, bearing their bright blossoms under protest, driven unwillingly to be gay by a fiery soil and a fiery sun. To the left, there was the high, dark wall of an *a-a* stream ; further yet, a tremendous volcanic fissure, at times the bed of a fiery river, and above this the towering dome of Mauna Loa, a brilliant cobalt blue, lined and shaded with indigo where innumerable lava streams have seamed his portentous sides : his whole beauty the effect of atmosphere, on an object in itself hideous. Ahead and to the right were rolling miles of a *pahoehoe* sea, bounded by the unseen Pacific 3000 feet below, with countless craters, fissures emitting vapour, and all other concomitants of volcanic action ; bounded to the north by the vast crater of Kilauea. On all this deadly region the sun poured his tropic light and heat from one of the bluest skies I ever saw.

The direction given me on leaving Kapapala was, that after the natives left me I was to keep a certain crater on the south-east till I saw the smoke of Kilauea; but there were many craters. Horses cross the sand and hummocks as nearly as possible on a bee line; but the lava rarely indicates that anything has passed over it, and this morning a strong breeze had rippled the sand, completely obliterating the hoof-marks of the last traveller, and at times I feared that losing myself, as many others have done, I should go mad with thirst. I examined the sand narrowly for hoof-marks, and every now and then found one, but always had the disappointment of finding that it was made by an unshod horse, therefore not a ridden one. Finding eyesight useless, I dismounted often, and felt with my finger along the rolling lava for the slightest marks of abrasion, which might show that shod animals had passed that way, got up into an *ohia* to look out for the smoke of Kilauea, and after three hours came out upon what I here learn is the old track, disused because of the insecurity of the ground.

It runs quite close to the edge of the crater, there 1000

feet in depth, and gives a magnificent view of the whole area, with the pit and the blowing cones. But the region through which the trail led was rather an alarming one, being hollow and porous, all cracks and fissures, nefariously concealed by scrub and ferns. I found a place, as I thought, free from risk, and gave Kahélé a feed of oats on my plaid, but before he had finished them there was a rumbling and vibration, and he went into the ground above his knees, so snatching up the plaid and jumping on him I galloped away, convinced that that crack was following me! However, either the crack thought better of it, or Kahélé travelled faster, for in another half-hour I arrived where the whole region steams, smokes, and fumes with sulphur, and was kindly welcomed here by Mr. Gilman, where he and the old Chinaman appear to be alone.

After a seven hours' ride the quiet and the log fire are very pleasant, and the host is a most intelligent and sympathising listener. It is a solemn night, for the earth quakes, and the sound of Halemaumau is like the surging of the sea.

HILO, *June* 11*th.*

Once more I am among palm and mango groves, and friendly faces, and sounds of softer surges than those of Kilauea. I had a dreary ride yesterday, as the rain was incessant, and I saw neither man, bird, or beast the whole way. Kahélé was so heavily loaded that I rode the thirty miles at a foot's pace, and he became so tired that I had to walk.

It has been a splendid week, with every circumstance favourable, nothing sordid or worrying to disturb the impressions received, kindness and goodwill everywhere, a travelling companion whose consideration, endurance, and calmness were beyond all praise, and at the end the cordial welcomes of my Hawaiian "home."

I. L. B.

LETTER XXX.*

RIDGE HOUSE, KONA, HAWAII, *June* 12.

I LANDED in Kealakakua Bay on a black lava block, on which tradition says that Captain Cook fell, struck with his death-wound, a century ago. The morning sun was flaming above the walls of lava 1000 feet in height which curve round the dark bay, the green, deep water rolled shorewards in lazy undulations, canoes piled full of pineapples poised themselves on the swell, ancient coco-palms glassed themselves in still waters—it was hot, silent, tropical.

The disturbance which made the bay famous is known to every schoolboy; how the great explorer, long supposed by the natives to be their vanished god *Lono*, betrayed his earthly lineage by groaning when he was wounded, and was then dispatched outright. A cocoanut stump, faced by a sheet of copper recording the circumstance, is the great circumnavigator's monument. A few miles beyond, is the enclosure of Haunaunau, the City of Refuge for western Hawaii. In this district there is a lava road ascribed to Umi, a legendary king, who is said to have lived 500 years ago. It is very perfect, well defined on both sides with kerb-stones, and greatly resembles the chariot ways in Pompeii. Near it are several structures formed of four stones, three being set upright, and the fourth forming the roof. In a northerly direction is the place where Liholiho, the king who died in England, excited

---

* Several letters are omitted here, as they contain repetitions of journeys and circumstances which have been amply detailed before. I went to the Kona district for a few days only, intending to return to friends on Kauai and Maui ; but owing to an alteration in the sailings of the *Kilauea*, was detained there for a month, and afterwards, owing to uncertainties connected with the San Francisco steamers, was obliged to leave the Islands abruptly, after a residence of nearly seven months.

by drink and the persuasions of Kaahumanu, broke *tabu*, and
made an end of the superstitions of heathenism. Not far off
is the battle field on which the adherents of the idols rallied
their forces against the iconoclasts, and were miserably and
finally defeated.   Recent lava streams have descended on
each side of the bay, and from the bare, black rock of the
landing a flow may be traced up the steep ascent as far as
a precipice, over which it falls in waves and twists, a cataract of stone.   A late lava river passed through the magnificent forest on the southerly slope, and the impressions of
the stems of coco and fan palms are stamped clearly on the
smooth rock.   The rainfall in Kona is heavy, but there is
no standing water, and only one stream in a distance of 100
miles.

This district is famous for oranges, coffee, pineapples, and
silence.   A flaming, palm-fringed shore with a prolific strip of
table land 1500 feet above it, a dense timber belt eight miles
in breadth, and a volcano smoking somewhere between that
and the heavens, and glaring through the trees at night, are
the salient points of Kona if anything about it be salient.   It
is a region where falls not

> ".   .   .   Hail or any snow,
> Or ever wind blows loudly."

Wind indeed, is a thing unknown.   The scarcely audible
whisper of soft airs through the trees morning and evening,
rain drops falling gently, and the murmur of drowsy surges far
below, alone break the stillness.   No ripple ever disturbs the
expanse of ocean which gleams through the still, thick trees.
Rose in the sweet cool morning, gold in the sweet cool evening, but always dreaming ; and white sails come and go, no
larger than a butterfly's wing on the horizon, of ships drifting
on ocean currents, dreaming too !   Nothing surely can ever
happen here : it is so dumb and quiet, and people speak in
hushed, thin voices, and move as in a lethargy, dreaming too !
No heat, cold, or wind, nothing emphasised or italicised, it is
truly a region of endless afternoons, " a land where all things
always seem the same."   Life is dead, and existence is a
languid swoon.

This is the only regular boarding house on Hawaii.   The
company is accidental and promiscuous.   The conversation
consists of speculations, varied and repeated with the hours, as
to the arrivals and departures of the Honolulu schooners

Uilama and *Prince*, who they will bring, who they will take,
and how long their respective passages will be. A certain
amount of local gossip is also hashed up at each meal, and
every stranger who has travelled through Hawaii for the last
ten years is picked to pieces and worn threadbare, and his
purse, weight, entertainers, and habits are thoroughly can-
vassed. On whatever subject the conversation begins it
always ends in dollars ; but even that most stimulating of
all topics only arouses a languid interest among my fellow
dreamers. I spend most of my time in riding in the forests,
or along the bridle path which trails along the height,
among grass and frame-houses, almost smothered by trees and
trailers.

Many of these are inhabited by white men, who, having
drifted to these shores, have married native women, and are
rearing a dusky race, of children who speak the maternal
tongue only, and grow up with native habits. Some of these
men came for health, others landed from whalers, but of all it
is true that, infatuated by the ease and lusciousness of this
languid region,

> " They sat them down upon the yellow sand,
>   Between the sun and moon upon the shore ;
> And sweet it was to dream of Fatherland,
>   . . . . ; but evermore
> Most weary seem'd the sea, weary the oar,
>   Weary the wandering fields of barren foam.
> Then some one said, ' We will return no more.' "

They have enough and more, and a life free from toil, but the
obvious tendency of these marriages is to sink the white man
to the level of native feelings and habits.

There are two or three educated residents, and there is a
small English church with daily service, conducted by a resident clergyman.

The beauty of this part of Kona is wonderful. The interminable forest is richer and greener than anything I have
yet seen, but penetrable only by narrow tracks which have been
made for hauling timber. The trees are so dense, and so
matted together with trailers, that no ray of noon-day sun
brightens the moist tangle of exquisite mosses and ferns which
covers the ground. Yams with their burnished leaves, and
the Polypodium spectrum, wind round every tree stem, and
the heavy *iè*, which here attains gigantic proportions, links the
tops of the tallest trees together by its knotted coils. Hot-

house flowers grow in rank profusion round every house, and
tea-roses, fuchsias, geraniums fifteen feet high, Nile lilies,
Chinese lantern plants, begonias, lantanas, hibiscus, passion-
flowers, Cape jasmine, the hoya, the tuberose, the beautiful but
overpoweringly sweet ginger plant, and a hundred others :
while the whole district is overrun with the Datura brug-
mansia (?), here an arborescent shrub fourteen feet high, bearing
seventy great, trumpet-shaped, white blossoms at a time, which
at night vie with those of the night-blowing Cereus in filling the
air with odours.

Pineapples and melons grow like weeds among the grass,
and everything that is good for food flourishes. Nothing can keep
under the redundancy of nature in Kona ; everything is profuse,
fervid, passionate, vivified and pervaded by sunshine. The
earth is restless in her productiveness, and forces up her hot-
house growth perpetually, so that the miracle of Jonah's gourd
is almost repeated nightly. All decay is hurried out of sight,
and through the glowing year flowers blossom and fruits ripen ;
ferns are always uncurling their young fronds, and bananas
unfolding their great shining leaves, and spring blends her
everlasting youth and promise with the fulfilment and maturity
of summer.

"Never comes the trader, never floats a European flag,
Slides the bird o'er lustrous woodland, swings the trailer from the crag :
Droops the heavy blossom'd bower, hangs the heavy-fruited tree—
Summer isles of Eden lying in dark purple spheres of sea."

HUALALAI, *July* 28*th.*

I very soon left the languid life of Kona for this sheep
station, 6000 feet high on the desolate slope of the dead
volcano of Hualalai, ("offspring of the shining sun,") on the
invitation of its hospitable owner, who said if I " could eat his
rough fare, and live his rough life, his house and horses were
at my disposal." He is married to a very attractive native
woman who eats at his table, but does not know a word of
English, but they are both away at a wool-shed eight miles off,
shearing sheep.

This house is in the great volcanic wilderness of which I
wrote from Kalaieha, a desert of drouth and barrenness.
There is no permanent track, and on the occasions when I
have ridden up here alone, the directions given me have been
to steer for an ox bone, and from that to a dwarf *ohia.* There

is no coming or going; it is seventeen miles from the nearest
settlement, and looks across a desert valley to Mauna Loa.
Woody trailers, harsh, hard grass in tufts, the Asplenium
trichomanes in rifts, the Pellea ternifolia in sand, and some
ohia and *mamané* scrub in hollow places sheltered from the
wind, all hard, crisp, unlovely growths, contrast with the lavish
greenery below. A brisk cool wind blows all day; every
afternoon a dense fog brings the horizon within 200 feet, but it
clears off with frost at dark, and the flames of the volcano
light the whole southern sky.

My companions are an amiable, rheumatic, native woman,
and a crone who must have lived a century, much shrivelled
and tattooed, and nearly childish. She talks to herself in
weird tones, stretches her lean limbs by the fire most of the
day, and in common with most of the old people has a prejudice against clothes, and prefers huddling herself up in a
blanket to wearing the ordinary dress of her sex. There is
also a dog, but he does not understand English, and for some
time I have not spoken any but Hawaiian words. I have
plenty to do, and find this a very satisfactory life.

I came up to within eight miles of this house with a laughing,
holiday-making rout of twelve natives, who rode madly along
the narrow forest trail at full gallop, up and down the hills,
through mire and over stones, leaping over the trunks of prostrate trees, and stooping under branches with loud laughter,
challenging me to reckless races over difficult ground, and
when they found that the *wahine haole* was not to be thrown
from her horse they patted me approvingly, and crowned me
with *leis* of *mailé*. I became acquainted with some of these at
Kilauea in the winter, and since I came to Kona they have
been very kind to me.

I thoroughly like living among them, taking meals with
them on their mats, and eating "two-fingered" *poi* as if I had
been used to it all my life. Their mirthfulness and kindliness
are most winning; their horses, food, clothes, and time are all
bestowed on one so freely, and one lives amongst them with
a most restful sense of security. They have many faults, but
living alone among them in their houses as I have done so
often on Hawaii, I have never seen or encountered a disagreeable thing. But the more I see of them the more impressed I am with their carelessness and love of pleasure, their
lack of ambition and a sense of responsibility, and the time
which they spend in doing nothing but talking and singing as

they bask in the sun, though spasmodically and under excite-ment they are capable of tremendous exertions in canoeing, surf-riding, and lassoing cattle.

While down below I joined three natives for the purpose of seeing this last sport. They all rode shod horses, and had lassoes of ox-hide attached to the horns of their saddles. I sat for an hour on horseback on a rocky hill while they hunted the woods ; then I heard the deep voices of bulls, and a great burst of cattle appeared, with hunters in pursuit, but the herd vanished over a dip of the hill side, and the natives joined me. By this time I wished myself safely at home, partly because my unshod horse was not fit for galloping over lava and rough ground, and I asked the men where I should stay to be out of danger. The leader replied, " Oh, just keep close behind me !" I had thought of some safe view-point, not of galloping on an unshod horse with a ruck of half-maddened cattle, but it was the safest plan, and there was no time to be lost, for as we rode slowly down, we sighted the herd dodging across the open to regain the shelter of the wood, and much on the alert.

Putting our horses into a gallop we dashed down the hill till we were close up with the chase ; then another tremendous gallop, and a brief wild rush, the grass shaking with the surge of cattle and horses. There was much whirling of tails and tearing up of the earth—a lasso spun three or four times round the head of the native who rode in front of me, and almost simultaneously a fine red bullock lay prostrate on the earth, nearly strangled, with his foreleg noosed to his throat. The other natives dismounted, and put two lassoes round his horns, slipping the first into the same position, and vaulted into their saddles before he was on his legs.

He got up, shook himself, put his head down, and made a blind rush, but his captors were too dexterous for him, and in that and each succeeding rush he was foiled. As he tore wildly from side to side, the natives dodged under the lasso, slipping it over their heads, and swung themselves over their saddles, hanging in one stirrup, to aid their trained horses to steady themselves as the bullock tugged violently against them. He was escorted thus for a mile, his strength failing with each useless effort, his tongue hanging out, blood and foam dropping from his mouth and nostrils, his flanks covered with foam and sweat, till blind and staggering, he was led to a tree, where he was at once stabbed, and two hours afterwards a part of him

was served at table. The natives were surprised that I
avoided seeing his death, as the native women greatly enjoy
such a spectacle. This mode of killing an animal while heated
and terrified, doubtless accounts for the dark colour and hardness of Hawaiian beef.

Numbers of the natives are expert with the lasso, and besides
capturing with it wild and half-wild cattle, they catch horses
with it, and since I came here my host caught a sheep with it,
singling out the one he wished to kill, from the rest of the
galloping flock with an unerring aim. It takes a whole ox hide
cut into strips to make a good lasso.

One of my native friends tells me that a native man who
attended on me in one of my earlier expeditions has since
been "prayed to death." One often hears this phrase, and it
appears that the superstition which it represents has by no
means died out. There are persons who are believed to have
the lives of others in their hands, and their services are procured by offerings of white fowls, brown hogs, and *awa*, as
well as money, by any one who has a grudge against another.
Several other instances have been told me of persons who have
actually died under the influence of the terror and despair
produced by being told that the *kahuna* was " praying them to
death." These over efficacious prayers are not addressed to
the true God, but to the ancient Hawaiian divinities. The
natives are very superstitious, and the late king, who was both
educated and intelligent, was much under the dominion of a
sorceress.

I have made the ascent of Hualalai twice from here, the first
time guided by my host and hostess, and the second rather
adventurously alone. Forests of *koa*, sandal-wood, and *ohia*,
with an undergrowth of raspberries and ferns, clothe its base,
the fragrant *mailé*, and the graceful sarsaparilla vine, with its
clustered coral-coloured buds, nearly smother many of the
trees, and in several places the heavy *ié* forms the semblance
of triumphal arches over the track. This forest terminates
abruptly on the great volcanic wilderness, with its starved
growth of unsightly scrub. But Hualalai, though 10,000 feet
in height, is covered with Pteris aquilina, *mamané*, coarse
bunch grass, and *pukeavé* to its very summit, which is crowned
by a small, solitary, blossoming *ohia*.

For two hours before reaching the top, the way lies over
countless flows and beds of lava, much disintegrated, and
almost entirely of the kind called *pahoehoe*. Countless pit-

craters extend over the whole mountain, all of them covered outside, and a few inside, with scraggy vegetation. The edges are often very ragged and picturesque. The depth varies from

Pit-craters on Hualalai.

300 to 700 feet, and the diameter from 700 to 1200. The walls of some are of a smooth grey stone, the bottoms flat, and very deep in sand, but others resemble the tufa cones of Mauna Kea. They are so crowded together in some places as to be divided only by a ridge so narrow that two mules can scarcely walk abreast upon it. The mountain was split by an earthquake in 1868, and a great fissure, with much treacherous ground about it, extends for some distance across it. It is very striking from every point of view on this side, being a complete wilderness of craters, and over 150 lateral cones have been counted.

The object of my second ascent was to visit one of the grandest of the summit craters, which we had not reached previously owing to fog. This crater is bordered by a narrow and very fantastic ridge of rock, in or on which there is a mound about 60 feet high, formed of fragments of black, orange, blue, red, and golden lava, with a cavity or blow-hole in the centre, estimated by Brigham as having a diameter of 25 feet, and a depth of 1800. The interior is dark brown, much grooved horizontally, and as smooth and regular as if turned. There are no steam cracks or signs of heat anywhere. Superb caves or lava-bubbles abound at a height of 6000 feet. These are moist with ferns, and the drip from their roofs is the water supply of this porous region.

Hualalai, owing to the vegetation sparsely sprinkled over it, looks as if it had been quiet for ages, but it has only slept since 1801, when there was a tremendous eruption from it, which flooded several villages, destroyed many plantations and fishponds, filled up a deep bay 20 miles in extent, and formed the present coast. The terrified inhabitants threw living nogs into the stream, and tried to propitiate the anger of the gods by more costly offerings, but without effect, till King Kame-hameha, attended by a large retinue of priests and chiefs, cut off some of his hair, which was considered sacred, and threw it into the torrent, which in two days ceased to run. This circumstance gave him a greatly increased ascendancy, from his supposed influence with the deities of the volcanoes.

I have explored the country pretty thoroughly for many miles round, but have not seen anything striking, except the remains of an immense *heiau* in the centre of the desert table-land, said to have been built in a day by the compulsory labour of 25,000 people : a lonely white man who lives among the lava, and believes he has discovered the secret of perpetual motion : and the lava-flow from Mauna Loa, which reached the sea 40 miles from its exit from the mountain.

I was riding through the brushwood with a native, and not able to see two yards in any direction, when emerging from the thick scrub, we came upon the torrent of 1859 within six feet of us, a huge, straggling, coal-black river, broken up into streams in our vicinity, but on the whole, presenting an iridescent, uphill expanse a mile wide. We had reached one of the divergent streams to which it had been said after its downward course of 9000 feet, " Hitherto shalt thou come and no further," while the main body had pursued its course to the ocean. Whatever force impelled it had ceased to act, and the last towering wave of fire had halted just there, and lies a black, arrested surge 10 feet high, with tender ferns at its feet, and a scarcely singed *ohia* bending over it. The flow, so far as we scrambled up it, is heaped in great surges of a fierce black, fiercely reflecting the torrid sun, cracked, and stained yellow and white, and its broad glistening surface forms an awful pathway to the dome-like crest of Mauna Loa, now throbbing with internal fires, and crowned with a white smoke wreath, that betokens the action of the same forces which pro-duced this gigantic inundation. Close to us the main river had parted above, and united below a small *mamané* tree with bracken under its shadow, and there are several oases of the same kind.

I have twice been down to the larger world of the woolshed,

when tired of strips of dried mutton and my own society. The hospitality there is as great as the accommodation is small. The first time, I slept on the floor of the shed with some native women who were up there, and was kept awake all night by the magnificence of the light on the volcano. The second time, several of us slept in a small, dark grass-wigwam, only intended as a temporary shelter, the lowliest dwelling in every sense of the word that I ever occupied. That evening was the finest I have seen on the islands; there was a less abrupt transition from day to night, and the three great mountains and the desert were etherealised and glorified by a lingering rose and violet light. When darkness came on, our great camp fire was hardly redder than the glare from the volcano, and its leaping flames illuminated as motley a group as you would wish to see; the native shearers, who, after shearing eighty sheep each in a day, washed, and changed their clothes before eating; a negro goat-herd with a native wife and swarthy children, two native women, my host and myself, all engaged in the rough cooking befitting the region, toasting strips of jerked mutton on sticks, broiling wild bullock on the coals, baking *kalo* under ground, and rolls in a rough stone oven, and all speaking that base mixture of English and Hawaiian which is current coin here. The meal was not less rude than the cookery. We ate it on the floor of the wigwam, with an old tin, with some fat in it, for a lamp, and a bit of rope for a wick, which kept tumbling into the fat and leaving us in darkness.

The next day I came up here alone, driving a pack-horse, and with a hind-quarter of sheep tied to my saddle. It is really difficult to find the way over this desert, though I have been several times across. When a breeze ripples the sand between the lava hummocks, the foot-prints are obliterated, and there are few landmarks except the " ox bone " and the small *ohia.*" It is a strange life up here on the mountain side, but I like it, and never yearn after civilization. The only drawback is my ignorance of the language, which not only places me sometimes in grotesque difficulties, but deprives me of much interest. I don't know what day it is, or how long I have been here, and quite understand how possible it would be to fall into an indolent and aimless life, in which time is of no account.

THE RECTORY, KONA, *August 1st.*

I left Hualalai yesterday morning, and dined with my kind host and hostess in the wigwam. It was the last taste of the wild Hawaiian life I have learned to love so well, the last meal on a mat, the last exercise of skill in eating "two-fingered" *poi.* I took leave gratefully of those who had been so truly kind to me, and with the friendly *aloha* from kindly lips in my ears, regretfully left the purple desert in which I have lived so serenely, and plunged into the forest gloom. Half way down, I met a string of my native acquaintances, who, as the courteous custom is, threw over me *leis* of *mailè* and roses, and since I arrived here, others have called to wish me good-bye, bringing presents of figs, cocoa-nuts and bananas.

This is one of the stations of the "Honolulu Mission," and Mr. Davies, the clergyman, has, besides Sunday and daily services, a day-school for boys and girls. The Sunday attendance at church, so far as I have seen, consists of three adults, though the white population within four miles is considerable, and at another station on Maui, the congregation was composed solely of the family of a planter. Among the whites who have sunk into the mire of an indolent and godless, if not an openly immoral life, there is an undoubted field for Evangelistic effort ; but it is very doubtful, I think, whether this class can be reached by services which appeal to higher culture and instincts than it possesses.

Kona looks unutterably beautiful, a languid dream of all fair things. Yet truly my heart warms to nothing so much as to a row of fat, English cabbages which grow in the rectory garden, with a complacent, self-asserting John Bullism about them. It is best to leave the islands now. I love them better every day, and dreams of Fatherland are growing fainter in this perfumed air and under this glittering sky. A little longer, and I too should say, like all who have made their homes here under the deep banana shade,—

> " We will return no more,
>   . . . our island home
> Is far beyond the wave, we will no longer roam."

I. L. B.

LETTER XXXI.

HAWAIIAN HOTEL, HONOLULU,
August 6th.

My fate is lying at the wharf in the shape of the Pacific Mail Steamer *Costa Rica*, and soon to me Hawaii-nei will be but a dream, "Summer Isles of Eden!" My heart warms towards them as I leave them, for they have been more like home than any part of the world since I left England. The moonlight is trickling through misty algarobas, and feathery tamarinds and palms, and shines on glossy leaves of breadfruit and citron; a cool breeze brings in at my open doors the perfumed air, and the soft murmur of the restful sea, and this beautiful Honolulu, whose lights are twinkling through the purple night, is at last, as it was at first, Paradise in the Pacific, a blossom of a summer sea.

I shall be in the Rocky Mountains before you receive my hastily-written reply to your proposal to come out here for a year, but I will add a few reasons against it, in addition to the one which I gave regarding the benefit which I now hope to derive from a change to a more stimulating climate. The strongest of all is, that if we were to stay here for a year, we should just sit down "between the sun and moon upon the shore," and forget "our island home," and be content to fall "asleep in a half dream," and "return no more!"

Of course you will have gathered from my letters that there are very many advantages here. Indeed, the mosquitos of the leeward coast, to whose attacks one becomes inured in a few months, are the only physical drawback. The open-air life is most conducive to health, and the climate is absolutely perfect, owing to its equability and purity. Whether the steady heat of

Honolulu, the languid airs of Hilo, the balmy breezes of Onomea, the cool bluster of Waimea, or the odorous stillness of Kona, it is always the same. The grim gloom of our anomalous winters, the harsh malignant winds of our springs, and the dismal rains and overpowering heats of our summers, have no counterpart in the endless spring-time of Hawaii.

Existence here is unclogged and easy, a small income goes a long way, and the simplicity, refinement, kindliness, and sociability of the foreign residents, render society very pleasant. The life here is truer, simpler, and happier than ours. The relation between the foreign and native population is a kindly and happy one, and the natives, in spite of their faults, are a most friendly and pleasant people to live among. With a knowledge of their easily-acquired language, they would be a ceaseless source of interest, and every white resident can have the satisfaction of helping them in their frequent distresses and illnesses.

The sense of security is a very special charm, and one enjoys it as well in lonely native houses, and solitary days and nights of travelling, as in the foreign homes, which are never locked throughout the year. There are no burglarious instincts to dread, and there is no such thing as "a broken sleep of fear beneath the stars." The person and property of a white man are everywhere secure, and a white woman is sure of unvarying respect and kindness.

There are no inevitable hardships. The necessaries, and even the luxuries of civilization can be obtained everywhere, and postal communication with America is regular and rapid.

When I began this letter, a long procession of counterbalancing disadvantages passed through my mind, but they become "beautifully less" as I set them down in black and white. If I put gossip first, it is because I seriously think that it is the canker of the foreign society on the islands. Its extent and universality are grotesque and amusing to a stranger, but to live in it, and share in it, and learn to enjoy it, would be both lowering and hurtful, and you can hardly be long here without being drawn into its vortex. By *gossip* I don't mean scandal or malignant misrepresentations, or reports of petty strifes, intrigues, and jealousies, such as are common in all cliques and communities, but *nuhou*, mere tattle, the perpetual talking about people, and the picking to tatters of every item of personal detail, whether gathered from fact or imagination.

A great deal of this is certainly harmless, and in some

measure arises from the intimate friendly relations which exist
between the scattered families, but over-indulgence in it de-
stroys the privacy of individual existence, and is deteriorating
in more ways than one. From the north of Kauai to the south
of Hawaii, everybody knows every other body's affairs, income,
expenditure, sales, purchases, debts, furniture, clothing, comings,
goings, borrowings, lendings, letters, correspondents, and every
thing else : and when there is nothing new to relate on any one
of these prolific subjects, supposed intentions afford abundant matter for speculation.   All gossip is focussed here,
being imported from every other district, and re-exported, with
additions and embellishments, by every inter-island mail.   The
ingenuity with which *nuhou* is circulated is worthy of a better
cause.

Some disadvantages arise from the presence on the islands of
heterogeneous and ill-assorted nationalities. The Americans, of
course, predominate, and even those who are Hawaiian born,
have, as elsewhere, a strongly national feeling. The far smaller
English community hangs together in a somewhat cliquish
fashion, and possibly cherishes a latent grudge against the
Americans for their paramount influence in island affairs. The
German residents, as everywhere, are cliquish too. Then, since
the establishment of the Honolulu Mission, church feeling has
run rather high, and here, as elsewhere, has a socially decisive
tendency.   Then there are drink and anti-drink, pro and anti-
missionary, and pro and anti-reciprocity-treaty parties, and
various other local naggings of no interest to you.

The civilization is exotic, and owing to various circumstances, the government and constitution are too experimental
and provisional in their nature, and possess too few elements of
permanence to engross the profound interest of the foreign
residents, although for reasons of policy they are well inclined
to sustain a barbaric throne. In spite of a king and court,
and titles and officials without number, and uniforms stiff with
gold lace, and Royal dinner parties with *menus* printed on white
silk, Americans, Republicans in feeling, really " run " the government, and in state affairs there is a taint of that combination of obsequious and flippant vulgarity, which none deplore
more deeply than the best among the Americans themselves.

It is a decided misfortune to a community to be divided in
its national leanings, and to have no great fusing interests
within or without itself, such as those which knit vigorous Victoria to the mother country, or distant Oregon to the heart of

the Republic at Washington. Except sugar and dollars, one rarely hears any subject spoken about with general interest. The downfall of an administration in England, or any important piece of national legislation, arouses almost no interest in American society here, and the English are ostentatiously apathetic regarding any piece of intelligence specially absorbing to Americans. The papers pick up every piece of gossip which drifts about the islands, and snarl with much wordiness over local matters, and in the absence of a telegraph one hardly but feels the beat of the pulses of the larger world. Those intellectual movements of the West which might provoke discussion and conversation are not cordially entered into, partly owing to the difference in theological beliefs, and partly from an indolence born of the climate, and the lack of mental stimulus.

After all, the gossip and the absence of large interests shared in common, are the only specialities which can be alleged against Hawaii, and I have never seen people among whom I should better like to live. The ladies are most charming, essentially womanly, and fulfil all domestic and social duties in a way worthy of imitation everywhere. The kindness and hospitality, too, are unbounded, and these cover "a multitude of sins."

There are very few strangers here now. It is the "dead season." I have met with none except Mr. Nordhoff, who is writing on the islands for *Harper's Monthly*, and his charming wife and children. She is a most expert horsewoman, and has adopted the Mexican saddle even in Honolulu, where few foreign ladies ride "cavalier fashion."

My friends all urge me to write on Hawaii, on the ground that I have seen the islands and lived the island life so thoroughly; but possibly they expect more indiscriminate praise than I could conscientiously bestow !

Honolulu is in the midst of the epidemic of letter writing, which sets in on the arrival of the steamer from "the coast," and people walk and drive as if they really had business on hand : and the farewell visits to be made and received, the pleasant presence of Mr. Thompson, and Mr. and Mrs. Severance, of Hilo, and the hasty doing of things which have been left to the last, make me a sharer in the spasmodic bustle, which, were it permanent, would metamorphose this dreamy, bowery, tropical capital. The undeserved and unexpected kindness shown me here, as everywhere on these islands, renders my last impressions even more delightful than my first. The people are as genial as their own sunny skies, and in more frigid regions I shall never sigh for the last without longing for the first. . . . .

S. S. Costa Rica, *August 7th.*

We sailed for San Francisco early this afternoon. Everything looked the same as when I landed in January, except that many of the then strange faces among the radiant crowd are now the faces of friends, that I know nearly everyone by sight, and that the pathos of farewell blended with every look and word. The air still rang with laughter and *alohas,* and the rippling music of the Hawaiian tongue ; bananas and pineapples were still piled in fragrant heaps ; the drifts of surf rolled in, as then, over the barrier reef, canoes with outriggers still poised themselves on the blue water ; the coral divers still plied their graceful trade, and the lazy ripples still flashed in light along the palm-fringed shore. The head-ropes were let go, we steamed through the violet channel into the broad Pacific, Lunalilo, who came out so far with Chief Justice Allen, returned to the shore, and when his kindly *aloha* was spoken, the last link with the islands was severed, and half an hour later Honolulu was out of sight. . . . .

. . . . The breeze is freshening, and the *Costa Rica's* head lies nearly due north. The sun is sinking, and on the far horizon the summit peaks of Oahu gleam like amethysts on a golden sea. Farewell for ever, my bright tropic dream ! *Aloha nui* to Hawaii-nei !

I. L. B.

LEPROSY AND THE LEPER SETTLEMENT ON MOLOKAI.

In 1865, the Hawaiian Legislature, recognizing the disastrous fact that leprosy is at once contagious and incurable, passed an act to prevent its spread, and eventually the Board of Health established a leper settlement on the island of Molokai for the isolation of lepers. In carrying out the painful task of weeding out and exiling the sufferers, the officials employed met with unusual difficulties ; and the general foreign community was not itself aware of the importance of making an attempt to "stamp out" the disease, until the beginning of Lunalilo's reign, when the apparently rapid spread of leprosy, and sundry rumours that others than natives were affected by it, excited general alarm, and not unreasonably, for medical science, after protracted investigation, knows less of leprosy than of cholera. Nor are medical men wholly agreed as to the manner in which infection is communicated ; and, as the white residents on the islands associate very freely and intimately with the natives, eating *poi* out of their calabashes, and sleeping in their houses and on their mats, there was just cause for uneasiness.

The natives themselves have been, and still are, perfectly reckless about the risk of contagion, and although the family instinct among them is singularly weak, the gregarious or social instinct is singularly strong, and it has been found impossible to induce them to give up smoking the pipes, wearing the clothes, and sleeping on the mats of lepers, which three things are universally regarded by medical men as undoubted sources of infection. At the beginning of 1873, it was estimated that nearly 400 lepers were scattered up and down the islands, living among their families and friends, and the healthy associated with them in complete apathy or fatalism. However bloated the face and glazed the eyes, or however swollen or decayed the limbs were, the persons so afflicted appeared neither to scare nor disgust their friends, and, therefore, Hawaii has absolutely needed the coercive segregation of these living *foci* of disease. When the search for lepers was made, the natives hid their friends away under mats, and in forests and caves, till the peril of separation was over, and if they sought medical advice, they rejected foreign educated aid in favour of the highly paid services of Chinese and native quacks, who professed to work a cure by means of loathsome ointments and decoctions, and abominable broths worthy of the witches' cauldron.

However, as the year passed on, lepers were " informed against," and it became the painful duty of the sheriffs of the islands, on the statement of a doctor that any individual was truly a leper, to commit him for life to Molokai. Some, whose swollen faces and glassy, goggle eyes left no room for hope of escape, gave themselves up ; and a few, who, like Mr. Rags-dale, might have remained among their fellows almost without suspicion, surrendered themselves in a way which reflects much credit upon them. Mr. Park, the Marshal, and Mr. Wilder, of the Board of Health, went round the islands repeatedly in the *Kilauea*, and performed the painful duty of collecting the victims, with true sympathy and kindness. The woe of those who were taken, the dismal wailings of those who were left, and the agonised partings, when friends and relatives clung to the swollen limbs and kissed the glistering, bloated faces of those who were exiled from them for ever, I shall never forget.

There were no individual distinctions made among the suf-ferers. Queen Emma's cousin, a man of property, and Mr. Ragsdale, the most influential lawyer among the half-whites, shared the same doom as poor Upa, the volcano guide, and stricken Chinamen and labourers from the plantations. Before the search slackened, between three and four hundred men, women, and children were gathered out from among their families, and placed on Molokai.

Between 1866 and April 1874, eleven hundred and forty-five lepers, five hundred and sixty of whom were sent from Kahili in the spring of 1872, have arrived on Molokai, of which number four hundred and forty-two have died, the ma-jority of the deaths having occurred since the beginning of

Lunalilo's reign, when the work of segregation was undertaken
in earnest. At the present time the number on the island is
703, including 22 children. These unfortunates are necessarily pauperised, and the small Hawaiian kingdom finds itself
much burdened by their support.* It is not surprising that
officials called upon to meet this sad emergency are assailed in
all quarters of the globe by sentimental criticisms and misstate-
ments regarding the provision made for the lepers on Molokai.
Most of these are unfounded, and the members of the Board
of Health deserve great credit both for their humanity and for
their prompt and careful attention to the complaints made by
the sufferers.

At present the two obvious blots on the system are, the
insufficient house accommodation, involving a herding together
which is repulsive to foreign, though not to native, ideas; and
the absence of a resident physician to prescribe for the ailments from which leprosy is no exemption. Molokai, the
island of exile, is *Molokai aina pali*, "the land of precipices,"
in the old native *mélés*, and its walls of rock rise perpendicularly from the sea to a height varying from 1000 to 2500 feet,
in extreme grandeur and picturesqueness, and are slashed, as
on Hawaii, by gulches opening out on natural lawns on the sea
level. The place chosen for the centralization and segregation of leprosy is a most singular plain of about 20,000
acres, hemmed in between the sea and a precipice 2000
feet high, passable only where a zigzag bridle track swings
over its face, so narrow and difficult that it has been found
impossible to get cattle down over it, so that the leper
settlement below has depended for its supplies of fresh meat
upon vessels. The settlement is accessible also by a very
difficult landing at Kalaupapa on the windward side of
Molokai.

Three miles inland from Kalaupapa is the leper village of
Kalawao, which may safely be pronounced one of the most
horrible spots on all the earth; a home of hideous disease and
slow coming death, with which science in despair has ceased
to grapple; a community of doomed beings, socially dead,
"whose only business is to perish;" wifeless husbands, hus-
bandless wives, children without parents, and parents without
children; men and women who have "no more a portion for
ever in anything that is done under the sun," condemned to

* In 1874 the expense of the leper establishment was $55,000.

watch the repulsive steps by which each of their doomed fellows goes down to a loathsome death, knowing that by the same they too must pass.

A small stone church near the landing, and another at Kalawao, tell of the extraordinary devotion of a Catholic priest, who, with every prospect of advancement in his Church, and with youth, culture, and refinement to hold him back from the sacrifice, is in this hideous valley, a self-exiled man, for Christ's sake. It was singular to hear the burst of spontaneous admiration which his act elicited. No unworthy motives were suggested, all envious speech was hushed; it was almost forgotten by the most rigid Protestants that Father Damiens, who has literally followed the example of Christ by "laying down his life for the brethren," is a Romish priest, and an intuition, higher than all reasoning, hastened to number him with "the noble army of martyrs."

In Kalawao are placed not only the greater number of the lepers, but the hospital buildings. Most of the victims are of the poorer classes and live in brown huts; but two of rank, Mrs. Napela and the Hon. P. Y. Kaeo, Queen Emma's cousin, have neat wooden cottages on the way from the landing, with every comfort which their means can provide for them. The hospital buildings are about twelve in number, well and airily situated on a height; they are built of wood thoroughly whitewashed, and are enclosed by a fence. Although it is hoped that a leper hospital is not to be a permanent institution of the kingdom, the soft green grass of the enclosure has been liberally planted with algaroba trees, which in a year or two will form a goodly shade, and water has been brought in from a distance at considerable expense, so that an abundant supply is always at hand. The lepers are dying fast, and the number of advanced cases in the hospital averages forty. In the centre of the hospital square there are the office buildings, including the dispensary, which is well supplied with medicines, so that in the absence of a doctor, common ailments may be treated by an intelligent English leper. The superintendent's office, where the accounts and statistics of the settlement are kept, and where the leper governor holds his leper court, and the post-office, are also within the enclosure; but the true governor and law-giver is Death.

When Mr. Ragsdale left Hilo as a leper, the course he was likely to take on Molokai could not be accurately forecasted; and it was felt that the presence in the leper community of a man of his gift of eloquence and influence might either be an invaluable assistance to the government, or else a serious embarrassment. In every position he had hitherto occupied, he had acquired and retained a remarkable notoriety ; and no stranger could visit the islands without hearing of poor " Bill Ragsdale's " gifts, and the grievous failings by which they were accompanied.

Hitherto the hopes of his well wishers have been fulfilled, and the government has found in him a most energetic as well as prudent agent. " It is better to be first in Britain than second in Rome ;" and probably this unfortunate man, superintendent of the leper settlement, and popularly known as " Governor Ragsdale," has found a nobler scope for his ambition among his doomed brethren than in any previous position. His remarkable power of influencing his countrymen is at present used for their well being ; and though his authority is practically almost absolute, owing to the isolation of the community, and its position almost outside the operation of law, he has hitherto used it with good faith and moderation. He is nominally assisted in his duties by a committee of twenty chosen from among the lepers themselves ; but from his superior education and native mental ascendancy, all immediate matters in the settlement are decided by his judgment alone.

The rations of food are ample and of good quality, and notwithstanding the increase in the number of lepers, and the difficulty of communication, there has not been any authenticated case of want. Each leper receives weekly 21 lbs. of *paiai*, and from 5 to 6 of beef, and when these fail to be landed, 9 lbs. of rice, 1 lb. of sugar, and 4 lbs. of salmon. Soap and clothing are also supplied ; but, for all beyond these necessaries, the lepers are dependent on their own industry, if they are able to exercise it, and the kindness of their friends. Coffee, tobacco, pipes, extra clothing, knives, toys, books, pictures, working implements and materials, have all been possessed by them in happier days ; and though packages of such things have been sent by the charitable for distribution by Father Damiens, it is not possible for island benevolence fully to meet an emergency and needs so disproportionate to the population and resources of the kingdom. Besides the two Catholic churches, there are a Protestant chapel, with a pastor, himself a leper, who is a regularly ordained minister of the Hawaiian Board, and two school-houses, where the twenty-two children of the settlement receive instruction in Hawaiian from a leper teacher. There is a store, too, where those who are assisted by their friends can purchase small luxuries, which are sold at just such an advance on cost as is sufficient to clear the expense of freight. The taste for ornament has not died out in either sex, and women are to be seen in Kalawao, hideous and bloated beyond description, decorated with *leis* of flowers, and looking for admiration out of their glazed and goggle eyes.

King Kalakaua and Queen Kapiolani have paid a visit to the settlement, and were received with hearty *alohas*, and the music of a leper band. The king made a short address to the lepers, the substance of which was " that his heart was grieved with the necessity which had separated these, his subjects, from their homes and families, a necessity which they themselves recognised and acquiesced in, and it should be the earnest desire of himself and his government to render their condition in exile as comfortable as possible." While he spoke, though it is supposed that a merciful apathy attends upon leprosy, his hideous audience showed signs of deep feeling, and many shed tears at his thoughtfulness in coming to visit those, who, to use their own touching expression, were " already in the grave."

The account which follows is from the pen of a gentleman who accompanied the king, and visited the hospital on the same occasion, in company with two members of the Board of Health.

" As our party stepped on shore, we found the lepers assembled to the number of two or three hundred—there are 697 all told in the settlement—for they had heard in advance of our coming, and our ears were greeted with the sound of lively music. This proceeded from the ' band,' consisting of a drum, a fife, and two flutes, rather skilfully played upon by four young lads, whose visages were horribly marked and disfigured with leprosy. The sprightly airs with which these poor creatures welcomed the arrival of the party, sounded strangely incongruous and out of place, and grated harshly upon our feelings. And then as we proceeded up the beach, and the crowd gathered about us, eager and anxious for a recognition or a kind word of greeting—oh, the repulsive and sickening libels and distorted caricatures of the human face divine upon which we looked ! And as they evidently read the ill-concealed aversion in our countenances, they withdrew the half-proffered hand, and slunk back with hanging heads. They felt again that they were *lepers,* the outcasts of society, and must not contaminate us with their touch. A few cheerful words of inquiry from the physician, Dr. Trousseau, addressed to individuals as to their particular cases, broke the embarrassment of this first meeting, and soon the crowd were chatting and laughing just like any other crowd of thoughtless Hawaiians, and with but few exceptions, these unfortunate exiles showed no signs of the settled melancholy that would naturally be looked for from people so hopelessly situated. Very happy were they when spoken to, and quite ready to answer any questions. We saw numbers whom we had known in years past, and who, having disappeared, we had thought dead. One we had known as a Representative, and a very intelligent one, too, in the Legislature of 1868. On greeting him as an old-time acquaintance, he observed, ' Yes, we meet again—in this living grave !' He is a man of no little consideration among the people, being entrusted by the Board of Health with the care of the store which is kept here for the sale of such goods as the people require. All do not appear to be lepers who are leprous. We saw numbers who might pass along our streets any day without being suspected of the taint. They had it, however, in one way or another. Sometimes on the extremities only, eating away the flesh and rotting the bones of the hands or feet ; and sometimes only appearing in black and indurated spots on the skin, noticed only on a somewhat close examination. This last sort is said to be the worst, as being most surely fatal and easiest transmitted. We saw women who had the disease in this stage, walking about, whom it was difficult to believe were lepers.

" If our sensibilities were shocked at the sight of the crowd of lepers we had met at the beach, walking about in physical strength and activity, how shall we describe our sensations in looking upon these loathsome creatures in the hospital, in whom it was indeed hard to recognise anything human ? The rooms were cleanly kept and well ventilated, but the atmosphere within was pervaded with the sickening odour of the grave. At each end, squatted or lying prone on their respective mats or mattresses, were the yet breathing corpses of lepers in the last stages of various forms of the disease, who glanced inquisitively at us for a moment out of their ghoul-like eyes—those who were not already beyond seeing—and then withdrew within their dreadful selves. Was there ever a more pitiful sight ?

"In one room we saw a sight that will ever remain fixed indelibly on the tablets of memory. A little blue-eyed, flaxen-haired child, apparently three or four years old, a half-caste, that looked up at us with an expression of timorous longing to be caressed and loved; but alas, in its glassy eyes and transparent cheeks were the unmistakable signs of the curse—the sin of the parents visited upon the child !

"In another room was one—a mass of rotting flesh, with but little semblance of humanity remaining—who was dying, and whose breath came hurried and obstructed. A few hours at most, and his troubles would be over, and his happy release arrive. There had been fourteen deaths in the settlement during the previous fortnight. On the day of our visit there were fifty-eight inmates of the hospital."

Though the lifting of the veil of mystery which hangs over the death valley of Molokai discloses some of the most woeful features of the curse, it is a relief to know the worst, and that the poor leprous outcasts in their "living grave" are not outside the pale of humanity and a judicious philanthropy. All that can be done for them is to encourage their remaining capacities for industry, and to smooth, as far as is possible, the journey of death. The Hawaiian Government is doing its best to "stamp out" the disease, and to provide for the comfort of those who are isolated; and, with the limited means at its disposal, has acted with an efficiency and humanity worthy of the foremost of civilised countries.

A CHAPTER ON HAWAIIAN AFFAIRS.

A FEW facts concerning the Hawaiian islands may serve to supplement the deficiencies of the previous letters. The group is an hereditary and constitutional monarchy. There is a House of Nobles, numbering twenty members, appointed by the Crown. The House of Representatives consists of not less than twenty-four, or more than forty members elected biennially. The Legislature fixes the number, and apportions the same. The Houses sit together, and constitute the Legislative Assembly. The property qualification for a representative is, real estate worth $500, or an annual income of $250 from property, and that for an elector is an annual income of $75. The Legislators are paid, and the expense of a session is about $15,000. There are three cabinet ministers appointed by the Crown, of the Interior, Finance, and Foreign Affairs respectively, and an Attorney-General, who may be regarded as a minister of justice. There is a Supreme Court with a Chief Justice and two associate justices, and there are circuit and district judges on all the larger islands, as well as sheriffs, prisons, and police. There is a standing army of sixty men, mainly for the purposes of guard duty, and rendering assistance to the police.

The question of "how to make ends meet" sorely exercises the little kingdom. All sorts of improvements involving a largely increased outlay are continually urged, while at the same time the burden of taxation presses increasingly heavily, and there is a constant clamour for the removal of some of the most lucrative imposts. Indeed, the Hawaiian dog, with his tax and his "tag," is seldom out of the Legislative Assembly.

What may be termed the *per capita* taxes are, an annual poll tax of one dollar levied on each male inhabitant between the ages of seventeen and sixty, an annual road tax of two dollars upon all persons between seventeen and fifty, and an annual school tax of two dollars upon all persons between twenty-one and sixty.   There is a direct tax upon property of ½ per cent. upon its valuation, and specific taxes of a dollar on every horse above two years old, and a dollar and a half on each dog.   Of the $206,000 raised by internal taxes during the last biennial period, the horses paid $50,000, the mules $6000, and the dogs $19,000 !

The indirect taxation in the shape of customs duties amounted to $350,000 in the same period.   The poor Hawaiian does not know the blessing of a " Free Breakfast Table."

The islands are large importers.   The value of imported goods was $1,184,054 in 1875, on which the Hawaiian Treasury received $213,285 as customs duties.   Forty-seven thousand dollars' worth of ale, porter, cider, and light wines, and forty-nine thousand dollars' worth of spirits, show that the foreign population of 6000 is more than sufficiently bibulous. The Chinamen, about 2000 in number, are, or ought to be, responsible for $22,000 worth of opium ; and the $42,000 worth of tobacco and cigars is doubtless distributed pretty equally over all the nationalities.   Twenty-one thousand gallons of spirits were taken out of bond for consumption in 1875. The licenses to sell spirits brought $18,000 into the Treasury in the last biennial period, but those for the sale of awa and opium brought in $55,000 during the same time.   These licenses are confined to Honolulu.

There are two interesting items of customs receipts, a sum of $924, the proceeds of a per capita tax of two dollars levied on passengers landing on the islands, for the support of the Queen's Hospital, and a sum of $1477, the proceeds of a tax levied on seamen for the support of the Marine Hospital. There is a sum of $700 for passports, as no Hawaiian or stranger can leave the kingdom without an official permit.

There are 51 vessels registered under the Hawaiian flag, of which 35 are coasters, and 16 engaged in foreign freighting and whaling.

The value of domestic exports, in 1875, was $1,774,082. Among these bananas, pineapples, pulu, cocoanuts, oranges, limes, sandal-wood, tamarinds, betel leaves, sharks' fins, paiai, whale oil, sperm oil, cocoanut oil, and whalebone.   Among other commodities there was exported, of coffee 165,000 lbs., of fungus 45,000 lbs., of peanuts 21,000 lbs., of rice 1,573,000 lbs., of paddy 556,000 lbs., of hides 22,000 packages, of goat-skins 60,000, of horns 13,000, and of tallow 851,000 lbs. The imports, in 1875, amounted to $1,184,054.

The expense of " keeping things going " on the islands for the two years ending March 1st, 1874, amounted to $1,193,276, but this included the funeral expenses of two kings, as well as of two extra sessions of the Legislature, which amounted to $42,000. The decrease in the revenue for the same period amounted to $45,000. The items of Hawaiian expenditure were as follows :—

For Civil List	$47,689.73
„ Permanent Settlements, Queen Emma	12,000.00
„ Legislature and Privy Council	15,288.50
„ Extra Legislative Expenses	19,011.87
„ Department of the Judiciary	72,245.64
„ „ of Foreign Affairs and War	78,145.85
„ „ of the Interior	389,009.08
„ „ of Finance	202,117.05
„ „ of the Attorney-General	97,097.00
„ Bureau of Public Instruction	89,432.40
„ Miscellaneous Expenditure	170,474.67
The balance on hand in the Treasury, March 31st 1874	764.57
	$1,193,276.36

That, under the head Finance, includes the interest on borrowed money. The funded national debt is $340,000. Of this sum a portion bears no stated interest, only such as may arise from the very dubious profits of the Hawaiian hotel. The interest charges are 12 per cent. on $25,000, and 9 per cent. on $272,000. The estimates for the present biennial period involve a large increase of debt. The present financial position of the kingdom is, an increasing expenditure and a decreasing revenue.

The statistics of the Judiciary Department for the last two years present a few features of interest. There were 4000 convictions out of 5764 cases brought before the courts, equal to a fourteenth part of the population. The total number of offences in the category is 125. Of these some are decidedly local: Thus, for " furnishing intoxicating liquors to Hawaiians " 92 persons were punished ; for " exhibition of *Hula*," 10 ; for " selling *awa* without licence," 12 ; for " selling opium without licence," 24. It is not surprising to those who know the habits of the people, that the convictions for violations of the marriage tie, though greatly diminished, should reach the numbei of 384, while under the head "Deserting Husbands and Wives," 67 convictions are recorded. For "practising medicine without a licence," 56 persons were punished; for "furious riding," 197; for "cruelty to animals," 37; for "gaming," 121; for "gross cheating," 32; for "violating the Sabbath," 61. We must remember that the returns include foreigners and Chinamen, or else the reputation for "harmlessness" which Hawaiians possess would suffer seriously when we read that within the last two years there were 178 convictions for "assault," 248 for "assault and battery," 12 for "assaults with dangerous weapons," 49 for "affray," 674 for "drunkenness," 87 for "disturbing quiet of the night," and 13 for "murder." Yet the number of criminal cases has largely diminished, and taking civil and criminal together, there has been a decrease of 656 for the last biennial period, as compared with that immediately preceding it.

The administration of justice is confessedly one of the most efficient departments of Hawaiian affairs. Chief Justice Allen, both as a lawyer and a gentleman, is worthy to fill the highest position in his native country (America), and the Associate Justices, as well as the native and foreign judges throughout the islands, are highly esteemed for honour and uprightness. I never heard an uttered suspicion of venality or unfairness against anyone of them, and apparently the Judiciary Department of Hawaii deserves the same confidence which we repose in our own.

The Educational System has been carefully modelled, and is carried out with tolerable efficiency. Eighty-seven per cent. of the whole school population are actually at school, and the inspector of schools states that a person who cannot read and write is rarely met with. Each common school is graded into two, three, or four classes, according to the intelligence and proficiency of the pupils, and the curriculum of study is as follows:—

CLASS I.—Reading, mental and written arithmetic, geography, penmanship, and composition.

CLASS II.—Reading, mental arithmetic, geography, penmanship.

CLASS III.—Reading, first principles of arithmetic, penmanship.

CLASS IV.—Primer, use of slate and pencil.

The youngest children are not classified until they can put letters together in syllables.

Vocal music is taught wherever competent teachers are found.

The total sum expended on education, including the grants to "family" and other schools, is about $40,000 a year.*

It has been remarked that the rising race of Hawaiians has an increased contempt for industry in the form of manual labour, and it is proposed by the Board of Education that such labour shall be made a part of common school education, so that on both girls and boys a desire to provide for their own wants in an honest way shall be officially inculcated. There is a Government Reformatory School, and industrial and family schools for both girls and boys are scattered over the islands. The supply of literature in the vernacular is meagre, and few of the natives have an intelligent comprehension of English.

The group has an area of about 4,000,000 acres, of which about 200,000 may be regarded as arable, and 150,000 as specially adapted for the culture of sugar-cane. Sugar, the great staple production, gives employment in its cultivation and manufacture to nearly 4000 hands. Only a fifteenth part of the estimated arable area is under cultivation. Over 6000 natives are returned as the possessors of *Kuleanas* or freeholds, but many of these are heavily mortgaged. Many of the larger lands are held on lease from the crown or chiefs, and there are difficulties attending the purchase of small properties.

Almost all the roots and fruits of the torrid and temperate zones can be grown upon the islands, and the banana, *kalo*, yam, sweet potato, cocoanut, breadfruit, arrowroot, sugar cane, strawberry, raspberry, whortleberry, and native apple, are said to be indigenous.

* The schools of the kingdom are as follows :

	Number Schools.	Boys.	Girls.	Total.
Common Schools	196	3193	2329	5522
Government Boarding Schools . . .	3	185	......	185
Government Haw.-Eng. Day Schools .	5	415	246	661
Subsidized Boarding Schools . . .	10	168	191	359
Subsidized Day Schools . . .	9	201	210	411
Independent Boarding Schools . . .	3	14	62	76
Independent Day Schools . . .	16	287	254	541
Total	242	4463	3292	7755

The indigenous *fauna* is small, consisting only of hogs, dogs, rats, and an anomalous bat which flies by day. There are few insects, except such as have been imported, and these, which consist of centipedes, scorpions, cockroaches, mosquitos, and fleas, are happily confined to certain localities, and the two first have left most of their venom behind them. A small lizard is abundant, but snakes, toads, and frogs have not yet effected a landing.

The ornithology of the islands is scanty. Domestic fowls are supposed to be indigenous. Wild geese are numerous among the mountains of Hawaii, and plovers, snipe, and wild ducks, are found on all the islands. A handsome owl, called the owl-hawk, is common. There is a paroquet with purple feathers, another with scarlet, a woodpecker with variegated plumage of red, green, and yellow, and a small black bird with a single yellow feather under each wing. There are few singing birds, but one of the few has as sweet a note as that of the English thrush. There are very few varieties of moths and butterflies.

The *flora* of the Hawaiian Islands is far scantier than that of the South Sea groups, and cannot compare with that of many other tropical as well as temperate regions. But all the islands are rich in cryptogamous plants, of which there is an almost infinite variety.

Hawaii is still in process of construction, and is subject to volcanic eruptions, earthquakes, and tidal waves. Hurricanes are unknown, and thunderstorms are rare and light.

Under favourable circumstances of moisture the soil is most prolific, and " patch cultivation " in glens and ravines, as well as on mountain sides, produces astonishing results. A *Kalo* patch of forty square feet will support a man for a year. An acre of favourably situated land will grow a thousand stems of bananas, which will produce annually ten tons of fruit. The sweet potato flourishes on the most unpromising lava, where soil can hardly be said to exist, and in good localities produces 200 barrels to the acre. On dry light soils the Irish potato grows anyhow and anywhere, with no other trouble than that of planting the sets. Most vegetable dyes, drugs, and spices can be raised. Forty diverse fruits present an overflowing cornucopia. The esculents of the temperate zones flourish. The coffee bush produces from three to five pounds of berries the third year after planting. The average yield of sugar is two and a half tons to the acre. Pineapples grow like weeds in some districts, and water melons are almost a drug. The bamboo is known to grow sixteen inches in a day. Wherever there is a sufficient rainfall, the earth teems with plenty.

Yet the Hawaiian Islands can hardly be regarded as a field for emigration, though nature is lavish, and the climate the most delicious and salubrious in the world. Farming, as we understand it, is unknown. The dearth of insectivorous birds seriously affects the cultivation of a soil naturally bounteous to excess. The narrow gorges in which terraced " patched cultivation " is so successful, offer no temptations to a man with the world before him. The larger areas require labour, and labour is not to be had. Though wheat and other cereals mature, attacks of weevil prevent their storage, and all the grain and flour consumed are imported from California.

Cacao, cinnamon, and allspice, are subject to an apparently ineradicable blight. The blight which has attacked the coffee shrub is so severe, that the larger plantations have been dug up, and coffee is now raised by patch culture, mainly among the guava scrub which fringes the forests. Oranges suffer from blight also, and some of the finest groves have been cut down. Cotton suffers from the ravages of a caterpillar. The mulberry tree, which, from its rapid growth, would be invaluable to silk growers, is covered with a black and white blight. Sheep are at present very successful, but in some localities the spread of a pestilent " oat-burr " is depreciating the value of their wool. The forests, which are essential to the well-being of the islands, are disappearing in some quarters, owing to the attacks of a grub, as well as the ravages of cattle.

Cocoanuts, bananas, yams, sweet potatoes, *kalo*, and breadfruit, the staple food of the native population, are free from blight, and so are potatoes and rice. Beef cattle can be raised for almost nothing, and in some districts beef can be bought for the cent or two per pound which pays for the cutting up of the carcase. Every one can live abundantly, and without the " sweat of the brow," but few can make money, owing to the various forms of blight, the scarcity of labour, and the lack of a profitable market.

There is little healthy activity in any department of business. The whaling fleet has deserted the islands. A general *pilikia* prevails. Settlements are disappearing, valley lands are falling out of cultivation, Hilo grass and guava scrub are burying the traces of a former population. The natives are rapidly diminishing,* the old industries are abandoned, and the inherent immorality of the race, the great outstanding cause of its decay, still resists the influence of Christian teaching and example.

An exotic civilization is having a fair trial on these islands. With the exception of the serious maladies introduced by foreigners in the early days, and the disastrous moral influence exercised by worthless whites, the Hawaiians have suffered none of the wrongs usually inflicted on the feebler by the stronger race. Their rights were in the first instance carefully secured to them, and have since been protected by equal laws, righteously administered. They have been aided towards independence in political matters, and the foreigners who framed

---

* The population by the last census, taken in 1872, is as follows : —

Total number of natives in 1872	. . . . .		49,044
,,	,,	half-castes in 1872	2,487
,,	,,	Chinese in 1872	1,938
,,	,,	Americans in 1872	889
,,	,,	Hawaiians born of foreign parents, 1872	849
,,	,,	Britons in 1872	619
,,	,,	Portuguese in 1872	395
,,	,,	Germans in 1872	224
,,	,,	French in 1872	88
,,	,,	other foreigners in 1872 . . .	364

Total population in 1872 56,897

Total number of natives, *including half-castes*, in 1866 . 58,765
,,   ,,   ,,   ,,   ,,   1872 . 51,531

Decrease since 1866 7,234

The excess of males over females is 6,403 *souls !*

AREA AND POPULATION OF EACH ISLAND.

	Acres.	Height in Feet.	Population in 1872.
Hawaii . .	2,500,000	13,953	16,001
Maui . . .	400,000	10,200	12,334
Oahu . .	350,000	3,800	20,671
Kauai . . .	350,000	about 6,000	4,961
Molokai . .	200,000	2,800	2,349
Lanai . . .	100,000	2,400	348
Niihau . .	70,000	800	233
Kahoolawe . .	30,000	400	......

Total 56,897

the laws and constitution, and have directed Hawaiian affairs, such as Richards, Lee, Judd, Allen, and Wyllie, were men above reproach; and missionary influence, of all others the most friendly to the natives, has predominated for fifty years.

The effects of missionary labour have been scarcely touched upon in the foregoing letters, and here, in preference to giving any opinion of my own, I quote from Mr. R. H. Dana,* an Episcopalian, and a barrister of the highest standing in America, well known in this country by his writings, who sums up his investigations on the Sandwich Islands in the following dispassionate words : " It is no small thing to say of the missionaries of the American Board, that in less than forty years they have taught this whole people to read and to write, to cipher and to sew. They have given them an alphabet, grammar, and dictionary; preserved their language from extinction; given it a literature, and translated into it the Bible, and works of devotion, science, and entertainment, &c. They have established schools, reared up native teachers, and so pressed their work, that now the proportion of inhabitants who can read and write is greater than in New England. And whereas they found these islanders a nation of half-naked savages, living in the surf and on the sand, eating raw fish, fighting among themselves, tyrannized over by feudal chiefs, and abandoned to sensuality, they now see them decently clothed, recognizing the law of marriage, knowing something of accounts, going to school and public worship more regularly than the people do at home, and the more elevated of them taking part in conducting the affairs of the constitutional monarchy under which they live, holding seats on the judicial bench and in the legislative chambers, and filling posts in the local magistracies."

If space permitted, the testimony of " Mark Twain," given in " Roughing It," might be added to the above, and the remaining missionaries may well point to the visible results of their labours, with the one word *Circumspice!*

---

* Author of " Two Years before the Mast," &c., &c.

A CHAPTER ON HAWAIIAN HISTORY.

———◆———

In the pre-historic days of Hawaii, for 500 years, as the bards sing, before Captain Cook landed, and indeed for some years afterwards, each island had its king, chiefs, and internal dissensions; and incessant wars, with a reckless waste of human life, kept the whole group in turmoil. Chaotic and legendary as early Hawaiian history is, there is enough to show that there must have been regularly organized communities on the islands for a very long period, with a civilization and polity which, though utterly unworthy of Christianity, were enlightened and advanced for Polynesian heathenism.

The kingly office was hereditary, and the king's power absolute. On the different islands the kings and chiefs who together constituted a privileged class, admitted the priesthood to some portion of their privileges, probably with the view of enslaving the people more completely through the agency of religion, and held the lower classes in absolute subserviency by the most rigorous of feudal systems, which included *hana poalima*, or forced labour, and the *tabu*, well known throughout Polynesia.

A very interesting history begins with Kamehameha the Great, the Conqueror, or the Terrible; the "Napoleon of the Pacific," as he has been called. He united an overmastering ambition to a singular gift of ruling, and without education, training, or the help of a single political precedent to guide him, animated not only by the lust of conquest, but by the desire to create a nationality, he subjugated every thing that his canoes could reach, and fused a rabble of savages and chieftaincies into a united nation, every individual of which to this day inherits something of the patriotism of the Conqueror.

His wars were by no means puny either in proportions or slaughter, as, for instance, when he meditated the conquest of Kauai, his expedition included seven thousand picked warriors, twenty-one schooners, forty swivels, six mortars, and an abundance of ammunition ! His victories are celebrated in countless *mélés* or unwritten songs, which are said to be marked by real poetic feeling and simplicity, and to resemble the Ossianic poems in majesty and melancholy. He founded the dynasty which for seventy years has stood as firmly, and exercised its functions for the welfare of the people on the whole as efficiently, as any other government.

The king was forty-five years old when, having "no more worlds to conquer," he devoted himself to the consolidation of his kingdom. He placed governors on each island, directly responsible to himself, who nominated chiefs of districts, heads of villages, and all petty officers; and tax-gatherers, who, for lack of the art of writing, kept their accounts by a method in use in the English exchequer in ancient times. He appointed a council of chiefs, with whom he advised on important matters, and a council of "wise men" who assisted him in framing laws, and in regulating concerns of minor importance. In all matters of national importance, the governors and high chiefs of the islands met with the sovereign in consultations. These were conducted with great privacy, and the results were promulgated through the islands by heralds whose office was hereditary.

Kamehameha enacted statutes against theft, murder, and oppression, and though he wielded oppressive and despotic authority himself, his people enjoyed a golden age as compared with those that were past. The king, governors, and chiefs constituted the magistracy, and there was an appeal from both chiefs and governors to the king. It was usual for both parties to be heard face to face in the enclosure in front of the house of the king or governor; no lawyers were employed, and every man advocated his own cause, sitting cross-legged before the judges. Swiftness and decision characterized the redress of grievances and the administration of justice.

Kamehameha reduced the feudal tenure of land, which had heretofore been the theory, into absolute practice, claiming for the crown the sole ownership of the land, and dividing it among his followers on the conditions of tribute and military service. The common people were attached to the soil and transferred with it. A chief might nominate his wife, or son, or any other person to succeed him in his possessions, but at his death they reverted to the king, whose order was required before the testamentary wish became of any value. There were some wise regulations generally applicable, concerning the planting of cocoanut trees, and a law that the water should be conducted over every plantation twice a week in general, and once a week during the dry season. This king constructed immense fish ponds on the sea coast, and devoted himself to commerce with such success that in one year he exported $400,000 of sandalwood (felled and shipped at the cost of much suffering to the common people), and on finding that a large proportion of the profit had been dissipated by harbour dues at Canton, he took up the idea and established harbour dues at Honolulu.

From Vancouver Kamehameha learned of the grandeur and power of Christian nations ; and in the idea that his people might grow great through Christianity, he asked him, in 1794, that Christian teachers might be sent from England. This request, if ever presented, was disregarded, as was another made by Captain Turnbull in 1803, and this exceptionally great Polynesian died the year before the light of the Gospel shone on Hawaiian shores.

Some persons, it does not appear whether they were English or American, attempted his conversion ; but the astute savage, after listening to their eloquent statements of the power of faith, pressed on them as a crucial test to throw themselves from the top of an adjacent precipice, making his reception of their religion contingent on their arrival unhurt at its base. He built large *heiaus*, amongst others the one at Kawaihae, at the dedication of which to his favourite war god eleven human sacrifices were offered. To the end he remained devoted to the state religion, and the last instances of capital punishment for breaking *tabu*, a thraldom deeply interwoven with the religious system, occurred in the last year of his reign, when one man was put to death for putting on a chief's girdle, another for eating of a tabooed dish, and a third for leaving a house under *tabu*, and entering one which was not so.

His last prayers were to his great red-feathered god Kukai limoku, and priests bringing idols crowded round him in his dying agony. His last words were " *Move on in my good way and* " —— In the death-room the high chiefs consulted, and one, to testify his great grief, proposed to eat the body raw, but was overruled by the majority. So the flesh was separated from the bones, and they were tied up in *tapa*, and concealed so effectually that they have never since been found. A holocaust of three hundred dogs gave splendour to his obsequies. "These are our gods whom I worship," he had said to Kotzebue, while showing him one of the temples. "Whether I do right or wrong I do not know, but I follow my faith, which cannot be wicked, as it commands me never to do wrong."

Kamehameha the Great died in 1819, and his son, Liholiho, who loved whisky and pleasure, was peaceably crowned king in his room, and by his name. He, with the powerful aid of the Queen Dowager Kaahumanu, abolished *tabu*, and his subjects cast away their idols, and fell into indifferent scepticism, the high priest Hewahewa being the first to light the iconoclastic torch, having previously given his opinion that there was only one great *akua* or spirit in *lani*, the heavens. This Kamehameha II. was the king who with his queen, died of measles in London in 1824, after which the *Blonde* frigate was sent to restore their bodies with much ceremony to Hawaiian soil.

Kamehameha III., a minor, another son of the Conqueror, succeeded, and reigned for thirty years, dividing the lands among the nobles and the people, and conferring upon his kingdom an equable constitution. The law officially abolishing idolatry was confirmed by him, and while complete religious toleration otherwise was granted, the Christian faith was established in these words :—" The religion of the Lord Jesus Christ shall continue to be the established national religion of the Hawaiian Islands." His words on July 31st, 1843, when the English colours, wrongfully hoisted, were lowered in favour of the Hawaiian flag, are the national motto :—" The life of the land is established in righteousness." In his reign Hawaiian independence was recognised by Great Britain, France, and America. His Premier for some time was Mr. Wyllie, who with a rare devotion and disinterestedness devoted his life and a large fortune to his adopted country.

Kamehameha IV., a grandson of the Conqueror, succeeded him in 1854. He was a patriotic prince, and strove hard to advance the civilisation of his people, and to arrest their decrease by reformatory and sanitary measures. He was the most accomplished prince of his line, and his death in 1863, soon after that of his only child, the Prince of Hawaii, was very deeply regretted. His widow, Queen Kaleleonalani, or Emma, visited England after his death.

He was succeeded by his brother, a man of a very different

stamp, who was buried on January 11, 1873, after a partial outbreak of the orgies wherewith the natives disgraced themselves after the death of a chief in the old heathen days. It is rare to meet with two people successively who hold the same opinion of Kamehameha V. He was evidently a man of some talent and strong will, intensely patriotic, and determined not to be a merely ornamental figure-head of a government administered by foreigners in his name. He ardently desired the encouragement of foreign immigration, and the opening of a free market in America for Hawaiian produce. He ruled, as well as reigned, and though he abrogated the constitution of 1852, and introduced several features of absolutism into the government, on the whole he seems to have done well by his people. He is said to have been regal and dignified, to have worked hard, to have written correct state papers, and to have been capable of the deportment of an educated Christian gentleman, but to have reimbursed himself for this subservience to conventionality by occasionally retiring to an undignified residence on the sea-shore, where he transformed himself into the likeness of one of his half-clad heathen ancestors, debased himself by whisky, and revelled in the *hula-hula.* He is said also to have been so far under the empire of the old superstitions as to consult an ancient witch on affairs of importance.

He died amidst the rejoicings incident to his birthday, and on the next day " lay in state in the throne-room of the palace, while his ministers, his staff, and the chiefs of the realm kept watch over him, and sombre *kahilis* waving at his head beat a rude and silent dead march for the crowds of people, subjects and aliens, who continuously filed through the apartment, for a curious farewell glance at the last of the Kamehamehas."

His death closed the first era of Hawaiian history, and the orderly succession of one recognised dynasty. No successor to the throne had been proclaimed, and the king left no nearer kin than the Princess Keelikolani, his half-sister, a lady not in the line of regal descent.

Under these novel circumstances, it devolved upon the Legislative Assembly to elect by ballot "some native *Alii* of the kingdom as successor to the throne." The candidates were the High Chief Kalakaua, the present King, and Prince Lunalilo, the late King, but the " Well-Beloved," as Lunalilo was called, was elected unanimously, amidst an outburst of popular enthusiasm.

From his high resolves and generous instincts much was expected, and the unhappy failing, to which, after the most painful struggles, he succumbed, on the solicitation of some bad or thoughtless foreigners, if it lessened him aught in the public esteem, abated nothing of the wonderful love that was felt for him.

He died, after a lingering illness, on February 3, 1874. Although the event had been expected for some time, its announcement was received with profound sorrow by the whole community, while the native subjects of the deceased sovereign, according to ancient custom, expressed their feelings in loud wailings, which echoed mournfully through the still, red air of early daylight. On the following evening the body was placed on a shrouded bier, and was escorted in solemn procession by the government officials and the late king's staff, to the Iolani Palace, there to lie in state. It was a cloudless moonlight; not a leaf stirred or bird sang, and the crowd, consisting of several thousands, opened to the right and left to let the dismal death-train pass, in a stillness which was only broken by the solemn tramp of the bearers.

The next day the corpse lay in state, in all the splendour that the islands could bestow, dressed in the clothes the king wore when he took the oath of office, and resting on the royal robe of yellow feathers, a fathom square.* Between eight and ten thousand persons passed through the palace during the morning, and foreigners as well as natives wept tears of genuine grief; while in the palace grounds the wailing knew no inter-mission, and many of the natives spent hours in reciting *kanakaus* in honour of the deceased. At midnight the king's remains were placed in a coffin, his aged father, His Highness Kanaina, who was broken-hearted for his loss, standing by. When the body was raised from the feather robe, he ordered that it should be wrapped in it, and thus be deposited in its resting place. "He is the last of our race," he said; "it belongs to him." The natives in attendance turned pale at this command, for the robe was the property of Kekauluohi, the dead king's mother, and had descended to her from her kingly ancestors.

Averse through his life to useless parade and display, Luna-

---

* Only one robe like this remains, that which is spread over the throne at the opening of Parliament. The one buried with Lunalilo could not be reproduced for one hundred thousand dollars.

lilo left directions for a simple funeral, and that none of the old heathenish observances should ensue upon his death. So, amidst unbounded grief, he was carried to the grave with hymns and anthems, and the hopes of Hawaii were buried with him.

He died without naming a successor, and thus for the second time within fourteen months, a king came to be elected by ballot.

The proceedings at the election of Lunalilo were marked by an order, regularity, and peaceableness which reflected extreme credit on the civilisation of the Hawaiians, but in the subsequent period the temper of the people had considerably changed, and they had been affected by influences to which some allusions were made in Letter XIX.

In politics, Lunalilo's views were essentially democratic, and he showed an almost undue deference to the will of the people, giving them a year's practical experience of democracy which they will never forget.

An antagonism to the foreign residents, or rather to their political influence, had grown rapidly. Some of the Americans had been unwise in their language, and the discussion on the proposed cession of Pearl River increased the popular discontent, and the jealousy of foreign interference in island affairs. "America gave us the light," said a native pastor, in a sermon which was reported over the islands, "but now that we have the light, we should be left to use it for ourselves." This sentence represented the bulk of the national feeling, which, if partially unenlightened, is intensely, passionately, almost fanatically patriotic.

The biennial election of delegates to the Legislative Assembly occurred shortly before Lunalilo's death, and the rallying-cry, "Hawaii for the Hawaiians," was used with such effect that the most respectable foreign candidates, even in the capital, had not a chance of success, and for the first time in Hawaiian constitutional history a house was elected, consisting, with one exception, of natives. Immediately on the king's death, Kalakaua, who was understood to represent the foreign interest as well as the policy indicated by the popular rallying-cry, and Queen Emma, came forward as candidates; the walls were placarded with addresses, mass meetings were held, canvassers were busy night and day, promises impossible of fulfilment were made, and for eight days the Hawaiian capital presented those scenes of excitement, wrangling, and mutual misrepresentation which we associate with popular elections elsewhere, and everywhere.

The day of election came, and thirty-nine votes were given for Kalakaua, and six for Emma. On the announcement of this result, a hoarse, indignant roar, mingled with cheers from the crowd without, was heard within the Assembly chamber, and on the committee appointed to convey to Kalakaua the news of his election, attempting to take their seats in a carriage, they were driven back, maimed and bleeding, into the Courthouse; the carriage was torn to pieces, and the spokes of the wheels were distributed as weapons among the rioters. The "gentle children of the sun" were seen under a new aspect; they became furious, the latent savagery came out, the doors of the Hall of Assembly were battered in, the windows were shattered with clubs and volleys of stones, nine of the representatives, who were known to have voted for Kalakaua, were severely injured; the chairs, tables, and furnishings of the rooms were broken up and thrown out of the windows, along with valuable public and private documents; kerosene was demanded to fire the buildings; the police remained neutral, and conflagration and murder would have followed, had not the ministers despatched an urgent request for assistance to the United States' ships of war, *Portsmouth* and *Tuscarora*, and H. B. M. ship *Tenedos*, which was promptly met by the landing of such a force of sailors and marines as dispersed the rioters.

Seventy arrests were made, the foreign marines held possession of the Courthouse, Palace, and Government offices, Kalakaua took the oath of office in private; the Representatives, with bandaged heads, and arms in slings, limped, and in some instances were supported to their desks, to be liberated from their duties by the king in person, and in ten days the joint protectorate was withdrawn.

Those who know the natives best were taken by surprise, and are compelled to recognise that a restive, half-sullen, half-defiant spirit is abroad among them, and that the task of governing them may not be the easy thing which it has been since the days of Kamehameha the Great.

Of King Kalakaua, who began his reign under such unfortunate auspices, little at present can be said. Though island affairs have settled down into their old quietude, party spirit, arising out of the election, has not died out among the natives. The king chose his advisers wisely, and made a concession to native feeling by appointing a native named Nahaolelua to a seat in the cabinet as Minister of Finance, but his first arrangement was upset, and a good deal of confusion subsequently prevailed.

The Queen, Kapiolani, is a Hawaiian lady of high character and extreme amiability, and both King and Queen have been exemplary in their domestic relations.

Kalakaua's first act was to proclaim his brother, Prince Leleiohoku, his successor, investing him at the same time with the title, " His Royal Highness," and his second was to reorganize the military service, with the view of making it an efficient and well-disciplined force.

There is something melancholy in the fact that this small Pacific kingdom has to fall back upon the old world resource of a standing army, as large, in proportion to its population, as that of the German Empire.

Those readers who have become interested in the Sandwich Islands through the foregoing Letters, will join me in the earnest wish that this people, which has advanced from heathenism and barbarism to Christianity and civilization in the short space of a single generation, may enjoy peace and prosperity under King Kalakaua, that the extinction which threatens the nation may be averted, and that under a gracious Divine Providence, Hawaii may still remain the inheritance of the Hawaiians.

Other TUT BOOKS available:

THE TEN FOOT SQUARE HUT AND TALES OF THE HEIKE: Being Two Thirteenth-century Japanese classics, the "Hojoki" and selections from the "Heike Monogatari" *translated by A. L. Sadler*

THE TOURIST AND THE REAL JAPAN *by Boye de Mente*

TYPHOON! TYPHOON! An Illustrated Haiku Sequence *by Lucile M. Bogue*

UNBEATEN TRACKS IN JAPAN: An Account of Travels in the Interior Including Visits to the Aborigines of Yezo and the Shrine of Nikko *by Isabella L. Bird*

Please order from your bookstore or write directly to:

CHARLES E. TUTTLE CO., INC.
Suido 1-chome, 2–6, Bunkyo-ku, Tokyo 112

or:

CHARLES E. TUTTLE CO., INC.
Rutland, Vermont 05701 U.S.A.